SCIPIO RISEN

BOOK FOUR OF THE SCIPIO AFRICANUS SAGA

MARTIN TESSMER

Copyright © 2016

Dedication

To the BookWyrm, editor par excellence.

Table of Contents

ACKNOWLEDGMENTS

Among 20th and 21st century historians, I am primarily indebted to Professor Richard Gabriel for his informative and readable *Scipio Africanus: Rome's Greatest General,* and *Ancient Arms and Armies of Antiquity.* Mary Beard's *SPQR* provided valuable insights into Roman life and politics during the Republican period. The same for David Gwynn's *The Roman Republic: A Very Short Introduction.*

H. Liddell Hart's *Scipio Africanus: Greater Than Napoleon* provided many valuable insights into Scipio the general and Scipio the man. John Peddle's *Hannibal's War* helped flesh out the personality, tactics, and motivations of Hannibal the Great. Nigel Bagnall's *The Punic Wars* provided confirmatory evidence for information I drew from Gabriel, Livy, Polybius, Mommsen, and others. Thanks to you all.

Among classic historians, I owe a deep debt of gratitude to Titus Livius (Livy) for *Hannibal's War: Books 21-30* (translated by J.C. Yardley) and Polybius for *The Histories* (translated by Robin Waterfield). Cassius Dio's *Roman History* provided additional details and confirmed some of Livy's and Polybius' assertions. Appian, Dodge, and Mommsen, thanks to you all for the many tidbits and corrections your works provided.

Cato the Elder's *De Agri Cultura* and Plutarch's *Roman Lives* provided insight into Cato, this simple but ruthless and powerful man that so influenced the course of Western History.

Ross Lecke has written two fine historical novels about Scipio and Hannibal: they are *Scipio Africanus: The Man Who Defeated Hannibal,* and *Hannibal.* Ross showed me that a writer can spin a good yarn and still stick to the facts, where there are facts to stick to.

Finally, I must give a tip of the hat to Wikipedia. Wikimedia, and the scores of websites about the people and countries of 200 BCE. The scholarship of our 21st century digital community is amazing.

Susan Sernau, your copyediting of my humble manuscript helped to evolve it from report to story. You are a wonder.

A Note on Historical Accuracy

Scipio Risen is a dramatization of the actual events surrounding Publius Cornelius Scipio's African campaign, as variously recorded by (in order of frequency) Livy, Polybius, Gabriel, Appian Mommsen, Bagnall, and Beard. This is a work of historical fiction, meaning it combines elements of historical fact (such as it is) and fiction. It is not a history textbook.

The book's major characters, places, events, battles, and timelines are real, meaning they are noted by at least one of our acknowledged historians. You will see footnotes scattered throughout the text to document various aspects of the book.

Whenever possible, I have included quotes of Scipio's and Hannibal's actual words, as described by Livy and Polybius, with a source footnote at the end of the quote. These were especially helpful in reconstructing the historic discussion between Scipio and Hannibal.

The story's Hellenic Party and Latin Party factions were created to capture the mood of the times, when there was real enmity between those favoring a more "decadent" Hellenic lifestyle and those of agrarian sympathies who disparaged it. The names are fictitious, but the disputes were real.

Similarly, the creation of hobnailed sandals, the cohort formation, cavalry formations, lighter packs, rudimentary steel, and the falcata sword seem to have occurred during this era, but it is difficult to know who invented them versus who popularized them. In this book Scipio Africanus is given attribution for them to help illustrate the military inventiveness that took place during the Punic wars. If he did not invent them, he certainly exploited their usage.

CREDITS

- Cover design by pro_ebookcovers at Fiverr.com

- Carthaginian helmet (cover) by NaughtyNut, purchased via iStockphoto.com

- Terrain maps created by wesdsd at Fiverr.com

- Back cover Scipio sculpture portrait "Ritratto di Scipione" by Mino da Fiesole, courtesy of Wikimedia Commons at commons.Wikimedia.org

- Inside cover Scipio bust by Shakko, courtesy of Wikimedia Commons at commons.Wikimedia.org

- Battle maps designed and developed by Martin Tessmer.

African Theatre 204-201 BCE

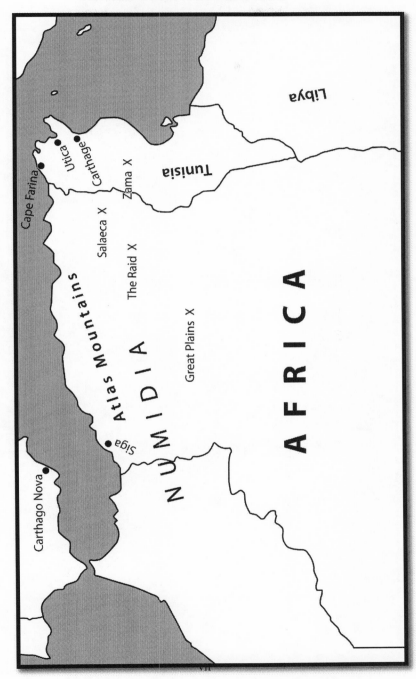

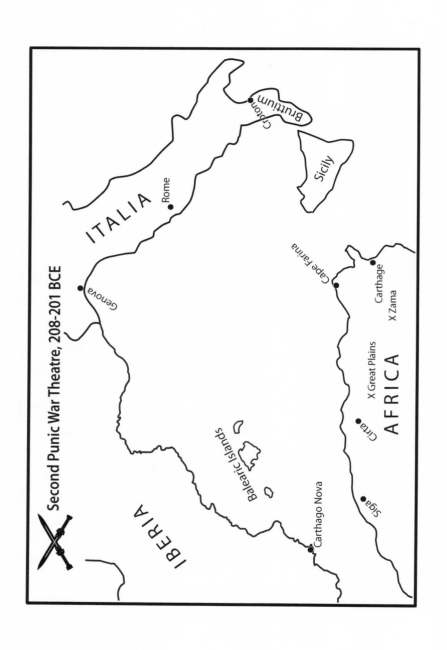

Second Punic War Theatre, 208-201 BCE

ITALIA

Rome

Genova

Croton

Bruttium

Sicily

Cape Farina

Carthage

X Zama

X Great Plains

Cirta

AFRICA

Siga

Balearic Islands

Carthago Nova

IBERIA

Scipio Africanus

I. THE LANDING

CAPE FARINA, NORTH AFRICA 204 BCE. Praxis stomps down the fog-shrouded gangplank and treads out onto the rough gray sands of the African seashore. The ex-gladiator draws his sword and squints into the shadowy beachside brush, looking for signs of the enemy. *There could an elephant in there and I couldn't see it*, the former slave thinks, shaking his head.

Praxis grabs one of the rounded beach rocks and pitches it into the brush, listening for a response. He pitches another, then shrugs. *Who in Hades would be out on this isolated spit of land, anyway?*

"Praxis! What do you see?" bellows Marcus Silenus from the flagship's railing. "Is it safe? Report!"

Romans! Always giving orders. "I see nothing, Legate," he replies. "But this fog is thicker than Vulcan's beard."

"Gods curse you, I'm coming down!" Marcus shouts. Within minutes, the stocky old warrior stands next to the rangy guard. "Get your men out into that boulder field to the left, Praxis. I'll take a century of men into the oak scrub. Make sure it is safe for the general to debark."

"You worry overmuch, my friends," says a deep baritone voice behind them. "I've planned it so no one would know we were landing here. If there's any Carthaginians out there, I'll kiss a Gaul's ass!"

General Publius Cornelius Scipio strides down the gangplank, tugging at the side straps on his torso-shaped bronze cuirass. A handsome and well-built man of thirty-two, Scipio's green eyes twinkle beneath his mop of graying black hair, amused at Marcus Silenus' concern.

"Before we left Sicily, we spent a lot of time declaring we would land over at Thapsus, just so Carthage's spies would report it," Scipio says.

1

"I'd like to think our ruse was not a waste of time!"

"Our general is right ... this time," says Admiral Laelius impishly. The tall and smoothly muscled man trudges out from behind Scipio and stands next to Marcus.

Laelius peers theatrically into the brush. "No, no Carthaginian phalanxes. Maybe there's a potato farmer with a hoe out there, somewhere. Think you could take him, Marcus?" Laelius grins at Rome's deadliest soldier.

Marcus spits at Laelius' feet, making him jump. "You need to be more cautious, boy. General Gisgo's army could be anywhere. Or Syphax' Numidians, who knows where that traitor is hiding?" He glares at Scipio. "Remember, we are but forty miles from Carthage itself."

"Ox droppings! No one knows we are here," replies Laelius. "My scout ships said that the Carthaginians are sailing all about Thapsus, looking for the dread Scipio and his invasion force." He laughs. "I'd hate to be the spy that told them about our 'secret' plans to land there!"

"I'm going to check around the shore," declares Marcus, waving over the legionnaires marching down from Scipio's ship. "It would be inauspicious to begin our campaign with an ambush."

The legate points toward at the boulders. "Praxis, get your men over there. I will take my men into the brush" Marcus draws his gleaming gladius and stalks toward the coastal scrub, his men trotting to catch up to him.

"Good luck, Marcus," Laelius shouts. "Let me know if you find Hannibal hiding out there. He was ever a master of ambush!"

Scipio stares at the forested promontory a hundred feet above them. "I can barely see the top in this fog. Too bad the men can't see the hills above us, or look into the clear blue-green waters here," he remarks. "The spot is called the Cape of the Beautiful One,[i] for good reason. The soldiers would take its beauty as a good omen."

"I'll tell you what is a good omen," says Laelius. "Unloading those hundreds of warships and transports without any of them crashing into one another. By Mars' cock, you can't see to take a piss out here!"

"Fortuna has been good to us," counters Scipio. "She has wrapped our fleet in a cloak of concealment. Did you learn nothing from fighting Hannibal all these years? Weather and terrain always holds an advantage for you, if you know how to use it."

Scipio shoves his old friend's shoulder. "Now get to the unloading, Admiral. We've got a war to win!"

"I'll see to unloading the ships' supplies, Pumpkin Head," says Laelius, checking to see that no one overhears his disrespect. "But you must find somewhere to take all that stuff."

Scipio wrinkles his nose at Laelius. "I'll take Marcus up to the plateau and find a place to build camp. Your advance scouts found some favorable locations up there."

While the crews unload the ships' tons of food and weaponry, Scipio and Marcus Silenus commandeer a squadron of equites and ride along the beach that borders the cape's long, high, ridge. Marcus and Scipio investigate every nook of the lowlands, searching for a strategic locale to build their camp.

"We'd be close to the ships here, but the earth is too loose," says Marcus, fingering the sandy earth. "The palisades would cave in with the first ram."

"Let's go to higher ground," Scipio says. "The scouts found wood and water there, and the ground is level." The two commanders plunge up the side of a rise with their cavalry, switch backing through the scrub trees to the top of the ridge.

As the morning sun burns off the fog, Scipio and Marcus search for a high, open area with fresh flowing water—a level plain with timber to build thick palisades around their camp. The two realize their army is far from home, without hope of military succor, against an enemy that will be triple their numbers. The camp walls must be strong, and their enemy visible from far away.

After an hour of reconnoitering Marcus and Scipio dismount and stand in the middle of a hill-bordered open space. Marcus walks back and forth, carrying a javelin. He studies the ground and the hills, estimating the distance to the nearby stream. He jabs the javelin into the earth.

"Here. The camp center should be here."

"Which way should the main gates face?" Scipio asks, "toward the sea or land?"

Marcus does not answer. He carefully appraises the surroundings, visualizing attacks from every direction. "The sea," he finally replies. "The Carthaginians will attack our supply ships coming in from Sicily. Our guard towers should face seaward."

"That leaves us more vulnerable on land. And the trees are thick toward the mainland."

"For our land assaults, we can establish some small outposts toward Carthage,"[ii] Marcus replies. "They will be our warning system."

Scipio looks out toward the sea, then over his shoulder at the distant mainland's sprawl of rolling, fertile plains. "We will mount our campaign immediately. Our best land defense is our aggression. If we keep the Carthaginians on the defensive, there will be no landward attacks."

"We must build a large ditch about our camp," Marcus notes. "Wide and deep enough to block any ladder attacks."

"Agreed. Tell the men to mound the excavated earth against the walls, to reinforce the stakes." The general prods his sandaled toe into the rocky soil. "It will not be an easy dig."

Marcus shrugs. "It will be an excellent conditioner for the recruits. A little shovel work may put some muscle on those powder-butts."

The legate picks up a large rounded pebble and hefts it. He flings it away, watching it arc into the swirling gray sky. "They will dig up lots of little rocks for the slingers, and we can build a camp altar with the bigger ones. This poor soil gives us all sorts of advantages!"

Scipio rolls his eyes. "If you say so. Can we finish the camp before the next full moon?"

For the first time since they left Sicily, Marcus grins. "As Laelius' marines are fond of saying, 'we will find a way or make one.' "

Scipio turns his horse toward the Cape Farina landing. "Then let us see to it, Legate. Get the ..."

"After them!" Marcus roars.

Scipio looks over his shoulder and sees his army commander racing away toward the mainland, javelin in hand. Scipio's guards storm out after him.

What in Hades are they doing? Scipio wonders. Then he sees their prey: three white-armored figures galloping out from a copse of nearby trees, heading southeast toward the mainland. *Carthaginian scouts!* Scipio kicks his horse into a full gallop and races after his men.

Spurring his stallion across the open plains, Marcus draws within yards of the rearmost rider. He grips his javelin tightly in his right hand and grasps his horse's mane in his left. *Have to get it through that cursed linen.* With a grunt of effort, Marcus hurls his spear at the Carthaginian.

The javelin crunches through the scout's lacquered linen armor and lodges in the rider's spine, sticking out like an enormous quill. The Carthaginian jerks back his head and screams, dropping his rope bridle. As Marcus races past him, the scout rolls off the back of his horse and crashes into the earth, scrabbling convulsively at the ground.

Marcus closes on the next rider and pulls another javelin from his saddle sleeve. Seconds later, another rider falls to the earth, to be dispatched by the pursuing equites.

The last scout veers toward the forested hills at the cape's edge. *I'll never find him in there*, it occurs to Marcus. *He'll be back at Carthage by nightfall, reporting to Gisgo.* Marcus slaps his horse's side and the mighty beast surges forward. As he closes on the barbarian, he rears his shoulder back and hurls his last spear.

The Carthaginian sees Marcus' spear slicing towards him. He jerks his horse to the right. The missile whistles past him.

A worthy move, Marcus thinks. *But you're not getting away.*

The legate offers a quick prayer to Epona, the Great Mare. *Lend your strength to my horse, Goddess.* He pats the side of his stallion's neck. "One more surge, then you can rest." He kicks his heels into his mount.

"Hyeeaaah!"

With a last burst of energy, Marcus' lathering stallion draws its head near the left side of the nimble Carthaginian pony. The black-bearded scout darts his small horse sideways but Marcus instantly follows, watching the man's knees to see which way he will guide it. The scout looks back and glowers at the legate, cursing him in Carthaginian. He stares into Marcus' yellow-green eyes and grins.

He's up to something, Marcus thinks. He crouches lower in his saddle, tensed for action.

The scout digs his left knee into his horse and while his right hand jerks on the rope around its neck. The horse whirls about and hurtles back past Marcus' mount. Marcus grabs for his sword but the Carthaginian has already passed him, wheeling about to close in on his back.

Eyes alight with triumph, the barbarian draws out a three foot curved sword and eases his galloping mount alongside Marcus' racing steed, following its every turn. The Carthaginian raises his blade high for a killing stroke into the back of Marcus' bare neck.

Marcus watches him raise the deadly blade, unperturbed. *Careful now*, he tells himself. *We need an informant.* His hand jumps to the left side of his belt, past the pommel of his sword.

Marcus' right hand flicks back toward the Carthaginian. There is a flash of bright metal. The scout screams with pain. His sword clatters to the ground as he grabs at the five-inch throwing knife that juts from his bleeding thigh.

Marcus Silenus crashes his horse sideways into the Carthaginian. The scout flies off the side of his horse and thumps into the rocky ground. Marcus pulls in his stallion and vaults to the ground. He strides over to the Carthaginian, who is pushing himself upright.

The blocky Roman grasps the knob on top of the Carthaginians' domed helmet, yanks his head back, and rams his iron fist twice into the Carthaginian's jaw. The scout collapses face first into the earth, unconscious before his head hits the ground.

A minute later Scipio and the guards pull up beside Marcus. He stands guard over his captive, massaging his swollen knuckles. Scipio slides off his horse and calmly walks over to his commander.

"What have you got there, Marcus?" Scipio asks.

"Someone to tell us about the outposts between here and Carthage," Marcus replies.

"Hmm, he may be reluctant to divulge such information."

Marcus snorts. "I have my cauldrons and skinning knives. I will tell him what I will do to him to encourage his cooperation. Then he can decide how 'reluctant' he wants to be."

"You have no such instruments," Scipio says, grinning. "And you would do no such thing."

"Ah, but I am one of those terrible, baby-eating Romans!" Marcus exclaims. "He believes I would feed his guts to the pigs—while he is still alive."

Scipio chuckles. "Well, you got all three of the scouts, that's the important thing. We will have a few more days before Carthage sends someone to look for them. We have to finish our defenses as soon as possible."

"I've got twenty thousand men we can put to work on building the camp and docks," says Marcus. "I suggest we start tonight. After we post some sentries around the headland."

"Let's get back to the landing, then," says Scipio, walking towards his horse. "The legends will speak of how our camp sprung up overnight!"

"Yes, let's go back," says Marcus. "I want to see Laelius' face when I bring back the 'potato farmer' I found."

For the next two weeks the beach and ridge are beehives of tree-felling, wall-building, and organizing the camp. The mules and packhorses are herded into stables that are being nailed together even as the beasts are led within.

The camp engineers draw out the streets and tent locations of the massive castra, starting with the location of the praetorium, Scipio's command tent. Hundreds of scowling recruits take out their pack shovels and begin to dig out the massive camp perimeter trench, twelve feet wide and nearly nine feet deep. With every shovelful they loudly curse Marcus Silenus—all the while looking over their shoulders to make sure he is not there.

Admiral Laelius spends his days marauding the seas about Cape Farina. Leading a quartet of sleek, hundred-foot triremes, Laelius patrols for Carthaginian ships, reveling in the excitement of exploring a foreign land. One fateful morning, he sights a Carthaginian warship patrolling near the seaside fortress of Utica, but the swift trireme runs back to Utica's sheltered harbor, much to the disappointment of Laelius' battle ready marines.

After days of exploring the coast, Laelius regretfully returns to oversee the unloading of two hundred transport ships onto the newly-completed docks. He spends much of his time arguing over supply allotments with irascible Cato, the obsessively punctilious army auditor.

Cato is never far from the docks, spending long hours scrutinizing the unloading of the army assets, meticulously retabulating every horse, mule, grain urn, and helmet. "Every item in our log must be accounted for," he tells his assistant accountants. "Down to the last sprig of rotten barley."

"We have already tallied everything in Sicily," protests a young scribe. "We finished our work there."

"Even though the work stops, the expenses run on," [iii] Cato replies. "I will know how much of everything has been used, and everything that remains. The Roman people deserve no less than we spend their taxes wisely."

"As you say," The scribe mutters.

Cato becomes Scipio's daily gadfly. He berates the general for transporting costly wines and foodstuffs, and encourages him to reduce the troop's daily wheat and corn allotments. Worst of all, he threatens to report Scipio to Rome if he holds any feasts or celebrations that are not on the religious calendar.

"You cannot use army resources for your indulgent little parties," he tells Scipio. "It's illegal. And it softens the men!"

Scipio stoically bears his quaestor's remonstrances, knowing that Cato's own life is more austere than the lowest of Scipio's soldiers. *The man is a fool, but he is no hypocrite*, Scipio thinks. *But Charon take me to Hades if I let him stand in the way of a good celebration!*

A week after the landing, Cato appears at Scipio's tent. Scipio raises his eyes heavenward. "What is it this time, Cato? I am busy organizing our campaign."

The sturdy redheaded man scowls at Scipio. "You have brought men with you who are of little military value, General. Those disgraced veterans of Cannae and Herdonia are too old for battle. You should ship them back to Sicily."

Scipio finally explodes. "Those men have one chance to redeem themselves before they die, their last chance to die with honor. And you would deny them that, just to save a few grains of barley?" Scipio throws up his hands. "How small is your spirit, Quaestor?"

"Your futile largesse shows who is small," a red-faced Cato replies. "I but fulfill my duty as quaestor. Can you say the same, protecting these men who disgraced themselves in defeat to Hannibal?"

"You overstep your bounds. And your knowledge. The fault was with their generals, not with them."

Scipio points his finger toward the tent exit. "Get out. You waste my time, and I have a war to win. The Cannenses will stay, and if you do not like it you can ship your own self back to Sicily—or Rome, or wherever you want!"

"Those men consume valuable resources," Cato grumbles as he stalks from Scipio's command tent. "Rome will hear of it."

"Senators Flaccus and Fabius will no doubt delight in your words," Scipio says to Cato's retreating back. "And just for that, we will hold a celebratory landing feast tomorrow, with tons of food and wine!"

When the tent flap closes on Cato's hunched back, Scipio steps over to his map table. He stares at the goatskin map of mighty Carthage, a mere three days' march from his budding camp. *They will be coming soon, unless we come at them first. We must venture forth and conquer.*

Scipio fills his bronze cup with undiluted wine. He downs it in a single draught and slams down the cup, still fuming over Cato's words. *Death comes too soon to all of us, little man. Would you drain the life from what living we have here? Tomorrow we feast. And then we strike.*

While the legionnaires hammer in the camp wall palisades and unload the last of the transports, Scipio instigates the next phase of his plan—taking control of the Carthaginian mainland.

Hundreds of soldiers and slaves venture out along the Bagradas River Valley beneath the coastal Atlas Mountains, plundering the bountiful farms. The foraging parties quickly replenish the army's forty-five-day food stores with a providence of wheat, barley, olives, and dates, agog at the fertile beauty of a land they were told was a barren desert.

The ground troops are soon followed by eight turmae of thirty cavalry each, Scipio's first African assault force. The equites range across the neighboring hills and valleys. They raid villages, destroy Carthaginian scouting patrols, and instigate terror into the region. [iv] The mainland peasants flee to Carthage and its neighboring towns, desperate to escape the Roman menace.

With the loss of King Syphax as his ally, Scipio knows he must draw Carthage into a battle as soon as possible, before they can muster more men—before Hannibal is recalled to join Gisgo and Syphax. Time becomes his worst enemy, and aggression his best defense.

* * * * *

CARTHAGE. "He is coming! Scipio is coming! There are Romans in the hills!" The panicky old merchant screams his dire warning to the hundreds of men and women in the public square, even as a Sacred Band guard yanks him from the bottom of the Senate steps.

"Silence!" the guard barks, shaking the old man, "The Romans are not anywhere near Carthage!"

The old man pushes away from the guard and straightens his birdlike frame. "That is a lie! The farmers say they saw Romans marching by the Bagradas River near Cape Farina! They are coming to get us, you will see!"

The elder's alarm spurs the anxious crowd to surge forward around him. They shout at the handful of Carthaginian senators who are ascending the steps to attend the morning Senate meeting.

"Keep them away from me!" blurts a portly older senator, flinging his pudgy arm at the commoners. "They are turning into a mob!"

The guards shove back dozens of Carthaginians but more scramble past them. Several manage to grab the hems of some senators' purple robes.

"Save us! The Romans are coming to destroy us!" a woman pleads, gripping a bewildered senator's toga.

"They will sell our children into slavery!" cries another.

"Bring back Hannibal," yells a wiry little man in the back of the crowd, prompting a chorus of agreements.

"We have to fight them!" yells a young man to the crowd, not specifying whether he means the Romans or the guards. A score of men push toward the steps, fists clenched.

"Get back now!" yells a young guard, his eyes shining with fear. He pulls out his bright curved sword, ready to strike.

Senator Salicar sees the glint of the blade. The stately senator realizes a massacre could erupt at any minute. "Get behind me, Mintho," he says to the coltish young senator who stands next to him.

"They're going to kill us," gasps Mintho.

Salicar slowly shakes his head. "No, no, they just want to be heard. They want someone in power to ease their fears." He smiles at Mintho. "Is that too much to expect from us, to simply talk to them?"

The middle-aged senator pauses halfway up the steps and faces the crowd. He smiles beatifically, spreading his hands as though he is blessing them.

The citizens halt their surge up the steps. Senator Salicar is one of Carthage's most esteemed leaders. In spite of their anger and fear, they are awed by his presence.

"Be at peace, noble Carthaginians," Salicar says confidently. "The Romans are still far north of us." He points toward the forty-foot walls that flank Carthage's house-sized front gates. "Why do you fear? Their army is small, and our walls are impenetrable."

"Then what about them, why are they all up there?" challenges a willowy young woman, pointing toward Carthage's walls.

The Landing

The civilians look back at the east wall of Carthage. They see the walkways are thick with patrolling sentries.

Salicar smiles. "Yes, yes, we have tripled our guards, but that is only to ensure that no spies sneak in on us. This Scipio knows he cannot defeat us in battle, so he resorts to intrigue and deception. But it will do him no good, I assure you."

Salicar sweeps his hand northwest, toward Utica. "Even as I talk to you, our army is building a dozen outposts along our rivers and hills, ready to alert us of any impending danger. We have squadrons of fleet Numidian scouts ranging across the plains. They will warn us if this boy Scipio should be foolish enough to approach Carthage."

Salicar pulls his toga back from his right arm, exposing a forearm stitched with battle scars. "You know I fought in the first war against the Romans, and helped drive them from our shores. As a general of Carthage let me remind you, you are part of the most powerful empire in the world. You live in the strongest fortress in the world. None can breach our treetop walls. None can match our mighty warriors!"

Most of the men halt their advance, but two muscular young men step toward the senators, glaring at the guards. "Who are you to tell us what to do?" blurts one of them.

"Get your men back up the steps and they'll quit coming at us," Salicar mutters to the nearby guard captain. When the soldier hesitates, Salicar fixes him with a stare. "Do it!" he growls. The officer withdraws his men to the top of the steps.

Salicar turns his attention to his fellow senators. "Go on up the steps. Walk slowly." With a benevolent wave at his people, Salicar turns and strides up the last steps, listening for any sounds that he is being pursued. When he is at the top to the walkway he pauses, blowing out his cheeks with relief.

"I wish I was as confident as I sound," he says to Mintho. "Scipio is a force to be reckoned with. We must decide what to do about him today."

13

Salicar treads across the marble tiled walkway and enters the enormous rectangular Senate chambers. Mintho follows, glancing anxiously at the milling crowd below.

The elder senator walks through the enormous bronze-studded Senate doors. He pads over to plunk down onto the chamber's lowest marble bench, a row reserved for the most influential of Carthage's senators, the Council of Elders.

Mintho scrambles up into the back rows, joining the rest of the junior senators. He leans down to hear the senior senators conversing below him. As befits a merchant empire, most of the senators are wealthy men who are lifelong businessmen. Others are veteran army leaders from military families such as the Barcids and the Gisgons, stern veterans of many battles. One faction fights to preserve the wealth of Carthage, the other to increase its might and reach.

The rail-thin Senate leader stands behind a tall stone table in the center of the chambers. "Seat yourselves quickly," the old man bawls. "We have much to discuss with the esteemed General Gisgo!"

Gisgo stands next to the Senate leader, clad in full battle armor. He watches the last of the senators file into the spacious chamber. *They look grim*, Gisgo muses. *I'm in for a long day of being questioned by idiots.* Gisgo fidgets with the edge of the phoenix-embroidered tunic that dangles below his white linen cuirass. He stares at the portly senior senators lining the front row benches. *Most of them are businessmen. They've never put hand to sword. And they dare to question me?*

When all are seated, Hamilcar Barca stands up in the front row. The one-legged senator will be the first to address the Senate, as is his right by seniority. The burly old general is a namesake cousin of the legendary Hamilcar the Thunderbolt who was Hannibal's father, and is almost as revered. All grows quiet when he starts to speak.

"General Gisgo, these Roman barbarians are on our doorstep, a bare two days' march from us. And this Scipio, the man who conquered the Three Generals, I fear he will not rest until he is camped beneath our walls, laying siege to our peerless city!"

Hamilcar turns to face his peers. "Now, we know that Carthage is impregnable, but our people are all in a panic, and our ships cannot leave port to do business!" The last comment elicits shouts of agreement from the merchant senators, who shake their bejeweled fists into the air.

Hamilcar turns back to face Gisgo. "We cannot just sit and wait for him to lay siege to us. What do you propose to do?"

"Attack him!" shouts a young senator.

"Bring back Hannibal and Mago to destroy him!" shouts another.

"We must send peace envoys to Rome," implores an elder senator, a wealthy dye merchant of some renown.

"I will confront Scipio, but my army is not yet ready," Gisgo declares. "At the present time we have about thirteen thousand Carthaginian and Libyan infantry, and twelve hundred cavalry.^{v} That is about half the number in Scipio's army, according to our spies in Sicily."

"Yes, but we are on our native soil, and our soldiers are more than a match of any Romans!" expostulates Hannum, a young Barcid senator. This elicits a smattering of agreement from the most hawkish senators.

These fools would lead me to my doom, Gisgo thinks, *I must stall them until I'm ready*. He straightens up and smiles confidently. "Oh, we certainly have the finest warriors in the world," he says, "When they are all properly trained!"

Gisgo wags his finger at the assembly. "We have many untested recruits in our army, and they require more weapons training, and more practice in horsemanship." *Just like Scipio's army, but they don't know that.* "I need time to recruit more men, and to properly train the ones I have."

"So what do you propose?" sneers the young Barcid. "Do we wait for Scipio to knock on our front gates, then invite him in?"

Gisgo closes his eyes and takes a deep breath. *The pup has never fought in a battle, and he presumes to chide me!* "No," he replies calmly, "I propose we wait for Syphax' army to join us. We will outnumber the Romans three to one and we can wipe them out. I will send a letter of alliance to Syphax this very night!"

"I think we should listen to General Gisgo and wait to engage Scipio," intones Salicar. "With Syphax' Numidian cavalry on our side, we could ride all over the Romans." He glances sideways at Gisgo. "And General Gisgo has more experience with Scipio than any of us," he adds, neglecting to mention Gisgo's three defeats at Scipio's hands.

"We cannot just sit around and do nothing!" fumes Hannum. Three of his fellow Barcids stand up, signaling their support of Hannum's statement.

Gisgo's mind races. *I have to buy time somehow.* "Very well, we will take action immediately. I will send out five hundred of our best cavalry. They can probe Scipio's position and impede his progress toward Carthage, should he dare to come here."

He sees the senators looking at each other and his voice rises excitedly, knowing he is on the cusp of convincing them. "Our men will leave within a few days. They will be led by the redoubtable Captain Hanno, son of Bomilcar."

The senators mutter among themselves. Just as they nod their agreement, Commander Hannum vaults up from his seat.

"General, I want to lead your contingent instead of Hanno. I have been trained on horse since I was a child, and I know the area around Utica." He smirks at his Barcid relatives. "As a Barca, I will truly test the mettle of this Roman cur."

Gisgo laughs to himself. *You think you will test Scipio?* He shrugs to himself. *If it will keep the Barcids quiet, so be it.*

"I think that is an excellent idea, Hannum" replies Gisgo, with a bow that hides his sarcastic smile. "With your skills and background, I do not doubt it will be a memorable venture."

16

*   *   *   *   *

CIRTA, NUMIDIA. "What a load of camel droppings!"

Syphax balls up the papyrus sheaf and bounces it off a stone wall of his chambers. "Can you believe it, Hasdrubal Gisgo wants me to bring him my entire army! And me in the midst of exterminating Masinissa's rebels!"

He spits onto his ornate horse hair rug. "Gods be cursed, I should have kept my alliance with Scipio."

Sophonisba stares at her husband, feigning dismay. "Gisgo does not understand how stubborn those Massylii rebels can be," she says soothingly. "That Masinissa keeps them all stirred up. They think he will return to conquer you and your Masaesyli."

Syphax stalks about his throne room like an angry boy, shoving guards out of his way. "Wait until I catch Masinissa!" he growls, "I will roast him inside a bronze bull, like Hasdrubal Barca did to those Romans!" He stops and rubs his black-bearded chin, panting with anger. "I'll make a rug of his skin and piss on it every day!"

Sophonisba shudders at the thought of her beloved inside a white-hot torture chamber. *How can I delay his pursuit of Masinissa?* she wonders. Then it occurs to her.

"It would not be wise to ignore Gisgo's request, husband. He promised you thousands of troops when Scipio is conquered. But you must show him that you are King Syphax, lord of the Masaesyli. Show him you will not be ordered about."

Sophonisba walks behind her husband and places her hands on his shoulders, gently massaging them. She leans near his ear. "Send him some of your elite cavalry. That will be a gesture of friendship and respect on your part, but without any conciliation to his demands."

Syphax pushes her head away. "Oh no! I'm not sending that little bastard my royal guard!" Syphax growls. "I've had two attempts on my life already."

"My gods no, don't do that!" exclaims Sophonisba. "I can't tell you what it would do to me if you were killed! Send him the ones that have been chasing after Masinissa these last two months."

Syphax looks sideways at her, his eyebrows arched. "You would like that, wouldn't you?" he says suspiciously. "Send your friend's pursuers to Carthage, so he won't be caught."

Sophonisba shrugs and looks away from him. "He is not my friend, I can promise you that. He can rot in an ant hill for all I care."

"Then why do you want to remove his pursuers, my love? Why is that best for me?" asks Syphax, his voice mixed with hope and doubt.

Sophonisba sidles up to Syphax. She pillows her breasts against his back and wraps her arms about his neck. "I only want you to be the mightiest king in Africa," she coos. "If you can appease Gisgo by sending him a few hundred men, you could keep your army intact and end this rebellion—and Masinissa. Then you could join Gisgo and crush Scipio! Once Scipio falls, Gisgo would help you conquer all Numidia, as he has promised."

"You expect me to believe that you want your old admirer to die for my sake?" Syphax says edgily.

Sophonisba squeezes his shoulder, and musters excitement into her voice. "There is more to it, I confess. With him gone I would be the true queen of all Numidia." She strokes the back of his head. "That is what I really want, not this sham throne of half a nation!"

"Hmph!" Syphax says, frowning at the tent wall. "I will consider it."

Sophonisba sniffs. "I care not what you do, although loaning Gisgo those men would benefit the both of us." She stalks towards the main door. "My elephant needs a bath. I am going to tend to Boodes."

Sophonisba pushes her way between Syphax' two gigantic guards and strides down the tapestried hallway, the clacking of her sandals fading into the distance. *Oh my beloved, where are you? Are you with Scipio? Take care, they are coming for you both.*

II. STRIKE AND COUNTERSTRIKE

BAGRADAS RIVER VALLEY, NORTHERN AFRICA.
Commander Hannum's cavalry gallop across the grassy open plains, elated with their recent triumph. His men have just destroyed a squadron of Roman scouts, surprising them in the narrow passage between the rocky hills at the valley's mouth.

Knowing the terrain like the back of his hand, it was an easy matter for Hannum to hide his men in the hillside ridges. When the thirty Romans filled the middle of the passage, his warriors cascaded down upon them. Hannum's ambitious young noblemen quickly encircled the heavily outnumbered Romans and rained javelins into them. When only a handful of dying legionnaires were left, his men drew lots for the privilege of administering the fatal spear thrust into their helpless victims.

The victorious Carthaginians stripped the dead equites of their armor and weapons, pulling off their rings and belts. They piled their plunder behind a ridge, aiming to recover their souvenirs upon their return home. Now they ride on, eager to massacre more of their enemies. They brag about taking heads and mounting them on spears as a grisly warning to the Roman invaders.

The Carthaginian horsemen do not have far to ride for their next confrontation. One of Hannum's scouts spies a Roman outpost at a branch of the Bagradas River. It is a simple fort of piled timbers and branches, populated with two score of Scipio's soldiers. The scout returns to Hannum with the news, bringing a smile to his face.

Hannum gathers his five hundred riders about him. "We attack all at once, at full speed. Blow into them like a desert storm, men. Leave no one alive, however much they beg for mercy."

With a snap of his reins Hannum charges across the plain, his men thundering in behind him. As they close on the camp, Hannum watches the Roman soldiers running about for their armor and weapons. *Look at those unprepared fools, did they think Carthage would hide behind our walls? They deserve to die.*

A Roman rider dashes out from the camp, heading north toward Scipio's camp. "Leave him!" Hannum shouts. "Get the rest of them before they escape. Kill them all."

Hannum's cavalry charge in with the vainglorious shouts of men still new to death and battle. They leap over the camp's rude palisade and swirl into the Romans, spearing them down as they dash for their horses and weapons. Dozens of Carthaginians dismount and draw their swords. They break into clusters and surround the few remaining soldiers. The noblemen jab their long, curved blades into the backs and sides of the legionnaires, laughing at their futile efforts to defend themselves.

Finally, only the lead tribune remains, a stocky redheaded man who has backed himself against the wall. His eyes glare defiantly at the smirking Carthaginians who stroll towards him, blades dangling at their sides.

"Come on, barbarian puke. I'll have your heads before I fall." The Carthaginians do not understand Latin, but they grasp the gist of his defiant message. They laugh and fling horse shit at the glowering tribune. A handsome young nobleman bends over and bares his buttocks at the soldier, pantomiming anal sex with him. The riders roar with laughter.

Hannum observes the defiant little man from atop his black stallion. "He's a plucky little rooster, isn't he? Well, it's time to pluck the chicken. Go have your fun. Then we move on."

The Carthaginians step toward the legionnaire. The tribune darts over and grabs a shield from a dead comrade. He stands back against the wall, legs planted wide and sword at the ready.

The riders encircle the man. "Take your time, he is the last one" says a young nobleman as he stalks toward the tribune. With a loud battle cry, the nobleman jumps forward. He cracks his sword against the tribune's rectangular shield, parrying the Roman's thrust with his round one. While their leader duels with the tribune, the others lunge forward from the sides. They jab into the Roman's thighs and back, stitching his body with wounds.

The tribune staggers about, bleeding from a dozen cuts, his blade held low. He raises his head and spits blood at the nobleman in front of him, speckling his face. "We beat you in the first war," he gasps, "and we'll do it again."

Amused at his valor, the Carthaginians dive in to whack him with the flat of their blades, laughing as he pitches about to confront his attackers.

Hannum looks at the sun's position in the sky and frowns. "Come on, boys. We have more conquests."

A fox-faced young nobleman nods at Hannum. "Let me venture into single combat against this dread Roman!" he declares.

Laughing, the Carthaginian steps over to the slumping tribune, his blade poised for a killing thrust to his heart. The Roman jerks up his shield and batters its iron boss into the young man's chest, knocking him flat.

The tribune hurls himself on top of him. With the last of his strength, he stabs his gladius through the nobleman's throat, impaling his neck into the earth.

"Laugh at that, bastard!" the legionnaire mutters, watching the Carthaginian gurgle out his life.

A dozen spears and blades pierce the Roman's back. He slumps on top of his victim, his corpse oblivious to the Carthaginians' cuts and blows.

"That Roman shit killed him!" Hannum yells. "Now what will I tell his mother?" He rubs his eyes and sighs, then waves his hand toward his men. "Come on, stake him out and we'll go get our revenge."

The Carthaginians saw off the tribune's head and stake it upon one of their javelins, placing it in the center of the outpost. They jump onto their horses and gallop after Hannum, who has already headed west across the plain.

Heady with conquest, Hannum leads his men into the open plains by Utica, intent on destroying one more outpost before he returns home with his victories. *These are the dread Romans I have heard about? Psh! Tomorrow we will attack Scipio's camp. His plodding cavalry can't catch us.*

Hannum's men head due north along the gulf coast, enjoying the vista of the open plains to their left and the shimmering Mediterranean waters far to their right. They see nothing but fields and farms about them, not a Roman in sight. Hannum grows restless. *We've got to get a kill soon, so I can be back for the evening feast. I hope we are having she-camel, I'm tired of chickpeas and mutton!*

He orders his men to increase their pace. The five hundred riders draw near another Roman outpost, but the rude hut shows signs of being hastily abandoned.

"That damned scout warned them," Hannum says to his men. The Carthaginians ride on while the sun draws near the horizon, recounting the day's kills. The riders finally approach the Utica fortress, squinting their eyes against the setting sun.

"Isn't it time we went back?" queries his captain. "We are nearing the Roman camp."

Hannum makes a face. "We need to take back some more plunder." He sees his captain frowning at him. "Don't be such a sheep! We'll turn around at the top of that rise. We'll see what we can attack tomorrow."

Hannum and his men trot to the top of the rise. They halt in their tracks, gaping at what they see below. There, within a mile of the Utica walls, Scipio's legions have arrayed themselves around the front of the port city,[vi] with a score of Roman warships blockading Utica's harbor.

The commander raises his hand to signal for a gallop back home. He notices a large dust cloud approaching from the plains to the left of them. *Well I'll be cursed, the Roman slugs have finally found us!*

"Back to Carthage!" Hannum shouts. He wheels around his mount and charges south toward Carthage.

The Carthaginians race back down the open plain, slowly widening the gap between them and their Roman pursuers. Hannum watches the Romans fade from sight. *Those fools should get rid of all that armor.*

Hannum toys with a curled strand of his hair, thinking of the triumphant report he will provide to the Senate, and of the accolades he will receive. *Perhaps they will give me a gold wreath. At the very least, I deserve a silver one. And a virgin!*

His men storm back toward the passage between the hills, racing for the faint outline of Carthage, its white walls glowing gold in the long-angled rays of the setting sun. They dash into the opening of the narrow valley.

"Leave the plunder," Hannum orders. "We'll get it tomorrow." The Carthaginians trample over the scattered Roman corpses and gallop toward the eastern end of the defile, their homeland looming before them.

As they ride through the passage between the forested hillsides, Hannum hears the brittle crack of branches breaking above him. *Is that a herd of deer? I can take one tomorrow, on the way home.* He halts his horse and looks up. His mouth drops open.

A horde of lean, dark, half-naked riders pours down from the mountainside trees on both sides of him, reprising Hannum's own ambush on the Romans. More horsemen flow into the mouth of the valley and blockade it, their long spears bristling in front of them.

Hannum sees that they are Massylii Numidians, led by a tall, sinewy man with a lion's head perched on top of his ornate bronze helmet. His heart leaps to his throat. *It's Masinissa!*

Masinissa kicks his horse forward. "For Numidia!" he shouts, brandishing his spear above his head.

The Numidians whirl into the Carthaginians, darting about for quick javelin strikes into their unprotected bodies. The young noblemen pull out their swords and plunge after their outnumbered foe, but the Massylii urge their nimble Numidian ponies up the slopes of the steep hills, eluding the Carthaginians' larger and slower mounts. When the noblemen retreat down the hillside, the Numidians gallop down and hurl spears into them. Droves of the young bravos fall from their horses, javelins dangling from their backs and chests.

The Carthaginian cavalry, so brave and exuberant an hour earlier, now mill about in panicked confusion. They ram into one another in their attempt to elude the Numidian lances, which seem to come from every direction.

We are trapped! Hannum thinks. His heart hammers in his ears. The young commander sees that there are only two score Numidians blocking the front passage. *Death or freedom, it's the only way.*

"Charge the front!" Hannum bellows, waving for his trumpeter to sound the call. The horn blows three times. The Carthaginians ride straight at Masinissa and his waiting tribesmen.

The two sides collide with a splintering crash of shield on shield, followed by the ringing scrapes of clashing swords. The Numidians pour down from the hillside and push the Carthaginians together. With little room to maneuver, the conflict becomes more a mounted brawl than a battle, with the close-packed riders barging into one other as they battle for position.

The superior numbers of the Carthaginians begin to tell. The Numidians in the front line drop from their saddles, bleeding from multiple wounds.

"Stay facing them!" Masinissa shouts from the front. He ducks a spear thrust and counters with a reaching stab that opens a lean young man's forearm to the bone. "Not much longer. Stay at your position!"

The Numidians close ranks as if they were infantry, creating a fence of spears to fend off the desperate attacks of the Carthaginians. The Numidians on the hillsides press into Hannum's men from both sides, but their limited numbers dwindle.

Minutes later, Masinissa hears the blare of a distant horn. He looks into the passage behind the Carthaginians, and grins with relief.

The Roman heavy cavalry hurtle into the back of the passage. The heavily armored equites gallop furiously at the men who killed their fellows, swords drawn and faces grim. They crash the Carthaginians' rear, wielding their gladii with deadly efficacy, striking madly to their right and left. Scores of Hannum's men fall beneath the Romans.

"Attack the front!" Hannum screams. "Everyone at the front!" With a desperate energy born of fear, the Carthaginians fight their way through the last of Masinissa's Numidians and break out of the passage.

Racing out into the open plain, Hannum waves for his men to follow him to Carthage. His surviving cavalry gallop desperately for the shelter of home, but they are chased by the ablest pursuit cavalry in the world, the relentless Numidians.

The Numidians fling their javelins into the backs of the rearmost riders. Dozens fall from their galloping mounts. Some crash to the earth so hard their heads bounce, dying from a shattered skull. Others land stunned and wounded, becoming easy prey for the Numidians who dismount and close on them with swords drawn. The lead Numidians gallop past the falling Carthaginians. They grab more javelins from their saddle slings and mow down the next line of riders.

Masinissa is in the fore of the pursuit. Eyes agleam, he yells encouragement to his men, exultant to finally be the pursuer instead of the pursued. *You will regret the day you allied yourself with Syphax, Carthaginians. And gave my Sophonisba to him.*

Young Hannum speeds ahead of his riders, urging them on toward the city. Behind him he can hear the thumps and cries of the falling casualties, and he frantically digs his heels into this mount. He sees a most blessed sight—the distant gates of Carthage are slowly opening. *Baal help me,* he prays, *send some men out to scare these bastards away.* As the gates widen he hears a roar of rage behind him.

Hannum looks over his shoulder and sees Masinissa closing in on him, the head of his horse is next to Hannum's left leg. Still at full gallop, Masinissa slides out his curved short sword. He raises it over his head to chop into the back of Hannum's neck.

Without breaking stride, Hannum yanks up the small round shield on his left arm, ready to wield off the blow. But Hannum's classical cavalry training could not prepare him for a fight with Masinissa, the prince of nomads, the man who rode horses before he could walk.

Masinissa springs onto the back of Hannum's mount and locks his arm about Hannum's neck. In one quick motion he slashes open the nobleman's throat and flings him to the ground. As Masinissa rides back to his horse, proud Hannum kicks out his life in the dust, his eyes bulging with the terror of death.

Seeing their leader fall, a dozen of Hannum's men pull up to help him. They see the gaping throat slash and the death spasms of his feet. They to flee, but they have tarried too long. The Numidians swarm around them. The Carthaginians soon join their commander in the uncaring dust.

Hordes of infantry and riders pour out from the Carthaginian gates, all rushing headlong at the Numidians. Masinissa spins his mount around and his horsemen follow him, riding away so fast their pursuers soon abandon the chase.

Hannum's surviving cavalry hurtle headlong through the gates as if demons are upon them, scattering their own men in their efforts to achieve safety. Several hundred Carthaginians have escaped the trap, but most of these proud young nobles will prove to be little use in the future, their minds haunted with the carnage of their first battle, with the mind-numbing terror of moving from slayer to slain in the blink of an eye.

The Roman cavalry commander sends a scout toward Scipio's camp with news of the victory, as the Massylii and Romans return together, riding along at a leisurely pace. They trot triumphantly into Scipio's camp by Utica, passing through the groups of carpenters and engineers who are finishing the camp walls and buildings. Scipio himself is standing at the spot where the gates will be built, surrounded by his tribunes.

"Welcome King Masinissa," Scipio exclaims, looking back at his officers. He faces Masinissa and winks at him. "I have told my men all about you, how you have lent the power of all Numidia to our cause!"

Masinissa is aware that Laelius told Scipio he had little more than two hundred men.[vii] He smiles at Scipio's ruse.

"It is an honor to join you, King Scipio, " Masinissa gushes. "All of my men are at your disposal, that we may conquer Africa together!"

"I am overjoyed to hear it," replies Scipio. He turns back to his men. "Do you see? Now we have allies here! Tell your fellows that Numidia has joined us, and that Nike will bless us with total victory!"

Scipio beckons for Masinissa to follow him. The two head into Scipio's praetorium. They will drink and tell stories long into the night, celebrating Rome's first victory of the African campaign.

*   *   *   *   *

ROME, 204 BCE. "I know I have advocated restraint," sputters Fabius. "But I was wrong. Hannibal has slain proconsul Manius Fabius, and he will kill more if given the chance. His army must be destroyed as soon as possible!"

The aged general stalks about the Senate floor, raging against Hannibal's latest victory in Bruttium—and the death of his beloved nephew. As this year's Princeps Senatus, Fabius is the first senator to speak on any issue. He has called this meeting to address the threat of Hannibal in south Italia, and—at Flaccus' urging—to assail the fiscal support of Scipio's African campaign.

"Yes, yes, Manius Fabius was my nephew, and my love for him does color my judgment. But you all knew his heart, how the young man ventured out to confront dread Hannibal and drive him from Italia."

The bent old man wipes a tear from his seamed face. "They told me he fought to the very end. He could have dropped his sword and begged for ransom, but he did not! He had the virtues of a true Roman!"

Fabius glances over at Flaccus, who is sprawled out in the front row, legs akimbo under his purple-bordered toga. Flaccus is savoring Fabius' speech in spite of his sorrowful face, knowing what Fabius will say next.

When Fabius looks at him, Flaccus slightly waggles the fingers of his right hand, which rests in his lap. *Go on,* he signals, *give them the rest of it.* Fabius looks at the Senate. He raises his Principes staff high above his head, as if leading a charge.

"Here is the question I pose to you honorable Senators: Are we true Romans, like Manius Fabius? Are we ready to exert our will upon Hannibal's cornered army, and attack him in full force?" He stands silent, letting his words sink in before he lowers his staff.

"Do you think we lack the men or money for such an assault?" he continues. "If so, the solution to that is simple. Recall Scipio from Africa! Next month we will have the New Year elections. We must urge the Popular Assembly to deny Scipio a military imperium for another year. Bring his army home, and bring our legions back from Macedonia! Those armies can join our South Italia legions in one massive assault on Hannibal. Then our northern armies could march west and wipe out his brother Mago. Once and for all, we will purge the Carthaginians from our shores!"

Amidst heavy applause, the exhausted Fabius shuffles to his seat, a small marble bench that faces the Senate. He eases into it and glowers at this peers, daring anyone to disagree with him.

Flaccus sees his opportunity and rises from his seat. His back is ramrod straight; his deep voice resonant with righteous anger. "You have heard our honored General. He has a sound strategy to end this war."

He bows his head toward Fabius. "Fabius was ever a man to seek truth over personal advantage. And now you hear him doing it again. He has abandoned his support for his own brilliant delaying strategy—the approach that earned him the honorific of Cunctuator—to advocate a direct assault on Hannibal, and Mago. Now he says we must muster all our resources for one mighty blow against our homeland invaders, and end this war."

"Scipio will end the war if he stays in Africa," shouts Senator Tiberius Julius, a wreathed veteran of the first Punic War. "He will finish what we started last time, and break Carthage's back!"

The chamber is filled with a smattering of approving cheers as scores of senators raise their fists in agreement.

Flaccus shakes his head. "Would it were so, but we are only doing what Hannibal desires—dividing our force and weakening his opposition. The same strategy Philip of Macedon used to conquer the Greeks. He called it 'divide and conquer'." [viii]

"I fully support Fabius' proposal. Destroy Mago and Hannibal before they can join forces against us! Now, at the new year, when the people's Popular Assembly gathers, we must urge them to revoke Scipio's imperium, and bring our Romans home!"

Flaccus resumes his seat to hearty applause from the Latins. He sits down gingerly. His scarred anus is an ever-present reminder of Pomponia's revenge upon his assault on her. *That vote will drag her spawn back here in disgrace,* he thinks, savoring the outcome of his plan. *That will hurt her enough until I can kill her.* Flaccus nods pleasantly at several party members watching him, the very picture of patrician grace and decorum. *And that bastard Silenus, he has a surprise waiting for him, too.*

Flaccus stretches out his arms and legs, feeling better than he has in weeks. *I must get myself a boy tonight to celebrate. Perhaps a Carthaginian.* He smirks. *I will wage my own assault.*

The morning after the senate meeting, Pomponia leads a one-armed messenger through her manse, halting him outside her office chamber. "Wait for me, I shall not be long," she commands.

The grizzled Cannae veteran nods and stands against a wall, grateful for his respite from clopping his aged horse along Rome's cobbled streets. He begins retying his new wooden arm onto his elbow stump, pulling the thin leather straps tight with his remaining front teeth.

Pomponia enters her office and sits down at her stone writing table. She grabs a foot-long roll of papyrus and unrolls it. Placing stones at each end to hold it, she dips her reed pen into a jar of octopus ink and writes a note in her elegant flowing hand, muttering with irritation.

Beloved Son:

The Latins work day and night to recall you from Africa. I swear, they are more concerned with preserving their power than providing for Rome's safety!

I do not doubt that you are still the people's favorite here, and that you will prevail in Africa, if given a chance. But the Senate is no less fickle than the goddess Fortuna. They have short memories, as do the citizenry. Both require frequent reminders of your past successes.

As you attain your conquests over there, you need to send us some reminders of them, be they wealth or prisoners. The evidence of your success will be no less potent than the weapons you wield, more so in our war for Rome's hearts and minds.

Please take care of your brother Lucius. I worry about him.

Your Loving Mother,

Pomponia

Pomponia sprinkles some chalk dust across the ink and blows it off, gently flapping the sheet to dry it. She rolls up the scroll, dabs some wax on it, and stamps in the family's owl's head signet.

Pomponia hurries out to the waiting messenger and shoves the scroll into his leathery hand, giving him a small purse of coins. "Three days. I want this in Scipio's hands by the Day of Saturn. Then you will have the other half of the payment."

The messenger turns to go. Pomponia clamps onto his shoulder and turns him about. "I will find out how long it took, I promise you!"

The abashed veteran trots out into the city street fronting the Scipio domus. He takes his horse's reins from the bent old house slave holding them. Grasping the horse's neck in his good arm, the messenger gracefully levers himself up onto his mount. The man races out toward the Ostia docks, where a bireme for Africa awaits him.

Pomponia stands at the doorway, watching him clatter down the cobbled street. She looks back inside at wall of the Scipio family death masks, where her husband Publius' face hangs above his ancestors' figures. She grins ruefully at it. *Now we have two wars to win, Beloved. At home and in Africa. If we lose either one of them we will doubtless lose the other.*

Pomponia waves over her main attendant, a statuesque Greek woman with ringlets of gray hair cascading past the shoulders of her thick indigo tunic. "Ask Amelia to come over at her earliest opportunity, she is over tending to her old home." Pomponia tells her.

The attendant departs, pacing down the street toward the Paullus domus. Pomponia returns to her writing desk, spreading out a new roll of papyrus. *Time for Amelia and I start the home campaign. Next month we have to conquer our own people.*

*   *   *   *   *

CARTHAGE, 204 BCE. By the time the survivors of Hannum's ill-fated cavalry raid have stabled their horses, the city's two governors have already sent orders to the Carthaginian Senate, commanding them to meet the next morning to discuss the disaster. As leader of all the

Carthaginian forces in Africa, General Gisgo is summoned to appear before them.

The next day Gisgo is again at the speaker's platform, facing an angry group of senators. This time, however, the general's demeanor is decidedly combative—he is determined not be blamed for Hannum's folly.

Gisgo resented Hannum's impulsive intrusion into his battle plans, and is secretly delighted at his misfortune. This time Gisgo will brook no more concessions to foolish noblemen who have never put hand to sword in combat...

The Principal Elder commences the military inquiry. Gisgo stands next to the old man on the large rectangular speaker's platform, wearing his best armor.

"The Romans have struck again, General," the Principal says. "This time we have lost noble Hannum, the pride of Carthage."

You mean the idiot of Carthage, Gisgo thinks, his face masked with false regret.

Senator Rosto Barca rises from his seat. The one-armed veteran sneers at Gisgo. "Would you say you are now ready to confront the Romans, General? Or perhaps we should wait until they show up at our gates! You can use me then, I've been properly trained. And I've still got my sword arm!"

There is chorus of laughter. Gisgo stoically waits for it to die down before he replies.

"We are still gathering new recruits from Carthage and Libya," Gisgo intones sarcastically, "as well you all know. Syphax has just destroyed a large part of Masinissa's rebel army, although Masinissa escaped with several hundred of his men. Syphax will soon join forces with us, then we will have an army twice our present size!" He glares at the senators. "Now is not the time to fight the Romans."

"Now is not the time to wait!" counters another retired warrior. "I fought in the first war, and I know those Italians. They will burn and plunder our land until they are at our gates. They cannot be gainsaid from aiming to destroy us."

Gisgo nods. "I agree, Fuano. Carthage will be their ultimate target. And this Scipio, he is persistent. But if we fight them before we are ready—and lose—there will be none left to stand in their way."

"Bring back Hannibal!" shouts one senator.

"Mago, too!" shouts another.

"Gisgo's army will be ready for battle before they can get here," counters a Gisgon senator. "Just wait until he is ready!"

For the fifth time that day, the senators erupt in bickering. While the Principal Elder shouts for order, a tall and regal man steps in next to Gisgo and whispers in his ear. Gisgo responds with a nod and a grimace. He steps back and yields the floor to the purple-togaed senator.

"You all know me. I am Hanno, the hero of our first war with Rome. I say it is folly to talk of recalling Hannibal to fight Scipio and his little army, when he may soon conquer Rome itself."

Hanno bows his head toward Gisgo. "Senators, you know I fought in our victories at Cannae and Trasimene. I tell you now, General Gisgo is right to wait until our army is fully ready, to wait until we have enough properly trained men—and to wait until Syphax joins him with his thousands of cavalry. We crushed the Romans at Cannae and Trasimene because their generals acted hastily—rushing to battle before their men were ready. Let us not do the same."

Hanno sees several senators rise to protest, and he sticks out his palms placatingly. "That does not mean we sit here like am ox waiting for slaughter. I volunteer to lead an expeditionary cavalry force against Scipio."

"You would attack Scipio when Gisgo says we do not have enough men to fight him?" blurts out one of the senators, looking incredulously at his fellows. "What men would you take? We do not have many veteran cavalry, and I would rather you did not risk them on another sortie."

"Hanno has discussed this with me before," says Gisgo. "We have a solution."

Gisgo waves to the guards at the chamber doors. They open the twin oak portals and step to the side. A light brown Numidian walks in, a heavyset man wearing a large bone necklace and a cheetah loincloth, the marks of a tribal leader.

Gisgo beckons the man forward. "This is Arat, the chieftain of one of the Masaesyli tribes. He has brought his tribal warriors to us at Syphax' behest. Syphax sent them as a gesture of solidarity."

Arat faces the Senate, his broad face imperious, looking at them as though they are his underlings. Hanno steps next to him.

"Arat has brought thirty-eight hundred Numidians with him, veteran warriors who have been fighting Masinissa's rebels. I already have two hundred more of Carthage's finest young nobles who will join the Numidians.[ix] These men are not timid recruits, they are expert riders who are anxious to avenge the loss of Hannum and their friends. We will be a formidable force."

The stout chieftain bows almost imperceptibly toward the senators, and sweeps out his thick, tattooed arm. "I lead out my men with you, Hanno," he says in his pidgin Carthaginian. "We drive Romans from Salaeca town. This Roman Scipio, he must beat us before he can come on to Carthage." He laughs loudly. "No chance! My men ride circles around Romans. They move like oxen!"

Hanno looks at the Senate. "See? Our presence will give my friend Gisgo time to muster and train his army. Then he can move on Scipio in full force." He grins wolfishly. "If there is anything left of them."

Gisgo stands to the side, impassively observing Hanno's introduction and Arat's oration. *Typical of Hanno*, he thinks. *We could have arranged all this without going before the Senate, but he had to bring*

*the chieftain in here for dramatic effect, and show off his plan. Ah, I
care not. Maybe they'll get lucky and kill the Roman bastard.*

"We have made a good plan," interjects Gisgo, weary of Arat's
theatrics. He looks at the Principal Elder. "I would ask for a vote upon
this matter."

The Elder looks at his fellow senators. "All who favor Hanno's
occupation of Salaeca raise your right hand."

Most of the senators raise their hand, enough that it is a clear majority.
"The plan is approved," says the Elder. "Hanno and Gisgo, you may
proceed as you see fit."

Hanno grins widely, eager for the glory of defeating the Romans.
"Arat and I will leave in the morning." He looks at Arat, and his smile
widens. "Rest assured, we two will give the Romans a good lesson
about attacking our homeland."

*   *   *   *   *

UTICA PLAINS, 204. BCE. Scipio, Masinissa, and his officers stand
out on the windswept plain by the front gates of camp. They watch the
winter rainsquall blow in from the sea towards the Utica fortress,
pulling rounded cloud shadows across its thirty-foot walls.

"I swear, winter here feels like summer back home," comments one of
the North Italia officers. "I could get used to this climate."

Marcus shakes his head. "The winter rains will be upon us, and the
plains will soon be quagmires. It will be very cold. We will have to stay
near camp until spring comes."

"Perhaps," Scipio replies, "but we can still take Utica during the
winter, and do it soon!"

Marcus Silenus looks sideways at Laelius. His eyes relay his doubt.
Laelius shrugs and raises his eyebrows. *It's possible*, he signals.

Marcus turns back to Scipio. "You say we are going to take Utica, honored General? Is that truly necessary?" Marcus is mindful that all the senior tribunes are watching him, and any disrespect from him could undermine his young commander's position.[x]

"We have to take Utica," Scipio enjoins. "It will be the perfect base for the spring campaign."

"That is a formidable city," says Marcus, looking over at its towering walls. "It will be much more difficult than last week's capture of the Membrone garrison, though their resistance was stiff."

"I am aware of that," says Scipio irritably. "Utica will be more like capturing Carthago Nova—which I did quite ably, by the way. And I will do the same to Utica!"

"Perhaps so," says Marcus evenly. "But that was before our enemies knew who you were. Now they are much more watchful and cautious, knowing you are prone to tricks and ruses."

"Do not be so pessimistic, you old foot soldier," quips Laelius. 'Our ships have already blockaded Utica harbor. A fish can't get out of there without me knowing about it!"

Marcus shrugs. "That will prevent the Uticans from receiving supplies, but I venture their fortress is already well stocked." He sweeps his hand across the wide plains. "Look about us. This Bagradas Valley is lush with grain and fruit. It might take a year to starve them out."

Scipio grimaces. "We cannot take a year, we must take Utica within three months, before the spring campaign. And when we conquer it, Rome will have an impregnable garrison in Africa. That could hasten a peace between us."

"If Utica is so impregnable," a young tribune pipes up. "How are we to 'impregnate' it? Who sticks their penis in Utica?" He smiles at his fellow officers, but his grin vanishes when he sees their disdain for his joke. To them, he has not yet earned the right to be as frivolous as Laelius, veteran of a dozen battles.

Scipio looks steadily at the youngster until he blushes and averts his eyes. "It is not impregnable, Decimus. Nothing is unconquerable to those who are bold and inventive."

"Still, Marcus' point is well taken," says Scipio. "We cannot just sit here for a year. We need to make inroads into the country, to keep Carthage on the defensive." He glances at Laelius. "And to give the people at home some tangible results of our progress." He laughs. "My mother has told me how important that is."

A senior tribune smirks at Scipio. "You take advice from your mother? A woman?"

"A woman such as you have never seen," growls Marcus Silenus, prompting the tribune to silence.

"My gods, Scipio. You just sent Rome eight thousand captives and a two shiploads of plunder," [xi] Laelius grouses. "Is this a campaign or a business expedition?"

Scipio rolls his eyes. "Both, I fear. The people want victory, but the Senate wants wealth. We must feed the beast that is the Roman treasury, and send Rome signs of our success. We need constant conquest and plunder."

"And our noble senators make jest of the Carthaginians as mercenaries!" laughs Laelius. "At least they are open about it!"

Masinissa shakes his head. "I do not see us doing this assault on Utica, King Scipio. Why do we not take Tunis? It overlooks Carthage from but a few miles away. It has lower walls. Our men could storm over it within days."

Scipio turns and looks at Utica. "Utica is the wealthiest city in Africa, save Carthage. Think of the resources we would secure, think of what it would mean back home!" He looks sheepishly at him men, embarrassed at the mercantilism of his comments. "Do not forget," he continues, "The Uticans defected to Rome in the last war, we just need to persuade them to do it again. A month's siege should do the convincing, as it did in Iberia."

While Scipio's officers discuss siege tactics, a large wooden wagon trundles past them and heads towards the camp. Scipio's eyes follow the wagon, curious at the cloud of flies that follows it.

A nervous-looking young peasant drives the wagon, looking fearfully at the armed legionnaires who gaze at him as he passes. The wagon continues to the camp entrance, passing through a knot of camp carpenters who are lashing together the timbers for the gates. The craftsmen glance curiously as the wagon, sniffing at the foul odor emanating from it.

Two sentries step out in front of the entrance. They march up and grab the wagon's reins. "What is your purpose here, boy?" barks one of the sentries. The young man babbles incoherently in his native tongue, his tone urging forgiveness.

The guards walk to the back of the wagon. The sentries pull off the cloth covering and peer inside. They stare at what they see for several long seconds before one of them steps back and vomits. "Jupiter save us," he says, as he bends over again.

The two walk back to the front of the wagon and cast the driver off it. They jump onto the wagon and snap the reins, leading it into camp. The gate carpenters drift over and glance into the uncovered back of the wagon. They recoil in horror, throw down their saws and hammers, and follow the wagon into camp.

As the wagon rolls through the main street, various soldiers peer into the back and join the following, until there is a large procession of angry and horrified legionnaires following it. The ubiquitous camp dogs circle it, their noses high in the air. The wagon halts at Scipio's tent headquarters.

"There is a distress in camp," Scipio says. "I must see to it." Scipio strides toward camp, intercepting the centurion.

"Carthage has answered our attack on them," the centurion says dourly, nodding at the wagon. Scipio walks over to the wagon and peers into the rear. When Scipio's officers hear him gasp, they rush over and join him—and draw back in horror.

A dozen torsos lie inside, piled up like pale, bloody logs. The bodies have no heads, arms, or legs. Were it not for the unfortunates' bloodied breastplates, Scipio would not know them to be legionnaires.

Marcus stands at Scipio's shoulder, calmly looking inside the wagon. "Bastards!" Marcus says, fingering the pommel of his sword. Laelius covers his face with his hand and rubs his eyes, as if trying to erase what he has seen.

An older tribune stares at one particular body. He looks at Scipio, his eyes shiny with tears. "These are the men from the outpost near Salaeca," he says. He points to the corpse. "I know that man by the scars on his neck stub. He is ... was ... Compus, a man with ten years of service and a wreath of valor." The tribune chokes out a sobbing laugh. "He fought his way out of the Cannae slaughter, only to fall victim to this humiliation."

Scipio's fists clench and unclench. His breath quickens. He pulls his eyes from the wagon. "Get the driver and get my interpreter," he commands, his voice edged with fury.

When the dusky-skinned driver is dragged before Scipio, the wiry little man breaks free of the guards' grasp and flings himself at Scipio's feet, groveling as if he were clawing out his own grave. He looks imploringly at Scipio, wailing for mercy.

"Why did you do bring this here?" Scipio asks through his interpreter. "You would not have done so of your own volition."

The peasant stares up at Scipio, his teary eyes bulging. His mouth works but no words come out.

Marcus steps forward and delivers a stinging slap that spins the peasant's head sideways. When the man's eyes clear he replies slowly and deliberately, clenching his hands in supplication.

"He says the Carthaginians have his family," explains the interpreter, "Their captain threatened to sacrifice them to Baal if he did not drive this wagon into camp."

"Where is this captain? Who is he?"

The peasant swallows. A stream of words gushes from him.

"He is a nobleman named Hanno. He has brought his cavalry into Salaeca, they have taken over all the homes inside it, and driven out the people. The people sleep in the streets, fearing to protest their treatment."

"How many?" asks Scipio. The peasant looks about frantically, as if searching for an answer from those attending. He blurts out a string of words, flashing the fingers of both hands.

"Many, many, he says," replies the interpreter. "He says the Numidians filled the plains in front of the town. Some Carthaginians, too."

"These Numidians, what tribe are they?" demands Masinissa. He looks at the man. "Masaesyli?" The peasant nods, pointing to his threadbare blue tunic.

"He says they wore indigo tunics and headdresses."

"They are from Syphax' tribe," declares Masinissa, grating his teeth. "They are inside Salaeca. There may be thousands of them."

With a gentle smile, Scipio bends over and lifts the man up. He places both his hands on his shoulders. "You are a brave man, son of Africa. I would do the same in your place. I have no quarrel with you."

Scipio reaches into his belt purse and extracts a handful of denarii. He reaches out to give them to the man.

The interpreter jumps forward and grasps Scipio's wrist, prompting several tribunes to flash out their swords. Unhanding Scipio's wrist, the interpreter gives the peasant a handful of his own money. "I have shekels to give him, General," says the interpreter. "He would be crucified as a traitor if he was found with Roman money."

Scipio nods, embarrassed at his mistake, and gives the interpreter his denarii. "Gratitude, Amacus. Sometimes I forget where I am. Give this man a mule to ride back."

He turns the peasant around and pushes him toward the gates. "Go now, and tell Hanno that I look forward to meeting him." As the interpreter delivers Scipio's words, several soldiers lead the little man toward the front of camp.

"Well, General Scipio, the gods have answered your prayer," says Laelius with grim smile. "You were worried about the men being inactive over the winter. And here the Carthaginians have taken Salaeca and butchered our soldiers! Now it is war in earnest!"

"We cannot afford to lay siege to two different towns," notes Marcus. "That would be stupid. But these town-dwelling soldiers may not be willing to battle outside of the city."

Scipio starts to reply when Masinissa steps in front of Scipio, his young face alight. "Syphax' Masaesyli are my tribe's mortal enemies. They hate me and they hate my rebels. And Syphax has put a large bounty on our heads. They would do anything to kill us!" He acts like he is pulling in a fish with both hands. "Me and my men, we can be the bait to draw them out of there."

Scipio is silent, envisioning different attack plans. He nods his gratitude at the Numidian prince. "Masinissa is right, enmity is a strong bait. I can see how his Numidians could lure out Hanno's little army."

Scipio points toward a rock prominence. "Prince Agathocles of Sicily[xii] perpetrated a similar trick on the Carthaginians a hundred years ago. You can see what's left of his tower there, near the shore. Those rocks are called the Tower of Agathocles."

The tribunes look at one another and shrug fatalistically, accustomed to Scipio's obscure historical references. Scipio sees the confusion on their faces. "I do not expect you to know him, it was a long time ago. I would hope the Carthaginians have forgotten him, too. My point is, we will try to draw them out to those hills just west of us, and spring our trap. What say you?"

Marcus nods. "I know not this Agathocles, but I trust your inventiveness—though some call it trickery!" he says, with a glint of humor in his eyes.

"If Marcus does favor it, I do, too," answers one of the tribunes. Several of the senior tribunes nod their mute assent. Scipio looks at Laelius, who appears to be seriously deliberating upon it. He catches Scipio's eye and grins.

"Well then," Laelius says, slapping Masinissa on the back. "Looks like it is time for you to go fishing. And I will join you for the catch!"

*   *   *   *   *

SALAECA. The mornings grow ever cooler, and the first winds of winter send a chill message that autumn is gone.

The two Carthaginian guards on the battlements need no such reminder: they huddle into their cloaks, waiting for the rising sun to warm the stone block pathways that they patrol. An hour later the sun's rays carve panes of gold across the scrabbly Salaeca Plains. The angular light cuts into the shadowed passages that lay between the tree-covered shoulders of the coastal hills nearby, striping them with shades of dark green and light.

"It's time for a fire and breakfast, Silom," grumbles Luli to his companion, rubbing his thick matted forearms. "Maybe there's some grasshoppers left over from last night's feast. Or even some antelope!" He looks out at the low-lying sun and curses it. "The sun is up, why are we still out here? Our replacements should be here by now!"

Silom's pie-faced features twist into a snarl. "You know why we're still here. Those bastards are sleeping off their drunk from last night's celebration."

Silom looks down the stone switchback and scans the town square beneath them. "I do not see anyone moving around down there, not even any of the Numidians, and they're always pacing about like caged lions. Look, why don't we patrol the walkway one more time, it will give us something to do—and warm us up!"

Silom and Luli pick up their spears and trudge east along the wide battlement walkway. Silom studies the distant hills in front of them. "Gods be cursed, there are more rain clouds gathering out there on the coast. Just when things have dried out."

Luli shoves Silom's shoulder. "Quit complaining! What do you expect? It's the rainy season! The farmers need the water, anyway."

Silom snorts. "Maybe so, but I'd think those travelers out there are hoping it stays dry for a while, at least until they get here." He leans over then squints to see the group, backlit by the morning sun. "What is that anyway, a caravan?"

The sentries head to the corner of the walkway and lean over the limestone parapet, studying the oncoming group. Silom shakes his head. "They don't have any armor. Could be some of our Numidian scouts, but there's too many to be a squadron. Maybe Carthage is sending us more Numidians."

Silom looks about to make sure he is not overheard. "Shit! As if we needed more of those horse-eating savages just to protect this old tomb!"

Luli says nothing, staring at the blurry black outline of the men riding towards them. Now he sees the silhouettes of the party. Their billowing dust clouds indicate that they riding hard toward Salaeca.

"Those are Numidians, certainly. Must be a couple hundred of them." He frowns. "Hanno will not be pleased to get more of them, he already has enough trouble keeping Arat's men in line."

The two guards watch the horsemen approach the garrison. They gossip desultorily about the Numidians' capers at last night's celebration, chuckling over some of their particularly obscene escapades.

Luli suddenly stands up and stares over the wall, puzzled. "Those

43

riders are spreading out into a line," he remarks. "Why would they be doing that?"

Silom waves away his question. "Who knows what those desert fools would do? Maybe some of them want to come into the side gates for some reason."

Luli and Silom get their answer soon enough. The Numidians heel up at a spear's cast from the front gates. Luli looks about and sees a dozen other sentries lining the walls, curious about the strangers below.

The Carthaginians watch as a tall, lithely muscled young man rides out from the middle of the pack. He wears a lion's head as his helmet, with the beast's tawny pelt flowing down his back like a cape. Silom notices he has a string of silver necklaces about his neck—the dress of royalty.

"That one there is a king or a prince," Silom says. Luli shrugs. "Maybe he just thinks he is. Numidians are crazier than a pet antelope."

The warrior carries an eight-foot ceremonial spear bolt upright. His burnished shield gleams in the morning rays. Silom looks down into the town square and spies a passing Sacred Band guard. "We have visitors. Get Hanno up here!"

"Who are you?" a wall sentry shouts. The regal man ignores him, mutely watching the town's front gates. One of the Carthaginians flings a large stone at him. It thuds inches from his mount's feet, but horse and man remain still as statues.

Long minutes later, Hanno's head appears over the wall above the gate, his hair tousled and his eyes sleepy. Arat appears next to him, and his eyes gape when he sees the warrior below him.

"You!" he snarls.

The man below them trots forward several paces, sneering a challenge as he looks up at Hanno. "I am Masinissa, the future king of all Numidia. In the name of General Publius Cornelius Scipio, I come to demand you relinquish the town to me. Surrender now, and none of you

44

will be killed."

Arat is apoplectic with fury. The hated Massylii rebel who has evaded him for months is right below him, demanding he give up. "None of *us* will be killed? I'll kill you myself for that!"

Arat clambers down the walkway steps, screaming for his officers. "Masinissa is out there! Get him before he runs!" Three of his captains rush up to him.

"Masinissa?" one asks incredulously. Arat shoves him backwards. "Get your horses and get your ass out that gate! A gold spear to the man that kills him! Get me my horse!"

Hanno walks over to Arat and grabs his shoulder. "Wait! Wait until we can gather all our men!"

Arat shrugs off Hanno's hand. "He is out there now!" Arat screams, spit flying from his mouth. "We don't need four thousand men for that bunch of traitors. I'll eat his liver tonight!"

Arat marches to his stone block headquarters in the town square. Even as he straps on his ostrich-plumed helmet, his Numidians gallop out through two of the town's side portals. Eager for the reward of a golden spear, they dash out without formation or standards.[xiii]

As soon as Arat's men fly out from the portals, they fling their spears at Masinissa's men. The Massylii raise their round shields and skillfully deflect the throws.

"Bunch together," Masinissa orders. "Shield to shield, form a wall across the front! Spears out! All together now! Forward!"

Masinissa and his men ride straight into their oncoming enemy, spears fixed in front of them. Masinissa eschews his usual hit-and-run tactics, using the straight-line formation he has learned from fighting with Scipio's legions.

The Numidian tribes crash together. Dozens of Arat's men fall to the spears of the Massylii, impaled on their spear wall. Arat's men back up several paces to regroup. It is the move Masinissa has been waiting for. "Fling!" he commands. His men hurtle their spears into the retreating tribesmen, and dozens more fall to the earth.

Arat storms out the front gate with hundreds of his men, his eyes fixed upon the Numidian prince. "Remember! A gold spear to the man that kills him!" he shouts.

"Away now!" Masinissa bawls to his men. As one, they turn and gallop away.

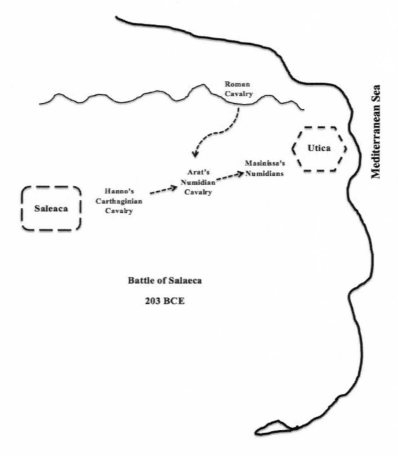

Battle of Salaeca

203 BCE

"After them!" Arat screams. "Gods curse you all, I want his head!"

Arat's cavalry hurtle after the Massylii. Soon, thousands more of Arat's men scramble out from Salaeca, racing to join their chief.

Hanno and his two hundred Carthaginians burst out from the town gates, rushing to catch up to Arat's riders. *What in Mot are we all doing out here, scattered all over the place?* Hanno curses to himself. *Out chasing a few Numidians because that big fool can't control his temper!*

With Arat's men strung out across in the plain in pursuit of the Massylii, they have little trouble in turning about to parry the assault of the Numidians closest to them and then dash away again, leaving a trail of bodies as they gallop east toward the Utica hills.

As his Carthaginians draw near to Arat's riders, Hanno veers off to the side, scanning the palm-covered hills for ambushes. He sees no men or mounts among the hillside's scrabbly foliage. *Good. No tricks.* He spurs his mount to catch up to Arat. The two meet and ride on together. They wave for their men to follow them as they dash past the scattered bodies of Masaesyli and Massylii.

The Carthaginians and Numidians gallop past an island of hills on their left, passing by a low-lying saddle that connects the two ranges. The two leaders close in on the rearmost of Masinissa's tribesmen.

"We have them, Hanno!" Arat exults. Arat digs his heels into his tiring horse's flanks, eager for a kill. He pulls out a spear from his camelskin sheath and hauls back his arm for a mighty throw, aiming at the naked back of a galloping Massylii warrior.

"Arat!" Hanno shouts. "They're coming behind you!"

The Numidian chief looks over his left shoulder and drops his spear. "Get back here!" he shouts, "It's a trap!"

Hundreds of Roman cavalry pour down from the saddle between the hills, emerging from their hiding places in its long, rocky ridges. Blowing their bronze battle trumpets, the equites hurtle onto the plain and cut into the middle of Arat's scattered pursuit force, slicing it into two milling groups of confused riders.

Masinissa hears the trumpets and yanks his horse to a stop. *Ammon be praised, it worked!*

"Back at them, my brothers! Attack!" the prince bawls. Masinissa whirls his pony about and leads his men on a headlong rush back into the pursuing Numidians.[xiv] His skilled warriors ram into their Masaesyli enemies, blocking them from escape.

The first wave of equites surrounds Hanno's rear force, as more of cavalry stampede down from the hills. The heavily armored Romans deflect the Numidians' lances and cut into Arat's lightly armed cavalry, hewing them down with sword and spear. The Masaesyli collide with each other in their haste to escape, knocking their own men to the ground.

Curse that Numidian fool for getting us into this trap! Hanno fumes. "Gather our men to me!" he shouts to his captains. "We'll fight our way back to Salaeca!"

Hanno sees a large group of Romans threshing their way through his flank, headed straight for him. He sees they are led by a tall young Roman in silver plated armor, grinning as if he were playing captain in some war game.

"The one with the purple plume is mine!" Hanno hears the man shout. He watches the equite swoop under a spear thrust and stick his sword into the side of an onrushing Carthaginian. *That Roman has an Iberian falcata* is all Hanno can think, as he shoves his spear into the neck of an attacking Roman's horse.

Laelius sees Hanno's purple-plumed helmet and heads for him. As he hurries across the plain, he spots Masinissa at the front of the attack, slashing down Arat's men as he battles to get at the Numidian chief. *We have the same notion, kill the leader and demoralize the troops. Pretty smart for a half-naked barbarian!*

When he draws within a spear cast of Hanno, Laelius halts his horse and sheathes his falcata. *I have a little surprise for you, Carthaginian!*

Laelius reaches behind his back and pulls out a short curved bow. He nocks an arrow and lets it fly. The arrow sails over Hanno's head, so high that the Hanno doesn't notice it. The second arcs past Hanno's shoulder and prompts a scream from a Carthaginian rider behind him. Hanno waves his javelin at Laelius.

"Come fight me like a man, Roman!" Hanno plunges towards Laelius, his spear at the ready.

You clumsy oaf! What was all that practice for? Laelius quickly nocks another arrow, lowers his bow angle, and releases. The iron-tipped arrow crunches through Hanno's linen cuirass and buries itself in his collarbone.

Hanno bellows with pain and slumps onto the neck of his mount. Laelius smiles with satisfaction and turns to find another foe. He hears Hanno shouting behind him.

"I'll cut your guts out for that, cur!"

Laelius looks back and sees a bloody Hanno grappling at the shaft that sticks out of his neck. The Carthaginian yanks out the arrow and holds it in front of him. "You think to kill me with your little toy, fancy man?"

Tough little bastard, Laelius muses, *Best finish this the old-fashioned way.* Laelius spins his horse about and spurs it forward. He dodges around an onrushing Sacred Band guard, and pulls out his falcata.

Hanno whips out his sword and kicks his horse into a gallop, blood streaming down his snow-white armor. He closes on Laelius, whirling his curved blade at Laelius' head. Instinctively, Laelius raises his shield, turning it sideways to deflect the blow. Hanno's blade screeches off the shield's burnished surface.

Laelius kicks his horse on the right side and rams him against the Carthaginian's mount, knocking Hanno sideways. As Hanno teeters uncertainly, Laelius levers his shield into the underside of Hanno's, shield, prying it away from Hanno's body.

With a grunt of effort, Laelius chops his sword into Hanno's exposed neck. The blade cleaves through muscle and bone. Hanno's head lolls sideways onto his shoulder, held to his body by a scrap of neck skin. He topples sideways, dead before he hits the ground.

Laelius yanks back his falcata and whirls to defend himself against any oncoming enemies, but there is no need. The Roman cavalry have followed his charge and have overwhelmed the Sacred Band defenders that surrounded Hanno.

"Get the Carthaginians' horses!" Laelius shouts. "They are better than ours!" Laelius pushes his way forward to help Masinissa get to Arat, but he sees he is too late.

A grinning Masinissa rides up to Laelius with Arat's head mounted on his spear. The blood-spattered prince raises his grisly trophy up for all to see, and Arat's remaining warriors cry out in dismay.

That is a good idea, Laelius thinks. He rides back and dismounts by Hanno's corpse. He yanks out his pugio and uses the dagger to sever the last flaps of Hanno's neck flesh.

Laelius grabs a lance from the ground and jams Hanno's head onto it, being careful to tie on Hanno's purple-plumed helmet so that all can see it. He pushes the helmet firmly onto Hanno's bloody skull and ties together its cheekpieces. *There. Now you look presentable!*

"Come on, men. Time for a parade!" Laelius remounts his horse and trots about the battlefield with his cavalry, holding Hanno's head high in the air. Masinissa joins him, brandishing Arat's head next to Hanno's.

"Arat is dead!" one Masaesyli shouts.

"The Romans killed Hanno!" a Carthaginian wails.

The laments wash across the milling battlefield, more destructive than any weapon. With their leaders gone, the surviving Numidians and Carthaginians stampede from the field, save for the unfortunates ringed in by the Romans' attack force.[xv]

"Hunt Arat's men down!" Masinissa bawls. "Do not return without a kill!"

The Numidians relentlessly hunt down Arat's fleeing cavalry. They strike down hundreds as they chase them across the plain, tossing spears into their backs as though they are hunting antelope. The Massylii do not turn back until they reach the gates of Salaeca, allowing the remnants of Arat's army to rush inside.

Laelius weaves through the final knots of battle, seeking Masinissa. He finds the prince kneeling on the ground, leaning over a disemboweled Masaesyli youth, the boy's oversized helmet half covering his face.

"Who are you?" the boy quails. "Please, do not hurt me!"

"Fear not, boy," Masinissa says, his voice quavering as he gently pulls away the helmet. "I am here to help you."

Masinissa grasps his spear with both hands, and places the tip of the leaf-shaped head over the youth's heaving chest.

"May the Sun God take to you to paradise, brave warrior," he says softly, "your pain is over." Masinissa turns his head sideways and shoves the spear through the youth's chest. The boy shrieks, once, and his head slumps.

Masinissa stands up and flings the spear from him. "Too young to be out here," he mutters angrily, looking away from Laelius as he wipes at his face. "All those men Syphax has, and he still recruits boys."

Laelius places his hand on the prince's shoulder. "Let's finish up and get out of here."

The two leaders ride over to the base of the hill saddle. Standing side by side on their mounts, they oversee the grisly proceedings of plunder, burial, and execution. The two chat casually, as if they were back at camp, answering questions from the officers that ride up to query them.

Masinissa glances at the bow on Laelius' back and raises an eyebrow.

"A bow and arrow? When did you Romans start to mimic the Parthians? Or have you decided to become Egyptians?"

Laelius chuckles. "I met a Greek horse archer while I was in Sicily. He taught me how to fight like a saggitarius, shooting arrows while I ride. I didn't have anything to do on the ships, so I started shooting into the ship beams while I ran around on deck!

"It is one way to pass the time on board, I would think."

"It annoyed my marines," Laelius says with a chuckle, "but it certainly sharpened my eye. And it is so enjoyable to use it. You should have seen that Carthaginian's face when I pulled out a bow!"

"Enjoyable?" says Masinissa. "You talk of enjoyment in the midst of a fight?"

Laelius shrugs, dabbing a stray bit of intestine off his breastplate. "We Romans, are way too immersed in this gravitas attitude. If you can't have fun during a war, when can you?"

Masinissa shakes his head. "It is as Marcus Silenus says. You are truly beyond reason."

Laelius and Masinissa lead the cavalry back to Scipio's main camp several miles away. The war party is received with great joy and honor, having killed thousands of the enemy with only a few score losses. Much to quaestor Cato's disgust, Scipio halts camp construction and hosts a celebratory feast. He bestows gifts upon the officers and cavalrymen. In particular he lavishes them upon his new friend and ally, Masinissa. [xvi]

The day after the celebration, Scipio leads out a massive expeditionary force of infantry and cavalry, intent on securing the Utica region. Scipio arrives at Salaeca, only to discover that the Carthaginians have forsaken it. His scouts report that the Carthaginians are reinforcing the towns and outposts nearest to Carthage.

They fear I will attack Carthage, Scipio concludes. *I can use that to my advantage.*

Scipio immediately garrisons Salaeca with his soldiers, sparing the inhabitants so that they may manage its daily operations. But the surrounding towns are not so fortunate. With no fear of Carthaginian retribution, the Romans capture and plunder each locale, ravaging the surrounding fields for their winter provisions.

Carthage, meanwhile, remains quiescent. Gisgo gathers his army for an overwhelming strike against his nemesis, but he does not venture them out for battle, or even a skirmish. Contrary to his fearful compatriots, Gisgo believes that Scipio will not attack Carthage; he is sure that Scipio's obsession with taking Utica will occupy his time. Gisgo bides his time and builds his strength.

Scipio returns from Salaeca and resumes his Utica siege. When he arrives at his Utica camp he is pleased to discover that his supply transports have returned from Sicily, hastening to Africa's shores before the winter sea storms arrive. The ships deliver troves of much-needed weapons and provisions. Slowly, inexorably, the strength of Scipio's small army builds.

Laelius hobbles over to the port to direct the transports' unloading, ignoring his battle-bruised body. When all the ships are emptied, Laelius reloads them with the army's plunder of coins, gold, silver, and slaves, reserving the captured cattle and grain for the spring campaign.

As soon as the last cart is trundled aboard, Scipio sends the transports back toward his base in Sicily, save for a solitary ship that is destined to go straight to Ostia—and Pomponia. As always, Scipio designates the largest part of his booty to be transferred from Sicily to Rome, mindful that the new year elections are coming and his imperium is at stake—as is his war.

III. HANNIBAL'S GAMBIT

CROTON, ITALIA, 204 BCE. *If I do not make them recall him, he will make them recall me!* Hannibal's flash of insight turns his stomach queasy. He has known that Scipio could not conquer mighty Carthage with his small army, but now he grasps the Roman's true purpose. *The boy knows those cowards in my Senate will bring me back to fight him.*

"Maharbal!" shouts Hannibal, calling for his second in command, "Where is Maharbal?"

"He is speaking to the Bruttian recruits about the punishments for those who desert their posts in battle, General," replies his attendant.

"Fetch him!" Hannibal commands, rubbing his eye patch.

Within the hour Hannibal's cavalry commander pushes his way through the tent flaps, irritated he has been diverted from his recruit training. *By Baal's balls, he has grown old*, Hannibal thinks, studying Maharbal's seamed face. *But then, we have all aged much with fifteen years of war.*

"What is it now? I have work to do!" grouses the sinewy little man. "I was trying give those Italians a fear of cowardice, so they don't run when they get in a real fight."

"We cannot spend any more time training them," replies Hannibal, his right fist clenched with frustration. "I have seen through Scipio's ruse. He is not out to conquer Africa, he is out to conquer our politicians! He wants them to draw me back to Carthage, to eliminate us as a threat to Rome."

"Hah!" barks Maharbal, "That certainly makes sense. If Scipio gets near Carthage's walls, those soft-handed senators will beg for us to come rescue them." He smirks. "And your precious Barcid relatives will not stop them from having their way! You'll have to go back to fight him. And Mago will get recalled, too!"

"But Gisgo is already there," Hannibal replies.

Maharbal rolls his eyes. "Oh yes, Gisgo is there!"

"I know," Hannibal says. "The boy Scipio has thrice defeated him, and I think Gisgo's afraid of him. But he can at least forestall Scipio's advance until I finish my mission."

A knowing light comes to Maharbal's eyes. "Ah, so you will march on Rome now, even though it is late summer! I am right, no?"

Hannibal looks north, his voice almost mournful. "Yes, the war season wanes. But we have to move before our Senate decides to call us back to Africa. If we move north, and Mago moves south, the Roman senators may prevent our Senate from doing it!"

Maharbal stares at Hannibal. "You confuse me."

"It is simple. If Rome feels threatened, the Latin Party senators may move to recall Scipio. Fabius and his ilk opposed his going to Africa in the first place." His eye lights with excitement. "Scipio's recall would calm our anxious Senate, and give Mago and I more time to join forces and assault Rome."

"Winter is coming, though," Maharbal says.

Hannibal sighs. "So it is. We must muster out our army within five days. I will send a message to Mago about our plans."

"That does not give us much time. Not much at all."

Hannibal shrugs. "It is all the time we have."

"You know, you are the finest General I have ever seen," says Maharbal, irritation creeping into his voice. "But we would not have this problem if you had taken my advice after our victory at Cannae, and marched on Rome." [xvii]

Hannibal shakes his head. "We were not ready." *I was not ready*, he thinks. "Killing takes its toll on men of conscience. More so when it is carnage. And Cannae was carnage. I will speak no more of it."

Maharbal opens his mouth. Hannibal shoves his open palm at him, commanding him to silence. "How many men for the march, counting the new Bruttians?"

Maharbal's scarred face contorts with his efforts to add and subtract. "Uhm, hmmm. With the usual troop allotments for Croton and the nearby garrisons, I would say we have about twenty thousand infantry and four thousand cavalry." He shakes his head. "But thousands of them have yet to see a battle."

"The novices still have value. If it comes to that, they can wear out the Romans in the first attack." Hannibal sighs. "I wish we had more Gauls with us. How I loved to see them rampaging into those stiff-ass Romans!"

"Well, we still have almost a thousand of them," replies Maharbal, "but they may desert if they don't fight someone soon! Then again, they may desert if we go north and get close to their homes. Who knows with Gauls?"

"I hope we find out. Because it would mean we are nearer Rome. And to my brother Mago and his army in the north." He smiles wistfully. "When we join forces with him, what a joyous reunion it will be! Nothing would stop us."

Hannibal walks to the tent entrance. He holds the flap open and points outside. "Prepare the men and beasts. We are bound for Rome."

Days later, Hannibal rides out from Croton, leading his army along the coastal road towards the region of Lucania. Riding atop his old war elephant Surus, Hannibal leans back in his saddle tower and enjoys the scenery about him. The deep blue Adriatic glistens in the morning sun to his right, with the low-lying valley hills rolling toward the horizon on his left.

Maharbal rides next to him on his favorite Numidian horse. The old warrior scans the terrain for potential ambushes. *Why do you bother?* he tells himself. *Romans are not prone to using such tactics, they think them to be cowardly and demeaning. Then again, there may be another Scipio out there, so we had best prepare for anything.*

Hannibal's army columns trudge along behind him. The tight phalanxes of his staunch Libyans are in the front, followed by the loose columns of Carthaginian citizen soldiers. They are unarmored young men from the city, carrying round bronze shields and a sling of javelins.

Thousands of roughshod Bruttians follow the Carthaginians. The Bruttian veterans wear cloaks fashioned from the pelts of wolves and bears, earned symbols of their battle experience. The Bruttian recruits wear the arms and armor that Hannibal has scavenged from the Roman dead. They look like more like unkempt Romans than Bruttians.

The Gauls follow the Bruttians, tramping along with their families and consorts, many already drunk with the morning's wine. The army's horses, mules and elephants bring up the rear, protected by scores of Bruttian recruits. Hannibal's marching formation is designed to put his best warriors ready for a frontal assault, although he knows Croton province should be free of Romans.

The march is pleasant and uneventful for the rest of the day. As dusk nears, Hannibal designates a beachside location near the plains of Petelia for the night camp, favoring its unobstructed view. He sends a messenger north to update Mago on his location and directs the building of the sprawling army camp.

That night, Hannibal pours over his terrain maps of Croton province, plotting his march toward Rome. He weighs the benefits of taking the Appian Way from Tarentum versus taking a coastal route and meeting Mago by Arminium. As he studies his maps Hannibal reaches into his belt pouch and places the figurine of his father Hamilcar on the map table, a reminder of his promise to protect Carthage from Rome.

On the second day of their march, the Carthaginian army heads to the northwest toward Caprasia, where Hannibal plans to camp before marching northeast. By late morning the army enters a hill-shrouded Caprasia valley. Maharbal sends out a dozen scouts to explore the surrounding area. Two scouts soon return from the valley road in front of them, their eyes wide with alarm.

"General, the Roman army has a camp at the other end of the valley. Their legions are marching toward the valley mouth, directly at us. They will be here within hours!"

Hannibal blinks in surprise. *Already?* He calls Maharbal over. "The Romans are coming. It must be Consul Publius Sempronius' army. No one else could get this far south so quickly. Our spies said he was coming to Bruttium to contain us."

Maharbal snorts in derision. "To 'contain' us as if we were dogs in a pen? Sounds like something that doddering Fabius would do!" He grins. "At least the Gauls will be happy, they can take some heads and plunder."

Then Maharbal looks at the road behind them. "You know, our way is clear back to Croton. We can return there safely, and give our recruits more time."

Hannibal's mouth tightens. "You mean retreat safely, don't you?" he snaps. "I am sick of being trapped down there like camels in a pen. We march on!"

Maharbal frowns. "You know I am not a man to avoid a battle. But this Sempronius, he likely has a consular army with two legions of Romans and two of allies. They will at least equal our strength." He looks back toward the rear lines "Almost a third of our men our green recruits."

Hannibal studies the foothills and mountains that border their passage. All is quiet for several minutes. "We will not ask our new men to fight on equal terms. We will catch the Romans on the march, where they can only fight with their front columns. Then they will have to contend with our best men, the Libyans and Gauls."

Maharbal nods toward the hills. "I can get our cavalry up there in the hillside trees. They can descend when the time is ripe."

"All the better," says Hannibal. "We'll use the valley's confined space to our advantage. The Roman scouts will soon find our army, so let's not give Sempronius time to prepare. We march double time, now!"

The Carthaginian army picks up its pace and speeds toward the oncoming Romans. Riding in the vanguard, Hannibal notices two Roman scouts watching him from an overlook a quarter mile in front of them. The riders silently watch the army, then whirl back the way they came. *So much for the element of surprise*, he says to himself. *As if that were possible with an army out in the open.* He shrugs. *We were fortunate we got this far undetected.*

Maharbal's scouts pick their way down the steep hillside and race over to Hannibal. "The Romans are coming, General. They will be here within the hour. It is a large army. Their marching line is almost ten miles long." [xviii]

Hannibal calls for a halt. He summons his infantry captains to the front and points his spear at the wide roadway in front of them. "They are marching straight at us. Get the Gauls up to the front immediately. Bring up the elephants. And bring me my elephant, Surus!"

The Gallic horde trundles up to the front of Hannibal's columns, followed by Hannibal's eight remaining elephants. Surus leads the herd, clad in a mask and body sheath of blood red mail.

Hannibal dismounts from his horse and clambers up a rope ladder onto his war elephant, closing the gate on his wooden battle tower. His attendant hands Hannibal a fourteen-foot sarissa, its silver head glinting in the sun. Hannibal waves the command spear over his head, its purple pennant summoning his men forward. As one, the army quickens its pace toward the Romans.

The scouts gallop in as the Carthaginian vanguard rounds a bend in the road. "They come, they come!" bellows one rider. He hurtles toward the rear columns to spread the alarm.

Hannibal takes a deep breath and tightens the cuirass straps about his shoulders. *Steady, old man. This may be your last obstacle to Rome. Hit them with everything.*

Hannibal slaps Surus' side with his spear and the elephant lurches forward, trumpeting its excitement. The soldiers fall silent. There is no sound save the tramping of thousands of sandaled feet along the narrow road.

The Carthaginian vanguard soon hears the uniform rumble of marching feet, growing ever louder. The clank of armor and weaponry become audible, then the neighing and braying of beasts. Minutes later the Roman heavy infantry appears, marching six abreast, filling the middle of the road.

From atop his perch, Hannibal looks across at the oncoming legions, searching for Publius Sempronius. He finds Sempronius five rows from the front, his blood red cape draped about his shoulders. Hannibal realizes the Romans are going to march straight into his Libyan phalanxes, seeking to cut their way through his staunchest warriors.

"Halt!" Hannibal commands. His men stop in place. "Close ranks," he orders.

The Libyans raise their tall oblong shields and draw a step closer together. As the Libyans reform their ranks, scores of velites dash out from the front lines of Roman infantry. The young legionnaires fling three volleys of javelins into the Libyans. The Africans quickly angle their shields over their heads. Several anguished cries attest that some spears have hit their mark, but most skid off the Libyans' shields.

The velites fling the last of their pila and dash back towards the main lines. The Roman columns tramp forward, their steps so coordinated it sounds as if one giant foot after another is stomping toward the Carthaginians.

The Roman infantry draws within a spear's cast of Hannibal's front line. Hannibal looks over his shoulder at his beast attendants and waves his sarissa. "Now, send them now!" he shouts, and his officers behind him echo his command.

The Libyans suddenly part wide in the middle. Seven elephants stampede through the opening, goaded on by the mahouts running alongside of them. The elephants trample dozens of legionnaires, caving in the Roman front.

The second line soldiers run in to jab their spears into the rampaging beasts. Trumpeting their rage and pain, the elephants careen through the back lines, throwing the hastati and principes into milling confusion.

Hannibal watches the rampage, and smiles. He sees that the elephants have broken the Roman front. *Time for the next wave.* He whirls his sarissa in a circle. "Bring on the Gauls!" he shouts to his officers.

The huge barbarians run forward, waving their long swords and thick-bladed axes. Most are bare-chested, attired only in blue plaid pants. Others are naked, showing their disdain for their enemy.

Bored with their extended inaction in Bruttium, the Gauls are lusting to hack into their long-standing enemies. They storm headlong into the disorganized Romans, slashing at anyone within arm's reach, fighting through the stabs and thrusts of the short-bladed Roman gladii.

With their lines broken by the elephants and pushed apart by the Gauls, the Roman defense becomes a long, narrow space of individual battles, and the fight becomes a swarming mass of individual duels.[xix]

"Prod those beasts off to the side," Sempronius calls to his lead tribune. "I want a century of men on each elephant!" Within minutes, groups of Romans surround each elephant. Poking into the beasts' sides and rear, they goad them off to the side of the road, driving them behind the Roman lines.

The Gallic warriors fight their way through more rows of legionnaires. Then they stop, pausing to take plunder and heads from their victims. The front line Romans step back, grateful for the respite.

The centurions blow their command whistles and reform the back lines. Sempronius' men reorganize into tight six-man columns and march forward to relieve the broken ranks ahead of them.

The fresh legionnaires step into the Gauls. They plunge their short swords into the exposed stomachs and legs of their foes, keeping a three-foot fighting space between themselves so they can ably maneuver in the confined space of the road. Many a Gaul tries to charge through the space between the soldiers, only to be stabbed by Romans on both sides. The Romans cut down scores of Gauls and the barbarians slowly retreat, losing interest in continuing the fight.

Hannibal can see Sempronius riding about the back lines, a tall and lean man with dark burning eyes, shouting for his men to continue their onslaught. *You are winning now but you will soon be mine.* Hannibal thinks. *I have more surprises for you.*

The Roman cavalry rides into the edges of the fray, galloping in singly along the sides of the road. They cut into the flanks of Hannibal's front lines, spearing the backs of Sacred Band warriors with their javelin casts, piercing the Gauls' unprotected shoulders and necks. Scores of the barbarians trot back from the front lines.

They lasted longer than I thought, Hannibal reflects. *Time for a fresh assault.*

"Call back the Gauls," Hannibal shouts to his trumpeter. The battle horns sound twice, then twice again. The barbarians walk back between the ranks of the stone-faced Libyans, carrying their plunder of ears, heads, and armor, bragging as if none of their kinsmen had been killed.

While the Gauls move behind the Libyans, Hannibal motions over his Sacred Band captain, "Take your men to the rear."

"We are retreating?" the captain asks.

"We retreat so we can attack," Hannibal replies, enjoying his captain's mystified look.

Hannibal reverses Surus and plods back through the waiting Libyans. His elite Carthaginians follow him. As he does, he catches the Libyan commander's eye and waves him forward. *Now!*

The Libyans step forward, shield to shield. They shove into the

Roman lines, their thick armor clanging against the stout Roman shields. The Africans fight as coldly and methodically as the Romans, exchanging carefully placed stabs and thrusts. After a half hour of furious combat the two sides step back, leaving a twenty-foot space between them.

When the two lines withdraw from each other, Hannibal leans down to his trumpeter. "Send the cavalry!" The stout young boy takes a deep breath and blows three mighty blasts. The hillsides above the road rustle with movement, then thunder with hooves.

The Numidians avalanche down the slopes. Maharbal leads them, his eyes agleam with battle lust. Half of the Numidians cut into the knots of Roman cavalry at the foot of the hills. The others dash into the open space between the Libyans and Romans and barge into the front row of the legionnaires. Soon the Numidians are swirling around the Roman vanguard, stampeding among their lines.

Sempronius watches his men mill about in confusion, trying to defend themselves from three sides. He sees scores of soldiers retreating along the sides of the columns behind him, and realizes slaughter is imminent.

"Crassus!" he shouts to his infantry legate, "Get the rear lines ready to withdraw!" Heedless of the mob scene about him, Sempronius rides to the front of his men and points his sword back toward the mouth of the valley. "Retreat!" he yells, as the cornicen trumpets the consul's command.

The Romans suddenly fight with renewed vigor, knowing they have a chance to withdraw with their lives. The front line centurions shove their men together into a semblance of a three-sided shield wall. They drag their dead and wounded from beneath the feet of the front-line soldiers so that they can maintain their stance while fighting.

Slowly, step by step, the Romans draw back from the Hannibal's infantry and cavalry. The Libyans labor to maintain an even front line but their men stumble and slip over the remaining corpses scattered along their path, leaving them open for the thrust of a Roman blade..

The retreating Romans have an unencumbered path behind them. They retreat in order and their shield wall holds.

The tribunes order fresh men to the front, and the Romans become the aggressors during their methodical retreat, pushing aside the shields of the tiring Libyans, scoring stabs into their unprotected legs and arms. Dozens of Libyans fall. Their replacements march forward but they are more cautious in their assault, and the Roman lines continue to hold.

Sempronius' army columns withdraw from the valley. General Sempronius orders the allies and legionnaires to reform next to a steep hill on the left, knowing it will protect them from a left flank attack. The officers direct the Romans and allies into maniple formations, with the cavalry and velites protecting the right flank. The last of Sempronius' front lines emerge from the defile and join a fully organized army on the plain.

Hannibal sees that the Romans have already reorganized into legionary battle formation, but his men are still streaming into the valley from the narrow road. He realizes it will take his miles-long army several hours to organize effectively for a pitched battle with the prepared Romans.

Hannibal looks up at the lowering sun, frowns, and raises his right arm. "Halt!" he shouts, looking at his captains. "Halt, I say!"

Jabnit rides up to Hannibal. The infantry commander's bloodied sword is still clenched in his fist. Jabnit nods toward the reforming Romans and looks inquisitively at Hannibal. "Should we send our Numidians at them?"

Hannibal shakes his head, frowning. "Let them go, we have lost the terrain advantage. We will camp here by the valley mouth. Tomorrow they will be ours."

The two watch somberly as Sempronius' fully formed army marches the miles back toward their old camp. Jabnit leads the Carthaginians, Gauls, and Libyans over to the side of the valley entrance, where the mercenaries begin to mark out camping territories for their respective factions.

Hannibal clambers down from his elephant and stands off to the side of the road, watching his caravan trail out from the passage and into their emerging camp. Maharbal rides up, his face flushed with excitement—and disappointment.

"Why did we stop?" he blurts, with his customary impatience. "My men can hit their flank while you go at their center!"

Hannibal shakes his head. "It would be a fool's move. They were better prepared for battle than we were. In a few days we'll challenge them to open battle and end this thing."

Hannibal's eye gleams excitedly, in spite of his weariness. He can see himself marching up the Appian Road to join Mago at Rome to end this war. And go home.

As dusk settles Sempronius' soldiers file to the remnants of the camp they thought they had permanently abandoned. Sempronius directs the men to pitch tents and reinforce the staked ramparts with a deeper trench. He calls for an immediate meeting with his legates and tribunes. The group stands in a circle off to the side of the main gate, talking as the rest of the army streams into the camp.

"How many dead?" demands Sempronius, his eyes blinking with anger. A tribune steps forward, his eyes downcast. "We lost almost a score of maniples, and some cavalry." He takes a deep breath." I would say twelve hundred men."

"Twelve hundred soldiers to that one-eyed old bastard and his tricks!" fumes Sempronius.

"They are making camp at the valley mouth," observes a bent old senior tribune. "They will be out to fight us in two or three days. We had best prepare, especially against all those cavalry."

Sempronius stalks about, thinking furiously. "We are not too far from proconsul Publius' Licinius' army, are we?"

"He is a long day's march north," replies one of his tribunes.

The consul nods his head, and the trace of a smile appears. "Then we'll prepare for battle, all right. But we'll use one of Hannibal's old tricks,"

Sempronius waves over one of his attendants. "Get me a messenger for General Licinius." The attendant darts from the tent, as Sempronius grins impishly then laughs. His officers watch, mystified. "Don't you see? We use a trick to catch the trickster!" He nods. "Scipio was right, we have to learn from Hannibal if we are to defeat him...."

IV. THE RAID

ROME, 203 BCE. **Keep Consul Scipio in Afric**a! shouts the mural on the apartment house wall.

Amelia finishes with a few brush strokes to the head of the double-eagle that sprawls across her painting. *Nothing like having an eagle to get them feeling patriotic.*

Chin in hand, Amelia steps back to admire her work. *I should add "Remember Iberia!" on the next one. Give the eagle bigger thunderbolts in his claws.* She hands her slave the paint pot and twig brushes. She stretches up and blows on the wet paint of her final flourishes. *There, that's ten of them today! I deserve a cup of wine!*

Amelia walks past the wall to the front door of the rickety mud brick apartment house that sports her mural. A freedman waits there, elegantly dressed in thick white tunic that is bordered with a broad red stripe. She drops a bulging purse into the insula owner's hands.

"That stays up until the People's Assembly concludes, agreed?"

The grey-haired landlord whisks the purse into his large belt pouch. "Of certitude, Domina Scipio. It will be there, or I will pluck out my own eye!"

Amelia laughs, and stares into his eyes. "It if does not, I will do it for you! I will return to see that no one has defaced it. If all is well, you will receive your next purse."

The landlord bows deeply, eager to please the wife of Rome's most famous personage. Amelia turns on her heel and paces down one of the many narrow side streets of this cramped and dirty Palatine Hill neighborhood. She hastens south to check on the work of her fellow Hellenics on the Aventine.

Amelia and her attendant carefully negotiate the strewn offal and broken cobbles. Within the hour, they arrive at the run-down and rowdy Aventine, an area densely populated with expatriates from all over the world—most of whom have good reason to leave their homeland. As she approaches the Temple of Juno Regina, a wispy young woman runs up to her, her green eyes alight with alarm. "Mistress! There is trouble! Come see!"

Hoisting up the hem of her skirt, Amelia scurries over to the apartment house opposite the temple. She sees that her four hired assistants are backed against the blank wall they were painting. Three burly men shove the young nobles sideways, gesturing for them to leave.

"Get away from them!" Amelia commands, standing in front of her assistants. "I have paid the owner to use that wall!"

A barrel-bellied man steps toward her, his yellow teeth glowing from his bushy black beard. "I don't care if you paid Jupiter for it, you cunt. You'll not be slapping your bullshit upon our walls!" He glowers at her "You don't leave now, I may just take myself a taste of patrician pussy..."

Amelia backs away from him, sneering her disgust. *A bunch of hired thugs! Flaccus and his cronies must have paid them. No way to reason with them, they only want to line their purses.*

"I will not tell you again," she growls, "get away from us!" The leader looks back at his amused men. "She likes it rough. Bet she likes it in the ass." He reaches for her shoulder.

The man howls with pain, staring at the knife blade sticking from the back of his hand. Amelia yanks her throwing knife from his wrist and stands with arms spread and her feet planted, ready to stab again. The thug clutches his hand to his grease-mottled tunic, trying to staunch the bleeding. "I'll break your neck!" blurts, and lunges at her.

Amelia jumps forward and sticks her knife into the join at the man's shoulder and neck, inches from his artery. The leader bends over and shrieks with pain, clapping his hands to his neck.

"Fucking bitch!' he snarls.

"The next one will be in your eye. Now get out of here!"

Groaning, he stumbles back to his two companions. The two henchmen push him behind them and head for Amelia. There is a flash, and one man clutches his shoulder, grappling at the hilt of the throwing knife embedded there.

Amelia crouches before them, her right hand thrust forward with another gleaming blade at the ready. Her face is a rictus of anger. "Come on! Try me!" she blazes.

The man with the bleeding shoulder hefts her bloody knife in his hand, his face red with rage.

"Go ahead," Amelia challenges. She cocks back her arm, her knife poised next to her ear.

The other man grabs his partner's bicep and yanks him back. "Let's go. We have our money. They don't pay us enough to put up with this shit!" The two men grab their wounded leader and stalk down the side streets. Amelia's helpers watch them retreat, dumbfounded.

When they are out of sight, Amelia doubles over and grasps her knees, her body shaking with repressed fear and anger. She takes several deep, shuddering, breaths. She rises and motions for one of her helpers to come over.

"Finish your work here, and then do the one on the Capitoline Hill. If there is any more trouble, send a runner to Scipio House. I'll be waiting."

The young men look wonderingly at her, then at the side street where the thugs retreated. "Whatever you say, Domina," one of them replies. They resume their work.

Now I know I deserve that wine! Amelia says to herself. She retraces her steps and heads toward the Scipio domus, eager to see how Pomponia has fared.

Walking along, she gestures for one of her female house slaves to give her a cloak, and bundles herself against the cool breezes of early winter. *It has been so cold this month,* she thinks, looking at the ice glazing the fountains and puddles. *The priests say it is a sign the gods are unhappy with Rome. But why? Have we not sacrificed enough, on the altar and the field? Has my husband displeased them?*

Entering the wide main street that leads to the Forum, Amelia sees Tiberius Gracchus approaching her. The young priest's face splits into a broad smile when he sees her. "Salve, Mistress Scipio! I am honored to see you!"

Amelia summons her composure and manages an awkward smile at the handsome man. "Salus, Tiberius Gracchus. It is a pleasure to behold you. I hear you are doing well!"

The haruspex shrugs noncommittally. "Fortuna has favored me. Many call upon me to assay their fate. Most seem pleased at what I have said, and find it to be true, in time. But I am just a mouthpiece of the gods, I merely see what they write in the signs."

Gracchus looks at Amelia's flushed face, tilting his head sideways as he studies her. The haruspex grasps her wrist and looks at the underside of her forearm. He slides his hand down across her palm and releases it, then peers into her eyes. Amelia blinks at him, surprised and flustered.

His face lights up with delight. "I am so happy for you, Sister, You are with child! A girl child, if I read the signs correctly."

Amelia's eyes start from her head. "What! You think I am pregnant? How can you tell?"

Tiberius Gracchus looks away. "You have missed your time, is that not so?"

Amelia blushes, and nods her head.

Gracchus beams. "Well, then, we must conduct an augury on the child's future. But I know she will be a momentous woman. Look at the stock from whence she springs!"

"You are kind, my priest, whether I be pregnant or not." Amelia favors him with a gentle smile. "The mere fact you show such interest touches me."

Gracchus is silent for a moment. He sighs, as if making a difficult decision. "I have more interest in you than you might expect, Amelia Scipio."

She looks questioningly into his eyes, but his gaze seems focused on some distant place.

"I have had dreams, visions of a daughter of yours being my wife." A flush creeps into his face. "I thought it silly, because you have no children, but the gods have shamed my doubt."

Amelia chuckles. "So, my husband is not the only one who follows his dreams!" She places her hand on Tiberius' forearm. "I do not know about you being in our lives, but I hope you are correct about me, haruspex. We will have such a celebration if it's true!"

Gracchus squeezes her hand. "As I once told your skeptical husband, our destinies are entwined. It is a thought that does not displease me."

Saying farewell to Tiberius Gracchus, a bemused Amelia walks to the Scipio domus where she finds Pomponia sitting on a low-slung couch by the atrium's piscinae, watching her prize eels undulating among the frenetic silver mullet. Amelia removes her street sandals and quietly pads in to sit next to her. Sensing Pomponia's morose mood, she says nothing about her meeting with Gracchus. They rest for a time, quiet together.

"They killed Sestertia," Pomponia says, still watching the fish.

Amelia turns her head and stares at Pomponia's expressionless profile. "Your house slave? She was such a dear old woman! Who would do such a thing?"

"She was with the several of the Hellenics, acting as my observer during our grain giveaway to re-elect my son. They were naught but some old men and women handing out bags of grain to the poor. Some men appeared and shoved their way to the front and began grabbing the bags, saying General Scipio was a thief and homosexual. The crowd berated them, and these horrid men began clubbing anyone they could reach. Someone bashed in Sesteria's skull—a harmless old woman!"

"The Latins?" Amelia asks.

Pomponia shrugs. "I cannot say if the party itself was involved, but I am fairly sure one of them was responsible."

"Flaccus?" asks Amelia.

Pomponia grimaces. "I cannot be sure. And that is what he is counting on—doubt. The bastard is free from Marcus' retribution—and mine— unless we know." She stands up, suddenly animated. "But we can secure our retribution in another fashion—we must ensure that my son has his imperium extended, whatever the cost!"

"I will double our banners and murals throughout the city," Amelia proposes. "We can work night and day for the rest of the month."

Pomponia squeezes her wrist. "That will certainly help, but we will need more than that. We have to remind the people of General Scipio's greatness. For that we need the Circus Maximus."

Amelia winces. "The Circus? That will cost a fortune to rent!"

Pomponia smiles tightly. "Yes, and my son has sent us a fortune for just such a purpose. We will gather all the plebs there, at the end of the Saturnalia." She grins wryly. "Nothing like a sporting event to attract the men."

"But for what? A chariot race? That will be held anyway during the first days of the fest."

"No, no more chariot races," muses Pomponia. "We have to give them something more memorable." She looks guiltily at Amelia. "We have to give them blood."

*　　*　　*　　*　　*

HANNIBAL'S CAMP, NORTHERN BRUTTIUM, 204 BCE.
Hannibal rides out from the darkened gates. He peers up into the indigo
sky, savoring the full moon that looms over him, its soft light
silhouetting the landscape of plains and rolling hills. His guards and
commanders follow him out onto the plain.

"Why are we out here at night?" asks a Bruttian.

"Baal take me if I know," replies the Carthaginian next to him.
"Hannibal has another wild plan, I am sure."

The war party rides for almost a mile until they see the twinkling
flickers of torches in the distance, high on the palisade of Sempronius'
camp.

Hannibal signals for his retinue to halt. He trots out a pace to stand
alone, sitting silently on his stallion. He scans the shadowed valley that
stretches before him, rehearsing the terrain features he has imprinted on
his mind. *The hills for our cavalry ambush are over there. We can
sneak more horses near them over by the adjoining ridge. Maharbal
can send the Bruttians out from behind the Libyans there, by the
stream, and engulf their flank.* As he always does, Hannibal plays out
the impending battle in his mind. He visualizes the Romans' counter
tactics to his moves, and decides how he would adjust to them.

Hannibal breathes deeply, enjoying the cool night air, savoring one
the few moments in his life when he is alone. Then he hears the soft
clop of approaching hooves.

"What is it?" Hannibal mumbles irritably, without looking back to see
whom it is.

"What are you doing out here?" asks Maharbal. "What are *we* doing
out here? We could have talked inside the tent." He squints about,
studying the gray outlines of the hills. "They could have men hiding
out there by the apple trees."

Hannibal laughs. "The Romans don't have night raiders. That is one of their problems, they are too predictable." He stares at the scattered Roman camp lights. "I needed to see the battle site to properly plan our attack. With Baal's blessing, this time I will destroy Sempronius."

Maharbal says nothing. His silence hangs in the air. "As you say," he finally replies. "So what will you do with the young Bruttians? They are not ready to be shock troops."

"You know. They will tire out the Romans, even if it's just by wearing out their sword arms from killing them," says Hannibal.

He turns his horse about. "Bring the captains up here, we have some planning to do. Tomorrow we challenge Sempronius to battle." He looks to the north. "Rome and Mago, they beckon us."

By late morning of the next day, the Carthaginian army is arrayed a half-mile from the Roman camp. They stand there for several hours, inviting battle. No one stirs from the Roman camp. His patience exhausted, Hannibal rides within a spear cast of the gates.

"Sempronius! Come out and fight, you cowardly dog!" shouts Hannibal. "If you make me break your gates, I shall spare no one!"

Hannibal spots two sentries at one of the gate towers. "You two!" he shouts, "Tell that coward of a general I await him with sword or fist, whatever he chooses!" They stare at the angry general for a moment, and then disappear. Hannibal waits, fist clenching his spear. He listens for the clanks of troops being mustered, but he hears nothing.

The light of realization comes to his eyes, and a sad grin comes to his face. He turns to Maharbal, shaking his head. "Gods curse them, they ran out in the night. That fucking camp is empty!"

Maharbal barks some orders. A quartet of Carthaginian light infantry trots in from the army, each pair lugging a tall wood limb ladder. The boys throw their ladders onto the eight-foot stake wall and scramble over it. Within minutes they push open the gates.

Hannibal rides inside and looks about. He sees the outlines of well-marked streets, bordered with the stake holes where hundreds of tents were mounted. In the rear he sees the open gates of the empty stables.

Hannibal laughs. "This Sempronius is becoming as tricky as that Scipio!" He slaps his horse's neck. "Ah well, he has saved us a battle. And much loss of life."

"Shall we go after them?" asks Maharbal. "They could not have gone far."

Hannibal shakes his head. "No, we do not have time to chase Romans. I have decided we head north, along the coast. That is where most of our allies live. We'll have enough battles when we join Mago's army, no need to seek any more." He turns back to Maharbal. "Send out our scouts. Locate Sempronius' army and follow him. This sly Roman may try to sneak back up on us!"

Two days later a Bruttian scout intercepts Hannibal while he is on the march with his army, heading in to build camp. "Forgive me, General, I bring news of the Roman general Sempronius. He is marching this way. He has many, many, men with him."

Hannibal's brows furrow. "More than we saw before?" The scout nods, wide-eyed. "Yes, general. Lots more."

"Go get Astegal, he is our best camp infiltrator," Hannibal orders. "You two go count them tonight. I want you both back here in the morning."

The scout and spy are back in Hannibal's tent by dawn. Astegal has a fresh linen bandage wrapped about entire right forearm, the cloth blooming with blood. "Sempronius has joined forces with General Publius Licinius," [xx] he says. "Their armies must have met on the march after Sempronius abandoned camp."

"Hmph!" Hannibal snorts. "That is a surprise indeed. How many?"

"Judging by their standards, General, they have four legions and at least that many in allied infantry. And thousands of cavalry." The spy avoids Hannibal's eye. "I would say double our force. At least."

"And they are coming for us?" Hannibal asks, unperturbed.

Astegal nods. "That is what their centurions were talking about when we prowled about their camp. They say that Sempronius was very ashamed to run from you. He is determined to destroy you and regain his honor."

"You are dismissed," Hannibal says. He looks at the spy's arm. "Go to the brown tent on the left and see my healer. He has some healing herbs for you." The spy nods and follows the scout out from the tent.

Hannibal sits for a long dawn hour, staring at the tent walls. He sips from a goblet of watered wine, a taste he has acquired from his long years in Italia. Finally, he heaves a deep sigh. "Bodemun!" he shouts, calling for his attendant. The one-legged old soldier limps in from outside the tent. "Fetch Maharbal."

Maharbal soon enters the command tent, already dressed and groomed. He cocks his eye inquisitively at Hannibal, who stares mutely at him, as if summoning himself for what he must say.

Maharbal shifts about, waiting for Hannibal to speak. "What is it? Just tell me," he finally says.

"We must retreat to Croton," Hannibal says quietly, staring at the ground. "Retreat," he repeats, not believing what he says. "There are two armies coming after us, with many more seasoned warriors than we have."

He looks apologetically at Maharbal. "I have turned this issue every way I can, considering our location, sun, dust, wind, and terrain. I can see no ploy or advantage that we can exploit enough to defeat all of them. We have to go."

"You are afraid we will lose? You have never been afraid of overwhelming odds."

"It is more that I consider the cost of the loss," answers Hannibal, wearily rubbing his eyes. "If we lose, we lose the war. If Carthage hears of our defeat, they would likely call me back—if I still lived. Or worse, they would finally capitulate to the Romans and make peace."

Hannibal looks northward. "And Mago, he would be all alone against them. Against all their legions. We must return to the south and recruit more men. And double our force, somehow."

Maharbal sees disappointment in Hannibal's eyes. And for the first time, doubt. "I do not question your decision, General," he says softly. "Someday, men will speak of you as the greatest general of all." He chuckles. "Thank the gods you were not born a Roman, they'd own the world by now!"

Hannibal stares at the tent wall, still thinking. "We must send a letter to Mago about our setback. It may give him more time to execute his own plans."

The next morning the Carthaginian army returns south toward Croton, leaving a burning camp behind them. Licinius and Sempronius' army stalk them on the way back, and hundreds of Hannibal's men are lost in the many skirmishes between them.[xxi] But even with their combined might, the two generals hesitate to attack the man who destroyed half of Rome's legions.

Hannibal returns safely to Croton. He immediately starts to replenish his army, his eyes ever north.

*   *   *   *   *

CIRTA, NUMIDIA, 203 BCE. The Numidian cavalry prance past Syphax' expansive palace, moving along in field-sized rectangles of a thousand men, each bearing their tribe's standard of a carved wooden elephant, lion, cheetah, or antelope. Gisgo and Syphax watch the parade from the comfort of their large padded thrones at the top the palace steps, idly conversing as the riders file past.

Gisgo yawns. "An impressive display, my king. But can they fight? The Romans are not impressed by fancy steps, I assure you."

Syphax sweeps his hand across his cavalry. "You look at the finest riders in the world, and I have thousands of them. How many men do you have in your army?"

The Carthaginian general grins, expecting Syphax would ask. He pulls a linen scrap from his robe sleeve. "Umm, let's see ... as of yesterday, about thirty thousand infantry and three thousand cavalry, with more joining every day." He pulls another small sheet from his robe and shows it to Syphax. "Here's a list of my siege equipment and elephants, if you'd care to look at it."

Syphax grunts approvingly. "You have been busy. The last message you sent me, you said you had thirteen thousand men and twelve hundred cavalry." [xxii]

Gisgo grunts. "My recruiting goes well, but I need even more. I want to outnumber Scipio's Romans at least two to one."

Sophonisba is standing behind her husband. Ostensibly she is watching the military parade of Syphax' warriors, but she is more intent on eavesdropping on the two commanders. She blinks in alarm at Gisgo's words. *He has an army the size of the Romans. He didn't tell me that.* Bending down, she touches her father's shoulder, wafting him in her spicy perfume. "That is laudable, Father. How did you gather so many, so soon?"

Gisgo smiles grimly. "Fear is a great motivator. After that cursed Scipio took Salaeca, thousands of Carthaginian youths massed in the city square and volunteered their service." He smiles. "Even the sons of the richest families in Carthage joined in. It was a stirring site."

"Sounds like you have large bunch of green recruits," notes Syphax skeptically. "Boys who have yet to sleep in the open or live in filthy underwear—much less take a wound and keep fighting! I'll take a farmer's son over a nobleman's, any day. They are used to persisting in all conditions."

"Our Carthaginians are strong warriors—just look at our Sacred Band! Many of these recruits may be pampered, but they have grown up fit and healthy. They were trained in sports and arms since childhood, and are quite capable of marching and fighting for days.

They are just finishing their javelin training, so they are almost ready for battle."

Gisgo leans toward Syphax. "My men and I have ridden everywhere to gather recruits," he says, grimacing at the memory of his saddle sores. "We rode up to Tunis and out to every outlying Carthaginian town. We even went south to get more of those tough Libyans. We have more than just some pampered city boys."

"Then you are ready for Scipio?" asks Syphax.

Gisgo looks at his daughter Sophonisba. "*We* are almost ready. You know our agreement, son-in-law. You and I dispose of Scipio and then we dispose of Masinissa."

Time to show your loyalty. Sophonisba decides. "He is right, husband. It was part of our wedding pact, though I needed no such guarantees to be with you." She smiles at Syphax. "If it will give you all Numidia, you must do it."

"Ah, such a devoted wife! She is worth it, is she not?" says Gisgo. Syphax nods mutely.

"So how many men can you bring me next month?" asks Gisgo.

"Well, all of those you see out there. With many more from the Masaesyli nation. And some from Masinissa's tribes, too!" Syphax grins proudly. "I will have fifty thousand infantry and ten thousand cavalry.[xxiii] Will that suffice?"

Gisgo gapes at him. "In truth?" he asks. "I can believe you have that many riders, but where would you get fifty thousand footmen?"

Syphax pulls his gold-embroidered cloak about his shoulders and sniffs. "You are not the only one who can recruit. I take the ones too poor to have a horse, and train them in spear and sword." He looks out on his splendid riders. "There are always plenty of poor men willing join the army and leave the bush. There are always hungry men who will risk their lives for food and glory. I have enough to drive Scipio out by myself."

Gisgo reaches behind himself and pats Sophonisba's hand. "You see? I mated you with the most powerful king in Africa! You are a lucky woman."

Mated! Sophonisba smiles tightly at her father, considering already how she will warn Masinissa.

"It is agreed, then," states Syphax, watching some riders dash past, standing atop their horses. "When should we move on Scipio? We should not let him gather strength."

"As soon as you can muster all those men you brag about," Gisgo replies. "We have to stop Scipio from taking Utica and making it his winter quarters. It would be impossible to get him out of there!"

Gisgo takes Sophonisba's hand and glares at Syphax. "You have no thoughts about renewing your treaty with Scipio, do you?" he says threateningly. "I could not have my daughter wedded to a traitor"

Syphax' eyes flare angrily. "I sent Scipio a message requesting he avoid waging war in Africa, because I would be obliged to defend my country against him. And he accused me of abandoning my honor by joining you!" [xxiv] His face colors. "I am ready to show him what it means to insult me!"

"My husband is not a traitor, Father!" blurts Sophonisba. "He will be loyal to your cause."

Syphax extends his arm. "The next full moon is soon upon us. We can join armies then, on the plains of Utica."

Gisgo drops Sophonisba's' had to grasp Syphax' forearm. "So be it. On the next moon we join forces and attack."

When she hears their words, Sophonisba's eyes grow wide with alarm. *They're going to destroy them all. I'll never see him again! Ah gods, what a life you have given me...*

Near midnight, Syphax rises from Sophonisba's damp body, grinning fatuously. "Ah, my treasure, I do so enjoy being in you—and with you," he adds hastily. "But I must go now, there are many preparations to make." Syphax eases his wife's doors shut.

As soon as he is gone, Sophonisba vaults from the bed and runs to her bathing room. She furiously scrubs herself from two urns of perfumed water, her face contorted with disgust. "Sweaty pig!" she mumbles as a slave gently dries her ravaged skin with a soft linen towel.

Sophonisba sends her attendant from the room. She slips into a sheer floor length robe and pads over to her special statue of the goddess Tanit. The queen shakes out her vial of belladonna and lovingly fingers it, looking at its ground up leaves and berries. *I am married to a pig,* she thinks. *An ignorant, sweaty, pig!*

Sophonisba steps into the hall. "Jezebel, bring me some mint tea," she orders. The slave returns with a silver goblet of the fragrant drink. Sophonisba waves her from the room. When the door is closed, she rushes over and slides its bolt into place.

The regal young woman places the cup down next to the vial for a moment, staring at it. She looks at the door that Syphax just exited, and heaves a deep sigh.

Sophonisba quickly uncorks the vial of belladonna and sprinkles it into the cup, stirring it with a quavering finger. She eases it to her lips, breathing in short gasps, and opens her mouth.

Suddenly, Sophonisba plunks the cup onto a window shelf. She draws back from it as if it were a serpent, her mouth a rictus of disgust --- and fear. As her hammering heart slows, she looks at the spread of African desert below her tower window, studying the waves of sand softly shadowed by the moonlit indigo sky. *How can I leave such beauty? But how can I spend my life in it as a king's whore, traded off by Father as if I were a prize cow?*

She grabs the cup with trembling hands and raises it to her lips. *I will not be controlled by them!*

Then the idea seizes her. *Your death does no good for your prince. You leave him when he most needs you. Are you such a coward?*

Sophonisba pitches the cup away, watching it clatter across the stone floor. She grabs a thick veil and dabs up the spill her hands shaking so violently she must grasp it with both. *I almost did it!*

She open the door and leans her head into the hallway. "Fetch Arsil," she barks, then her voice softens. "Fetch him when you are done with your cleaning, Jezebel. There is no hurry—not now." After her attendant leaves, Sophonisba rushes to her desk and grabs her quill pen. Writing furiously, she inks out a message on a sheaf of camelskin and stamps it with her family seal.

Soon a gangly, rawboned Sicilian boy stands before his mistress. Sophonisba knows that Arsil is in love with her, she has seen his eyes following her everywhere she goes. Now it is time for her to exploit her slave's affection.

"I must ask you to go on a mission of great danger, Arsil. One that is very important to me."

The young man's eyes light with eagerness to please her. "My life is yours, my queen. I ask nothing more than to sacrifice it for you."

Sophonisba lays the message in Arsil's hands and softly strokes his cheek, watching his eyes glaze with pleasure. "You are a remarkable rider, all know that. I need you to ride for me tonight. Take this message to the Roman camp and deliver it to General Scipio. Give it to Prince Masinissa if Scipio is gone."

Arsil nods, his eyes growing large with the dawning knowledge of his danger.

Sophonisba touches his shoulder and abruptly shakes it. "When you are there I command you to surrender yourself to the Romans, that you may return home. You are not to return here, is that understood?"

She gives him her signet ring and two bags of coins, and gently shoves him toward the door. "Go to our south exit. There is a stable there with a worthy stallion. Give the ring and one of the bags to the gate attendant. You keep the other for your new life."

Arsil nods, too scared to speak, and darts out the door.

With a deep sigh she walks to the window overlooking the desert and leans her head into her hands. Sophonisba watches the scythed moon cut into a dark gray cloud that drifts along the deep blue sky. And she waits.

*   *   *   *   *

UTICA, 203 BCE. "Sixty days. We have been here sixty fucking days!" grouses the grizzled senior tribune, staring challengingly at his thirty-three year old general. "We came here to storm over Carthage and conquer Africa, didn't we? But here we sit, not twenty miles from where we started, while we fling rocks at those stubborn fools inside that pisspot town!"

Scipio sighs reprovingly. "Crassus, that 'pisspot town' is strategically located right above Carthage. If we take it we can keep our supply lines open forever. That is more important than winning some skirmishes out on the plains, Tribune."

Scipio shakes his head, as if convincing himself of what he says. "I will not fall prey to poor logistics, as our other generals have done."

"The rainy season is upon us, anyway," remarks Laelius. "It would be stupid to campaign far from our base camp where we landed. The terrain could become mud in a minute."

He looks at Scipio. "But if we stay here we have no victories or plunder to give to Rome." He waggles his finger at his commander. "Was it not you who extolled the necessity of sending constant reminders to the folks back home?"

"Yes, and that's why we have to take Utica," Scipio says. "That would be a great political and military victory." He looks at Marcus Silenus. "What if we tried a night attack with our escaladers, as we did at Carthago Nova?"

Marcus shakes his head. "Their walls are thick with night sentries, I have never seen the like." His lips twitch with the barest of smiles. "I fear your reputation has caught up with you. The Carthaginians are well aware of your tactics."

"Then think up some new ones!" barks Scipio, his face reddening with frustration.

Marcus merely stares at him. "You can give up on Utica," he replies. "We could stay here and prepare for the spring campaign."

"There is wisdom in his words, King Scipio," adds Masinissa. "The rains will soon turn the roads to mud. My men know how to ride in this weather, but your wagons and infantry would be bogged down."

"General Scipio! By your leave, I approach." Praxis barges into the tent with two other members of Scipio's Honor Guard. The two carry a bedraggled youth with a linen bandage belted around his waist, a belt with a widening blood stain on the side.

"He was speared by a Carthaginian when he went by one of their outposts," says Praxis. "He says his name is Arsil. He came from Cirta with a message from Sophonisba."

"What!" Masinissa vaults from his chair and rushes to the reeling youth. "Is she well? What does she have to say?"

Scipio steps between the two and leads the boy to a sleeping platform, stretching him out upon it. The boy suddenly vaults up. "I have a message for you, General!" he blurts dazedly.

Scipio gently pushes him down. "Easy, boy. You can tell me from here." He looks at one of the Honor Guard. "Fetch my medicus."

Praxis walks over and hands Scipio a blood spattered sheepskin roll. "This was in his satchel. This Arsil here said he was to give it to you personally."

Scipio starts to break the seal. Praxis snatches it from his hand, breaks it open and unrolls it, then gives it back to Scipio. "Apologies, Imperator. There could have been a serpent inside, or a scorpion."

Scipio stares at him, mildly amused. "Gratitude, Praxis. You are a very careful man."

"I only have your welfare in mind," Praxis responds, bowing his head as he steps back from his general. Marcus catches Laelius' eye and nods his head toward Praxis. *Why did he do that?* his expression says. Laelius merely shrugs, bewildered.

Scipio scans the brief document. He turns to his officers. "Men, the message says that Gisgo and Syphax are heading towards us with an army of a hundred thousand men."

"A hundred thousand!" exclaims Laelius. "Sophonisba must be exaggerating."

"She is not one to use words idly," bristles Masinissa. "Syphax has most of Numidia at his disposal. It is not impossible he would have tens of thousands of men. With many, many, cavalry."

Scipio says nothing. He walks to his map table and slumps onto a stool. He looks at the clay figurines of soldiers and siege engines arrayed about the tower shape of Utica. Scipio picks up a soldier and taps it upon the map, lost in thought. He surveys the expectant faces of his officers, and pauses to study Marcus' stolid expression. Then he flips the infantry figure back onto the map and stands up.

"Even if Sophonisba's figures are exaggerated, they likely have twice the size of our army, with many more cavalry than we do. That is crucial in these conditions." He reaches over and flicks his finger into the Utica icon, cartwheeling it off the table. "The siege is over for now. We must organize our forces to defend ourselves."

Masinissa puts his arm on Scipio's shoulder. "My men can scout them tonight. By tomorrow we will know how many."

Scipio nods. "Send them out, but I already know the answer. There are too many."

Masinissa strides from the tent as Scipio turns back to his tribunes. "See that your men have their arms at the ready. Tell them a battle is coming. We will meet after breakfast to discuss this."

The officers hurry out of the tent while Scipio returns to the Arsil's bedside. "You have done well," he says to the young man.

The medicus enters and immediately unrolls the boy's bandage, checking the wound with probing fingers.

The youth gasps, but he keeps his fearful eyes fixed on Scipio's face. "Queen Sophonisba, she said I am not to return to her. That I should stay with you," he says expectantly.

Scipio spares a quick glance to the medicus, who briefly nods his head—the boy will recover. Scipio exhales, smiles, and strokes Arsil's thick black hair. "You will stay here for now, young warrior. But you will soon be on the next ship for Sicily. Admiral Laelius will see to that."

Scipio rises from his bedside and steps out from the tent, gesturing for his horse. He takes Praxis and his Honor Guard on a ride out onto the plains. They pause at a gentle rise overlooking the front gates of unyielding Utica, observing the Roman siege sprawled around it.

The general watches his ballistarii winching back the bowstrings of their siege engines, releasing them to hurl their spear-sized bolts at Utica's stout walls. He can see the catapult's rocks arc down onto the battlements, knocking holes in the top wall. But he can also see the Carthaginians scrambling about to rebuild the damage, shoving fresh limestone blocks into place as the bolts swoosh by their heads.

They will not give up, he concludes. He scans the walls for areas with the least concentration of soldiers, looking for a weakness. Minutes later, Scipio snorts a bitter laugh and shakes his head in frustration. *The place is as solid as a block of rock. This may require a full-scale frontal assault. We'd lose thousands.*

Scipio raises his right arm, palm out. He salutes the Utica defenders. "Come on, Praxis. It's time for me to get back."

The former gladiator studies the mobs of men bustling by them. "Wait until I get the rest of the guards over here. This would be a good spot for an assassin."

Scipio smiles wearily. "You are ever attentive to my safety. It has not gone unnoticed." Scipio studies Praxis' face. "You know, I do regret having to kill those two guards who used to fight in the ring with you.[xxv] But they made an attempt on my life."

"As soon as they broke our oath to protect you, they were no longer my friends," replies Praxis. "I swear by all my gods, I would never let harm come to you." *But my oath is only to protect you, my General.*

"I believe you." Scipio heads back towards his tent with Praxis trotting near his side.

Near dawn, Masinissa's scouts appear at Scipio's tent. Their faces show they have disappointing news.

"Gisgo has blocked the valley entrance into Carthage," says a bleary-eyed Numidian, almost asleep on his feet. "King Syphax is a day's march from joining him there. The Numidian has a force of at least fifty thousand men.[xxvi] He has thousands of cavalry, far more than we do." The other scout nods his agreement. "And Hasdrubal Gisgo has almost as many soldiers as Syphax."

"Gods above, when has a scout ever brought me good news?" Scipio grouses, rubbing the sleep from his eyes. He sees Masinissa frowning at him. "You did well, men," Scipio says sheepishly.

Scipio exits his tent. "Summon the military council," he orders Praxis, who is standing guard outside. "I don't care if you have to drag them from their beds."

When Marcus, Laelius, and his senior officers are gathered, Scipio gives them the enemy troop figures.

"We must retreat to the landing," urges one of the tribunes. "They can attack us from here at any moment."

"They seem more intent on building a defensive position," replies

Masinissa. "My men say the Carthaginians are building a permanent camp. They may be satisfied with simply defending Carthage and the valley."

"You have defeated Gisgo three times," states Marcus. "He may be afraid to fight you again, even with an overwhelming force."

"I would agree," says Laelius. "The poor devil probably wouldn't be there at all if he wasn't Carthage's army commander. He's probably praying for you to run back to Sicily."

"If he is loath to attack," says Scipio, "that would give us more time to lay siege to Utica. Then we might take it."

The room is quiet. Marcus finally speaks. "We would be out there on an open plain, with our force divided between preparing for a battle and laying siege to a stubborn fortress. Against a numerically superior foe. Is that what you are saying we should do?"

Scipio looks at Marcus' impassive face. He glances over at Laelius, but he will not meet Scipio's eyes. Scipio takes a deep breath. "I hear what you say, men. And what you have not said. Perhaps Utica has been my folly, and I have been too stubborn to recognize it. But if we take it, we could win the war with far fewer casualties."

The officers' silence shouts out their disagreement.

Don't be stubborn, he tells himself. *You are going to lose their respect.* "Very well. Winter is coming, and it does leave us vulnerable on the plains. Much as it may pain our engineers, tell them to move camp to the high ground two miles north of us, on the coastal peninsula.[xxvii] We can deal with Gisgo and Syphax from a more advantageous position."

"We could attack their camps," says one of the younger tribunes, breaking the silence. "Our men are better fighters!"

Scipio smiles tolerantly. "Creesus, I am sorely tempted to do so. If we defeated them our path would be open to besiege Carthage. But we are not sure of their numbers, other than they are many more than us. No, we shall use these few winter months to scout them out and prepare the spring campaign."

"After hearing all that has been said, I must disagree," says Laelius. "Next month the people will vote upon your imperium to continue the campaign here. You could be recalled. You need to make some good news, not hide in a hole!"

Scipio's eyes flare at him for a moment, and then he smirks. "Yes, and I am tempted to make the same mistake as my predecessors and rush to battle for glory's sake—but I will not." He looks north. "I can only hope that Pomponia and Amelia can win Rome on my behalf."

"Well," sniffs Laelius. "If we can't give the people victories, those two must give them entertainment. If they want to win the commoners, they'd best give them a circus!"

*   *   *   *   *

CIRCUS MAXIMUS, 203 BCE. The citizens of Rome clamber onto the plank seating that surrounds the Forum Square, taking their places in a rudely constructed amphitheater that has seemingly sprung up overnight. The plebs are curious about this extemporaneous festival— the wooden signs in the Forum promise a rare spectacle to celebrate today's winter solstice, the closing day of the Saturnalia.

After days of feasting, street performances, sacrifices, and races, the commoners are ready for something different. Tens of thousands have filed into the stands during the early afternoon hours, anxious for a new diversion.

The street hawkers scramble about the wooden planks like mountain goats. They lug wicker baskets of the crowd's favorites: roast dormice and boiled snails. The amphitheater is alive with noise: the citizens chat, gamble, and argue while waiting for their show. Anticipation hangs heavy in the air.

At the appointed hour the trumpets blare from the central dais. A tall, rangy man walks up the back steps onto the front platform, carrying a twelve-foot scythe over his bony shoulder. The bent figure sports a flowing white robe and wears an enormous curly black headpiece and false beard. The man is costumed to look like Saturn, the god of bounty, wealth, and harvest. He is the host god of the Saturnalia.

The "god" steps over to a flower-lined couch facing the square. He slowly waves his scythe over the people and stretches out upon the couch, a sign that Saturn has blessed the games.

Minutes later, Pomponia and Amelia walk to the front seats of the dais. Rome's two censors, Marcus Livius Drusus and Gaius Claudius Nero, parade in behind them. Both are former consuls, well known throughout the Republic. Pomponia has paid handsomely for these high-ranking officials to attend her fete, and she has paid even more to persuade them to halt their perpetual bickering and sit together.

Pomponia is a goddess herself today, resplendent in a floor-length robe of darkest purple. Her ample bosom is crossed with shimmering gold chains, and her flaming red hair is graced with a silver and emerald diadem. Amelia is more demurely dressed, as is her custom, but she has donned several silver necklaces over her forest green gown. Her hair is wreathed with the laurel branches of victory.

The two have dressed to flaunt their rank and importance. They know this public festival is a rare opportunity for a woman to publicly display her power and status—and to clarify that they are the ones sponsoring the event that will soon be the talk of the city.

Pomponia claps her hands, and the first pair of gladiators march in from a space between the stands. They tramp out into the center of the square, followed by two gray-tuniced referees. The gladiators are soon joined by a barrel-bodied giant in a simple loincloth and leather belt, carrying a leg-sized wooden cudgel. The man wears the Hermes mask of the merciful executioner. He will watch each match for his opportunity.

Nero steps to the edge of the dais, spreads his hands, and smiles beatifically at the people. "We wish to thank the Scipios for the entertainment they provide us, in celebration of our bountiful and beneficent god."

Livius pushes himself up from his chair and stands next to Nero, frowning at him before he turns and beams at the crowd. "We also wish to thank the Scipios for the remembrance this event provides. This festival celebrates Rome's recent triumphs—and celebrates her son Publius, who has brought us so many victories in Africa and Iberia."

At the mention of Scipio, the crowd roars their approval and begins to chant his name. Pomponia and Amelia smile at the honor, their eyes glinting with triumph.

Livius spreads his arms wide and stares heavenward, as if speaking to the gods. "And now, let the games begin!"

The crowd roars even louder. The consuls resume their seats and lean forward expectantly, ready for the fights.

The first match pits a Greek-style hoplomachus gladiator with a spear and a round shield against a murmillo, who is attired as a Roman legionary, bearing a scutum and a gladius. The small and lean hoplomachus darts about his stockier armored opponent, scoring half a dozen minor cuts and jabs, using his bronze arm guard to adroitly block the murmillo's sword thrusts.

The hoplomachus turns his shield sideways, essaying a feint move, but the alert murmillo slides his sword over the shield and into the gladiator's triceps, the blade sticking out the other side of the man's spear arm. The wounded hoplomachus raises his forefinger, signaling his surrender. The referee quickly runs in to separate the two and raises the hand of the murmillo. The crowd roars with delight, always happy to see a Roman defeat a Greek, even if both are actually Macedonians.

A dozen more matches follow. Many of them feature combats between two thraex, Thracian style gladiators that employ short swords and shields. All the matches end with one of the opponents wounded or beaten to the ground, save for one bare-torsoed thraex who takes a gladius deep into his bowels, prompting the man with the Hermes mask to rush out and cave in his skull to end his agony.

The crowd is clearly exhilarated, buzzing with discussions about the matches they have witnessed and the bets they have won and lost. Pomponia knows it is time to play her final political gambit. She stands up from her seat and spreads her hands.

"Honored citizens, it is time for our main event! Now we will celebrate Rome's greatest triumph—the conquest of Iberia! The domination of the Three Generals, by the peerless Publius Cornelius Scipio!"

A dozen gladiators march into the blood-doused ring. Half of them are outfitted like Iberians, carrying oblong shields and thick falcatas. The other six are armored as Carthage's Sacred Band warriors, wearing shining linen cuirasses and domed helmets to go with their round shields and short swords.

Three of the Carthaginians have purple-plumed helmets. Two of the three have the Barcid thunderbolt upon their shields. The third bears the Gisgon lion. The crowd knows they are portraying the infamous Three Generals, and they jeer them accordingly.

A dozen new fighters stride out from the other end of the ring. The broad-bodied men are garbed as Roman legionnaires, each brandishing the new wasp-waisted gladius that Scipio had developed for the Iberian wars.

A scarred older man in immaculate silver armor leads the dozen, his helmet bearing the owl's head signet of the Scipio family. Clearly, he is meant to be General Scipio. The leathery warrior is that rarest and most skilled of all gladiators, the dimachaerus. He grasps a sword in each of his sinewy hands, dangling them loosely at his sides. Many of the citizens stare wonderingly at him, having never seen a warrior forego his shield.

The gladiators arrange themselves in two rows opposite one another, their swords at the ready. Several gladiators stamp their feet and wave their swords, nervous and eager. The others shift from side to side, testing their balance. Only the dimachaerus stands still as a statue, oblivious to the screaming multitude about him. He looks down, kicks away a severed finger that lies near his right foot, and resumes his stance.

Pomponia rises and walks to the front of the dais, smiling at the populace. "And now, beloved citizens, I bring you our finale. A reenactment of the Battle of Ilipa, in which General Scipio conquered Iberia and restored it to Rome."

Pomponia looks across the sea of waiting faces, and raises her hand for quiet. "As with any war, this is a battle to the death. And there are no rules!"

She waves away the referees. A thousand eyes follow them as they walk into the stands and sit down. Pomponia's eyes gleam with feral anticipation.

Pomponia claps her hands together. Two battle trumpets blare the attack signal, and the gladiators rush forward. Within seconds the arena becomes a scene of feinting, dodging, thrusting, and slashing blades. The men from the two gladiatorial schools dart into and away from each other, feeling out their opponents' strengths and weaknesses.

An Iberian fighter dips low and slashes the back of his Roman opponent's knee, bringing his opponent crashing to the earth. The Iberian eagerly rushes at the Roman and pulls off his helmet. Even as the fallen fighter raises his finger in surrender, the Iberian crunches his cleaver like blade into the man's forehead, bringing a horrified—and delighted—roar from the crowd.

The gladiators are now dueling in earnest, fighting with all their skill. Men drop on both sides, some dead before they hit the ground, others killed as they grovel for mercy.

One combatant stands out. The Scipio warrior is a whirling maelstrom of action. His blades strike like serpents, flashing in to cut an exposed arm or leg before snapping back to defend him from a counterstroke. Two, then three, then four fall before him, bleeding from a dozen cuts.

Pomponia watches with a smile. She has paid a small fortune to the gladiatorial school to engage the man only known as The Parthian. He is known to all of Rome to be the school's most deadly warrior. *I made a good investment*, she reflects smugly, watching him slay man after man.

When his fourth opponent falls, The Parthian jumps over to team up with another Roman-clad warrior and then pairs with another, the duos killing their solitary opponents without conscience. Now only one opponent remains to the Romans, a man bearing the purple helmet plume of the Three Generals.

"Fuck you!" the Carthaginian shouts at the Roman gladiators. "Take me by yourself, if you have the balls!"

The Scipio fighter looks to the stands and sees their rapt attention. He waves his fellows back and walks toward the Carthaginian fighter. He halts five paces from the General and slowly unstraps his chest armor, then his greaves. Finally, he removes his helmet. The ropy-muscled old fighter stands in loincloth and sandals. He taps a sword against his iron-muscled thigh, a wry smile upon his seamed, tanned face. Bobbing his blades in his hand, he walks toward the Carthaginian.

"So, who are you supposed to be? Mago or Gisgo? Maybe Hasdrubal? It is all the same to me, because I'm going to kill you."

The Parthian leaps forward, swords over his head, and swings them toward the gladiator's helmet. The Carthaginian lifts his shield to block one blow and clangs his sword against the other. He has blocked both of the blades, but his torso is exposed.

The Parthian plants his left foot and scoops his right into the back of the Carthaginian's left knee. He yanks the man's leg out from under him, sending him crashing to the ground. The dimachaerus is upon him in an instant, knocking the Carthaginian's shield askew and shoving his sword into the opening between his opponent's linen cuirass and his shoulder protector. The blade cuts deep into the man's left underarm and plunges into his chest. The Carthaginian rolls onto his side and curls into a fetal ball, coughing out blood as his death throes commence.

"Death to the Carthaginians," the Scipio warrior shouts theatrically.

"Carthage must be destroyed!" he screams, echoing Cato's famous enjoinder. He smears the blood from one sword onto the other and raises them high, exultant.

"Scipio! Scipio! Scipio!" the crowd cheers, not knowing the gladiator's real name.

Flaccus and Fabius watch from the top of the Curiae Hostilia steps. "That bitch has turned them all to Scipio!" Flaccus spits. "Just when we had a chance to recall him!"

Fabius places a consoling hand on his shoulder. "Be not so hasty, Senator. The election has not been conducted. Our Forum speakers will be railing against him in the weeks to come."

Several weeks later, at the start of the new year, the plebians and patricians gather beneath the cool morning drizzle at the Campus Martius, bunching into the geographic voting tribes that comprise the Popular Assembly. One of the issues they vote upon is for the extension of Scipio's African command.

Each voter walks up a temporarily constructed gangway to face the elector, who hands him a wooden tablet covered with wax. The voter takes the proffered stylus and marks either "as you propose," or "I vote against," and drops it into a large urn.

As afternoon turns to dusk, the voting is completed and tallied. The vote is so overwhelmingly in favor of Scipio's command being extended that the magistrates extend Scipio's imperium until the end of the war, whenever that occurs. [xxviii]

Pomponia immediately sends a messenger to her two sons. She and Amelia celebrate long into the night. They quaff many cups of unwatered wine, joyous in their victory.

Among other election results, Rome has voted for a new city augur, one Tiberius Sempronius Gracchus.[xxix] It is a remarkable occurrence to elect one so young as a priest, but his reputation for morality and perspicacity has already made him a people's favorite. The man who predicts he will marry Scipio's daughter quickly becomes one of

Rome's most influential people.

When Amelia hears the result the next day, she can't help but wonder at the haruspex' prophecy that his fate is inextricably tied to Scipio's. *What if I do have a daughter?* She reflects. *Will the priest become my son-in-law?* Her right hand wanders down to stroke her swelling belly. She contemplates the fate of the child within her, and of her children's children.

*   *   *   *   *

CASTRA CORNELIA, NORTH AFRICA, 203 BCE. "Scipio, where are you hiding?" Laelius barges into Scipio's command tent, eyes wide with excitement.

Scipio is seated at his map table. He looks up from his goatskin map of Gisgo's and Syphax' camp emplacements, irritated at the intrusion. "Here I am, you pumpkin. Hiding in plain sight."

"I just heard! Rome has extended your command until you finish the campaign here! Congratulations!"

"Well, yes, I guess that is good news," says Scipio distractedly, running his fingers along a roadway on the map. "Did you know that Syphax' and Gisgo's camps are only a mile from each other?"

Laelius shrugs. "We looked at that before. Syphax has placed his men nearer to his Numidian empire on the west, and Gisgo has his camp nearer to Carthage.[xxx] It makes sense to me, much as any African's thinking ever has!"

"It also makes for an opportunity to divide and conquer, because they are not so close that they may readily succor each other," says Scipio, his eyes distant with thought. He grins suddenly. "Yes, that certainly gives us some possibilities!"

"Possibilities for the spring? That's two months away. They could have moved by then. They might even come over and attack us!"

"Yes, yes, but we have to start planning while have winter time, that we may move quickly when Fortuna blesses us with an opportunity," says Scipio, resting his chin in his hand. "Now is the time for diplomacy, before the fighting starts. I want to make absolutely sure our old friend Syphax will not change his mind and ally himself with us."

Laelius shakes his head. "Why waste your time? He would have to give up Sophonisba."

"Regardless, I am going to make him a proposal." Scipio smirks. "Maybe he has grown tired of that wife of his by now, it would not be the first time."

"I imagine it is worth a try, now that we have more time on our hands." Laelius wrinkles his nose. "At least *you* have more time! I have to finish beaching our fleet so that we may begin winter maintenance." He throws up his hands. "The bottoms on some of those ships' are more moss encrusted than a Scythian's behind!"

Laelius heads for the tent exit. "Anyway, congratulations. I insist we celebrate tonight, even if I have to burn all your maps and scrolls to get you to do it!"

Scipio watches him go, laughing. *What would I do without you? I know you joke to ease my burden, and hide your own pain.*

Scipio grabs an ink stylus and a sheaf of papyrus. He fingers the papyrus' texture. Frowning, he casts it away. Scipio walks over to rummage in his map baskets. He extracts a roll of finest goatskin. Plopping himself back at the table, he carefully inks out his message to Syphax, frequently pausing to worry over the words.

Honored King Syphax:

I write you as a former colleague, not as an enemy. In truth, I still carry the treaty we both signed at Siga, and I treasure the bond we had made with it. But now you have joined Carthage and voided our agreement. Now my friend has become my enemy.

I know time and circumstances change, and I must ask you to reconsider your alliance with Gisgo. Let us renew our treaty. If we join armies, Africa will be ours within a fortnight. And peace will be upon the land.

May your gods smile upon you.

General and Proconsul Publius Cornelius Scipio

Scipio is rolling up his message when an angry Cato stalks into the tent, brandishing a papyrus scroll as if it were a club. Scipio's two guards halt Cato just inside the entrance. Cato stands there, stamping his feet impatiently, waiting to be recognized.

Scipio rolls up his message. He warms his sealing wax and carefully stamps his owl's head seal upon the roll, seemingly oblivious to his sputtering auditor. *Let the pissant wait. We take our little victories where we may.* Finally, he beckons Cato forward. "What is it this time, Quaestor?"

Cato shakes the scroll at Scipio, unfurls it, and shoves it in his face. "Missing monies, missing plunder! I monitored every load that went onto those ships bound for Sicily. There is a fortune missing. As General, you must give an accounting for it!"

Scipio places his hands on the table and stares heavenward. He faces Cato, looking at him as if he were a disobedient child. "You know, Cato, the last thing I need is a persnickety quaestor. Rome will require an accounting of my achievements, not my costs." [xxxi]

Cato snorts derisively. "There will be few enough of those, the way you coddle your men.[xxxii] I have it in mind to return to Rome and voice my complaints to the Senate. They will not tolerate your wastefulness."

He glowers at Scipio. "There was a ship that left from here but did not reach Sicily. Where was it bound, General?"

Scipio points south, toward the docks. "You do not approve of the way I conduct my campaign? There is a transport sailing in two days, Quaestor. It is yours to board for Rome. But if you go, do not return."

A red-faced Cato starts to reply when Scipio shoves his palm out at him, commanding him to silence. Scipio turns to a guard. "Bring me a messenger, Brutus." He looks back at Cato and nods imperiously toward the exit, holding Cato's eyes until the sturdy little man stalks from the tent.

"Do not think I will not consider it," Cato says over his shoulder, as he shoves the flaps aside. "You may have an imperium to continue here, but you can be recalled for breaches of morality!"

Scipio finally loses patience "Out of here, now!" he commands loudly. "Leave or I'll assign you to a tent with Laelius!"

With a final scowl Cato stomps out, shouldering aside one of the guards. Scipio hisses out his breath and chuckles ruefully. "Gods above, must I fight my own men, too?"

Three days later an elegantly dressed Numidian dwarf rides into the Roman camp, dressed in the finest silks of indigo and gold. He halts his small pony before the camp sentries at the entrance.

"I bear a message for General Scipio!" the dwarf pronounces to the grinning guards. "Take me to him immediately!"

"As you wish, Dominus," replies the burly captain of the guard. He strides forward and pulls the struggling man off his mount. After searching the messenger for weapons, he carries him to Scipio's tent.

Seeing the dwarf, Scipio sighs. He knows the answer to his request even before he opens the message. *Shit*, he thinks, and morosely opens the sealed papyrus.

General Publius Cornelius Scipio:

I am honored and humbled that you would remember our agreement. I told you then that Africa's interests were ever foremost in my mind.

There is only one way for Rome and Carthage to achieve a lasting peace. Carthage must leave Italia and Rome must leave Africa. Each of you would keep the lands you have already won there, but each must leave the other's homeland.[xxxiii]

The rebel Masinissa has joined you, so I cannot come to your camp. I would welcome you to our emplacement, however. You could discuss peace terms with General Hasdrubal Gisgo and myself.

I eagerly await your response.

Syphax, Absolute and Rightful Ruler of Numidia

That evening Scipio reads Syphax' message to his officers. They receive it with a mixture of rage and disappointment.

"He sends a dwarf, and tells you to come to him," growls Marcus Silenus. "We should march over there and teach him some respect. I'll fight his best champion myself."

"I have a better idea, General. Let me return to eastern Numidia," urges Masinissa. "He could come to your camp then, and I can gather hundreds more men to my side. Then we can attack them both. Why wait for spring?"

Scipio rolls up the message and smiles slyly. "Ah, let us not act too hastily. I would welcome the chance to visit Syphax' camp. And Gisgo's too. We will go there with our minds open to their proposals." He pitches the message into a corner. "And our eyes open to their camp arrangements."

* * * * *

MILAN, NORTH ITALIA, 203 BCE. Mago's speech to the towering Gaul is brief but impassioned.

"Spring will be here soon, Chief. I have twenty thousand men at the ready, thirty thousand if your army joins me. In two months we will march down to Rome and join my brother. When Rome falls, you and your warriors will have first pick of the plunder—and the women!" Mago rubs his hands eagerly. "Think of it! You can sack Rome, just as the mighty Brennus did!"

"The idea appeals to me," says Morcant, chief of the Insubrian Gauls. "And we are grateful for the cartload of silver you have given to us. But that new consul, that Marcus Cornelius, he blocks the way south to Rome." The bull-necked giant pulls at the thick auburn braid behind his right ear, pondering Mago's words. He shakes his head. "No, I think it best we send you some men a little at a time, so that the Romans do not notice us. Then we could all take more time to prepare."

"I cannot wait any longer!" sputters Mago. "We have sat around all winter while the Romans dance across Africa, plundering as they go." He shakes his finger at Morcant. "And when they are done in Africa they will come here and do the same to you! They will not stop until they have conquered Gaul, you know that is the way they are!"

Mago's words make Morcant's chieftains mutter with alarm. "We should fight them now!" a rangy old warrior says.

Morcant raises his hand and the chiefs quiet. "We will send you a thousand more men, Mago. Maybe two thousand. That is all for now."

Mago flaps his hands, exasperated. "That is not enough! You must commit your army, Morcant. Then we will have enough men to completely destroy them!"

Morcant looks at the ten chieftains sitting around the lodge's enormous oval feasting table. He sees only skepticism in their faces. "We have already discussed this among ourselves. My scouts say Rome has seven legions in North Italia. Four of them are nearby, commanded by this general Cornelius and that praetor Quinctilius Varus. That is almost twenty thousand Romans. And they have just as many allied troops." The chieftains nod solemnly.

Mago sniffs audibly, his nose high in the air. "I cannot believe what I am hearing! The fearsome Gauls are afraid of the Romans! Do you fear they will chop you all up with their pointy little swords?"

Morcant manages a wry smile. "We are not worried that they would defeat *us* in a battle, were we two to join forces." Several chieftains grin at his words.

"Ah, I see," Mago says. "Perhaps you doubt my Ligurian allies. But you have warred with them and know their power. That can only mean you question the might of my own men." Mago looks at one of his Sacred Band guards. "Go get the sack."

The guard pushes through the hall doors and disappears. "There is something I want to show you," says Gisgo.

The guard quickly returns with a large woven sack. The Carthaginian general unties the rope from around its neck and holds it in front of him, staring at the Insubres. "Here is what happened when my men fought the Romans."

Mago upends the heavy bag. Thousands of gleaming gold rings pour out onto lodge floor, chiming off its thick oak planks. The Gauls blink at the ringing cascade. They look at Mago, a question in their eyes.

Mago sweeps his hand over the rings. "These were taken off the fingers of Roman knights during Hannibal's battles in Italia, ones from which he always emerged victorious. This is the fate of any Romans who will oppose us." He barks a laugh. "Besides, half of these so-called Roman legions up here are slaves! Did you know that? Rome is so desperate they have slaves fighting for them!"

Morcant rises from the table and walks to the sprawled mound of rings. He is followed by several of his chieftains. They dip their large calloused palms into the glittering pile, letting the rings slide through their fingers. They stare at the engraved Latin words on them, slogans of love and victory worn by men who are long years dead. Morcant looks at his fellows. They mutely nod.

"At the first frost you will have our army here, Mago. But you must promise we can plunder the fields and towns along the way, that we may send food to our families back home."

Mago laughs. "Oh, you can sack all of Italia for all I care, as long as your plundering does not slow us down. Hannibal awaits us, and Rome will fall."

*   *   *   *   *

The Raid

SYPHAX' CAMP, BAGRADAS RIVER VALLEY. "Welcome, honored envoys, welcome!" gushes Syphax. "We have eagerly awaited your arrival. Perhaps peace is possible, after all."

"I am honored to be here," replies Laelius dryly, slightly bowing his head. "General Scipio is most anxious to discuss your proposals." He nods towards Cato, who is frowning at the gold cloths bedecking Syphax' palatial tent. "We are here as Scipio's envoys. We hope to meet with your delegates in the upcoming weeks, that we might negotiate a permanent treaty."

Laelius motions to one of his two attending slaves. "Calvus, bring me the box!" The bald slave bows obsequiously and shuffles from the tent. He quickly returns with a small gold-bordered container of polished oak.

Laelius takes the box and waves toward the exit. "Appius, Calvus, you two wait outside," he orders. The two middle-aged slaves hurriedly exit through the tent's ten-foot high flaps, eyes downcast.

"With the sincere compliments of General Scipio," purrs Laelius, as he extends the box to Syphax.

"This is an affront to the gods! He deserves nothing!" Cato snorts. Laelius fixes the quaestor with a look, and he quiets.

Syphax opens the box to find a gold-embroidered tunic of a soft, thick material. "It is made by an Egyptian weaver, from what they call 'cotton.' It is very soft."

Syphax carefully fingers the fabric. He smiles. "I have wanted some of this wondrous material. My thanks to Scipio. Now, please come with me. My tribal elders are anxious to talk to you."

"We are anticipating a pleasant and fruitful dialogue, aren't we, Cato?" says Laelius, smiling threateningly at his crusty colleague. *Why Scipio insisted that I bring him along is beyond me. I don't care how observant he is—a pig is a pig!*

"Hmph!" growls Cato, as the group moves out the rear exit to a hall-sized conference tent. "From lightest words sometimes the direst quarrel springs." [xxxiv]

While Laelius and Cato are engaged with the Numidians, the two slaves shuffle about the campgrounds, watching the construction of the camp buildings. Calvus stops to tug at the branches of a freshly constructed hut, noticing how it sways when he pulls at it, how brittle and dry it is. A rough hand shoves him from behind, and he lurches forward.

"Here, what are you doing?" barks a stolid little Numidian carpenter, his wood ax gripped in his hand.

Calvus blinks in ignorance at the foreign tongue, and shrugs, his head downcast. "I meant no harm, master," he mutters.

"Ignore them. They are nothing but slaves," says a Numidian guard.

"I don't care if they are cup bearers to the gods," rejoins the craftsman, "I just put that stick hut together!"

Calvus starts to shuffle away. He stoops his back, but his eyes are aflame with anger. The carpenter kicks him in the buttocks, spurring laughter from the nearby soldiers. He cowers away from the angry little man and scurries back toward the main tent, followed by his alarmed companion. The Numidian returns to chopping up branches—unaware of Calvus' parting glare.

Calvus turns a corner and stops, panting with fury. "I will kill that little shit-eater with my bare hands," he growls, rubbing his backside. "Then I'll kill Scipio for making me pose as a slave!"

The other slave nods, "Easy, soldier. You must find the courage to be a coward."

He pulls the sleeve of Calvus' worn grey toga. "Come, let's go over by the stables, and count their stock." The two men slump down and shuffle toward the rear of the enormous camp, as hundreds of enemy soldiers bustle past them.

Late that afternoon, Laelius and Cato exit the meeting tent and find the two slaves waiting by the horses. A regally dressed Syphax parades out from his headquarters and shakes Laelius and Cato's forearms before they mount their horses.

"I trust the discussions went well?" asks Syphax.

"Oh, it was a good start for us," answers Laelius brightly. "But there are still many things to be discussed. I would like our infantry commander to come to the next session. He could talk better about scheduling our troop evacuations from Africa, should we arrive at a treaty. Perhaps he could talk with Gisgo's commander?"

"Of course," says Syphax. "Gisgo is presently in Carthage, but we could go meet at his camp when he returns."

"What a pity he is not here," Laelius says.

Syphax shifts about uncomfortably. "Please excuse General Gisgo. He is, uh, uncomfortable coming here to meet you. He thinks that would be a loss of status."

Laelius smiles. "Of course. We understand. We are more than willing to go to his camp."

The Romans leave camp with an escort of Syphax' elite guard around them. When they exit the gates Laelius looks about the perimeter of the quarter-mile clearing outside the camp. He watches groups of Numidians constructing new reed huts around the hundreds already built there.

Syphax' army grows larger every day, Laelius thinks, trying to count the sea of rude shelters. *And the new arrivals are all camped outside his walls.*

Laelius examines base of the palisades, where scores of rude huts border the trench around the walls.[xxxv] *Hmm! They are piled right up by the gates!* He sees Cato studying the sea of brittle shelters and stares at him until he catches Cato's eye. Cato nods silently at Laelius—*this is important to remember*, he signals.

The Romans' Numidian escort accompanies them for the first mile back to Castra Cornelia. When the group draws near to a Roman outpost, the Numidians wordlessly turn about and ride back toward their camp. The envoys send a scout hurrying ahead of them as they trot on towards Scipio's command tent.

When Cato and Laelius arrive at Scipio's praetorium they find Masinissa, Marcus Silenus, and Scipio awaiting them at the tent entrance. Scipio waves them over to sit at a large oval table he has brought in for their meeting. Cato and Laelius pull up two heavy oak stools and sit down with the rest of the group.

"So, was your visit productive?" queries Scipio.

Laelius crooks his finger at Cato, "What do you think, noble Quaestor?" Laelius lilts sarcastically. "You are ever the man with high standards."

"I would say so," Cato replies. "They want to continue negotiations at their camps, as we hoped. We have requested they meet with Marcus Silenus."

Scipio nods. "Excellent. If we can prolong these talks for a month, then we will be ready." He looks at Calvus and Appius. "What have you learned, Centurions?"

"It is as Masinissa predicted," says Appius. "The Numidians are using native plants for their shelters. The nearby river is blanketed with reed filled marshes. The camp huts are all built out of dried reeds." [xxxvi] He looks intently at the group. "The huts are all pushed together, with several sharing the same wall."

"And," interjects Laelius, "most of these huts are outside of camp, clustered about the walls. The new arrivals have to build their shelters in a big clearing."

"There is a front and rear exit for escape, but the rear could be blocked by a single cohort of our men," remarks Calvus. "There are miles of trees and brush around the camp clearing, thick enough for men to hide in."

Calvus rises puts his finger on a map, at a spot near Syphax' camp, "There are hills here, and here. A legion could be concealed in them."

"Ah, that is good to hear," Scipio says. "That is why I wanted you two centurions to pose as slaves.[xxxvii] I needed wise eyes looking at that camp."

"When I go to Gisgo's encampment, I shall bring some my own 'slaves,' " says Marcus. "I know of a tribune and a centurion who understand Carthaginian. They can listen in on the camp soldiers."

"All the better, Marcus." says Scipio. "Just remember, you should argue about the treaty conditions, and demand that you consult with me before you make a decision. We have to prolong the discussions so we can learn more about their assets and vulnerabilities."

Marcus shrugs resignedly, and grins. "Wouldn't it just be easier if I killed them all right there? I'd wager I could take out their entire command before they got to me."

"Not if I'm there you won't!" rejoins Laelius. "I'm too beautiful to be flayed and crucified!"

Marcus studies the ceiling. "On that, there is serious disagreement..."

"Masinissa will go with Marcus," says Scipio. "He has an eye for Numidian vulnerabilities, wouldn't you say?"

Laelius laughs. "Oh, now I do want to go! Imagine Syphax' face if he is there to see Masinissa!"

The next week, Marcus and Masinissa arrive at Hasdrubal Gisgo's camp, accompanied two tribunes and two slaves. After a day of deliberately fruitless negotiations, the envoys return to meet with Scipio.

"Gisgo's huts are built from sticks and boughs, not reeds" Marcus reports, "They are a bit stouter than the Numidians' reed shacks outside, but they are not reinforced with earth about their walls." [xxxviii]

"They are quite vulnerable to fire, then," notes Scipio, "that is all we need to know." He hands the men a papyrus sheet and points to his map table. "Draw a map of the inside of their camp." Scipio plops himself onto a stool next to the table and sips some watered wine while the six men sketch out a rude map, arguing about several of its details.

"The Carthaginian camp seems better protected than Syphax' camp," comments Appius, one of Marcus' slave spies. "They have more guard towers along the palisades, and stronger walls"

Scipio counts the tower rectangles on the map. "Hmm. It would be less vulnerable to a surprise attack. That is not good news. We have to take them both."

Masinissa stands up. "There is another way. When I was a child, a neighboring tribe raided my father's village and stole all our horses. The tribe was too powerful for us to fight, and well they knew it."

Cato blinks at him. "There is a purpose to this story, Numidian?" he inquires.

The Numidian prince deigns a slit-eyed glance at Cato before he continues. "The invaders celebrated their raid long into the night. When the fell into a drunken sleep, our men crept up and set fire to their corral. When the raiders stumbled out to extinguish the fire, we sprang upon them." He smiles grimly. "There was much weeping in their village the next day."

Scipio is still for a minute, and then he nods. "I see the implication, Masinissa. We can draw them from a position of strength to a position of weakness." His eyes gleam with excitement. "Just how far apart are the two camps?"

"We rode a little over a mile from Syphax' camp over to Gisgo's," notes Marcus. He smirks "Syphax followed later, he would not travel with Masinissa." Marcus trails his finger from the map outline of Gisgo's camp to the one of the Numidians. "The road cuts between these low hills."

Scipio nods, and sits quietly for a moment. He looks intently at each man in the room. "Tell no one what we have discussed, understand? We will continue the negotiations for another month, that we may get some detailed drawings of each camp." He grins. "Perhaps we can put Masinissa's little fable into action."

"General Scipio, we have a truce with these people," says Cato. "Yet you use it to plan to attack them. You violate our honor. Romans do not break truces."

"True enough, Cato," Scipio answers. "I can always count on you to be our conscience, can't I?"

He looks expectantly at the other men. "Truces can be broken, if one of the parties makes unreasonable demands. And I daresay that will happen sometime soon, from us or them."

He looks at Cato. "We will not violate our truce, we will declare an end to it. And when a truce is ended, its conditions no longer hold." He stares harder at Cato. "Would you find that acceptable?"

"It smacks of sophistry more than morality," replies Cato.

"And you smack of self-righteousness more than inspiration," snipes Laelius. "May the gods preserve Rome if you ever become a general. You would rather we all die than besmirch your precious honor."

Cato starts to retort when Scipio raises his hand. "You think you are the only man possessed of a conscience?" Scipio says.

"I only say I am one who follows its dictates," replies Cato.

"And are not torn by its consequences," mutters Laelius. "Whatever the costs to others." He chuckles darkly. "You act more like a censor than a quaestor."

Scipio leans forward, hands on the map table, and looks at all of his officers. "It is possible that Gisgo and Syphax will propose a peace that we can accept. But such a peace must conform to conditions that make for a lasting peace—with terms that so weakens Carthage that it will pose no future threat to Rome. It is my dream that such would occur."

He shakes his head. "Unfortunately, I cannot see that happening without a decisive victory in the field." ^{xxxix}

"Carthage must be destroyed, burned to the ground!" blusters Cato. "Level their walls and salt their grounds so it never returns to power."

"Carthage must be preserved," counters Scipio, with a ferocity that temporarily silences the doughty quaestor. "The city is a magnificence of art and culture that must be saved from the likes of you. You speak of honor, yet you would destroy an entire nation!"

The officers are silent, taken aback at Scipio's temper.

"What next?" Marcus finally interjects.

Scipio looks south, toward the enemy camps. "If the truce is broken, we must prepare to act at once, before the two of them can mount a concerted attack on us."

"So we will take the battle to them," a tribune says.

Scipio shakes his head, as if a child had made a silly statement. "Not a battle, there are too many of them. It will be a raid; a surprise attack. Tomorrow we begin our plans." He stares at them. "Plans we will keep secret."

The officers rise from the table and march towards the door. As the guards open the tent flaps for them to leave, Scipio casts one final comment. "And gods help us if the raid is no surprise!"

After the final tribune departs his tent, Scipio rummages inside a wicker basket of his treasured scrolls. "Ah!" he exclaims. He eases two thick yellowed papyrus rolls from the bottom of the worn basket and blows the dust off them.

Cradling the scrolls like a child, Scipio takes them to the map table and gingerly unrolls the first, a record of Greek wars in Africa. He runs his finger along its rows of words, mumbling to himself, searching for something. Eventually he rolls it back up and carefully restores it to the bin.

He unrolls the second and runs his finger over its scrawled lines. His finger halts at a particular passage. He bends closer and mouths the words out loud as he reads. He leans back, satisfied. *Good old Agathocles. He said it burned like a torch!* Scipio's eyes grow distant, his mind drawn inward to the plans taking shape in his head.

Scipio rushes outside and crawls around the perimeter of his tent. He grabs handfuls of twigs and branches, bending them to ensure he has the driest ones. He makes three fist-sized piles from them on the ground, each a hands-breadth from the others.

"There!" he says. Scipio runs inside to fetch a torch. He lightly touches the torch to the first pile. The twigs flare to life. The flame quickly spreads its fingers to the second pile, which flames up and reaches to the third. Scipio laughs giddily as he watches the little fires burn.

*   *   *   *   *

CASTRA CORNELIA, 203 BCE. The camp guards loll out in front of the open gates, gazing at the stubble of spring wheat that has seemingly sprouted overnight from the rich earth of the river-fed valley.

"It won't be long, now," observes the young socii, an allied soldier from Umbria. "General Scipio, he's not one to sit around in camp all winter, he's going to do something soon, I can feel it."

The other young soldier laughs. "You can tell something is going on. The tribunes are buzzing around camp like flies around a mule pile, sticking their noses in everything." He sighs as he looks out on the plain. "I'd be weeding fields if I were back in Latium right now. When sprouts arise like those out there, it's time to work from dawn to dusk! I wonder what my father is plowing right now?"

"Probably your wife," quips the other.

The guards' banter is interrupted by the sight of a Numidian hurtling across the plain toward them. "Is that one of Masinissa's men?" asks the Umbrian.

"Who can say? They don't carry proper standards, riding around half naked on those skinny little horses. Better to be safe, anyway." The Latin steps inside the gate opening. "Squad to the front!" he shouts, and six more guards appear from inside, straddling the entrance.

The rider halts his lathered mount in front of the stolid wall of guards, his face evidencing his frustration. "I have a message from King Syphax," he says in broken Latin, "Rightful Ruler of Numidia, Light of Africa, Leader of ...."

"Yes, yes, yes," says the Latium guard, waving his right hand impatiently. "Suppose you drop all that title shit, and your spear. Then we'll let you in."

The sneering messenger holds out his silver tipped ceremonial spear, and lets in drop in the dust. "Do you feel safe now, Romans?"

The guards lead the Numidian into the camp square, where Praxis and his Honor Guard intercept him.

"You have news? What is it?" Praxis asks the messenger, his hand on his sword pommel.

"News for your leader, and no one else," the messenger replies

Praxis steps forward and shoves him toward Scipio's tent. "Get on with you, then." The Guard surrounds the messenger and leads him to Scipio's tent.

Scipio is sitting at his table, playing a solitary game of latrunculi. He jumps a black pebble over two white ones on the checkered board, and smiles up at Praxis. "There!" he preens. "I've just taken two Libyan phalanxes!"

"Would it were that easy for you, General." Praxis replies.

Scipio eyes the Numidian. "What did you bring me, Praxis?"

"Charon take me if I know." The old gladiator glowers at the Numidian. "Go on, give it to him."

The messenger stares haughtily at Praxis, then faces Scipio. He hands a sealed sheepskin roll to him. "I am to wait for your reply," he says.

Scipio breaks the seal and scans the roll. His breath quickens as he reads it. "Praxis, give this man food and water, and a safe place to rest." He turns toward another guard. "Summon my council, they are to be here immediately."

As the men rush off to fulfill their orders, Scipio steps inside his tent and pulls out a papyrus roll and his writing stylus, ready to write his reply. Marcus, Laelius, Lucius, Cato, and the senior tribunes soon join Scipio. He holds Syphax' message in his hand, his eyes flashing with excitement.

"Syphax and Gisgo have returned their final version of the peace terms we have discussed," he says, his face at once grim and expectant. "As I expected, they have added a number of unreasonable expectations to our proposal, thinking we are eager for peace." [xl]

"You mean, as you had hoped," snipes Cato.

Scipio goes to his desk and holds up a blank sheet of papyrus. "I will keep the messenger here for the night. In the meantime I will write a formal reply that the truce between us is ended. That signifies that the war between us has resumed." He steps toward his men. "But now, right now, we take action!"

Scipio turns to Laelius. "Tomorrow morning, take our warships and blockade the Port of Utica. Take the catapults with you, as if we are going to lay siege to it from the water."

He turns to Marcus Silenus. "We'll put two thousand men atop the hill over by Utica, where they can be readily seen. It will look as if we are preparing for a land attack. That should distract Gisgo and Syphax' scouts from our true intentions." He grins at his men. "Perhaps what you see as my 'preoccupation' with Utica will be to our advantage, after all."

Scipio's face flushes. His eyes gleam with the excitement of preparing for battle. Even staid Cato can feel his own heart beat faster at the challenge awaiting them—a life or death engagement against a vastly superior force.

"With your permission, I would join your cohort in this venture, General," Cato blurts, surprising himself. "As a line officer with the legion."

Scipio gapes at him, then nods. "Of course, Quaestor. You are an experienced warrior. I am pleased to have you."

Laelius rolls his eyes. He opens his mouth to say something, but Scipio silences him with a glare.

"Two nights hence, we meet for a final war council, to review our tactics. After that meeting we will inform the tribunes of our plans. Then you lead the legions out from camp at sunset, when you hear the trumpets blow. [xli] I know it will be difficult to prepare your men with so little time, but we cannot risk being discovered."

Scipio turns to one of his tribunes. "Publius, I will need two hundred torches, heavy with pitch. Go and prepare them." He motions for his officers to follow him to the map table, where they crane their necks over the maps of the two enemy camps.

The general sketches a map of the hill-bordered passage between the two camps, and inserts the fresh map between the other two. "There may be a hundred thousand men in those two camps, and they are only a mile apart. But that proximity is to our advantage, because we can quickly move from one to the other."

Laelius smirks. "It is a marked disadvantage, because they can move quickly to help each other!"

Scipio grins. "And that is what we are counting on, we want them coming to assist each other!"

He stands back from the map. "I liked your story, Masinissa. As you say, deception and surprise are most important with a superior foe. If this raid does not fool Gisgo and Syphax we will lose—the fight, our lives, the war."

He takes a deep breath and looks at his men, his face eager with the anticipation of purposeful action. "No more sitting around Utica. We are taking the war to Carthage. Now go!"

*   *   *   *   *

GISGO'S CAMP, BAGRADAS RIVER VALLEY. "Here, let me do that. We don't need a slave pouring for us. I'd rather have the jug near me!"

Hasdrubal Gisgo refills Syphax' wine goblet and then his own, brimming them with dark red wine. He lies back on his dining couch, quaffing deeply from his cup. Syphax nods his thanks and lies back on his own seat, sipping thoughtfully—thinking of what they should do about Scipio.

"I knew it. That bastard resumed his siege on Utica today. And Roman ships are in the Utica port!"

"Well, we did add quite a few demands to the proposal," soothes Syphax. "We can remove that demand for him to leave Africa immediately, and take out the one for him to cede Bruttium to Hannibal." Syphax drains his cup. "We may then come to agreement."

Gisgo shakes his head. "We outnumber the Romans better than two to one. I am thinking we just storm into his camp tomorrow, while his men are up near Utica." He reads Syphax' face. "I know what you are thinking, it would be a costly battle. But we have him backed against the sea, with twice his numbers. What could be a better time?"

Her men have informed her that the slaves wandered over to the camp's back walls and exits, conversing with the guards stationed there. Her beloved Masinissa has told her about wily Publius Scipio, how his spying undid the Three Generals in Iberia. Sophonisba suspects that Scipio and Masinissa have a plan for attacking one of the camps.

Sophonisba's father betrayed her, and her husband stole her from the man she truly loves. She is not of a mind to protect either Gisgo or Syphax, especially if it bodes ill for Masinissa. She says nothing of what she surmises, waiting to play her part.

Sophonisba sees that the two are becoming bleary-eyed with drink. She walks to Gisgo's couch and stands behind him, placing her hands on his shoulders. "Should we not try for peace one more time, Father? Think of it. You could be the man who ended the war. You, not that overrated Hannibal Barca."

Syphax belches wetly. Sophonisba's upper lip rises into a sneer that she quickly stifles. *Pig! I should give you the poison!*

"Her idea has merit, Gisgo." Syphax says. "I do hate to attack without one more attempt to settle this. The truce with the Romans has been so quiet: no fights, no skirmishes. The few sentries we have had to post report nothing. It is almost like peace has already happened."

He leans toward Gisgo. "Let us make a counter proposal tomorrow, with fewer demands. If Scipio rejects it, we will try it your way." He sighs. "I would rather keep as many of my men as I can, that I may finally capture that pestiferous Masinissa."

Gisgo grabs the wine jug and splashes the final drops into his goblet. "One more time, then. But I will not wait much longer. The winter seas are calming, and Scipio may soon get more troops from Sicily."

Gisgo holds up three fingers. "Three days. I give him three days to accept our new proposal. Then we wipe him out, whether he answers or not."

*   *   *   *   *

SYPHAX' CAMP, BAGRADAS RIVER VALLEY. "Here they come!" hisses Laelius. Two Numidian guards walk towards one another from opposite directions, marching along the earthen walkway between the ten-foot camp walls and their protective trench. The guards sidle past each other, oblivious to the five pairs of eyes that scrutinize them from the brush. When the two guards meet at the gates they reverse course, heading to the ends of the ten-foot high palisade. They soon disappear from sight.

"Where are the rest of the sentries?" whispers Marcus Silenus, crouching in the scrub.

"They are the only two," replies Scipio. "Masinissa's spies say those two walk to meet the guards around the corner and then come back here." He looks at Marcus. "They do it very slowly, thanks be to Fortuna."

"Camp vigilance has fallen since the truce," observes Masinissa, his voice low. "They have grown lazy with the confidence of their numbers. See up at the corner towers? The sentries left some time ago and no one has replaced them. We can slip inside easily, if we time it right."

"And so we will," says Scipio. He motions for his compatriots to step farther back into the bushes that border hut-filled clearing around the Numidian camp. They trudge through the head-high weeds and reeds, passing the still-warm body of an enemy night scout. A Numidian spear juts from his spine.

Scipio pauses a hundred yards back from the sprawling camp, to stand beneath the tall pine he has used as a centering point for his hidden army. The men huddle together to see each other's faces.

Scipio turns to Marcus Silenus. "Lucius and I will head for the passage between the camps. We will hide our men in the hills on each side of the road. Marcus, you take the other legion and surround Gisgo's camp."

"His camp is more strongly fortified than this one," worries Lucius. "It will be difficult to break inside it."

Scipio looks at his brother and pats his shoulder. "Just so, Lucius. We intend for them to break out of their camp, not for us to break into it. They will rush to help Syphax' camp, because it will be a tower of fire."

"You are sure this will work?" asks Lucius dubiously. "There are thousands of Numidians here to put out a fire."

"Psh!" replies Scipio. "Last night I reread a story about Agathocles' campaign against Carthage a century ago. He told how the Carthaginian camp was built of reeds and straw, and how everyone ran from it as it burned to the ground from an accidental flame." [xlii]

Lucius blinks empty eyes at his brother, and then shrugs. "If you say so. I have learned to expect the unexpected from you. I will be ready."

"Enough talk," mutters Marcus, looking back toward his men. "It is already past midnight. We need all the darkness we can get."

Scipio nods, and turns to go. He looks back at Laelius and Masinissa. "I'll send a runner to you when we are in place. Then we will wait until we see your signal."

"Remember," says Scipio, "your men have to cover all of the exits, especially the one by the river, where Syphax' men will go for water."

Masinissa grins. "We will look forward to meeting the Masaesyli again," he says.

"Do not attack! Your men are not to enter the camp, whatever they hear," orders Scipio. "Tell them to stand at the edge of the clearing. If Fortuna smiles on us, this will not be a battle, it will be a slaughter."

"Are there any children in camp?" asks Lucius anxiously. Laelius and Marcus avert their eyes from him. Scipio looks sadly at Lucius and shakes his head, knowing Lucius cannot see him in the dark. "No, brother. There are no children."

Lucius sniffs. "Good. I could not bear.... good."

Scipio, Lucius, and Marcus disappear into the undergrowth. Laelius and Masinissa return to the edge of the clearing, listening to the rustle of seven thousand soldiers silently stalking to their places about its edges. Once they are at their stations the foot soldiers crouch down. They wait for their prey to emerge.

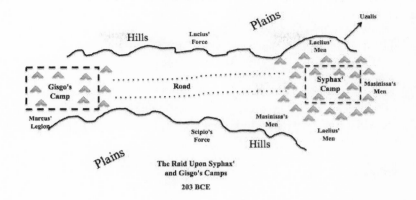

The Raid Upon Syphax'
and Gisgo's Camps
203 BCE

Laelius and Masinissa reach Syphax' camp without incident. They watch two guards desultorily patrolling the top of the wall, searching for a change in the guards' patrol pattern. They find none. "You think they would at least change their routine out of boredom," Laelius mutters.

"A change could mean their heads," replies Masinissa. "You do not know Syphax."

A wiry young velite thrashes in from the brush behind them, panting from his run. "They are ready!"

Masinissa disappears sideways into the brush as Laelius watches the exit. The guards at the base of the walls round the walkway and disappear around the wall corners.

As soon as they are out of sight, Ziri and Amalu step lightly through the thick maze of reed huts, crouching low as they move. The lanky young Numidians are silent, listening to the snoring inhabitants of the haphazard camp. They carry a long, soot-blackened ladder near their slim hips.

The two Massylii pause when they reach the trench, and crouch beneath an antelope head stuck on a spear, the boundary mark for a chieftain's tribe.

"Where are the other two men?" asks Ziri.

"How do I know?" whispers Amalu. He is the taller boy, two months older than his fourteen year old friend. "They'll be here soon, don't worry."

Off to the side of the boys, two Massylii men enter the maze of huts about the clearing. They stroll through the jumble, confident that no one will notice them. They lug along a long plank of notched wood.

Ziri is the first to see them coming. "There they are!" he whispers with relief.

"What are you doing with that ladder?" blurts a voice behind the boys.

They look over their shoulders and see a portly Masaesyli guard eyeing them, a spear clenched in his thick fist.

"The captain up there told us to bring this ladder here," stammers Amalu.

The guard steps closer to them, eyeing them suspiciously. He stares at little Amalu. "What captain? What's his name?"

"Brotina, the second chieftain of the guard" replies Amalu, answering with the name Scipio's spies provided them. He looks at the ground.

The guard stares at him. "Why?" he demands.

"We are boys. You think he would tell us?" replies Ziri irritably. "He just told us to bring it here."

The two Massylii men walk out from the perimeter of huts and approach the guard, carrying their plank. "You, guard, what are those boys doing with that ladder?" one of them says.

The guard no sooner turns to face them than a curved dagger flashes out from behind him, wielded by a slim brown hand. The razored blade opens a yawning cut in the guard's throat.

The guard grabs at his neck, his mouth agape. The two men run up and push him to the ground, their hands muffling his lips. But there is no need.

"He's done." one mutters to the other. The men roll the body into the trench, where he lands with a soft thud.

Amalu stands next to them. His shaking hand grips a bloody dagger. He stares dazedly at the blade as if it were a serpent.

Ziri stands by his side, patting Amalu's back. "You had to," he says. "You did good."

One of the men walks over to Amalu and pulls the dagger from his hand. He wipes it off in the dirt and gives it back to the boy.

"You are a warrior now," he whispers. "And you must act like one. You still have a task to finish."

The four Massylii crouch among the huts nearest to the trench, watching the walls. They watch the shadowy wall sentries marching away toward the other corners of the wall.

When the guards' footsteps fade from earshot, the two men rush forward and straddle the trench with their plank. Ziri and Amalu run in and jam the foot of their ladder into the notches cut into the plank. They lean the ladder forward, bracing it against the wall.

The wiry boys scramble over the wall in the blink of an eye, pulling out their daggers as they mount the top. When they disappear inside, the other two Numidians ease the plank and ladder into the dark trench. They nonchalantly stroll back toward the scrub on the edge of the clearing, nodding at the occasional passer-by.

All is silent for several minutes. There is a heavy thump against the thick doors, then a slow scraping of wood being pulled from iron. The gates crack open. Ziri's and Amalu's heads pop out. Amalu waves a scrap of white linen.

Four of Masinissa's Massylii spring out into the clearing and hasten toward the opening. Each clutches a brace of unlit torches. Padding barefoot through the maze of huts, they rush towards the gates and squeeze through the opening. The last two men grab the inside door handles and ease the gates closed.

The six Numidians trot silently towards the rear of camp, fading back into alleyways whenever they hear someone approaching. When they near the back of the camp they creep between the buildings, looking for the four sentries that Scipio's envoys noticed on their visits.

The Numidians see two men standing at the base of the rear gates and two more patrolling a rickety walkway along the top, moving along the wall in different directions.

One of the torch carriers points to himself and his fellow, then points upward. The others nod. They creep off to the sides of the wall and soon appear on top of it, tiptoeing above the two unsuspecting guards. The remaining four Numidians steal in behind the gate guards, with knotted choking ropes tightened in their fists.

There is a scuffle. A strangled shriek is followed by a muffled cry, then the sound of something heavy being dragged along. The four Numidians ease the gate bolts sideways then crack open the rear gates. The two other men return from the walkway, wiping their daggers on their loincloths. They take their place next to the gate opening and nod their heads, signaling that they are all ready for the most important phase of the assault.

The Numidians tiptoe over to a torch that is lighting a nearby latrine trench. Each kindles one of their pitch-covered brands, waiting until the head is awash in flame.

With a final nod to each other, the men begin their mad dash through the camp. Amalu and two of the Numidians run to the right. Ziri and the others dash to the left. The six Numidians fling the first of their torches into the middle of the tinder-dry camp huts. They pause, waiting until the fire—and the cries—spring to life. Then they dash toward their starting point, flinging newly lit brands as they go.

Willowy orange flames leap above the huts and race from one roof to another. Screams erupt behind the running Numidians, screams of alarm, then of agony, and finally of panic. Horses stampede past the runners, desperate to escape the flames.

Amalu trips and falls onto his face. As he pushes himself up he hears the thunder of hooves behind him. "No!" he cries, just as a herd of fear-maddened horses tramples over him. His fellows rush past his still form.

The remaining Numidians reach the front gates, yank them open, and dash into the field of huts. They loop back towards the rear gates where they find Masinissa and the rest of the Massylii walking out of the brush and making their way toward the rear gates. The Numidians' swords are drawn, ready to execute their grim task.

Up near the front gates, Laelius sees the signal he has anticipated, a faint orange flickering near the back of Syphax lengthy camp. "Light them!" he commands quietly.

A centurion bends down and strikes iron to flint, the sparks falling on his tinder pile. A flame springs to life and the twelve velites lean in as one to light their torches. "Go!" urges Laelius. "Run like the wind!"

The young soldiers dash along the perimeter of the hut field and hurl their torches into the flimsy reed shacks. The fire engulfs everything around it,[xliii] including the thousands within the huts. The terrified Masaesyli warriors race out from every direction. They leap over the scores of their fellows that roll screaming upon the ground, trying to quench their burning bodies.

The interior of Syphax' camp has become a flaming inferno. Thousands of unfortunates awake to find themselves engulfed in flames, burning alive before they can rise from their beds. Hundreds more run out from the camp shacks, wailing manically from the agony of their burns.

The Masaesyli flee toward the front and rear exits, leaving arms and armor behind. They crash open the gates and bolt out from the camp, seeking surcease from the pandemonium. What they find is death.

At the rear gates, Masinissa's Numidians stalk into their onrushing tribal enemies, stabbing down any who cross their path. Syphax' tribesmen only know that there are killers stalking them in the lurid light of the fires. They run, crazed and terrified, unable to escape the screams that come from everywhere. They trample over their fallen and wounded comrades, only to run into a waiting Massylii. Soon Masinissa's men are left chasing after the scores of survivors who flee into the bush, racing from the field of burning corpses behind them.

The Masaesyli who barge out from the front gates fare no better. They burst out from the entryway into the field of flames that has enveloped the clearing in front of them, with human torches careening through the field of smoldering huts. The terrified Masaesyli dash for any area that is free of flames, zigzagging among the burning hovels. Those who make it to the edge of the clearing find a wall of armored Romans with swords and spears at the ready.

"Spare no one!" shouts Laelius. He stands at the front of his double row of soldiers, his face grim as an executioner's. The legionnaires raise their shields and gladii, and march in as a solid wall. The Romans stab down the hundreds of naked Numidians who beat at them with fists and stones.

When the first alarms sound, Syphax bolts from his command tent near the front gates. "Guards, guards! Where are my men?" he screams.

Dozens of Syphax' personal guards rush to encircle him. He stares fearfully about the camp, dazed by the towers of flame rising behind him. An older guard gently shoves Syphax back to awareness. He pushes a horse's reins into his king's hands.

"The Romans are at the gates, Master," the guard shouts over the din. "We have to charge through them."

Syphax nods mutely, his eyes darting about in confusion. "What happened, Izem? Who did this?"

Izem shakes him again. "The Romans," he says. "The Romans are out there!"

Syphax' lips move spasmodically, but no words come.

Izem looks up at his mounted fellows. "We have to get him out of here." He sweeps his hand toward his fellow foot soldiers. "We will go first. You ride through while we occupy them."

Izem turns toward the gates and yells over his shoulder. "You men! Defend your king! Follow me!"

The Numidians trot through the gaping front gates and out into the screaming inferno, shields and swords at the ready. They wedge into the center of Laelius' legionnaires, crashing their shields into them and flailing furiously with their swords, buying time for their king. As the Romans rush to surround the foot soldiers, Syphax' mounted guards hurtle out through the gates, their king in the center.

Izem bucks his shield into the legionnaire in front of him and quickly looks over his shoulder for Syphax. He watches the guards break through the Romans and gallop into the clear, with naked Syphax hugging onto the neck of his horse.

"Take him to Uzalis!" Izem screams out. He turns back in time to see the centurion's sword blade plunge into the join of his throat and chest. Izem stares at the shining blade as he chokes out his life. He glances over to see if his king is safe but his vision darkens, and he falls.

A panicky Syphax breaks ahead of his men and gallops north. He rides heedless of direction or distance, only knowing he wants to get as far as he can from the burning abattoir that was his camp. One of his officers grabs the rope bridle of his mount, gently steering it northeast toward Uzalis,[xliv] one of Syphax' allied towns.

Thousands of unarmed Numidians follow Syphax into the night, running across the plains. Masinissa's mounted Massylii hunt them down as if they were antelope. The riders barely break stride as they lean sideways to deliver a mortal sword cut or spear thrust. Before their victims hit the ground they are galloping on to the next target, hooting with the joy of the kill.

The towering flames brighten the night sky A mile away, Gisgo's tower guards watch the horizon turn into a midnight sunrise of flickering orange. They grab their warning horns and trumpet the fire alarm.

"Fire! Fire at Syphax' camp!" scream the camp sentries. "Get up! Get over and help them!"

Scores of woozy Carthaginians pour out of the main gates, running and stumbling toward the flames of their allies' camp. Naked and unarmed, they dash down the connecting road between the two camps, with hundreds more joining them.

Crouched in the hills between the two camps, Scipio watches the first strings of Carthaginians hasten along the road in front of him, carrying torches to light their way. His eyes grow feral at the sight of his unarmed prey, and at the heady realization that his grim plan is succeeding. *They are tempting bait*, Scipio thinks. *But bigger prey will come.*

Scipio turns to Lucius. "Remind our men that they are to wait for the horn!" he whispers, Lucius crawls towards the legionnaires strung out inside the hill foliage, looking to alert the tribunes.

Scipio reaches over and takes the cornicen's long, curved battle trumpet from his attendant. He sticks his head inside its loop and pauses, watching the roadway. Then Scipio sees exactly what he has been hoping for. The string of Carthaginian rescuers has turned into a flood. Thousands fill the depression below him, men rushing by with buckets, hoes, and shovels—but few weapons.[xlv]

Scipio takes a deep breath and blows a mighty blast on the battle horn. His call is quickly echoed from the other side if the hill.

The Carthaginians halt, staring towards the blasts emanating from the darkened hills around them. The dread sounds of clanking armor and weapons soon follow, and the Carthaginians gape in terror at the waves of shadowy figures that flow down from the trees and bushes above them, their bared swords gleaming softly in the moonlight.

Scipio is at the fore of the descent. He leads his men down from his hillside while grim Cato commandeers the descent of his cohort on the other. There are few words exchanged among the legionnaires. They descend with their eyes fixed on their quarry.

The panicky Carthaginians look to their left, and their right. They see nothing but the silhouettes of armed enemies. Many sob with terror and despair, realizing their fate. Some begin their death prayers to Baal. Others hurtle down the road, only to find each end blockaded with waiting Romans. The Africans begin to scrabble about for limbs, rocks, or handfuls of earth—anything that feels like a weapon, anything that makes them feel less vulnerable.

The Romans descend onto the roadway and thresh into the milling mob, stabbing down anyone within sword's reach. Many Carthaginians rush toward the legionnaires, determined to die a warrior's death. They pound their fists onto the legionnaires' shields or beat futilely on their helmets with sticks and stones, fighting until a gladius transfixes them. Others fall to their knees and raise their hands in supplication, begging for mercy or promising gold. The legionnaires dispatch them with a quick stab to the throat, and move on.

Over at Gisgo's camp, Marcus Silenus hears the faint trumpet calls of Scipio's ambush. He knows his time has come. Picking some twigs off his gold-enameled white linen cuirass, the legate stalks back through the brush to a small clearing. Six horses wait next to five other men in the armor of Sacred Band guards. Each horse has a long, bulging saddle pouch hanging from its neck.

Marcus walks up to a tall swarthy man and shoves him backwards. "You try any tricks and I'll your neck open," Marcus whispers hoarsely, craning his neck to stare up into the man's eyes.

The Carthaginian defector nods mutely. Marcus unhobbles his Carthaginian horse and vaults onto it, motioning for his men follow suit. The six men mount, then ride out from the scrub trees that surround the clearing. They trot calmly towards the masses teeming out from the camp gates.

Marcus rides in the lead. *By Jupiter's cock, how can they wear this shit?* he grouses to himself, yanking at the stiff linen cuirass that is two sizes too large for him. He hefts the Carthaginian short sword he has sharpened to a hair-splitting edge. *At least this is a proper weapon. I must train our men to wield it, so they'll know how to defend against it.* He grins. *If I survive this mad scheme.*

The imposters approach the gates. Marcus leans sideways on his horse, next to the Carthaginian collaborator. "Now!" he hisses.

"Fire!" The Carthaginian yells loudly to the teeming masses. "There is a big fire Syphax camp! Run and help him!"

The rider looks up at the sentries. "We just found out that Masinissa and Scipio are over there! Go tell Gisgo!"

The sentries disappear from the wall. Marcus' men enter the gates, pushing their way through the half-naked soldiers running towards Syphax' camp. They gallop down the dirt path that borders the inside perimeter of the camp, with the Carthaginian bellowing his warning to the guards perched above them.

The cavalry party pulls up next to the stables and jumps off their horses. With a finger to his lips, Marcus draws his sword and points it at the horse pens. His men nod. Marcus grabs the nervous Carthaginian and pulls him toward the high-walled elephant pen at the side of the stables.

Two Libyans stand guard next to the roped corral gate, lolling under the torches burning above their head. They look curiously at the approaching Sacred Band guards, wondering why these elite soldiers are coming to the pens. But they do not look for long, for Marcus is upon them.

There is a torchlight flash from Marcus' thrusting blade, followed by an orange flamed back cut. The Libyans crumple to the earth, one futilely choking out an alarm through a mouthful of blood, the other lying decapitated.

The Carthaginian deserter gapes as Marcus wipes off his Carthaginian blade on one of the Libyans' loincloths. *No, not a bad weapon at all.*

Marcus raises his sword high and hatchets it across the finger-thick corral ropes, splitting them asunder. He pushes the tall gates wide and stares in at the twelve war elephants facing him. The monstrous beasts placidly observe their midnight visitor.

"The elephants are ready," Marcus mutters. "Let's see to the horses." They trot over the adjoining horse stables, where two of his men are dragging off the bloodied bodies of the stable attendants.

The legate waves for his men to join him. He raises his hand for silence, listening. He can hear the shouts and calls at the front of the camp but he hears no approaching horses. Satisfied, Marcus jumps onto his horse and his men follow him onto theirs.

Marcus reaches into his saddle pouch and pulls out a fistful of stubby torches. His men follow suit. He trots his horse over to the stable torches and lights one of his faggots, passing it along until all of his men heft a burning brand. He points to the Carthaginian and to another Roman rider, then points to himself and to the right. *You two, follow me there.*

Marcus throws one of his torches into the stick huts across from the animal pens, watching until the flames leap high. He gallops off with his two riders while the other three hurtle off the left. The two groups fling their torches into the stick huts as they loop around the perimeter toward the main gates. Flames sprout, grow, and spread behind them, counterpointed with the earth-shaking thuds of fleeing beasts.

Scores of horses crash through the tents and huts along the side streets, killing and maiming the soldiers who have lingered behind. The elephants trample through the very center of the camp, crushing men and structures in their frenzied attempts to avoid the raging inferno.

The Carthaginians dash through the exits and out into the night. But everywhere they run they encounter the same welcoming party as Syphax' men: centuries of fully armed Romans waiting in the brush outside the walls.

"Forward!" a tribune yells, knowing there is no need for secrecy now.

The Romans march out from the brush and methodically slaughter the enemy before them. Caught between the twin hells of fire and blades, thousands dispiritedly fall to their knees and beg for mercy.

It is denied.

Scipio's deadly plan is unfolding successfully, but the dense flow of creatures exiting through Gisgo's main gates proves to be problematic. Elephants, mules, and horses stampede out among alongside the fleeing men, giving hundreds of Carthaginians enough protection to escape the Romans.

Many more of the enemy are out in the open and vulnerable, however. The Romans mow down hundreds of them, then thousands. Many of the legionnaires rush forward to kill the flaming unfortunates who roll and scream with the severity of their burns. Some do it to end their agony, others to end their conscience-rending cries. With the night alight from the burning camp flames, there is nowhere to hide. Soon, Carthaginian bodies layer the fields like new-mown hay. The Romans begin to tire of the killing, their sword arms aching from weariness.

The last of the Carthaginians stumble out from the flaming camp. Many of them are officers who stayed to organize rescue efforts. They see the hopelessness of their plight and prostrate themselves among the bodies in the clearing, wailing for clemency.

"Enough!" bellows Marcus Silenus, sheathing his gore-spattered sword. "We can use the officers for ransom!"

The Romans rope scores of dispirited warriors and noblemen into human chains and shuffle them off toward Castra Cornelia. The captives depart to the haunting wails of the beasts and men trapped inside the conflagration.

"Move faster!" one of the tribunes commands, desperate to escape the tortured sounds.

Marcus watches his men march off toward the dawn lit east. Off to his right he sees scores of unarmed Carthaginians plunging frantically through the low scrub bushes past the clearing, ignoring the slashes of bramble and thorn.

"Shall we go after them?" asks a young tribune, his downy cheeks grimed with the night's soot and blood.

Marcus' head turns slowly. He stares into the boy's soft eyes. "Those men will be no danger to us, boy. They are broken. Let them live with their memories." He turns back to watch the rising sun.

As high morning illuminates the charnel fields of Gisgo's camp, the Romans return to finish their work. A knot of equites rides about the scrub, collecting any wandering horses and elephants. They herd them back to Scipio's castra.[xlvi]

Squadrons of legionnaires step carefully through the field of dead and dying, javelins poised. Their job is to collect plunder, hasten enemy deaths, and locate wounded comrades. More than once a wounded Carthaginian springs from a mound of bodies, biting and clawing at a Roman stepping past them, determined to kill them before he dies. Several of these brave men extract a price, managing to sink their teeth into an unwary soldier's jugular before a blade ends their existence.

Later that day, Scipio trots out from Castra Cornelia, flanked by Lucius, Laelius, and Marcus. His sword arm is bandaged from wrist to forearm, covering the slashes that a knife wielding Carthaginian gave him while Scipio cut his throat.

Scipio rides past the field of blackened timbers and skeletons that was once a sprawling Numidian camp, past the hordes of Carthaginian bodies strewn along the roadway to Syphax' gates. He trots up to a rise overlooking Gisgo's smoldering emplacement. A gentle spring breeze wafts the stench of charred flesh over them. Lucius abruptly turns and gallops away.

Scipio sits immobile on his horse. His eyes roam across the killing fields. *Is this horror what it takes to bring peace? Why didn't I offer them one more proposal, one more chance to make a proper peace? My gods, what have I done?*

Laelius draws his horse closer to Scipio's and leans in. "We cannot locate Syphax, but Gisgo has fled to a small garrison north of here.^{xlvii} Our scouts say he is holed up there with several thousand of his men."

Scipio does not reply.

Laelius looks into Scipio's distant eyes. He reaches out and gently pushes his shoulder. "Did you hear me? We can wipe them out, get him before he flees for Carthage!"

Scipio turns slowly, mechanically. He stares at Laelius and Marcus. His face bears a twisted smile that shocks them both.

"Now I know. Now I know why Hannibal didn't attack Rome after he slaughtered us at Cannae." He swallows hard and bows his head, his eyes clenched shut. Marcus and Laelius study the scudding morning clouds, looking everywhere but at their general.

"No, no more killing right now," Scipio finally replies, his voice distant. "We'll set out after Hasdrubal Gisgo tomorrow." *Perhaps it will give him time to escape, and I will not have to do this again.*

Laelius forces a jaunty tone into his voice. "Well, then, I think it's time for us to go back to camp. You have to hand out the award to the most valiant fighters. And the men will want to celebrate their great victory!"

Laelius leans close to Scipio, His voice is urgent. "They will want to celebrate that so few of them died today ... thanks to you." He shakes Scipio's shoulder. "Do you hear me, Scippy? You saved them!"

Scipio stares into infinity. "I am glad I saved someone."

Laelius kisses Scipio's cheek. "I'm heading back. I expect to be drinking wine with you before the night is out. Perhaps a game of latrunculi?"

He rides off, singing a mournful battle song. Scipio grabs his horse's reins and starts to follow. He feels an iron hand grasp his bicep. He looks back to see Marcus' yellow-green eyes boring into his.

Marcus shakes Scipio's arm so hard his entire body quivers. "It was just like Carthago Nova, just like it! No matter what you did, people would die. There was no other choice."

Marcus slides his calloused hand down to grasp Scipio's. "You destroyed their armies. Many of our men will wake to another day because of your plan." The blocky legate spurs his horse with his heels and trots off to catch up to Laelius.

Alone, Scipio reaches into his pouch and pulls out his figurine of Nike, the winged goddess of victory. He turns it slowly in his fingers, scratching off a fleck of blood between the goddess' robed breasts.

Scipio clenches it and draws back his arm to throw it away, to hurl it into the stinking human ashes about him.

He thinks of what he will have to tell Amelia about its loss. That he will have to tell her what he has seen—and done—to bring about his "victory." He fumbles it back into his pouch.

"Fuck!" he sobs. Scipio snaps the reins of his horse and drops them, letting his beast lead him back to camp.

V. THE PLAINS

CASTRA CORNELIA, NORTH AFRICA, 203 BCE. *Just one quick thrust into his liver, then pull the blade across. He'd bleed out in minutes.*

Praxis studies Marcus Silenus' broad back, searching for vulnerabilities in the legate's ceremonial armor. Praxis' face is calm, but his mind boils with plans to assassinate the old legionnaire. *If I can bring him down, an entire Sabina farm will be mine. Then I will be the one with slaves!*

The day before Scipio's army left for Sicily, a man named Flaccus had dropped a heavy purse into Praxis' man-killing hands. The money was Praxis' initial recompense for his deadly assignment, and for notifying Flaccus when it was done.

Praxis had only to see the man's uncalloused palms to know he was a patrician, likely a senator. *Why would a Roman senator want this man dead?* the Thracian wonders. *Marcus Silenus is Rome personified.*

Praxis has watched Marcus train men and kill enemies these last months, and he still does not have an answer to that question. He only has a heightened respect for his target. *Ah well. Another dead legate will make my countrymen happy. And this Flaccus will get me a farm.*

As if feeling Praxis' eyes upon him, Marcus looks over his shoulder. His baleful eyes fix on Praxis' face. The old gladiator quickly looks away and stares at the tribunes in the front row, his heart hammering.

Over the years, Praxis has slit the throats of a half dozen men at the behest of the shadowy figures who paid him. He has out-dueled many able warriors. But this sturdy little ex-centurion, he disturbs Praxis with his stone-faced gaze, with his dazzling speed and strength. Praxis knows he must move as if he is stalking a deadly serpent, and bide his

134

time.

He turns his gaze beyond Marcus, listening to the final words of
Scipio's celebratory speech to the army. *I will have my moment with
you, Marcus Silenus.*

Scipio stands in an open space outside the newly finished gates of
Castra Cornelia, facing a field of Romans and allies. He holds a silver
medallion in his hand, imprinted with the owl's head signature of the
Scipio gens.

"Quintus Susculpius, step forward," shouts Scipio. A middle-aged
centurion marches out from his cohort, self-consciously pulling at the
brown-spotted bandages that cover both his forearms. Quintus is a
slight man with a homely froglike face, but he walks forward like a
king to be crowned, head high. His red-plumed helmet and carefully
polished armor shine like a noonday star.

Scipio holds the medallion high over his head. "Centurion Susculpius
did drag two of his wounded comrades out from the deadly fires of the
Carthaginian camp. This man stuck his arms into the embers that
covered them, ignoring the grievous pain. For that he earns my badge
of honor!"

The centurion stands at rigid attention as Scipio fixes the medallion
onto the centurion's belt and kisses him on both cheeks.

"Gratitude, General," Susculpius mumbles. "I would gladly die for
you." Eyes moist and shining, the centurion raises his right arm in a
return salute and marches back to his post, stoically savoring the honor
of his life.

After handing out several more badges for outstanding bravery and
sacrifice, Scipio turns to distributing the silver headed spears of honor,
given to men for exemplary combat achievements. His armorers have
been busy all night, preparing Scipio's awards for the conquest over
Gisgo and Syphax.

Now that he has recovered from the torpor that engulfed him after the
slaughter, Scipio has taken pains to host a victory celebration. He

knows that he must cultivate the loyalty and bravery of his green recruits, if he is to make them an instrument of his will. And so he spends the day lauding his soldiers' achievements from an engagement that reminds him more of a cattle slaughter than a battle.

After all the awards are handed out, the ceremony concludes with a parade of prisoners and captive elephants. Thousands of empty-eyed Carthaginians and Numidians shuffle past their victors, knowing they are bound for Rome and a life of slavery.

Scores of captured noblemen are inside a corral off to the side of the camp gates, watching the commoners shamble by. They know they will be held until their families ransom them, and that they will return to their privileged life. Many swear to themselves that they will restore their honor on the field of battle. Still more swear they will never draw a sword against Scipio again.

The six captive elephants trundle by legionnaires and allies, who eye them nervously. A Carthaginian straddles each pachyderm's neck, guiding it forward with skillful touches of their twelve-foot poles.

Laelius leans to Scipio's ear. "Where did you get the mahouts?"

Scipio smiles. "From the prisoners, of course. I asked for volunteer drovers. I promised they could stay here instead of boarding the slave ships." He looks at Laelius and grins darkly. "Everyone volunteered. You should have seen the ones that never rode an elephant! Two of them died in the trying."

Laelius shakes his head. "I sympathize with them. But what shall we do with the elephants? Are you going to kill them? They are such noble looking beasts!"

He draws back an imaginary bow, grinning. "You know, I could see myself riding atop one. I could be garbed in red and gold armor, shooting arrows into our unworthy enemy!" He grabs Scipio's arm. "Think of it! I could become Rome's first elephant saggitarius!"

Scipio rolls his eyes. "Why don't you broach that topic to Cato? I'd be anxious to hear his response."

Laelius shifts his attention to Marcus, who is standing next to him. "They are beautiful in their own way, are they not? They look so wise!"

Marcus blinks at Laelius. He leans toward Scipio. "What does elephant meat taste like?"

Laelius gasps. "You are a savage!" he sputters. The barest of smiles cracks Marcus' face.

Scipio chuckles. "Marcus plays the fool on this—I think. We shall take good care of the beasts, Laelius. They have a purpose. We will ride our horses next to them, that we can accustom them to the smell of elephants. And accustom our infantry to their presence."

His face tightens. "I remember what Hannibal did to us in Italia. Never again will our lines be broken by elephants."

Marcus nods. "It will be done. I have some ideas on how to control them when they attack. I will talk to some soldiers who were farmers."

Scipio exhales. "Good, I fear that will soon become very important." An impish gleam momentarily brightens his care-worn eyes. "I know how we can use them to trick the Carthaginians!"

"Of course you do!" Laelius replies. "You always have 'some ideas' about everything! Do you really think Hannibal is coming over from Italia?"

Marcus looks at him. "What choice does Carthage have, Laelius? They have no one left to fight us." He looks at the sky. "It will be dusk soon. The men should bed down early after all that feasting. And drinking. We can sound the retirement early tonight."

"Good, the new men will need a respite," replies Scipio. "The horror of doing all that killing does drain a man's strength and heart. And we have to march out on the morrow."

Are we to pursue Gisgo at Uzalis?" asks Marcus. "We must move on him soon, or lose our opportunity to get to him."

"I will take out some of our veterans late tomorrow morning," replies Scipio. "And we will not return until we control all the towns and garrisons near Carthage. That will leave only Tunis, Utica, and Carthage."

Laelius frowns. "I fear we have delayed too long about Uzalis. Gisgo may be gone."

Scipio looks away from his two commanders. "I would hope so. I hope he escapes to Carthage."

Marcus' head turns slightly towards Scipio, then snaps back to face the legions, his face a stone.

Scipio understands Marcus' expression of doubt. "Gisgo is more of an asset to us as a general than a captive," Scipio explains. "With all his defeats he has become a man of fear and desperation. That makes him vulnerable. And very predictable." He chuckles. "I would rather have him leading their army than someone braver or more resourceful!"

"If we take all those towns Carthage may abandon hope of defeating us," says Laelius. "It would give you a chance to force peace on them, on your terms. Wouldn't that be your dream? Our dream?"

"There is logic to that," states Marcus. "But how much longer can Carthage tolerate defeat, before they recall Mago and Hannibal? Would they sue for peace with those two armies waiting to come at us?"

"Who knows the mind of a politician?" Laelius retorts. "It may depend on what General Gisgo tells them he can do—or cannot."

*   *   *   *   *

CARTHAGE. *One more chance. I have one more chance, Gisgo muses glumly.* He laughs bitterly as he snaps the reins on his horse. *Oh, that prissy Council of Elders wouldn't be so rude as to openly threaten me, would they? That would mean they were no better than the rest of us. But I know what they meant with their polite warnings. I'll be crucified if I fail again.*

Gisgo is riding southeast from Carthage on a recruiting expedition, heading to the Carthage's allied towns. The Elders were very clear with him: do not return without five thousand more men. *I should kill myself. Restore my honor and deny them the pleasure of doing it to me. Better than another defeat to that bookish little Roman bastard.*

Gisgo had returned to Carthage three days ago, leading his remaining troops on their flight from Uzalis. When he entered Carthage's gates he found a Senate's delegation waiting for him. He was ushered to the Senate chambers to await the next day's meeting.

Carthage's two ruling sufetes had called an emergency Senate session, urging them to decide what Carthage should do next in light of the destruction of Gisgo's and Syphax' armies.

Once again, the Senate was divided over three courses of action. They fought about whether to send envoys to Rome for peace, to build another army for Gisgo to attack Scipio, or to recall Hannibal and Mago.

Once again, the powerful Barcids prevailed in their wishes for Gisgo to further the war here,[xlviii] so that Hannibal and Mago would have a chance to conquer Italia. Gisgo and the other members of the Gisgons supported them, his relatives aching to restore the family honor that Gisgo has lost.

The Barcids had their way, but the Senate's peace proponents were more numerous and vocal than ever. After sixteen years of war, proud Carthage has drawn closer to capitulation, and farther away from continuing the fight. Gisgo was granted funds to hire another army, but he would need to build it himself.

Hours after departing on his recruiting mission, Gisgo enters the dry plains of Carthage's southern empire. He approaches the garrisoned port town of Sabratha. Its twenty warships bob gently from their ties along its quarter-mile dock, ready for action.

Gisgo draws up near Sabratha's open gates, and his hundred cavalry pause behind him. Two tall and muscular old men ride out to meet

Gisgo. Each wears the head of a lion over their domed Carthaginian helmet. Gisgo recognizes them as the two sufetes who rule Sabratha,[xlix] Carthaginians who wear the uniform of the dark-skinned Libyans they rule.

Gisgo had sent an order to the sufetes: muster every man who wants to earn pay and plunder by fighting the Romans, regardless of age, infirmity, or tribal affiliation. He is ready to accept anyone that can hold up a shield. He has already made plans to use the weakest as initial attack forces.

The two sufetes raise their right arms in salute as they draw near to Gisgo, who curtly returns their salute. "How many?" he blurts, surveying the river of men behind them. The line flows all the way back into the city.

The two rulers exchange a glance. "Five thousand," replies the tallest sufete, scowling at Gisgo's rudeness. "Three thousand Carthaginians from Thapsus, Thaenae, and far Aras. And maybe two thousand Libyans."

Gisgo nods, then looks expectantly at them. "How many can fight?"

"The Libyans—they are good fighters, though many have not fought many battles. The others—not so good."

"I'll take them all," Gisgo replies. "We'll do some initial training tomorrow." He grins. *Thank Baal for Libyans, they'll make up for the rest of this lot! I hope my envoys have better luck with Syphax.*

*   *   *   *   *

ABBA, NUMIDIA. Syphax and his weary entourage plod their horses into Abba, seeking refuge for the night. The fortified town is a safe stopping point on Syphax' retreat back to his capitol at Cirta.

The Numidian king collected hundreds more of his dispersed troops and cavalry as he marched southeast from the burning camps. His ragtag army has grown to six thousand men, with more wandering in every day. But it is a dispirited force, filled with men haunted by the memory of their brothers in arms being burned alive or helplessly slaughtered. They march silently, shields slung over their backs, spear butts dragging on the ground. Syphax cares nothing for their mood; he only wants to obtain surcease and rest within Abba's welcoming gates.

The foot-thick entry gates creak open. Syphax marches through a human corridor of wide-eyed, dark-skinned citizens. They watch his army quietly, as if they are not sure the Numidians are friend or foe. Syphax forces his chin high and summons his best commander's voice, the rictus of a smile pasted onto his face.

"Hail, good citizens, hail! I seek rest and food for my mighty army, that we may gain strength and finish destroying the Roman menace!"

There is a scattering of cheers. Most of the townspeople eye the downcast mien of the cavalry and infantry filing into their well-tended city, wondering who has repelled whom.

Syphax dismounts and walks over to the town's headquarters, a tall, square building of blocky limestone. The town magistrate is there, garbed in a flowing white linen robe, a simple gold circlet upon his grey-grizzled hair. He enthusiastically embraces his revered king, but Syphax takes little notice.

"Is she here?" he asks anxiously. "Is she?"

The magistrate smiles. "She arrived under guard just this morning, as you had ordered." He sweeps him arm upward. "She is waiting for you in your chambers."

"I am in your debt," Syphax gushes. He steps up the oak plank stairway.

"Are you going to rejoin Gisgo's army?" the magistrate calls out.

Syphax looks back at him. He shrugs forlornly. "I do not know. I truly do not. I think we are losing more than we gain in this alliance."

Syphax hurries up the stairs and pushes open the tapestried door to his wife's chamber.

Smiling tightly, Sophonisba rises from her dressing stand to meet him, pulling her golden gown about her. "My king," she says softly. "You have returned. I trust you are well—after all that has happened."

"I have returned to you. All else fades." Syphax shoves the door closed. He shoulders off his dusty robes, His eyes crawl over Sophonisba's body as she stoically watches him undress.

There is a knock at the chamber door. A naked Syphax grabs his sword and opens it. One of his captains stands outside.

"What should we do about the men?" he asks.

"I don't care," Syphax says. "Get them some food and a place to sleep, and don't bother me until morning!"

Hearing his words, Sophonisba grimaces. *Come on. He needs to trust you.* She stalks to the door and glowers at the captain.

"Leave me alone with my husband!" Sophonisba yells. Alarmed, the captain slams the door shut. "I need you alone," she says. "I have been thinking about you, and what I would like to do to you." *That much is no lie,* she thinks.

Syphax' eyes shine with lust. His breath quickens. "My queen, my heart sings to hear of your desire."

Sophonisba slowly disrobes as Syphax watches. Finally, she stands nude. "You will do more than hear of it," she says. Biting her lower lip, she kneels before him ....

The dawn light creeps over Syphax' huddled form. Sophonisba rises from her sleeping husband and steps softly to the window overlooking the vast plains of eastern Numidia. Her eyes search for a glimpse of a band of Massylii riders, led by a tall handsome prince who is coming to rescue her. She sees nothing but a few antelope.

Sophonisba glances back at her dressing stand, at the statue of Tanit that rests in a corner. *It would be so easy. One drink of tea, and you would be free. No more indignities.* She walks to the statue and shakes out the vial in its bottom, glancing at its contents. She abruptly shoves he vial back inside. *Hope yet remains. Masinissa and Scipio may sweep all before them.*

Sophonisba looks over at a snoring Syphax, and frowns with disgust. She sees his sword belt piled by the head of the bed. *One thrust under that stinking beard of his, right up into his skull. It would be worth the torture.*

She walks to the window and looks out. *If he returns to Cirta and stays there, Masinissa may never take the throne from him.* Her eyes begin to cloud with tears, but she wills them away. *Get him to go back and join your father, he'd have to leave Cirta.*

"Come back to bed, Wife," comes a voice behind her.

Sophonisba stiffens, closes her eyes tightly. She takes a deep breath, turns to face King Syphax, and smiles. "In a bit, my king. Right now I am aggrieved by your losses to Scipio's treachery." She purses her lips. "You are not thinking of reneging on your pact with my father, are you?"

Syphax pushes himself from the bed and pulls an indigo robe over his stout and hairy frame. He walks over and faces Sophonisba, his face abashed. "I have thought of it, I confess. I could concentrate on taking the rest of Numidia, now that Masinissa is occupied with fighting Carthage. Then I could destroy him if he dared venture back home."

He rubs his thickly bearded chin. "I could do that without having to fight that cursed Scipio."

Syphax looks at Sophonisba, his face distressed. "But then I think: what if Scipio should defeat Carthage? And then try to take Numidia? He would likely give the crown to Masinissa. And I would have nothing. Nothing."

"Think of my poor father," Sophonisba replies. "I beg you, do not let down my father and my country." [1] She splays her long, tapered fingers gently across his chest. "Father might order me to come home, and I would have to obey!" She strokes his neck. "It would shatter me if I lost you."

Syphax' reply is interrupted by loud banging on the door.

"My king! An army is coming, we can see them on the horizon! There are thousands of them!"

Syphax throws open the door to see a dozen of his personal guard awaiting him. "Who are they? Romans?"

"They march in formation like Romans, but it is too far away to tell, with all the dust they make, we cannot see!"

Syphax grimaces. "Get me up to the wall," he orders. "Get my attendants and my armor!"

Within minutes Syphax rushes out to the courtyard. He scrambles up to the walkway that surrounds Abba's twenty-foot walls, and squints out into the horizon.

"Send out some scouts," Syphax commands, peering into the approaching dust cloud.

Two Numidians hurl out on their swift little ponies, dust streaming behind them as they hurry towards the shadowy rectangle of troops. *Strange, they have no cavalry with them*, Syphax considers. *Who marches way out here without them? Even Roman cavalry are better than none at all.*

The two Numidians soon gallop back into town and trot over to the walkway, pulling up beneath Syphax.

"Well?" he asks irritably. His face is stern but his heart beats with dread. *This could be another of Scipio's tricks. We are sixty miles from his camp, but who knows what he'll try?*

"We do not know who they are," the one scout replies. "We have never seen the like." The other nods his agreement. "These soldiers took no notice of us, even when we approached them."

"May Ammon take you both to the underworld!" Syphax curses. He spins around and glares at the trembling magistrate of Abba. "Get every one of your men armed and ready!"

As the magistrate rushes down the stairs, Syphax peers out at the approaching horde. Now he can discern the armament of the troops. He stares harder, not believing what he sees. There are row upon row of thick-bodied warriors with domed brass helmets, carrying oblong shields decorated with intricate swirling patterns. The men are armored in thick leather cuirasses studded with iron and silver discs. From each man's belt hangs a swoop-bladed falcata.

By Mot's breath, those are Celtiberians! What are northern Iberians doing out here in Africa?

"Gauda, cease the muster! Those men are friendly." Syphax steps carefully down the rickety plank stairs and motions for his horse. He rides out with a squadron of men, heading for the lone figure that leads the dense lines of somber warriors. Behind Syphax, hundreds of Numidians peer out from the walls, fearful of these forbidding-looking soldiers tramping silently towards them.

As Syphax approaches, the lead rider halts his men and waits. Syphax can see he is a blocky man with a long tail of gray hair flowing from a hole in the back of his helmet. The leader bears the same shield and sword as his warriors but he also sports the gold medallions of an officer on his leather cuirass.

When Syphax draws near, the Celtiberian raises his arms high in greeting, showing he bears no weapon. He beckons for his interpreter to join him as Syphax rides up and clasps arms with the leader.

"Hail, Celtiberian. I am King Syphax, ruler of all Numidia."

"I know who you are, enemy of Rome. I am Anton, chieftain of the Celtiberii. We have come from home to fight for Carthage."

Syphax blinks at him. "How did you get here?" He bristles. "Did you invade my shores?"

"I can best answer that," comes a voice from the rear. A thin older man rides out from behind the stoic Celtiberians. He wears a purple-bordered white linen tunic with an empty sleeve where his shield arm would be. The man is without weapon or armor, with only a white linen cap as his helmet. He walks his horse up to face Syphax, and bows deeply.

"My name is Haggith, noble king. I am one of Carthage's mercenary recruiters. Carthage has paid these men to join Gisgo's army. We are heading to the city to join him."

Haggith notices Syphax is examining the rows of soldiers. "There are four thousand of them, King. All are veteran warriors." [li] Anton grins. "Veterans at fighting Romans, I should add. Before their tribe's treaty with Scipio, they fought with Hasdrubal and Mago Barca. And with Gisgo, your ally."

Syphax sees they are all strong and in the prime of life, their shields bearing the nicks and shreds of many battles. He smiles. *These are worthy allies.*

"Well, then. This is welcome news." He points at the recruiter. "Tell Gisgo I will remain here and await his call while I rebuild my army into a mighty force. I will call up all the young men in my kingdom." [lii]

He snorts. "Besides, Scipio did not defeat us, the fire did. He did not beat us in a real battle." [liii]

"It will be my pleasure to relay your message," replies Haggith. He turns back to Anton. "Onward." The officer swoops down his arm and the Celtiberian phalanx marches forward, heading toward Carthage.

Syphax watches them go, invigorated with renewed hope for conquering Scipio and regaining all of Numidia. *Sophonisba will be pleased*, he says to himself. *I will rejoin her father and she will soon be queen of all Numidia! What more could she want?*

Thirty days later, Gisgo's envoys summon Syphax to join Gisgo's new forces at Camp Magni near the Bagradas River, seventy-five miles south from Utica.

Syphax musters out his new army of twelve thousand men. He soon arrives at Camp Magni, joining Gisgo's force of the Celtiberians and his newly minted army of over ten thousand infantry and three thousand cavalry.[liv] Now, with thirty thousand men under them, they begin their plans to destroy Scipio's army.

*   *   *   *   *

UTICA, 203 BCE. "You will take a least one bite of each, I command it!"

One by one, two dozen battle-hardened tribunes shuffle reluctantly past Scipio's map table, staring at the platters on it. Each picks up a dried fig and pops it into his mouth. Next, each samples one of the dried dates that are mounded next to the figs. They then sample slices of lemon, watermelon and—last of all—roasted grasshoppers.

Several tribunes grab more pieces of watermelon and lemon, delighting in their tart and crisp flavors. But many pause before the grasshoppers, summoning their will before they dart their hand out and pop one into their mouth. The officers moodily crunch into them, chiding Scipio with their eyes.

Scipio watches them with arms crossed over his breast like a stern mother, making sure everyone samples the local foods.

Laelius and Marcus are the last to file past. "Ah, what a feast!" Laelius exclaims. Accustomed to such delicacies at the Scipio domus, he gleefully chomps into several pieces from each platter. He smacks his lips loudly—and irritatingly—at the other officers, enjoying their discomfiture.

Marcus picks one item from each platter and impassively consumes them. The tribunes carefully watch their hero's reaction. Marcus picks up two more figs and dates, eats them, and then turns to Scipio. "The fruits will suffice," he says flatly. "The insects—no!"

"Suffice?" Laelius exclaims, "They are delicious! The men will love them."

Marcus' head barely turns in Laelius' direction. "They are not here to enjoy. Give them grain, cheese, fruit, and oil, and they will march across the earth. They need nothing else!" He wrinkles his nose. "Next you will have us eating dog, like those repulsive Carthaginians!" [lv]

"It is important that we draw nourishment from the foods of the lands in which we fight," interjects Scipio, ending a potential argument. "The fruits are lightweight and invigorating. And ubiquitous."

He looks sheepishly at his officers. "I have already purchased a dozen wagonloads of figs and dates from the local farmers, to win their support for us. They are tired of being taxed to support this war,[lvi] and have welcomed the Carthaginian money I give them."

He grins. "When the coins descended from my hand into theirs, an enemy fell and rose as a friend."

"I am not sure what those dates or figs will do to their innards," grouses one tribune. "We can't have men running to the bushes every few minutes when we are on the march, much less in a battle!"

Scipio snorts derisively. "We had plates of both at the camp feast, and the men consumed them. They suffered no ill consequences."

Scipio waves over Praxis, the captain of his guard. "Praxis! You are a Thracian. Doubtless you have had some of these foods when you were at home?"

"We ate figs as part of our daily army ration," Praxis replies. He looks at the complaining tribune. "In truth, they were good at binding loose bowels."

Laelius sighs. "What a discussion! I am a long way from my genteel conversations at the Temple of Vesta!"

"How do these taste?" asks Scipio. Praxis pops a fig into his mouth and chews thoughtfully. "Very good. Much like the ones from Greece."

Praxis steps to the rear of the tent and resumes his watch over Scipio. *He is a democratic leader*, Praxis thinks. *Serving him, he would give me a chance to become a tribune, or even a praetor.*

He looks at the scars on his forearms, at the broken knuckles that jut from his battle-worn fists. *But Flaccus would give me my own farm, and wealth. I would be a nobleman.*

Praxis looks at Marcus Silenus. *I just have to do one task for him. Some may suspect me, but no one would know.*

He studies Scipio's tribunes, laughing as they try to stuff the foreign foods in each other's mouths. A smile creeps onto his face. Then he reminds himself: *They are Romans, fool. They made you a slave, made you fight for your life. You will never be one of them.*

Praxis snaps out of his reverie. Scipio is saying his name.

"You heard what Praxis said. I say it is done! Figs and dates will go into our men's daily allotment. Dried fruit is light and will not spoil. Our packs will be even lighter than before."

"We may have need of that sooner than you think," states Marcus Silenus. "Gisgo and Syphax are massing another army south of us, on the great plains near the desert. They have about thirty thousand men."

Scipio looks at him, surprised and angered. "Why have I not heard of this?"

Marcus looks at him as if he were an idiot. "You are hearing it now. The scouts returned just this morning."

"We just destroyed them," marvels one of the tribunes. "And now they have another army?"

"A young army, I would wager," counters Laelius. He looks at Scipio. "They are not going to give up. Peace is not an option, as much as I hate to say it. At least not until they run out of men."

Scipio sighs heavily, rubbing his eyes. "I thought we had a respite from another major conflict."

He shakes his head. "Gisgo is a persistent fool. But then again, perhaps he has no choice but to fight us, if he is to live."

"You can redouble your siege efforts on Utica," notes one young tribune. "Then, when Utica falls, we can go after them with our entire army."

Scipio's face tightens with resolve. He stares at his men. "No, we will do both, while the weather allows. As Laelius says, they are likely a young army. We cannot allow them to get any older with experience, especially since they outnumber us. We march the day after tomorrow. Two legions with cavalry, the rest stay and give the appearance we are all here at the siege. Light packs, all food on our backs, no pack animals. Just like Iberia."

"Maybe we should wait until we can send our entire army," says Laelius.

"We can do this with a reduced force," replies Scipio. "Don't forget, we have a secret weapon!" Seeing their blanks stares, he grins. "We have Gisgo leading their army!"

Amid their laughter, Scipio walks over to an adjoining table and begins rolling up his scrolls, a sign that their meeting is done.

Marcus and Laelius walk out together. They head down the wide main path that runs past Scipio's praetorium and the tribunes' tents, seeking a good night's sleep before the restless nights of marching and battle. They see Cato returning to his quaestor's tent.

"I wager he's just returned from another of his endless audits of our supplies and plunder," mutters Marcus.

Laelius snorts. "Yes, and he is no doubt preparing to write another scathing report about Scipio and send it back to Rome on the next boat."

The two legates nod at Cato as he approaches.

"Pleasant eve, Quaestor," ventures Laelius, grinning.

"Hmph!" Cato retorts. He ducks into his tent.

"I do think he is warming to me," Laelius says.

"Who cares? We have another battle on our hands. That should dominate your mind."

"If the scouts were not drunk when they spied on Gisgo's army, then he will have a force at least twice our size, with thrice the cavalry," says Laelius, shaking his head. "I still don't know how he got them all so quickly."

"Gisgo has lost four times to Scipio." Marcus says, pausing to glower at two centurions who are laughing loudly. The men's smiles fall from their face. "I venture Gisgo is one step away from the cross, so he had to take the field immediately. He's probably given a sword to everyone who has a penis. But those Celtiberians will be trouble."

Laelius looks about the camp as Marcus talks, surveying the field of low tents where the legionnaires sleep, the dark rows speckled with the occasional cook fire of men preparing a late meal. The buccina sounds the new watch, and he can see the fires start to wink out.

A quick movement behind him catches Laelius' eye, a flicker of motion by Cato's tent, as if someone had darted from the path behind it. *Who skulks about like a thief in the night? Perhaps it is nothing. Still...*

Laelius turns back to Marcus. "The god Somnus is coming upon me, I think I shall return to my tent for some sleep."

Marcus nods and turns left, heading toward the spacious walkway that circles the camp palisades. "I need to patrol the perimeter, see that all the sentries are about their duties. Until tomorrow."

Laelius walks back toward Scipio's tent. As he approaches Cato's tent he quickly steps into the side path where he saw movement, scanning the low tents about Cato's quaestorium.

Five tent rows away, a hunched shadow ducks below a legionnaires' tent, almost invisible in the faint shadows of the half-moon night.

Laelius quickly paces to the spot, his hand on his dagger. He jumps around the corner, but sees nothing but tents. Then he stops. *Was that someone ducking down there by the tribunes' tents?*

Laelius shrugs off his concern. He takes his hand off his dagger, walking back to the main path. *Well, if someone is stalking Marcus or me, we won't have to search for him. He will come to us.*

He grins to himself. *What fool would try to sneak up on Marcus Silenus? I should tell him anyway, just in case.*

* * * * *

CAMP MAGNI, 203 BCE. "The Romans are here already, Kandaulo?" Gisgo gapes at his cavalry commander. "It cannot be!"

The dark and wiry little man spreads wide his leathered hands, as if apologizing. "Yes, they here already! They build a camp on a hill nearby. Our scouts track them from Utica. They do eighty miles in four days!" [lvii]

He shakes his head again. "The scouts say all they do was march, eat, and sleep. Didn't build camp at night. They hurry, hurry, hurry."

"Well, we will give them reason to pause," growls Syphax. "My Numidians will wash over them like storm waves on the shore."

Gisgo raises his hand and waggles his index finger at Syphax. "Hold on, King. Let us not rush into this. We can send out some raiding parties to test their strength."

Syphax glares at him. "We have them outnumbered, with five times the horse. What else do we need to know? We can settle this before any more of them get here."

"Scipio is clever for a Roman," warns Gisgo. "We should scout all the terrain around the plain of battle, to see if he is hiding anyone."

Syphax stares at him for a long moment, then holds up three

bejeweled fingers. "Three days. If he does not come out to fight by then, I will go after him myself!"

Gisgo sighs. *He is so impatient. But he's right, the time is opportune to attack.* "Very well, three days hence," he replies. "Tomorrow I will send out a large scouting party, let us see what they tell us."

The next morning the Carthaginian camp awakes to find the Roman army on the move towards their camp. Scipio's men have marched down the hill and are heading across the Great Plains. Gisgo and Syphax frantically muster their defenses to the front gates, but their haste proves to be unnecessary.

Scipio's men halt two miles from the sprawling Carthaginian camp. They begin building a camp as their enemy watches, fascinated at the Romans' organized bustle. By early afternoon the camp is laid out in neat squares and the palisade timbers are being lowered into the trench dug to hold them.

"Those maniacs are almost done," Gisgo notes.

"Let's get at them before they finish the walls," Syphax replies.

Two squadrons of Syphax' finest Numidians storm out to harass the Romans. They hurtle into the tunic-clad laborers and fling javelins into them as they run for their pile of arms and armor. The camp horns sound the alarm, and Masinissa's men stampede out to engage their enemies.

Both camps pause in their labors to watch the flowing, circling battle of expert horsemen dueling each other with sword and javelin, crashing horses into one another, ducking spears thrown at full gallop. An hour later, Syphax' men hustle back to their camp, only to resume the attack the next day. The skirmishes continue for the next several days,[lviii] while Gisgo and Syphax plan their deployment of forces for battle.

Syphax' camp raiders confirm the scouts' earlier reports: the army outnumbers the Romans by almost three to one. Gisgo's confidence swells. "I will follow your recommendations," he tells Syphax. "We attack tomorrow morning."

"That is good," says Syphax. "We'll empty our camp for this battle. We fight until all are killed or captured!" His eyes darken with anger. "This Masinissa, I need him dead. Tell your men I will give a gold spear to the man that brings me his head."

"Gladly," replies Gisgo. He is still wary of Scipio's tricks, however, so he will only engage the Romans on two conditions. They will not attack until Scipio has brought his entire army into battle formation and the center lines are engaged. Gisgo worries that Scipio will employ another sudden flanking maneuver, as he did in his victory over him at Ilipa.[lix]

That night Gisgo sends hundreds of scouts into the scrublands and low hills between the two camps. He orders them to investigate every hiding place that a cavalry squadron might lurk or a maniple might be stashed. Gisgo is taking no chances that Scipio will ambush him.

The next morning Gisgo, Anton, Kandaulo, and Syphax convene inside the Carthaginian's command tent for a final meeting. They converse as the sounds of battle preparations churn around them; hundreds of horses neighing and snorting as they are led to the front gates, the tramping of thousands of heavily sandaled feet, the gnashing ring of bronze and iron as heavy infantry passes by them.

Gisgo looks out the open tent and watches the troops pass. *This will be my last battle, either way*, he reflects.

"What traps did the scouts find?" asks Syphax sarcastically, breaking Gisgo's thoughts. "Were hundreds of Romans buried in the ground, or were they out there disguised as bushes?"

Gisgo winces. "We had to be sure. You do not know him like I do. He does nothing a Roman would do."

"So, we are ready?" asks Anton the Celtiberian. His tone indicates it is more of a command than a question.

Gisgo bites his lower lip. His eyes dart about, his mind racing to think if there is something he has overlooked. *There is no excuse not to fight, and there is nowhere to run anyway*, he chides himself. *It is your time.*

Gisgo raises his head, his eyes anxious but determined. "We are ready. I will do what no Barca has been able to accomplish: I will destroy Scipio."

"It is done, then," says Syphax. "I will take my Numidian cavalry on the left wing, next to our foot soldiers," he says. "They know how to fight together."

"My horsemen will take the right flank," adds Kandaulo, Gisgo's cavalry leader. "They can help out our foot recruits next to them."

Gisgo sniffs haughtily. "They will not need help. The recruits have been training for a month, and the veterans are mixed in with them." Gisgo faces Anton. "As we agreed, your Celtiberians will take the center, with our infantry on each side of you. We have twenty thousand men along the front lines."

"They shall not pass," Anton says through his interpreter. Gisgo pauses, waiting for him to say more, but Anton merely stares at him.

Well, you are certainly more a man of action than words, Gisgo thinks. He leans back and takes a deep breath. "No more talk, then. Let us attend to it. Get every available cavalryman on the flanks, leave no one in camp. We will ride them down or we do not return!"

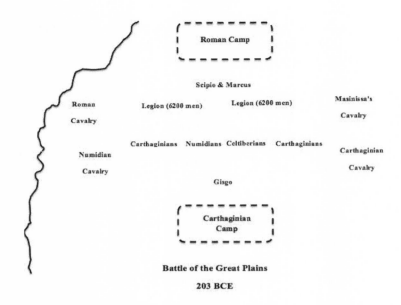

Battle of the Great Plains

203 BCE

By late morning the Carthaginian and Numidian army is out upon the plains, thirty thousand soldiers marching toward Scipio's waiting forces. When Gisgo is within a quarter mile of the Roman army he signals for a stop. Syphax rides over to him. "What is it?"

"Nothing, I just want to assess his formation again." replies Gisgo.

"It is no more than what you see," Syphax replies impatiently. "It is a typical Roman front with infantry in the middle and cavalry on the sides. Not very many cavalry, either. As soon as I dispose of the Roman cavalry I'll move my men over to finish off Masinissa, if your men have not finished him first." He points to the middle of the infantry. "See? Scipio is over there, behind the cohorts in the middle."

Gisgo peers at the distant hills. "The scouts found nothing out there?"

King Syphax sighs. "I have two hundred of my men up there right now, combing through the hills. You will hear their horns if they find anyone." Syphax' brows furrow. "Enough worrying, it is time. I'm going to..."

Syphax' words are interrupted by the blare of a dozen Roman battle trumpets, their three short notes echoing across the plains. The Roman lines tramp forward in unison, two legions of 6200 infantry in the center, with six hundred Roman cavalry opposite Syphax' riders. As always, the younger hastati are in the front line, with the battle-tested principes behind them, and the older veteran triarii protecting the rear.

As he did at Ilipa, Scipio has made each legions' ten cohorts larger than normal, filled with three maniples heavy infantry and one of velites.[lx] Each cohort a small army of six hundred men.

Gisgo stares into the dust clouds of the marching Romans, trying to ascertain the position of every cohort. He can see Masinissa to his right, leading his few hundred Numidians against Gisgo's thousands of Carthaginian riders. He smiles at the imbalance. To his left he can see Laelius leading the Roman and allied cavalry. His burnished armor shines like a beacon in the bright morning sun. His horsemen move slowly toward Syphax and his hordes.[lxi]

And there, in the middle, rides Scipio and a graying commander that can only be Marcus Silenus.

Gisgo breathes a sigh of relief. *They are still in a standard formation.*

Gisgo and Syphax' plan is simple: overwhelm Scipio's cavalry with their superior numbers while the staunch Celtiberians hold the Roman infantry in the center, enabling their cavalry to cut into the Roman flanks for a deadly encirclement. Scipio used such a stratagem in Iberia to defeat Gisgo, Hasdrubal, and Mago, and the veteran general has not forgotten it. Now, with growing confidence, he can visualize the destruction of Scipio's army, and the restoration of the Gisgon family honor.

Gisgo looks over toward Syphax, riding behind his cavalry, and sees that the king is watching him, impatient to charge ahead. Gisgo waves his hand at Syphax to signal he is ready. Then he does the same to Anton standing in front of his Celtiberians, and to Kandaulo on his right. All return his signal.

Gisgo barks the order to his trumpeter. The barrel-chested warrior raises his curved brass trumpet to lips and blows a long, extended blast, echoed by a dozen of his fellows across the half-mile line.

The first blast is not even finished before Scipio's cavalry surge forward from each side, as if Gisgo's battle horns were their signal to attack. Gisgo and Syphax' thousands of riders plunge toward their enemies, filling the rolling plains.

Anton waves his bright spear at his men and the Celtiberian infantry marches forward, their lines as straight as if they were chained together. Looking past Anton, Gisgo can see Marcus Silenus and Scipio trot their horses to the front lines of the legions' cohorts, with Scipio pointing his sword at the oncoming Celtiberians.

Masinissa and his Numidians hurtle into the young Carthaginian riders, screaming at the top of their lungs. Some of the Massylii battle with the riders in the front, but Masinissa and the bulk of his small force wedge through them, cutting into the heart of their untrained foes.

Kandaulo screams for his men to encircle them, but it is already too late. The Numidians have infiltrated the Carthaginian cavalry.

Masinissa's men dash from one confused foe to another. They swirl around a rider long enough to administer a telling spear stab or sword cut. Then they dash off inflict another casualty, always moving.

The armored Carthaginians gallop about trying to catch their elusive enemy, often colliding with their fellows in their vain efforts to corner Masinissa' men.

Masinissa hears Kandaulo shouting orders to his officers, and immediately spurs his horse towards him, knowing he is all that holds these panicky young men together. Kandaulo spies him coming and gallops directly toward Masinissa, eager to fell him and dishearten his men.

The two captains slide past each other at full gallop. Kandaulo hammers Masinissa's shield with his sword, knocking the Numidian prince sideways. Masinissa's spear thrust sails over his head. The combatants rein in their horses and charge again.

From the corner of his eye Masinissa sees Kandaulo's guards crossing the field to come to his rescue. He knows he has little time. *Remember what Laelius did in his last battle. No one expects madness.*

The Carthaginian and Numidian close on each other. Masinissa takes a deep breath. *Gods save me, here we go!*

When Kandaulo moves his shield aside to swing his sword, Masinissa vaults sideways into Kandaulo's chest, grabbing him with both arms. The two plummet to the ground, with Masinissa landing on top of his bewildered opponent. In a flash, Masinissa pulls out his dagger and stabs it into Kandaulo's face, feeling his blade crunch through the Kandaulo's eye socket. Kandaulo wails with anguish and rolls about the ground.

Masinissa scrambles from his writhing opponent. He slides onto his horse and dashes away before Kandaulo's guards can catch up to him.

"Kandaulo has fallen!" yells a cavalryman, his voice high with despair.

"Silence!" shouts a captain. "Don't let them know!"

"Kandaulo is dead," cries another.

The call echoes through the Carthaginian riders. Already demoralized at fighting the swirling death around them, the recruits panic. Throngs of Carthaginian cavalry flee toward their home city. The Numidians give chase and spear them down from behind, adding to their terrified flight.

As soon as the Carthaginians flee the field, Masinissa calls over a score of his finest riders. "Follow me to Syphax," he shouts. They hurtle across the legions' back lines towards the swirling dust clouds of the cavalry fight.

On the other side of the battle, Syphax and his hordes are faring as badly as the Carthaginian cavalry. Syphax' hastily recruited forces are filled with Numidian peasants who have never seen battle, and Laelius is capitalizing upon their inexperience.

"Into the center, men," Laelius screams to his commanders. "Ride all the way through them!"

Laelius directs his thousand men on a wedge attack into the heart of the unarmored Numidian riders. They cut deep into the Numidian center before Syphax can organize them for a counterattack. The Romans and allies cast their handfuls of pila with deadly effect, littering the field with groaning victims.

The Romans exhaust their javelins and pull out their swords. The densely packed Numidians cannot ably maneuver, and the armored Romans find it easy to draw close to the green recruits, slashing freely into their unprotected stomachs and necks. Wherever the Romans ride, Numidians fall.

Syphax himself rides to the front with his guard. He fights off the Romans' foremost attackers, roaring his defiance. His men swiftly regroup around him. They stampede into the Romans and beat them back, trampling down scores of wounded enemies—and their own men.

"Bring up the rear forces," shouts Syphax, as his mounted attendant hands him another brace of spears. "Get all of our men to the front, we have them now!"

Syphax can see dozens of the Romans fall, swarmed over by groups of Numidians frenzied in their first bloodlust of battle, heedlessly hacking Roman bodies even after they are dead. His heart quickens at the thought of victory.

Then, to his left, Syphax hears the clash of swords on shields, and the yodeling cry of the feared Massylii. He glances over to see Masinissa and his men stampeding towards him, the rebel prince staring murderously at Syphax.

"Masinissa is coming," shouts one of his guards. The cry echoes through the Masaesyli riders, who fear they are beset by another army. Syphax watches his young cavalry flee toward the hills, with more following them. He sees Laelius chopping his falcata deep into the collarbone of a Numidian captain, eyeing the king with fatal intent.

Syphax grabs one of his senior chieftains. "Get all your best men over there," he yells, pointing at Masinissa." He turns to another. "Take your men and kill that Roman over there in the shiny armor! Whoever does it gets a gold lance!"

As the two commanders ride off to execute their duty, Syphax turns to the captain of his guard. He points west, toward Numidia. "We ride that way. Now!" Syphax kicks his horse and gallops away.

When Syphax' men see him riding from the battle, they lose their last scraps of courage. The Romans and Numidians rout the last of Gisgo's and Syphax' cavalry, and watch them race for the hills.

In the center of the infantry battle, Marcus Silenus has dismounted and leads his men toward the oncoming Celtiberians. He pulls out his sword and stalks forward as if determined to defeat them by himself.

"Commander, wait for us!" screams his senior tribune, as the front line hastati race to join him.

"For Rome and for victory!" Marcus yells.

The hastati pound on their shields with their swords, setting up a deafening din. Shouting all the way, the Romans march across the hundred-yard gap and crash into the tightly contained ranks of the redoubtable Celtiberians.

The barbarians step forward as one and shove their shields and spears into the oncoming wave of legionnaires, knocking back their line.

"Into them!" screams Anton, brandishing his four-foot falcata. The Iberian warriors slash into the Romans, who counterthrust with their gladii. Dozens of men fall on both fronts, writhing on the ground as their compatriots battle above them.

The Celtiberians step back to reform, opening a thirty-foot gap between the two lines. "Spears at the ready!" shouts the First Tribune. "Get them before they come after us again!"

The trumpets sound and the Romans in the second line pitch their pila over the heads of the legionnaires in the front. As the spears rain into the Celtiberians, the front line Romans march in and cut into their distracted foe. Scores of Celtiberians fall along the front, to be quickly replaced by the undaunted warriors behind them.

The infantry battle rages unevenly along the half-mile line of fighters. The Roman lines are straight and unbroken on the sides, where they thresh methodically through the inferior Carthaginian and Numidian recruits. The Roman lines in the center begin to break apart, as the knots of Celtiberians fight their way into the legions' second line.

The alarmed centurions dash about the front lines, frantic to restore order. They shove the retreating hastati back toward the front, pausing only to help their soldiers stab down whatever enemies they are fighting. The centurions have been given orders from Scipio himself: the hastati must hold the front line, because the principes cannot relieve them.

Marcus Silenus rages across the center of the battle front. He dodges sword blows, batters opponents off their feet, and deftly slides his gladius into a half-dozen throats and torsos. The young hastati rally behind Marcus and the centurions, digging in their feet and refusing to give any more ground. The fighting becomes furious. The warriors bash at each other's shields, the Celtiberians battering at the Romans with their heavy long swords and the Romans stabbing under their guard to score wounding blows to their legs and arms.

Anton stalks across the front line of his men, shouting for them to push forward. He notices that a tall and muscular tribune is mustering one of the retreating maniples across from him, and quickly strides over to engage him. The tribune sees him and grasps Anton's purpose—the Celtiberian captain is coming to kill him and break the ranks. He turns to one of his centurions.

"Hammer the men back into place. Do not back up no matter what you see!" The patrician tightens the strings on his cheek plates and strides out to meet Anton, his gladius bared at his side.

With a mighty bellow, Anton sprints at the tribune. He raises his heavy sword high and batters it upon the Roman's shield, knocking him backwards. The tribune deftly deflects the next arm-numbing sword blow and remains calm, knowing the Celtiberian must soon tire from using such force. *When he holds his sword low, I will strike.*

Anton steps to the right and continues his onslaught, driving the tribune into another direction, axing his blows at the tribune's head. The tribune gradually steps backwards, maintaining his balance, countering with quick slashes and stabs that nick into Anton's bare thighs and forearms. The Celtiberian chieftain is soon bleeding from a half-dozen shallow cuts. Undaunted, Anton continues to batter at the Roman, even as his breaths come heavier. He wipes the blood from his sword arm so that he does not lose his grip.

The young tribune knows he is winning this war of attrition, and he watches the Celtiberian's body, seeking an opening for a mortal thrust. The tribune is so intent that he does not see the enemy corpse lying behind him. But Anton does.

The Celtiberian suddenly redoubles his efforts, screaming and hacking like a madman. The tribune staggers back. As Anton intended, the officer stumbles over the body behind him, sprawling on top of it.

Anton springs upon the tribune, knocking his shield aside with a wide sweep of his own, planting a knee on the Roman's sword arm. The chieftain grasps his sword with both hands and batters it into top of the Roman's gleaming bronze helmet, denting it deep into the tribune's skull. The young tribune's eyes glaze over, blood trickles from his nose, into his gaping mouth. When Anton sees the tribune's head loll sideways he jumps up and stalks back toward his men, knowing the Roman is good as dead. Anton does not venture very far before he finds his path blocked.

Marcus Silenus stands before him, his vengeful eyes fixed upon the Celtiberian commander. The legate holds sword and shield wide away from his body, challenging Anton to fight.

The Celtiberian takes one look at his diminutive foe and snorts his derision. He stalks forward, idly swinging his broad-bladed sword that drips with the tribune's blood.

The chieftain repeats his attack tactic, dashing at the legate like a maddened Gaul, raising his sword high. Marcus does not move.

When the Celtiberian begins his downward stroke, Marcus jumps inside and rams his rock hard body into his taller foe's midriff, knocking him off his feet. The Celtiberian's blade swooshes through the air behind Marcus. Anton crashes onto his back, with Marcus Silenus upon him. Before he can raise his head, Marcus' sword plunges into the underside of the Celtiberian's chin and up into his brain, the point jutting from the top of his domed helmet. Anton's eyes bulge from his head. With a despairing choke, his head falls to the side.

Marcus plants a knee into the corpse's chest and pushes himself up, his face expressionless. "That tribune was a fine boy. I knew his mother!" he barks.

Marcus Silenus carefully wipes his sword upon the skirt of the body's linen tunic, and strides back to the front line of hastati.

The legate stalks behind the front row of the cohorts, shouting encouragement, stepping forward to batter back a knot of Celtiberian who threaten to break through the hastati. He trudges into the very center of the cohorts, where Scipio is directing the troops from his horse.

"General! He shouts, I..." Marcus halts in mid-sentence, yelling in agony. He gapes at the slim blade sticking out of his stomach, and reaches around to yank it out, staring at it in wonderment. He crumples to one knee but quickly pushes himself upright, his face murderous with intent. But there is no one there to kill.

Marcus totters to his feet, swaying like a drunken man, and slowly walks toward Scipio, his sword dragging at his side. Dimly, fuzzily, Marcus hears shouts of dismay and alarm. He feels strong hands reaching for him, and he finds himself carried along by two sturdy legionnaires. He can hear Scipio shout something to his men, but he cannot tell what.

Marcus feels himself laid upon some stiff, firm, fabric, and carried off. *That was a pugio, a Roman dagger*, he thinks, before night descends on him.

The front line battle rages for over an hour, with men cursing and screaming as they fight through the clouds of dust that surround them. Gisgo ranges behind the front lines, shouting encouragement to his Carthaginian and Numidian foot soldiers. He promises gold and land for those who break the Roman lines, but the legionnaires still bend them back.

Riding to the center of the discomfited Celtiberians, Gisgo orders the men in the rear to replace the first line. He knows he has far more fresh troops than the Romans, and the hastati will soon be weary and vulnerable. *Scipio has not brought up his principes to spell them,* he wonders momentarily. *What is he saving them for?*

Gisgo soon has his answer. He rides over to the Carthaginian infantry at the far right battlefront, seeking to send them on a flanking maneuver. As he nears the end of the Carthaginian line he sees a sight that makes him freeze. The plains in front of him are empty of Carthaginian cavalry, there are only a bands of Masinissa's Numidians galloping away in the distance, chasing away the remnants of his riders. A thick wall of Roman principes are marching in on the flank, backed by hedgehog rows of the triarii's long spears. Thousands of fresh troops are heading into the sides of his untested Carthaginian infantry.[lxii]

In a flash, Gisgo grasps Scipio's strategy. Under the cover of the battle's dust clouds, Scipio has moved his principes and triarii out from behind the hastati while the front liners kept the Celtiberians engaged. Scipio's most experienced warriors are now closing in on the vulnerable flanks of Gisgo's weakest soldiers.

Gisgo bellows for his infantry officers to reorganize their lines and charge the Romans en masse, but it is too late. The first wave of javelins rains into the Carthaginians, followed by a second wave, and a third. Then the battle-tested principes are upon them, cutting down hundreds of infantrymen. Within minutes the Romans have caved in Gisgo's hastily-drawn formations, setting his men to flight.

Gisgo gallops back through the battling Celtiberians and Numidians, desperate to get Syphax and his cavalry to have them come to the aid his men. As he nears the other end of the battle he sees hundreds of the Numidian infantry running madly toward him.

"Turn around, you cowards!" he yells, but the men hurtle madly past him. Gisgo tries to push his horse through the fear-maddened Africans, but his path is blocked by the flood of deserters. One of them grabs Gisgo's bridle, eager to take his horse. The general's curved blade flashes downward, and the man is left with a bleeding stump.

"Guards!" Gisgo shouts to his Sacred Band officers. "Clear these vermin out my way!" The Sacred Band warriors draw their swords and cut a path through Numidians in front of him.

Looking at plains in front of him, Gisgo sees they are empty of any of Syphax' cavalry. *Those bastards have fled, too. And Syphax went with them.* All he sees are the oncoming maniples of the implacable Roman principes and triarii, executing the other half of Scipio's deadly pincers movement.

The legionaries march directly into the milling Numidians, jabbing them down with swords and spears, stampeding the Africans like cattle. Realizing their end has come, scores of proud Numidians march into the Romans, battling until they are stabbed down where they stand. Many more drop their arms and armor so they can flee more quickly from the Roman machine.

Soon, the Romans have driven all the Carthaginian and Numidian infantry from the field. Only the Celtiberians remain. The Romans on the flanks and rear march in as the exhausted hastati hold the centerline, and the Roman army closes in upon the unyielding tribesmen.

The Iberian warriors have nowhere to flee in this strange land. They know they cannot expect mercy from Scipio, having betrayed his trust by coming here to fight for Carthage. They can only sell their lives as dearly as possible, and die as warriors.

The surviving Romans have no wish to gamble their lives by fighting singly against such a fierce foe, now that victory is in hand. They are content to bring them down with spear throws, or to essay single warriors in pairs.

Soon, only a handful of Celtiberians remain, surrounded by a mound of their countrymen. These last stand defiant while knee-deep in gore. They spit insults at the approaching legionnaires, waving their phalli at them and baring their buttocks, laughing through their yellowed, blood-stained teeth.

Scores of Romans surround them and carefully step forward, as if approaching a pack of cornered wolves. A Celtiberian chieftain stands in front of his men, a leather-muscled older man holds his falcata against his gashed shoulder. He points his blade at the Romans and barks a command. The tribesmen charge forward, screaming their final battle cry, hurtling themselves upon the surprised legionnaires.

The Celtiberians fall, each pierced from a dozen blades,. The chieftain watches his men die a warrior's death. When his last man falls, the chieftain stands alone in the circle of bodies. He laughs derisively at the oncoming Romans, spewing invectives in his native tongue. When two centurions close on him, he holds his blade upright in front of them and falls upon it, driving it deep into his heart.

Out on the plains, Gisgo and his guard have joined the thousands fleeing back toward Carthage. There are so many that even the relentless Numidians cannot slay them all, although the plain is littered with Carthaginian bodies as if they were grain tossed to show Gisgo's path of flight.

Gisgo and his Sacred Band guards are soon galloping through the narrow pass where Hannum met his end, rushing for the gates of Carthage. Seeing there is no pursuit, Gisgo soon slows down and walks his horse toward the city's entry, suddenly reticent to return. *I have lost again. What will the Elders do to me?*

He laughs grimly to himself. *What would you do, if you were they?*

VI. LOSS AND RECOVERY

CAMP MAGNI. "How is he?" asks Scipio, hovering over Marcus' blood-stained body.

"Let me be!" the medicus barks, waving the general away. "I've got to finish sewing up his wound. It's wide as a trench!" The medicus pulls his curved bone needle through the back wound's skin flaps. "There!" he exclaims. His spiderlike fingers deftly tie up the last knot of flax.

The medicus looks up from his patient and grimaces at Scipio. "It is in the hands of the gods," he says, repeating the phrase that often signifies the patient is dying.

Scipio wipes his eyes and faces his somber officers. "I want him kept here until he is able to move. I want a full maniple about him, he is to be under constant guard, do you hear me? Constant guard!"

Masinissa and the tribunes are silent, but Laelius steps forward. "These men would give their lives for him, General," he says quietly. "You do not have to order them to protect him."

Scipio bites his lower lip. "Apologies, I am distraught. Of course you would."

Creesus, one of the elder tribunes, carefully examines the other officers' faces before he speaks. "We know Marcus' life is in the hands of the gods, General. And we will all be making sacrifices to Hygieia tonight, that the goddess of health may come to him."

He shifts uncomfortably. "But what are we to do next? Carthage's army is destroyed. We are out on these plains, with few supplies or protections. Do we return to Castra Cornelia, to continue besieging Utica? Do we march on Carthage itself?"

Scipio sniffs heavily, and swallows. "It is well you asked, Creesus. Our work here is done." He walks toward the exit of his tent. "Come out here, so we do not disturb him."

His guards and officers follow him outside. In the distance they can hear the revelry of the men, enjoying the feast Scipio has cobbled together from the enemy camp's plunder, including the Carthaginians' stores of rich red wine. In spite of his heavy heart, Scipio would not begrudge his men their celebration and their rewards. Now he will reward he who is most deserving.

"Masinissa, these men are to bear witness to what I tell you," Scipio says. "The tall prince steps forward, not knowing what to expect. "Your men fought bravely and well," Scipio says. "You have kept your promise to help us. Now it is time for me to keep mine."

Scipio motions for Laelius to join them. "Laelius, you are to help Masinissa seek out Syphax. Take our cavalry and light infantry. Do not return until he is dead or captured."

Masinissa's bows, his face is impassive but his eyes shine with tears. "I am most grateful, Imperator. I will not return without Syphax—or his head."

Laelius snorts. "So, I am to wander about that dry old desert, while you sit back at Castra Cornelia, flinging stones at Utica and sipping wine?" In spite of the somber mood, several tribunes chuckle.

Scipio manages a slight smile. "I have ceased that fool's errand. It's time for a bolder stroke, now that Carthage has no army."

He glances back at the tent. "I will do what Marcus urged me to do before. Two days hence we set out for Tunis, at Carthage's doorstep. If we can take that city, it's the end of the war. We depart in three days."

The officers disband and Scipio returns to his tent, intending to watch over Marcus through the night. He sits at his table, writing a report about the victory for Rome. Late that night he stamps his wax seal on the scroll and scrawls its destination outside of it. He summons his messenger. The young man soon arrives, rubbing sleep from his eyes.

"Get this to Rome," Scipio says, "with all haste."

The messenger steps out of his tent and heads for his horse, walking past the quaestor's tent. The young rider is preparing to jump onto his mount when he feels a rough hand on his shoulder, jerking him back.

Praxis stands there, holding a sealed scroll. "General Scipio forgot to give you this one, he just finished it," says Praxis. "He says it is critical that no one knows who you gave it to. No one, do you understand?"

The messenger nods nervously, taken aback by Praxis' intense tone. He stuffs it into his satchel, and gallops out into the night, venturing a quick glance behind him. Praxis is still there, watching him go.

The messenger turns around and shakes his head. *Why was he so cursed serious about keeping that scroll a secret? Who really cares if this Lucius Valerius Flaccus is getting a message?*

*   *   *   *   *

CARTHAGE, 203 BCE. "Look out Mintho, he'll run you over!" exclaims Salicar, pulling the young senator from the path of a trundling wagon loaded with limestone blocks. "Where are the street guards when you need them?" the elder politician mutters.

Salicar guides his alarmed young colleague into a side street. "Here now, let's take a side route to the Senate," he says soothingly, brushing limestone dust from his purple robe. He frowns as another wagon rumbles hastily through the street they just vacated, the passers-by darting out of its way. "All this cursed traffic! It's not safe to walk the streets today, everyone is rushing about like madmen, trying to prepare for Scipio's attack."

The two senators turn from one narrow street into another even narrower passageway. They stroll between the immaculate stone apartment buildings that tower over them. The apartments windows are festooned with small rugs and tapestries, with brightly painted gods and animals on the walls facing the street.

Salicar smiles at the modest adornments of the commoners. *Carthage is such a city of art, I have never seen the like.*

The senators emerge into the square that encircles the statuesque Senate building. They patter up the Senate's narrow limestone steps. Salicar halts at the top of the stairs. Mintho stops with him, puzzled at their pause.

Salicar's attention is taken by the beehive of activity that surrounds the city entrance. Workmen lever huge stone blocks against Carthage's forty-foot walls, buttressing them against Roman attacks. [lxiii] Hundreds of North African peasants flow into the open gates, dragging mules and horses laden with sacks of their possessions. They move with the endless train of food wagons that have arrived to fortify the city against a siege.

Carthage, serene and mighty Carthage, has become a city in panic. The citizenry knows that Gisgo's army was destroyed, and that they have lost their last means of protection. Now the rumor has spread that Scipio is marching his army towards the capitol. The news has stirred the people into frantic action as they seek to do something, anything, to protect themselves from the feared Romans.

Salicar's eyes travel to the temples, which are mobbed with thousands of people carrying chickens and goats to sacrifice to Baal. A motley group of self-appointed militia surrounds the supplicants, men and boys carrying rusty swords, kitchen knives, pitchforks, and garden hoes. They have all vowed to fight Scipio to the death.

The government forum is also overwhelmed with angry citizens. They clamor for their senators to hire more mercenaries, or to bring the two Barcas back to protect them. Or at the very least, to crucify Gisgo and find another commander.

Salicar purses his lips, dismayed at the chaos he sees below him. "We will have to make a decision today," he says regretfully. "We must decide upon peace or war, and figure out what price we will pay to get it."

Mintho nods. "I fear the price will be more than money."

Salicar blinks at the young senator. *The boy is wiser than I have given him credit for. Ah, the arrogance of age!*

"General Gisgo will have a hard time today," Mintho continues. "The Senate will demand an explanation of his latest failure."

Salicar shakes his head, his face grim. "Gisgo will not be there today," he replies, looking down at his feet. "He is awaiting judgment by the Council of Elders."

Mintho's eyes widen. "You think they will..."

Salicar raises his hand, interrupting Mintho. "It is entirely possible. I am one of the Elders and I tell you it is entirely possible."

The Senate meeting opens with the Senate priest's sacrifice of a bull, that Baal may help the Senate find wisdom for a good decision. As the unfortunate beast collapses onto the floor of the sacrificial ring, its throat blood is collected into a golden chalice. The priest tastes it, then nods his head: the blood is good, there are no evil portents.

The septuagenarian senate leader hobbles up the three steps to the room-sized limestone slab that serves as the Senate speaking platform. He bangs his bronze-bottomed Speaker's Staff onto the stone floor. The sound rings through the semicircular chamber, calling the meeting to order.

"The auguries have been propitious, and the sacrifice has been made," he rasps. "We start with our most pressing issue: how can we stop Publius Cornelius Scipio?"

As soon as the lead Elder opens the floor for discussion, the Senate decorum is shattered with a shouted exchange of opposing viewpoints.

"Recall Hannibal and Mago," bellow a number of senators, including several of the Magonids and Gisgons.

"If we recall them, we lose Italia! All of Rome's legions will join Scipio," shouts Hamilcar Barca.

"We should send our warships out to destroy Scipio's landing camp," another Barca declares, with supporting shouts from his family. "That will draw the bastard away from us. Then we have time to bring in some mercenaries from Phillip of Macedonia."

"This insanity has gone on long enough. We must seek peace," replies Akbar, one of the eldest and wealthiest senators. Akbar is the major representative of Carthage's powerful merchant class.

Akbar raises the silver hook that serves as his right hand, and waves it at the benches of the seated senators. "We have to admit it, my friends," he says. "We cannot win this war. We need to send our envoys to Rome and broker a treaty while we still have bargaining power."

He points toward the west. "If Scipio surrounds Carthage while we hide behind its walls, we will have little to say when we want to make a treaty."

The Senate argues late into the afternoon. They vigorously dispute the best course of action. Finally, a compromise is reached. Carthage will pursue one last attempt to defend itself and win the war.

The senators call in the fleet Admiral and notify him that he is to attack Scipio's anchored fleet at Utica, and proceed on to his naval camp.[lxiv] The senators also designate envoys to sail out the next day to Hannibal and Mago's outposts. They are to recall them both to Carthage.

In a nod to their fearful citizenry, the Senate allots more funds to bolster the city's defenses and prepare for a siege. [lxv] Though many of them think it unnecessary, they know that taking action, however ineffective, will placate the people and make the Senate seem decisive.

The peace faction is silenced for the time being, despite their dire warnings that Carthage will lose its chance for favorable peace terms by continuing the conflict. For now, Carthage still plots to win the war.

Led by the powerful Barcid and Magonid families, Carthage prepares to lure Scipio from their walls, even as Scipio plots to lure Hannibal back to his homeland.

*   *   *   *   *

SABINA HILLS, OUTSKIRTS OF ROME, 203 BCE. Flaccus takes the sealed scroll from the messenger and gestures for him to wait. He breaks open the seal and scans the brief message. His eyes stare intently at its contents, then flare with excitement.

He rolls the scroll up. "Just a minute," he says. Flaccus fumbles inside the purse attached to the silver ringmail belt that binds his immaculate white tunic. He extends a bejeweled hand that clutches a dozen denarii. The messenger opens his palm to receive the money, but Flaccus jerks his hand back.

"Did anyone ask you about the contents of this message, or to whom it was delivered?" Flaccus asks, studying the messenger's face. The one armed veteran merely shrugs. "No one ever asks about what I have, just who sent me the one that they got."

Flaccus nods, and drops the coins into the messenger's hand. "Gratitude. It was good to hear from, uh, from my old friend Scipio."

The messenger quickly marches down the wide marble steps of Flaccus' villa. Flaccus hears the sound of a horse galloping away. He paces out to the spacious courtyard that overlooks his acres of grain fields and olive groves. He unrolls his message from Praxis and rereads it, savoring its brief contents:

The deed is done. Your threat has been eliminated.

Px

Flaccus walks across his veranda and into the kitchen. He sticks the papyrus scroll into a house torch hanging above the stone oven. Flaccus watches the scroll flare and turn to ashes. He drops the remains into the oven's maw and strolls back to his courtyard to look out over his fields.

His eyes linger on the spot where unknown assailants ambushed him several years ago. He grimaces, remembering the pain and shock of a marble phallus jammed deep into his rectum. Unconsciously, he reaches back and rubs himself. *I did not forget what you did to me, bitch. Now your protector is gone.*

Whistling a drinking tune, the patrician walks into the courtyard's adjoining herb garden. Fabius Maximus sits on a stone bench in the center of the garden circle, sunning his aged bones among Flaccus' array of sage, basil, and chicory.

"Who was that?" asks Fabius, bending over to pinch off a basil leaf and snuffle it. "Did you have a visitor here?"

Flaccus smiles. "Yes, yes indeed. A messenger from the gods, as it were." He sits next to Fabius and grins triumphantly. "Marcus Silenus is dead, he died of a ... battle wound."

Fabius blinks his rheumy eyes. "Our legate is dead? Marcus Silenus? He was our finest soldier, and you smile as if Hannibal himself had perished!" He shakes his head. "I do not know you any more, I swear to the gods I do not."

Flaccus rolls his eyes. "Ah, yes, it was a great loss, for certain. I am sorry if I appeared happy. But he was Pomponia's protector. He has kept me from extracting my deserved revenge on that meddling Hellenic!"

Fabius' toothless mouth snaps shut like a turtle's. His face flushes with anger. He reaches over and grabs his oak staff, levering himself up from his seat next to Flaccus.

"You speak of 'revenge' against a woman? Against the matriarch of the Scipios? I do not like her politics either, but she is not deserving of whatever you plot against her!" He straightens himself, his bony chin held high, and for just a moment he again becomes the unrelenting General Fabius, the man who kept Hannibal from destroying Rome.

"If misfortune should befall her, I swear I will make your intentions known to all, Flaccus. And that includes our party members!" Fabius stamps his staff against the stone tiles. "My slaves! Where are my slaves?" He hobbles towards the front door.

Flaccus stands and watches him go. "I am sorry to hear you say that," he murmurs to the old man's back. "Truly, truly, sorry."

*   *   *   *   *

TUNIS, AFRICA, 203 BCE. Now they can see it.

The Roman vanguard stares at the small fortress standing alone atop a low hill overlooking a large shimmering lake. The citadel of Tunis beckons them to approach, to finish their three mile march to it.

"Look at that, General," says a veteran centurion. "There's not a soldier or ship around it"

"Nothing but flat earth all the way to the walls," chimes in Pontius, a bantam-sized man with a shock of unruly red hair. "This will be easier than Utica, or I'm a Nubian!" Amidst the legionnaires' laughter, Scipio waves his men to a halt.

"It appears very vulnerable, but Gnaeus and I had best take closer look." He grins. "Who knows? Hannibal may be hiding behind that hill over there!"

"And if he was, you'd paddle his ass!" retorts Pontius, prompting further laughter.

  Scipio and Legate Gnaeus Octavius study the lakeside city, its phoenix-emblazoned flags proudly waving over the ramparts of its twenty-foot limestone walls. Off to their left they discern the mist-shrouded outline of Carthage, its indomitable inner citadel of Byrsa towering above Carthage's impregnable walls. Scipio is heartened to see that the eleven-mile road between the two cities is darkened with Tunisians fleeing northeast to the capitol. *Less men to defend it*, he muses. *Fewer people to die.*

  General Scipio leans sideways from his horse to draw nearer to Octavius, the tribune who is acting in Marcus Silenus' place. He points to a slight rise in the plain around Tunis' front gates. "First thing today, we build camp on that slope facing the main gates. Then we surround their walls so no soldiers or wagons can get into it. But let them leave if

176

they want."

"When do we commence the siege?" asks Octavius. He is a thoughtful but outspoken young patrician who has garnered Scipio's favor with his valor in battle and his keen eye for tactics.

"Two days." Our supply trains will make the trip from Castra Cornelia in one day, rain permitting. Tomorrow they will bring up any rams and ballistae that haven't been loaded onto the ships blockading Utica. We'll pound Tunis' walls at dusk. Then we bring up our escaladers for a night assault.

Gnaeus' mouth tightens skeptically. "Imperator, do you think it's worth another six month siege to take this little city?"

Scipio grins at his boldness. "It is worth it, and it will not take that long. I have studied Carthage's history. In the last century, Agathocles and Regulus both seized Tunis,[lxvi] and they did it without undue effort. If we take Tunis we command the hills about Carthage's land entry.[lxvii] We can cut off their supplies and make it easier to levy a peace in our favor." His reddened eyes flash momentarily. "And bring Hannibal back from Italy."

"So we conduct two sieges," replies the legate, with a whisper of sarcasm.

Scipio gives Octavius a stare that makes him blush. "I am not that foolish," he says coldly. "If we have Tunis we do not need Utica." [lxviii] He shakes his head regretfully. I should have seen that earlier, but the past is past."

Wisely, Legate Octavius says nothing.

Scipio rubs his eyes. "I think I'll retire early tonight, Gnaeus. The labor of taking all those towns en route to Carthage has worn me down."

Gnaeus bows his head. "Forgive my brashness, General. I did not mean to question your decisions. You have conquered all before you. I merely wondered."

Scipio smirks. "I am but a man. Perhaps if your voice had joined the others who challenged me about Utica, we might be camped at Carthage's walls right now, and Hannibal would be rushing to the rescue."

Scipio turns his mount around. "I see my tent is finished. I am to bed for the night, Legate. Call a strategy meet for the morning."

Within the hour Scipio reclines on a makeshift couch made from tent materials, wearing the white cotton tunic his mother gave to him before he left Rome. He listlessly dips his flatbread into some herbed olive oil, chewing it slowly, half asleep.

Forcing his eyes open, he shuffles to his map table. For the fourth time, he studies the terrain between Carthage and Tunis, trying to think of a land assault tactic the Carthaginians might employ. *What would Hannibal do, were he here? How would he use the terrain and the sun? Or those coastal winds?* He laughs to himself. *Were Hannibal here, we might still be pinned back at our landing point. Thanks the gods there is only one of him!*

Scipio pushes away the finger-worn goatskin map and lurches over to his sleeping platform. He flings himself face down onto its straw mattress. In the blink of an eye, he is fast asleep.

But Scipio is not destined for rest this night, for Febris has chosen to visit him. The goddess of fever returns after many months away, bringing the fever dreams that have plagued Scipio since he was a child.

Murky shifting shadows flit about in his agitated mind, supplicating images backdropped by the cries of burning soldiers and people. Scipio shivers and thrashes, but he remains asleep. The images quiet, the voices fade, and peace returns to his slumber. Momentarily.

Scipio's beloved tutor, the long dead Asclepius, appears before him. The Greek shuffles in from the shadows, wearing his familiar gold-edged mantle. The muscular old warrior angrily waggles his finger at Scipio.

"Did I teach you nothing all those years? Do you even remember one single lesson?" He wrinkles his nose. "Remember Aesop, remember his fable about the Dog and the Shadow?"

He glares at Scipio and taps his foot, as if waiting for a reply. Finally, he flaps his hands in frustration. "Do you not remember the moral, Pumpkin Head? By chasing the shadow you ignore the substance!"

The ghost looks off to his left. "This Tunis, its plains and hills, they are but shadows. The true threat lies beyond them, under your very nose!" The aged tutor stalks back into the dark, muttering to himself.

Scipio blinks awake, staring at the tent roof. *What did he say? The dog and the shadow?* He pulls himself from his sweat stained sleeping pad and walks outside his command tent. Praxis and the rest of his Honor Guard follow him into the rising dawn.

He rubs the sleep from his eyes and draws the cool dawn air deep into his lungs. "Fetch me my horse," he tells a puzzled Praxis. "We ride toward Tunis."

A half hour later Scipio is galloping out toward the sunrise, followed by a squadron of his guards and officers. The plain is already bustling with Roman foragers and Tunisian refugees, but Scipio pays them no mind. He stares out toward the sea, looking for the key to his dream.

The waters behind Tunis are empty, save for a few small fishing boats tacking out from the shore. Scipio looks all about him, searching for some Carthaginian advantage he has overlooked. Finally he shrugs. *Not all your dreams are portents, boy*, he reminds himself. *Time to get some breakfast, and start preparing the siege.*

Scipio clears his throat and spits off the side of his horse. Praxis hands him a waterskin and he tilts it high, drinking thirstily. As he lowers the skin he glances over toward Carthage, looking about its dimly-lit walls, searching for signs of enemy activity. He notices a faint twinkling in its nearby waters, as if a small galaxy of stars had fallen down into its enormous harbor, winking on and off. *Something is going on over there.*

Scipio nods his head toward Carthage and his men follow as he trots closer to it, pausing after atop one of the hills above the road.

Now he sees that the winking lights are ships' lanterns, bobbing up and down in the faint morning light—lanterns from scores of harbor warships. He sees a dozen already floating out to sea, making room for their fellows to launch behind them. *They're going after my camp!* he realizes. *They don't have an army, so they're sending the navy to attack my force at Utica.*[lxix]

Scipio's heart thumps in his chest. *Gods below, the entire campaign is in danger.* He puts heels to his mount and gallops back toward his camp, past the men constructing the camp ramparts. [lxx]

"Gnaeus Octavius!" he shouts, "Find Gnaeus Octavius!" Several sentries dash over to the legate's tent and Gnaeus is soon facing Scipio, wearing only his gray wool sleeping tunic.

"Gnaeus, Carthage is sailing out to attack our camp!" Scipio blurts. "I am riding for Utica, bring the army after me. Forced march rations and no equipment!"

Gnaeus blinks. "What about the siege?"

"Let Pluto have the siege!" Scipio curses, already turning his horse southwest. "Our ships are heavy with siege equipment, they will be easy prey for the Carthaginians!" [lxxi] He gulps. "We could lose the entire fleet!"

A bewildered Gnaeus turns toward the knot of tribunes that have gathered. "You heard his words, men. Prepare for the march—double rations for breakfast, light packs only."

Scipio laughs to himself. *Now I see why Carthage has the phoenix symbol. Just when you think they are destroyed, they rise again from the ashes!*

* * * * *

CARTHAGE. "Here now, fill this one more time," orders Gisgo, bobbing his silver wine goblet at the Senate Chambers slave. The Roman boy rushes over with his tall bronze pitcher. He carefully refills Gisgo's cup with rich red Iberian wine.

At least this is one Roman I can control, Gisgo muses ruefully, as he quaffs deeply of his personal favorite. He leans back on the gold embroidered reclining couch in the Senate's elegantly appointed waiting room for dignitaries, and ponders his fate.

Within the hour Gisgo will be standing before the Elders' Council of the Hundred and Four, Carthage's highest judicial body. He will be tried for his repeated defeats at the hands of Scipio, and they will pass sentence upon him. *As if I did not know what it is already,* he smirks.

Try as he might, Gisgo cannot forget the fate of a general who was tried for cowardice while fighting to take back Sardinia: how he hung for days in the Forum square, the victim of countless taunts and insults from passers-by. *Is that to be my fate? Me, a scion of the Gisgons? My life ended by scrawny businessmen who couldn't outfight a one-eyed crone?*

He takes another deep drink of wine and swirls the remainder about the goblet's glimmering bowl, studying it as if it contained some portent. *Will they turn me over to that angry mob that gathers here every day, demanding my death? As if I have not already died the death of dishonor. Ah, fair Carthage! You are a city without pity.*

Gisgo recalls each of his battles—and losses—to young Scipio, how he and the other Three Generals were beaten time and again in Iberia. *But none as often as I,* he coldly reminds himself. *And none here in Africa but me.*

Gisgo takes another drink, and waves for the slave to refill his cup. *They all want Hannibal to come here. They think precious Hannibal will save them. I wish I had fought the dull Roman generals he had fought, and he had Scipio instead of me. We'd see who is the genius then!* His lips curl into a bitter smile. *But then, Hannibal is coming here. He'll find out.*

Gisgo shakes himself from his reverie. *I am whining like an old woman. What could have happened, did happen. Fuck it. Fuck it all.* He motions for the slave to leave him, and the boy scurries out. When the slave closes the heavy oak door, Gisgo fumbles inside his thick purple robes. He slides out his treasured Roman gladius, a souvenir from a patrician tribune he killed at his triumphant battle near Iberian Castulo, where General Publius Scipio was killed. *Got the whelp's father, anyway.*

Gisgo lovingly fondles the shining sword, studying the intricate battle scenes inscribed on its wide blade. *Look at that, each one has a winner and a loser. There has to be a loser. Even Alexander the Great lost battles, but no one talks of that.*

He slips off his luxurious purple robe, carefully folds it up, and lays it on the couch. He unbuckles the wide belt that circles his white linen tunic and pulls the crisp cloth over his head, laying them both on top of the robe. *No sense making a mess.*

He pitches the gladius' scabbard on top of them. *A Roman sword. I hope they appreciate the irony of this.*

Gisgo stands naked with his naked blade. He knows he must thrust strongly and decisively, else his enemies talk about how his death was botched as much as his battles. He is determined not give them that satisfaction. *I was just on the dark side of fate and fortune, as so many are. But now I control my destiny.*

The Carthaginian general walks over to the wine table and moves the flagon and goblets from the table's edge. He bends over and clenches the sword pommel with his wiry fingers.

Gisgo eases its tip into his ribs, just above his heart. He leans slightly forward and grimaces. Blood trickles down the gladius' gleaming edge, and pools darkly upon the oak plank table. *Daughter, forgive me.*

Gisgo pivots forward, thrusting the sword upward with all the strength of forlorn desperation. He gasps, his mouth agape as the keen blade slides into the bottom of his heart.

Gisgo rolls his dazed eyes about the ceiling, as if searching for something, someone. He crumbles onto the stone floor and kicks out the last seconds of life.

General Hasdrubal Gisgo, former commander of Iberia, member of the once-invincible Three Generals—lies still.

*   *   *   *   *

CASTRA CORNELIA, 203 BCE. The afternoon sun is high in the sky by the time Scipio arrives at the gates of his main camp. He dismounts and quickly strides over to Cato's tent. Cato sits inside, carefully reviewing the camp spending accounts, sipping from a clay cup of watered vinegar. He glances up when Scipio enters, and looks back down at his work.

"Quaestor, give me your attention," Scipio fumes.

"You have come for more money, haven't you?" Cato says without looking up. "For that damned siege at Tunis."

"I need to know where Taurus is," Scipio says, referring to the stocky marine left in charge of Laelius' fleet. "The Carthaginians fleet is coming upon us!"

Cato stares at him in surprise, then lowers his eyes. "Apologies, General. Taurus is leading our ships out to surround Utica's walls, in the event you want to resume the attack."

Scipio nods and starts from the tent. Cato jumps up and joins him, much to Scipio's surprise.

"I will accompany you," is all he says, knowing that Scipio is preparing for battle.

Then grab your horse, Cato," says Scipio. "There is no time for enmity now."

The two men hurtle southeast from camp, heading to a small dock the Romans have built near Utica. Within the hour Cato and Scipio are sailing out on a bireme, heading towards the warships and transports massed about Utica. They clamber aboard Taurus' new quadrireme and find the veteran seafarer waiting for them on the deck.

"Salus, General Scipio. Salus, Quaestor. Have you come to review our progress? The ships are loaded with every ballistae and scorpio we could fit onto them, with many loads of stone. We are ready to pound Utica's walls."

Scipio shakes his head furiously. "No, no, this is not about the siege. The Carthaginian fleet is coming at you, they may have a hundred warships on the way, loaded with men and weapons!"

Taurus gnashes his teeth. "What cursed fortune is this? My ships are weighted and heavy as a pregnant sow!" He points over at a nearby transport. "See how low she floats in the water? The ship is too heavy to maneuver."

Scipio looks at the transport and scratches his head. "Hm. We could cast off the siege equipment, and the missiles," he offers.

"You would throw our valuable equipment into the bay?" asks Cato. "That would certainly hearten the Uticans. And leave us helpless."

Taurus nods. "It would take days to do that, General. And the Carthaginians are fully armed for a sea battle. We are only staffed for a siege. We need all our weapons."

"Hmm," Scipio mutters, slapping his palm against his leg. "This is very unfortunate." He walks to the prow of the ship and stares out toward Carthage, as if he can already see their navy arriving to destroy him. "We can't lose our warships. We would lose control of the seas."

Cato nods. "They will choke off our supply ships, and open their lines to their allies." He grimaces sourly. "All we accomplished is going to be undone."

"Perhaps not. We still have time to prepare for them," Scipio says. "Their fleet admiral will wait until all his ships arrive from Carthage. I would wager it will be another day or two before they strike."

He looks southward. "I wish Laelius weren't out chasing Syphax, I would love to hear what he would do."

"Apologies, General, but you do not need him here," Taurus replies. "I know his mind. He and I have talked about a possible sea attack. He said that you two had studied the Greek wars as children, how Sparta used what he calls a 'wall of ships' to stop Athens' attack." [lxxii] He thought that would be a good defensive tactic if we were left vulnerable during the siege."

Scipio's face reddens, and he laughs. "I should have remembered that myself! But then, he was always more interested about ships and sailors. What did you two plan?"

Taurus motions for Scipio and Cato to follow him to the opposite side of the deck, where he sweeps his hand across Utica entry port. "We can sail in our freighters over there, and pile them outside the mouth of the harbor. We will keep our warships right where they are, near Utica's seaward walls. The transports can protect them."

"Another wall of ships, then," says Scipio.

"Yes," replies Taurus. "We have some creaky old ships that we can put in the front."

Scipio shakes his head. "No, let us be more offensive. Put the ones with siege equipment out in front. They can fling stones and missiles at their ships. Do that tonight."

"It will be done," says Taurus, "But we should prepare for losses. The Carthaginians may ram their way through them. Or use blockade runners to sneak in between. Or even tow some of them away! Most of our transports are laden with the plunder we were going to ship back to Sicily and Rome."

Scipio blinks, and begins rubbing his chin. Then he shrugs. "If we have to lose freighters to save warships, it must be done. Make four rows of them.[lxxiii] We will do our best to repel any penetration."

Cato walks up behind Scipio and stands silently for a minute, shifting his sandaled feet. Scipio turns and eyes him. "You have something to say, Quaestor?"

"Yoke them together," Cato states. "Just like I do with oxen on my farm. That will make a solid wall of ships, hard for them to sneak in between them." Cato stalks off, leaving Scipio staring at his back.

Scipio chuckles, shaking his head. *That stern little man has some imagination in him, after all.*

Scipio turns to his captain. "You heard him, Taurus. We take every available man and mount the blockade by end of day tomorrow. Bring up the transports into the harbor mouth tonight. Lash the ships front to back." Scipio grins. "The Carthaginians will have a little surprise waiting for them."

By early morning Utica harbor is a swarm of activity. The terrified Uticans watch from the ramparts as thousands of Romans bustle about the ships moored inside Utica's harbor.

Dozens of Roman quadriremes bob placidly inside the inner harbor, while scores of tall and bulky transports sail in from the Mediterranean to join them, arranging themselves across the wide harbor mouth.

As one ship's prow nears another's stern, a squad of marines scrambles to the other's prow, lugging along ropes that are tied to the mast of their ship. They lash the ropes onto the prow of the other ship, yoking the two together. Similarly, the marines on the other ship lash their mast to the other's stern. The process is repeated with each arriving freighter, until a thick fence of ships forms a rough semicircle about the Utica harbor.

Out at sea, Carthage's fleet admiral watches the blockade unfold, looking on with great surprise. *What is Mot are they doing out there? Where are their quadriremes and quinqueremes?*

"Baal curse them, they're blocking the harbor," he says to his captain. The admiral calls a strategy conference with his fleet officers. They argue into the late afternoon, trying to decide how to attack the ship wall, trying to figure out if it is another of Scipio's traps. The scout ships return with news that there are no warships hiding in the bays or coves about Utica; they are all inside the harbor.

"We were sent to destroy their war fleet and we will do it," the admiral declares. "We'll ram through those old transports and corner them in the bay."

With the entire day left to finish their preparations, the Romans load extra siege engines onto the freighter decks, lining the seaward side with catapults and scorpios. The marines and legionnaires spend the night piling head-sized catapult stones and spear-shaped scorpio bolts onto the decks, preparing to launch a deadly onslaught.

Morning breaks with scores of Carthaginian warships surging toward the Romans with full sails and stroking oars. When the Carthaginians draw within shooting range of the broadside freighters, the Romans unleash a hail of small boulders upon them, followed by flights of their deadly scorpio bolts. The hurtling stones crush scores of sailors. Dozens more fall to the deadly scorpio bolts, split asunder by the monstrous arrows that fly across the decks.

The Carthaginians catapult their own stones at the unmoving transports, but their warships have few catapults and their volleys bring only a handful of casualties. For hours the battle is more like a floating siege than a naval encounter, as the two sides batter one another with flying missiles.

Carthage's admiral tires of the stalemate. He calls his fleet captain to him. "We have to break that wall. Send our ships in!" The flagship's horn sounds thrice, and the warships churn straight at the transports.

"Prepare to be boarded!" Taurus shouts from the middle transport. "Swords and shields for all."

Scipio has stationed a thousand marines on the lead freighters' decks, and the veterans quickly mobilize for action.

The Carthaginian ships draw so close that the Romans can see the face of Yamm, their serpent-headed sea god, snarling at them from the sailors' shields. Taurus raises his right hand high, signaling a pending command. When the Carthaginian sailors move to the prows of their boats and grab their grappling hooks, Taurus chops his hand down.

"Loose!" he shouts. The soldiers hurl their javelins into the Carthaginian sailors, [lxxiv] slowing the assault. The enemy sailors hastily form a deckside shield wall and deflect most of the javelins, flinging back those that have their spearheads intact. When the projectile rain lessens, the flagship captain hurries over to the Carthaginian admiral.

"They are all tied together!" he exclaims. "We can't ram through!"

The Carthaginian fleet commander gnashes his teeth in frustration. "Gods curse them! We can't break through four walls of ships. But I can't go back empty handed. Yank them out!"

The Carthaginian quinqueremes turn sideways and edge toward the transports, each targeting a ship. The Carthaginians hurl their harpagones onto the decks and side rails of the transports, long poles tipped with starfish-shaped iron hooks, attached to a thick chain.

When several chains are secured on a transport, the captain of the enemy ship orders the oarsmen to row out with all their might. The quinqueremes surge backward, yanking their chained grappling hooks tight.

The Carthaginian warships snap off the transports' masts and yoke ropes, breaking the ships out from the ones behind them. Hundreds of Romans run across planks from their dislodged ship to the ones in the next row, [lxxv] escaping capture.

"Hurl everything we have, anything that will maim or kill!" cries Taurus.

The transports erupt with another storm of stones, bolts, and javelins. Scores of Carthaginian sailors fall, but their captains urge them on, ignoring the death that flies about them. The sailors continue to lash into the front wall of ships with their grappling weapons.

Eager for victory, the Carthaginians repeat the sally time and again, though the sea floats with the corpses of those struck down by the

Romans. First a dozen, then a score, then three score transports are pulled out from the ship wall, [lxxvi] as the late afternoon light creeps away from the seas.

Scipio watches the battle from a promontory above the harbor, his messengers waiting to dispatch his orders to the fleet below him. One of Scipio's tribunes anxiously watches as another two transports are towed from the second row of the ship wall.

"General, they are capturing our ships, and many are laden with supplies and plunder! Should we send the warships after them?"

Scipio turns slowly, and looks at his officer, unperturbed. "Why? So we can lose them, too? No, let them have their little victory, our warships are safe."

He looks west. "Darkness will end their folly. Many of their ships are damaged. An army of their men's bodies float beneath us. They will not soon return."

At sunset the Carthaginian fleet sails back towards Carthage, proudly towing their sixty captive vessels. When the fleet docks, Carthage celebrates with a triumphal parade. The senators know that the citizens are desperate for a victory, any victory, and so they make a great display of unloading the plunder from the Roman ships.

The next day, scores of wagons parade through the main streets of Carthage, displaying the ships' plunder of weapons, foodstuffs, gold, coins, and art. Thousands of cheering Carthaginians look on, ignoring the fact that much of the plunder is from the outlying towns that Scipio has only recently ransacked. The Council of Elders decrees a public holiday to celebrate Carthage's great naval victory. The downtrodden citizenry celebrates long into the night.

Carthage not only gains plunder with the victory, it acquires a renewed and overweening confidence in its military power. Several senators propose a recall of the peace envoys sent to Rome, but the envoys have already arrived in Italy and the other senators vote them down. Not a few senators declare that peace is still desirable, but that

Carthage should reject any peace terms that are not favorable to them, ones that do not preserve all their military prowess and shipping lanes.

In the space of a week, the Senate mood has changed from despair to arrogance.

Though the Senate has renewed confidence, the majority still agree that Hannibal should be recalled to Carthage so that he can destroy Scipio, and bring Rome to its knees.

*   *   *   *   *

CASTRA CORNELIA. "How many did we lose?" Scipio asks.

"Sixty transports, twelve scout biremes, and one warship that hit another of ours and sunk," Taurus replies. He holds up a clay tablet. "The transports' holdings are listed here. We lost a lot of food, weapons, and money."

"Yes, but not as much as we gained from the towns we took over while we marched here," notes Scipio.

"A loss is a loss," grouses Cato. "We lost enough resources to supply this army for a year, and you act like the Carthaginians stole a couple of cows from us!"

"They stole some cows," Scipio coolly replies. "But we still have our bulls. We have our warships."

"Laelius would approve." replies Taurus. "Our ships can raid the coast and regain our supplies, if it comes to that."

"Pfah!" replies Cato. "Carthage is probably crowing about their big victory over the Roman fleet, how we refused to come out and fight. Such cowardice is un-Roman, be it on the land or the sea!"

Scipio waves his hand dismissively. "That horse has left the stable," he says, "We have more pressing matters. My spies in Carthage tell me that Carthage is recalling Hannibal and his brother Mago. They will soon be upon Carthage's shores."

The officers stare at each other, dumbfounded. "We should take Carthage before they land," declares Atilius, pointing his three-fingered hand toward it.

A young tribune shakes his head. "Apologies, but I think not. Best we eliminate Syphax before he can join them," he says.

"Find out where Hannibal is landing, and get them coming off their ships!" proposes Taurus. "Get him before he gets the chance to recruit more men—and elephants!"

Scipio stands calmly in front of them, letting them argue among themselves. After years of command he has come to learn that his officers need the opportunity to be heard, even if he does not accept their complaint or recommendation. It is also best for them to hear their peers disagree with them before he does.

As the officers dispute strategy, Scipio walks to the wine table and fills half his goblet, topping it off with water. Taurus follows him, and bends over to fill his own cup.

"We have more opinions than assholes in this room today," Scipio mutters petulantly.

Taurus chuckles. "That sounds like something Laelius would say! They argue now, but they will readily follow your lead, General. That is the truth of it."

Scipio nods mutely and returns to the group. After several more exchanges the tribunes begin looking toward him, tiring of their harangues.

Time to intervene. Scipio raises his glass to them. "I do not say it enough, but I am very grateful to have you fighting by my side." He smiles wryly at Cato. "All of you." Scipio's comment causes several younger tribunes to laugh. Cato's neck reddens, though his face is a stone.

"We have accomplished much this year," Scipio continues. "Fortuna is truly smiling down upon us."

Scipio takes a deep sip of his wine, using the silence to organize his words. He smacks his lips and considers his men, his face stern. "I have heard what you have said. And I have carefully considered all your proposals, do not think otherwise. It is my duty to make the final decision, not to count votes for a particular course of action."

Scipio walks back and refreshes his glass. The room is silent. *This is it. We'll win or lose this war with what I'm going to say.*

He walks back and lays both his hands on the table. "I consider Hannibal and Mago's arrival as a glorious victory for us, not a cause for alarm. If the Carthaginians are gone from our homeland, it is as much a triumph as any of our victories in Africa."

"So we are to prepare for battle against them?" asks Atilius. Scipio shakes his head.

"Not yet. Not until we know when and where they land, and the strength of their forces. It would be folly to do otherwise" Scipio nods his head toward the west. "For now, we have more pressing threats to resolve. We will return to besiege Tunis, and forget about Utica. If Tunis falls, Carthage may press for peace."

Scipio gulps more wine. He belches loudly, and his men chuckle with surprise. "Apologies, men. I find myself relaxed, now that no battle portends us."

"So we squat around Tunis and wait for the Carthaginians to come after us, because you think there is no one left to fight?" Cato snipes.

Scipio shrugs. "Possibly. But Syphax and his minions are still at large. He still rules the Numidians, though many would join Masinissa if they had the chance."

He sweeps his hand toward a knot of younger tribunes. "Several of you have argued that Syphax must be vanquished before he can join Mago and Hannibal. I agree, and it will be so."

"I can muster our cavalry from the camp and the garrisons," says Gnaeus Octavius. "We can send out thousands of cavalry to help

Laelius and Masinissa. They can return if Hannibal or Mago lands."

Scipio reaches into his belt pouch and fingers his figurine of Nike,. *Goddess, grant me wisdom. I hope I am not dooming my friends.*

"No, Legate, they are on their own. The scouts say that Laelius and Masinissa are deep into Numidia, at least a week's ride from us. We would not arrive in time to help them."

Scipio drains the last of his wine, and gestures for his men to leave. "Our work is done tonight. This fight is in their hands, wherever they are. We will lose an enemy or lose an army, though I cannot say which."

VII. VICTORY AND TRAGEDY

NUMIDIA, WESTERN AFRICA, 203 BCE. "By Jupiter above," Laelius exclaims, "That bastard's got another batch of soldiers!"

He squints his dusty eyes at the army arrayed across the dry plains in front of him. "Syphax must have another ten thousand men out there, and most of them are cavalry! Where does he get them?"

"Numidia is vaster than you know," Masinissa replies, "And Syphax is a king on the verge of losing his kingdom. He grabbed every Masaesyli that stands to piss and has given him a horse."

"Then thanks to the gods we ran him out of your tribe's lands before he got even more of them," replies Laelius. He leans out from his stallion and slaps Masinissa on the back. "And your tribe acknowledged you as their king![lxxvii] You have regained the Massylii!"

Masinissa looks at the half-mile line of Numidian infantry. He notices that Syphax has arranged them in cohorts, mimicking the Roman formation. "I have nothing if Syphax beats us today. And everything if he doesn't."

He puts his hand on Laelius' shoulder. "My friend, I cannot leave this battle alive without resolving this one way or the other. It has been too many years."

Laelius surveys the Numidian horde. "It's going to be our cavalry against his, and most of his army is cavalry. His infantry looks more like a mob than a cohort. Look at that! They're trying to stand in legionary formation,[lxxviii] but they can't maintain the proper distance. They're bunched up in some places and spread apart in others! Our velites should just attack them head on and break through them—none of this throwing javelins and retreating crap!"

Masinissa nods. "I trust your tactics for that. You must trust me about the cavalry. And I tell you now, he has many experienced riders out there, and thrice our number. Your foot soldiers must come after his riders, once you disperse his infantry. If not, we will lose."

"So, you are daunted by ten to one odds?" Laelius says. "I swear to Hera, you take all the fun out of a battle!" He smiles. "Very well, it will be done. Just hold them for a while, and we will join you." His mouth tightens. "Besides, we have to win. We have no camp or palisades. There is nowhere to run."

Masinissa smiles grimly. "Good, no retreat. What better way to build determination?"

Laelius laughs as Masinissa snaps the reins of his horse and trots forward. "Let us go now, Laelius, and seize the advantage!"

The Numidian prince rides off to the right wing of their small army, preparing to lead the charge of his three hundred Numidians. Laelius looks to his left across his cohort of five thousand light infantry. He sees Sextus Gracchus, his slender young cavalry captain, waiting for Laelius' signal. Sextus will command the thousand Roman and Italian cavalry waiting behind him.

Laelius slowly rides to the front of his velites, unarmored young men with small round shields, a gladius, and a brace of javelins. *At least they are battle tested*, Laelius thinks, *more than that rabble across from us.*

He eyes the thousands of enemy infantry standing with oval shields and spears at the ready. *Still, just once I would like to outnumber those bastards, and not have to worry about strategy! Just swarm all over them like the Gauls. Well, at least we have a little trick in store for Syphax.* Laelius smiles and raises his right arm, preparing his men for the signal.

After a last glance at his cohorts, Laelius flings his arm down. The battle trumpets blare twice, sounding the attack. Masinissa and Sextus charge into the half-mile gap separating the two armies, leading their cavalry directly at Syphax' unwary foot soldiers. Syphax' cavalry plunge in from the sides to fend off the attackers. The Numidian riders gallop in and intercept Sextus and Masinissa's men. A free-form cavalry fight erupts in between the infantry lines.

Syphax' infantry stand apprehensively in place. They stare at the Roman infantry tramping towards them through the milling cavalry, their boar's-head standards bobbing in the hands of their wolfskin-capped bearers.

The armored equites fend off Syphax' nimble attackers, staying in squadrons to block off any rear attacks from their quicker opponents. Masinissa's men dash through and around their Numidian counterparts. The Numidians thrust their javelins at each other as they ride past, eager to slash a rib, thigh, or shoulder before they turn around and charge back.

Laelius rides at the head of his front line infantry, joking and chatting as if he were riding into a garden feast. Three of Syphax' Numidians veer off from the cavalry conflict and ride straight at the man with the shining armor.

Laelius whips his bow off his back and shoots an arrow into the shoulder of the lead horseman, knocking him off his mount. The stunned Numidian staggers to his feet, just as a second arrow thunks into his heart. As the Masaesyli drops onto his face his two companions spin about and ride back to the cavalry battle, seeking easier prey.

"Come back here, curse you! I need more practice!" Laelius shouts. His men hoot at the fleeing Numidians.

The velites close in on the cavalry battle in front of the Numidian infantry. Laelius shoulders his bow and draws his Iberian falcata.

"Sound the attack!" he orders his cornicen. The trumpeter blasts out two short calls and repeats them.

Hearing the signal, Sextus and Masinissa order their men to move to the Roman infantry flanks. Syphax' cavalry chase after them, leaving his untrained infantry to face the thousands of grim Romans marching towards them.

"Give them some shield music!" Laelius shouts. "I want to hear you!"

The legionnaires strike their javelins against their shields in a rhythmic tattoo, clanking forward like a giant machine.

The Numidian foot soldiers stir restlessly, looking anxiously for their cavalry.

When the Romans draw within a spear's cast of the Numidians, the battle horns sound again. Instantly, the Romans erupt with wild battle cries and charge at their opponents. They fling two rounds of javelins into the Numidian front lines and bash into them, using their wooden shields like battering rams.

The green soldiers buckle at the first impact. Scores are knocked to the ground with the unexpected violence of the Roman assault, and are stabbed down before they can rise. The Numidians panic and turn to flee.

The front line velites fling the last of their javelins into the backs of their retreating enemy, and more Numidians fall to the earth. Without breaking step, the velites draw their swords and cut into the Masaesylli's backs and sides. Hundreds of terrified Numidians career into their fellows, frantic to escape the murderous onslaught.

Riding at the back of his infantry lines, Syphax sees the members of his infantry fleeing the battle. "Gods damn those cowards!" He motions over the captain of his guard. "Follow me in. We've got to stop those Italian bastards from killing everyone!"

The warrior king crashes his stallion into the center of the velites, knocking several to the ground. He whirls through the light Roman infantry, lancing down one velite after another. His guards desperately fight their way through to assist him, as a ring of Roman bodies forms around their leader.

"King Syphax is here!" shout the Numidians. Seeing their king repelling the dread Romans, many of the foot soldiers take heart and charge back into the battle. They wield their curved swords with desperate energy, wounding scores of Romans. The velites waver, beaten back by swarms of warriors who come at them from every angle.

It is Dorsuo who turns the tide. The Sabina Hills farm boy gapes in alarm at the sight of his brothers in arms being cut down in front of him. *I will not watch them die!* he swears to himself.

Dorsuo lunges forward, ignoring his centurion's command to halt. He shoulders his way through the remaining infantrymen, clenching three javelins in his broad fist, his small round shield dangling from his forearm. His eyes are fixed on Syphax.

Dorsuo finds an open spot between the first and second lines and plants his feet. *Here, vermin!* He flings his first javelin at Syphax, who is moving sideways across the line. The pilum flies past his back, clattering to the earth.

Cursing his own impatience, Dorsuo grabs his second spear. He rocks back and arrows the javelin at Syphax. The Numidian king bends over to lance down a legionnaire. Dorsuo's spear whistles over his head.

"Pluto take me!" Dorsuo mutters. He drops his shield and draws back to throw his final javelin, watching Syphax' movements. When the front line velites retreat from the Numidian riders' attack, Syphax momentarily stands alone in the clearing.

Now!

Dorsuo throws this final spear, seeking direction more than speed, and releases it with a breathed prayer to Mars. The iron-headed pilum arcs over the heads of the front-liners and lands squarely in the nostril of Syphax' charger. [lxxix]

The warhorse rears back and screams. It beats the air with its forefeet and tumbles to the ground, rolling its head to dislodge the agonizing projectile. Syphax flies from his mount. He crashes the earth and rolls towards the Roman front.

"Get him!" shouts an alert centurion.

The centurion and his century sprint toward Syphax, fighting their way into to the center of the Numidian front. In the blink of an eye, seventy Romans pour over Syphax and his guards, fighting with every ounce of strength left in them.

Syphax dazedly pushes himself up. He raises his sword, only to be tackled to the ground by a heavyset velite. Two legionnaires yank Syphax' blade from his hands and strap their belts about his wrists and arms.

"Get away from me, dogs!" Syphax rages, writhing on the ground.

The centurion rams his sword pommel into Syphax' upper cheekpiece. Syphax' eyes roll into his head.

"This dog bites," the centurion replies. "Now get him to the back!"

The legionaries grab the Numidian king and drag him back behind Roman lines. He is quickly bound with chains and fetters. [lxxx]

"Stand about him, men. You have our victory in your hands!" the centurion shouts, clutching his bleeding forearm as he eases himself to the ground.

"They have our king!" cries Syphax' captain of the guard.

Syphax' guards spear their way through the velites' lines, blind to their losses. Several riders leap from their horses to hurl themselves onto the backs of the Romans, enabling their compatriots to plunge onwards towards the century protecting Syphax.

Laelius is off to the left of the battle center. He notices a swirling maelstrom of Numidians battling with the velites in the rear lines, with a wriggling black lump lying in the middle of the Roman defenders. *What are they fighting over? Is that one of our men on the ground?*

He squints his eyes and trots his horse forward, watching the fight. He discerns it is a Numidian lying on the ground, wrapped in chains. A bushy-bearded man with silver armor and a gold diadem on his helmet. Laelius' mouth falls open. *My gods, they have him!*

"With me, all of you, with me!" he screams, and kicks his horse forward.

Laelius' stallion breasts its way through a sea of battling bodies, trampling heedlessly over the wounded and dead. His cavalry and infantry scramble after him.

Laelius swings his falcata with all the coordinated might of his wrestler's body, cleaving the heads and shoulders of any who stand in his way. He pulls up next to Syphax and leaps off his horse, running over to the captive king. He pulls Syphax up from the ground.

"Well, I am certainly surprised to see you here," Laelius says. "But I am delighted, nonetheless!"

Syphax glowers at him. "My men will have your head for this!"

"All of you, circle about me." Laelius commands. The legionnaires form a thick circle of defenders around the two men. Standing shield to shield, they batter away the Numidian guards.

The Numidian infantry have watched their king dragged away, and their disheartened lines quickly disintegrate. The untrained foot soldiers run from the Romans, screaming about the capture of their king. Soon Syphax' entire army is in flight, leaving five thousand dead upon the field.

Masinissa's tribesmen set after them, leaving hundreds more strewn along the path of flight.

With the battle won, the Romans set about the grim task of rescuing their wounded from the piles of enemy dead. The legionnaires bandage their men on the spot and carry them out on litters, taking them to the improvised medical tents at the rear lines.

Cursing and weeping, the soldiers pause to dispatch their own comrades, men so maimed and wounded that they beg for a quick and honorable end at a Roman soldier's hands. Most soldiers comply, but some do not have the courage. They beg a compatriot to do it for them.

As the velites finish their grim task, Masinissa rides over to join Laelius, who is dabbing at a cut on his chest. The Numidian gazes across the battle site, taking census of the dead.

"I confess, Roman, I think we might have lost this fight, had not you captured Syphax." Masinissa shakes his head. "He had so many horsemen out there. I have lost seventy tribesmen—seventy friends."

"Fortuna has smiled upon us, as she often does to the brave," says Laelius. "I hear his horse was felled with a lucky shot from the back ranks, [lxxxi] as if Jupiter himself had sent a thunderbolt at him."

He smiles tightly. "Your kingdom is in your hands now, friend. Tomorrow we will complete its taking."

One of the equites rides up to Laelius, his face somber. "Commander, you should come with me. Sextus is asking for you."

Laelius sniffs. "Tell him to come over to me, I have another attack to plan."

The cavalryman's voice softens. "He cannot."

Laelius takes one look into the man's face and turns his horse about, following the equite to the rear lines.

He arrives at wide ring of centurions and tribunes, encircling a prone figure. Laelius dismounts and shoulders his way through the somber crowd.

In the center lies Sextus, holding his hand over a gash in the side of his neck. Laelius swallows hard, and kneels next to him. Sextus gapes at Laelius from fear-glazed eyes, the ground pooled red beneath his head.

Laelius looks at a tribune kneeling next to him, his eyes questioning. "He took a spear to the backside of his neck, after he was knocked from his horse." The tribune clenches Laelius' forearm. "He cannot move his legs or arms."

Laelius bends over and peers into Sextus' eyes, willing a smile to his face. "I am here, friend. The fight is all over! We have won a great battle! Can you get up now? We have to celebrate!"

Sextus grimaces, then laughs wetly. "Would that I could, Commander. If for no other reason than to kick that Numidian king bastard in the ass for betraying us to the Carthaginians!"

Laelius summons all his will and forces a hollow laugh. "Well, maybe I can prop you up and we can hobble over there. You can give him your foot before we ship him out to Rome!" Laelius reaches down to grasp Sextus' broad calloused palm. *My gods, it is like squeezing a piece of cold meat.*

Sextus' face contorts in a rictus of pain, his eyes clenched shut. He forces them open and smiles weakly. "Commander, my time here is done. I can but end it my way—as a soldier."

His watery eyes stare hopefully at Laelius. "I don't want to lie helpless in a bed. Will you do it for me?"

Laelius feels his heart hammering against his chest. Bile rises to his throat. *Steady, boy. He needs you.* He swallows. "You want me to..." he pauses, afraid to say the words.

Sextus nods. "Iuglatio. Please."

Laelius looks desperately about, suddenly a scared boy. He sees only grim and pitying faces. Faces that tell him this horrific task must be his. He staunches his rising gorge.

"Lift him up," he orders, not trusting his own arms. Two tribunes bend over and lift Sextus to a sitting position. They remove the top of his armor, gently unbuckling each strap.

Sextus' breath comes shallow and quick. Fear races across his ravaged face. "Please, quickly." he mutters. The men hear a gurgling beneath

Sextus, and look to see he has soiled himself. "Quickly," he says again.

Laelius flashes out his sword. He steps behind Sextus and places the blade point at the join of his shoulder and neck. The sword quakes in his steely fingers.

Laelius takes a deep breath and grasps his falcata with both hands. "Aaaugh!" he shouts in sorrowed agony.

Laelius delves his sword through Sextus' upper back, driving it deep into his heart. Sextus eyes bulge with shock; blood geysers from his gaping mouth. His eyes glaze and he slumps, lifeless, into the tribunes' arms.

Laelius throws down the sword and stalks away, tears streaming down his face. He walks through his men, his eyes seeing nothing, back to the center of the erstwhile battle. Masinissa is standing there, holding a fresh horse. He is surrounded by a contingent of his Numidian fighters, mounted and ready to depart.

A downy-cheeked velite runs after Laelius. He lugs Laelius' falcata in his hands, its blade wiped clean. "Apologies, Commander. You left your sword."

"Get that fucking thing away from me," he chokes out. "I don't want to see it again." Laelius stumbles on, leaving the bewildered youth in his wake.

Laelius straightens his back as he approaches Masinissa, and solemnly waves at him. He can see the eagerness on the Numidian prince's face, his teeth flashing against his dark, sun-browned face. *He is happy with today's victory, as he should be. But how can I celebrate this? How can I celebrate anything in this fucking war?*

"Laelius! My men and I are ready to ride for Cirta, Syphax' capitol," says the Numidian king. He looks imploringly at Laelius. "I would bring Syphax with us, that we may show his people that he is truly vanquished.[lxxxii] It would prove that I am the victor, the rightful king." He waves over toward the legionnaires. "You and your men could follow me later, at your own pace."

Laelius blinks at him. "What? You want to take him with you?" He looks back at the knot of Romans he just left, and sees them carrying Sextus' covered body on a stick litter towards camp. A red cape covers the body, blotched with a darker hue.

His shoulders slump. "Yes, of course. Why not? Take him."

"You are well, friend?" Masinissa asks. He steps closer to Laelius.

"Go Masinissa, just do it," mutters Laelius distractedly. "Grasp your glory while life yet allows. I will send my cavalry along, after we take over Syphax' old camp." He looks back at the procession carrying Sextus' corpse. "After I name a new Master of Horse."

Masinissa's eyes probe Laelius' face. "What can I do for you?"

Laelius blusters up a grin. "Nothing, nothing," he replies, but he does not meet Masinissa's eyes.

There is a short silence between them, as Masinissa waits for more.

"Very well," the prince finally says. "I shall see you in western Numidia, at Cirta. I hope Sophonisba is there so you can meet her."

The regal young prince suddenly steps forward and embraces Laelius, clutching him to his breast. Laelius shudders for a moment, stifling a sob. He raises his head and kisses Masinissa's cheek. Then he pulls back, staring at the ground, waving Masinissa away.

"Fare thee well, my friend," Laelius says his voice indicating it is more an order than a goodbye.

With a final wave the Numidian jumps onto his pony and trots from the charnel fields, his lean warriors following. Laelius watches him go, standing silently while the prince fades from view.

"Gather the officers at my tent tonight," says Laelius to one of his senior tribunes. "Tomorrow we destroy what's left of Syphax' camp— and any who remain there. Then we march on to Cirta." He smiles wearily. "Tell the men they fought gloriously today."

The veteran officer nods. "Gratitude, Legate. They will happy to hear that." He looks awkwardly at his commander. "You know, they very much appreciate having you as commander. Your humor and laughter have sustained them throughout this tedious march."

Laelius laughs bitterly. "Laughter? My days as a clown are gone, Tribune, and so is my humor. Perhaps it will return in Rome, should we ever get there again."

Laelius remounts his borrowed horse and trots from the battlefield, heading for a verdant stream he saw by the foothills. His men watch him go. They know not to follow.

*   *   *   *   *

ROME, 203 BCE. The mile-long funeral procession gradually wends its way from the Verrocusus manse toward the Forum square. Thousands of mourners fill Rome's main streets. Rome has lost its beloved old general, Fabius Maximus Verrocusus—the famed Cunctuator that was the scion of the revered Fabia family.

Nobles and commoners alike are thunderstruck at his sudden passing. Though increasingly feeble with age he nevertheless had not taken a sick day from the Senate in years, a man who could still deliver an extended oration when the mood came upon him. Now he is gone, struck down by some mysterious malady, his slaves finding him dead in his bed.

The Romans file into the Forum, there to listen to Fabius' good friend Flaccus deliver the funeral eulogy from the top of the Senate steps. Flaccus praises Fabius as war hero who saved Rome with his brilliant delaying strategy, hounding Hannibal on the march while refusing to do battle. Flaccus lauds Fabius' stern resolve to maintain a traditionally ascetic lifestyle. Several lissome prostitutes to chuckle under their breath and smile knowingly at one another.

When Flaccus finishes, the honor guard places the funeral pallet on their shoulders and carries the old general's body out the city gates to the cemetery, taking it to the front of the house-sized family tomb. The old man's draped body is carefully lifted onto a rectangular pyre of tree limbs. After the priests sacrifice a sow to the gods, a lit torch is touched to Fabius' pyre.

The citizens sing a funeral song while the flames flicker up towards the late summer sun, their voices blending with tubas and trumpets playing their mournful notes. When the flames die down, the citizenry tramps back to the city, leaving Fabius' family to collect his ashes in a marble urn and store them in the elegant tomb of the Fabii.

Pomponia and Amelia trudge along the edge of the crowd, moving slowly because Amelia is heavy with child. "I will miss the old bastard," Pomponia comments. "He at least had a sense of morality and duty, unlike that slippery Flaccus."

Amelia stops for a minute, grimacing as she pushes at her lower back. She raises herself upright.

"We should have taken a carriage," Pomponia says. "You are nine months heavy with child."

Amelia smiles. "I am fine, I just have a tendency to stoop nowadays. You know, I still do not understand his death. They say Fabius was at the Roman baths just the day before he died, wrestling about with some of the boys. And then he dies overnight? He must have displeased one of the gods."

"Perhaps the strain of wrestling was too great," Pomponia answers. "But it is odd. They say his face had a sickly, contorted appearance to it, as if some dread disease had suddenly seized him." She looks about to make sure they are not overheard. "Or perhaps he had some help in sending him on his journey."

Amelia looks puzzled. "Who would do such a thing? Even those who disagreed with his politics respected his service to Rome. And he ... oh, oh!" Amelia doubles over, grasping her belly. There is a trickling sound, and a tiny puddle appears beneath her feet.

"The baby is coming," she gasps. "It's coming!"

Pomponia whirls to her female slaves. "Fetch a litter! I don't care if you have to steal one, go get it!" She points her finger at two girl slaves. "You! Bring the midwife to my house. And you, prepare the birthing chair, see that the opening in the bottom is clean, and there is fresh linen below the hole. Go!" Pomponia's slaves scatter to their tasks as she bends to help her daughter-in-law.

Amelia waves her off and straightens up, her face set. She takes a deep breath and walks on. "I am fine, Mother," she says firmly. "I will make it to your house."

"I know you will," Pomponia consoles, knowing her daughter in law can be as stubborn as a mule. "But just in case you need it, the litter will be here soon." Pomponia puts her arm lightly around Amelia's waist. The two shuffle toward the nearby Scipio domus. Each prays to Lucina, the goddess of childbirth, that the baby will wait until they get home.

Pomponia guides Amelia down a side street shortcut that leads directly to the front door of her manse. They enter the sideway and walk quickly toward the bustling main street visible at its end.

A cloaked man steps in behind them, softly padding toward the distracted women. When Pomponia looks warily over her shoulder, he ducks into an alleyway off the narrow street.

Pomponia turns back to Amelia, and the figure tiptoes closer to them. He reaches into his gray robe and pulls out a long-bladed sica, dangling the dagger near his cloaked hip. He draws close to Pomponia's back, and raises the dagger in his clenched fist.

Two of Pomponia's male slaves appear at the end of the street, carrying a wicker litter from the Scipio home.

"Over here!" Pomponia calls, and the men trot over to her. The sicarius dissolves into another alleyway, softly cursing his luck.

Amelia waves the litter away. "I am fine." She doubles over for a minute, gasping, then pushes herself upright and staggers on, her eyes fixed on the twin blue doors of the Scipio manse.

Pomponia grins wryly. "The haruspex said you would have a daughter, eh? If she has half your resolve, she will make her mark in history!"

Amelia grimaces a smile and picks up her pace. The party enters the domus. Minutes later, an indigo-robed midwife hurries in. She quickly unpacks her birthing potions of hyena loin, sow dung, and goose semen. [lxxxiii] The thick doors boom shut behind her.

The sicarius pulls his beggars' cloak over his head and shuffles toward the Scipio house, moving with the gait of an elderly crippled beggar. He plops himself near the Scipio doors, his hand stretched out for alms.

Dusk's angular shadows creep down the street, harbinger of the nightfall. The bustling street quiets. The silence is broken by the cry of an infant, heartily announcing its entry into the world.

The Scipio doors fly open and Rufus struts into the street. The ancient red-headed slave cups his hands to his mouth. "A child is born to the Scipio family!" he shouts, drawing looks from the few passersby who are down the street. "It is a beautiful girl child! All is well!"

Rufus starts to step back into the house when he spies the crumpled beggar squatting by the doors. "You there, away with you! You are bad luck for this day!"

The stocky old slave glowers at the hooded figure who sits completely still, as if deciding his next move. The beggar slowly rises and shuffles away, glaring back at the old man.

The old slave walks back into the house. He does not see the man suddenly straighten upright and leap agilely into the side street from which he came, there to resume his vigil.

*   *   *   *   *

CASTRA CORNELIA, 203 BCE. Scipio stoops over the unmoving figure of Marcus Silenus, his brow furrowed with concern.

"Is there is nothing more you can do for him?" he asks the Greek medicus. "He has been immersed in the sleep of death for several weeks." He glowers at the old man. "Why in Olympus did it take you so long to get here?"

"The seas were rough, and the Carthaginians were out patrolling again," the old man replies peevishly. "Besides, there is little I can do. Corruption has set inside him. It is amazing he still clings to a thread of life." He sees the disappointment on Scipio's face and flaps his hands. "But this is Marcus Silenus we are talking about, the man Mars favors above all others. Perhaps the war god will intervene."

Scipio recalls the haruspex' prediction at the augury back in Rome, that two loved ones would die for his cause. *Laelius is still out there, somewhere. And Marcus is almost dead.*

Scipio feels his right hand begin to shake. *Was the boy right? Will I lose my best friends to my ambitions? I was a fool to think I could conquer Africa.*

"You must do something," Scipio blurts, his hand clenching the pommel of his sword. "You cannot just let him die!"

The wizened old man blinks at Scipio, taken aback at his fury. He glares at Scipio, angry with himself for being cowed.

"Very well, General. You are known as a man of risks." The Greek looks into Scipio's demanding eyes. "There is a new poultice I have made. I have not tried it on serious wounds, although it has been efficacious on minor cuts. I don't know what it would do."

He runs his finger along Marcus' back. "I would have to cut him open back here, where the blade entered."

"His wound has just healed!" Scipio exclaims, "It has finally closed."

The medicus sniffs. "It is a pustulent, suppurating mess, that is what it is!" He pulls out his bronze scalpel and a small flesh hook, brandishing them as though they are weapons. "And I will cut out all that corruption while I'm back there."

He considers Marcus' inert body, gazing at his colorless skin. His left hand reaches over to still his shaking right arm.

"His spirit will depart soon. You must decide."

Scipio's eyes moisten. He studies the chalk-white face of Rome's finest soldier. *He would not want to go out without a battle. I can at least give him that.*

"Do what you must," Scipio says. "Just give him a chance."

The Greek doctor nods. "Fetch me a flagon of your strongest wine," he says.

Scipio barks an order. Within minutes a centurion appears with a squat bronze pitcher.

"This would get the gods drunk," the soldier comments wryly, before he departs.

The medicus gestures for his two slave attendants to follow him to the bed. They roll Marcus onto his stomach.

Marcus groans faintly, and his eyes momentarily flutter open. He sees Scipio and the doctor and feebly raises his hand, trying to speak. His hand falls and he lapses back into unconsciousness.

Scipio feels the tears start from his eyes.

The medicus unrolls a spotless linen bandage and places his raft of surgical tools upon it. He pours out a cup of wine and douses Marcus' lower back with it, cascading it upon the wound. Marcus' body spasms, but he is silent. The medicus fills the cup again and drains the rest in a single swallow. He smacks his lips appreciatively as Scipio glowers at him.

"Get on with it," Scipio commands. "I'll burn you alive if you take another drink!"

The medicus grabs one of his scalpels and begins cutting off the gray-green lips of flesh that surround Marcus' back wound, humming softly to himself. "Mix me that poultice," he orders his attendant. "Use willow, garlic, gentian, and aloe. Twice the aloe as usual."

Tired of watching helplessly, Scipio exits his command tent. He finds several hundred legionnaires surrounding it, anxiously waiting for news about their revered commander.

Cato paces about in front of them, his seamed face bearing his usual expression of disgust. "You brought in one of those evil doctors!" [lxxxiv] Cato fumes. "And a Greek one besides! Likely another decadent who takes it in the ass! Rome is not paying for your medicus, I tell you now!"

Scipio rubs the tears from his eyes and looks at the vinegary little auditor. He balls his fist and begins to draw it back. *You could be tried for hitting a fellow officer. Send him back to Rome.*

Scipio relaxes his hand. *He's lucky Laelius is not here to hear this, he would beat him to death and laugh while he did it.*

"I will pay for the medicus, Quaestor. Now get out of my sight."

He turns to the gathered legionnaires. "Marcus is somewhere between our world and Hades. But the doctor is trying to bring him back to us. If anything changes, you will know soon as I do. Now return to your duties."

The soldiers walk off, many heading toward the camp altar to give sacrifice and prayer. Praxis steps next to Scipio.

"If it please you, General, I will personally stand guard over Marcus tonight, in case he should awaken or need assistance."

Something in his guard's tone gives Scipio pause. *He seems very eager to watch him.*

"That is much appreciated, Praxis. But I want three of you there, at all times."

"Of course, whatever your wish," says Praxis.

Scipio walks to the small tent adjoining his praetorium. "Wake me if anything happens," Scipio says. The general crawls inside, his mind still turning over the haruspex' prediction about two deaths.

Praxis and two other guards walk to the front of the command tent and resume their watch. They listen to the medicus working inside Scipio's command tent, muttering and cursing.

Several hours later a tunic-clad Scipio returns to his command tent, anxious to check on Marcus. He sees him laying quietly, his face peaceful. Scipio glances hopefully at the doctor. The old Greek is carefully wrapping his tools in linen and placing them in his doctor's pouch. His slaves gather up the remnants of the herbs and plants they mashed together for Marcus' poultice.

"How is he?" asks Scipio.

The Greek frowns, and shakes his head. "His wound is clean now. He seems a little stronger, but only the gods know his fate. He did wake twice and show some awareness, but then off he went!"

The medicus scrabbles about the bloody bandages underneath Marcus' back. "Where did I put that other scalpel? Mm. No matter, it is not where he would roll onto it."

The Greek picks up his bundle of implements and stalks toward the exit. "I am for some wine and sleep. My slaves will sit watch with him tonight, they will alert me if there is any change to his condition." He eyes Scipio's drawn face. "And I will alert you, General. You should get some rest now."

"I will be in that tent over there," says Scipio. "Wake me if there is the slightest change."

Scipio takes a final look at his friend and exits his praetorium. He strolls about the camp, drawing the cool night air deep inside him. *Will both of them die? What will I do then?*

Scipio notices a shadowy figure is walking behind him. He stops, his hand resting lightly on his dagger. "Come here near the torch," he orders.

A thin young man materializes from the shadows, grinning nervously. "Apologies, General. I know it is late, but I was to give you this message as soon as you awoke." Scipio waves the boy forward. He takes the papyrus scroll from him and sighs.

"I was told it is good news!" the messenger says consolingly.

"Humph! Most news is good for one person yet bad for another," Scipio grouses. *By the gods,* he thinks, *I'm beginning to sound like Cato!*

Scipio breaks the seal and scans its three lines. He looks heavenward and smiles. "I am a father! A father to a girl child!"

Scipio hugs the amazed young legionnaire, whose eyes bulge with confusion and alarm. The messenger awkwardly pats his general's back, then jerks his hand away as if he has committed a sacrilege.

Scipio releases him and laughs. "I did not mean to cause you discomfort. You have brought me the best news I've had since leaving Rome," Scipio says. "Go in peace, boy."

The messenger bobs his head and trots off, eager to tell others of his encounter with the great Scipio.

Scipio slaps the scroll against his hip as he walks on, his step jaunty. *Cornelia, we were to call her Cornelia. And Amelia is fine, thank the Gods.*

Then he stops. *Marcus and Laelius are still in jeopardy, though. He shakes his head. You pay too much attention to a young priest's meanderings.*

As dawn approaches, Praxis steps softly into Scipio's command tent. For hours he has surreptitiously peered inside it, watching the medicus' attendants, waiting for them to fall asleep. His bored fellow guards have just left for the latrine. He realizes he has a rare opportunity to finish his task.

Praxis steps softly past the snoring slaves. He pauses over Marcus Silenus' silent body, listening to his ragged breaths.

The assassin withdraws a small glass bottle from his belt purse. He uncorks the bottle and sniffs its colorless contents. The odor makes his head jerk back. *It smells as potent as the herbalist said it was. Two drops should do it.* Praxis bends over Marcus and puts the bottle to the commander's open mouth.

Praxis jerks his head back, howling in anguish. He clutches at the side of his head as he plunges to the ground, screaming in pain.

The slaves scramble up and look woozily about the tent. They see Praxis convulsing on the ground, the muscular gladiator mewling like a babe. Blood streams from his left ear hole, flowing around the scalpel that has been jammed there to the hilt.

The two Honor Guards barge through the tent flaps, swords bared. They raise their weapons at the cowering slaves.

"Leave them alone," rasps a voice. They see Marcus Silenus leaning on his elbow, looking at the guards with bleary yellowed eyes.

"He is an assassin," Marcus mumbles. He stares at Praxis' still form. "*Was* an assassin."

With that, he collapses onto his sleeping mat, breathing stentoriously.

"Master, Master!" the slaves cry. as they run from the tent, past the stunned guards. "He is alive!"

*　　*　　*　　*　　*

CARTHAGE, 203 BCE. "He is dead," Salicar reminds the Senate.

"Gisgo is dead by his own hand and Syphax is captured. Their armies are destroyed." The senior senator spreads his hands beseechingly. "What choice do we have but to surrender?"

"Be not so hasty, Salicar," booms Danel, a veteran senator from the Barcid family. "We pillaged Scipio's ships at Utica and captured many of his transports, with few losses on our side."

The portly senator draws himself fully upright and continues. "The Romans should be worried about us, not the other way around." He sweeps his hand toward the Bay of Carthage. "Our navy can hold Scipio at bay until Hannibal arrives and destroys this soft-handed patrician."

Danel snorts theatrically. "I hear the young man is more student than warrior, always poking his nose into scrolls and tablets."

"As Hannibal himself does," Salicar replies. "They learn from their predecessors and their enemies. That is what makes them both so dangerous."

"Scipio is not the measure of Hannibal, the destroyer of all he opposes," Danel retorts. "And his brother Mago has taken his own toll of Roman armies! You are all too fearful of this boy. When the Barca brothers return, Rome will sue *us* for peace!"

Salicar raises his eyes heavenward, weary of the same arguments from the same factions. *The Barcas would risk our empire to gain honor. What price glory to them?*

Mintho stands up. The young senator rarely speaks, but the other senators heed his opinion, knowing it reflects the wealthy and powerful merchant class he represents.

"Scipio has taken every town and garrison around Carthage." He says, his voice echoing his frustration. "He has us surrounded! You talk of our Navy stopping him? He has all his warships intact, and he still controls most of the shipping lanes."

"We have our own warships out there," Danel growls. "And Carthage is impregnable. He cannot win!"

Dozens of senators mutter their agreement, but Mintho is undaunted.

"Yes, our walls are sturdy and our food stores are vast. But we cannot do business with the rest of the world, and he has plundered the wealth from our outlying towns. This Scipio, he is draining our economy. We do not have enough money to hire soldiers and defend ourselves. He does not have to breach our walls to win, he will starve us out—by starving our finances!"

Salicar watches in amazed delight as scores of senators rise and raise their fists skyward, shouting down Mintho's dissenters. *By Baal's balls, I have underestimated that boy.*

The elder senator knows the time is ripe to quell the Barcid clan once and for all. He steps to the center of the chamber, a prerogative of the eldest members. "Let us hear no more talk of war, or conquest.[lxxxv] Our primary objective is to protect the realm from destruction!"

Salicar walks across the front row of senators, looking them in the eye. "My friends, we cannot wait for our peace envoys to return from Rome. That may take months, now that the winter winds have come. We must go to Scipio himself and sue for peace. And I will be the first to go!"

Most cheer Salicar's proposal, but one-armed Balon Barca waves his hand back and forth, as if wiping Salicar's suggestion from the air.

"I see that this capitulation cannot be avoided," he sneers. "Very well, mighty Carthage will prostrate itself in front of Scipio and beg him for peace. But we need a wider representation of interests than Salicar. I propose we send the inner circle of our Council of Elders, all thirty of them." [lxxxvi]

Salicar looks about him, and sees that most of the Senators are nodding their agreement. "I think that is a fine idea," he says resignedly.

The Senate votes that the Council of Elders will leave immediately to sue Scipio for peace. After approving additional funds to reinforce the city's defenses, the Senate concludes for the day.

Several senators hurry over to Salicar and congratulate him on securing his bid for peace, but Salicar is not happy. *There are four Barcas in our inner circle, they may become difficult during negotiations.* Salicar joins Mintho after the senators have dispersed, and the two exit the Senate chambers.

As they step down the hundred steps to the forum square, Salicar puts his arm around Mintho's shoulders. "You were very impressive today," he says warmly. "I would not believe you could sway some of those crusty old men with such a short speech."

Mintho grins widely. "Well, perhaps it was the power of my words. Perhaps it was the well-placed 'gifts' my merchant friends gave to five of the Barca sympathizers!"

Salicar halts in his tracks, staring at his protégé. Mintho wrinkles his nose reproachfully. "What? You did not think I knew the way of politics?" He laughs. "I swear to Baal, for a wise man you are sometimes naive."

"You bought votes?" Salicar asks.

"I bought peace," Minto replies, a sardonic grin on his face. "And Scipio is the best Roman to grant it. He is an educated man, I believe he will be merciful."

Salicar chuckles. "It will likely be a Roman's version of 'mercy', nonetheless."

"He will likely insist we disband our military," Mintho replies, "But he would be willing to preserve our culture, I am sure of it. And Carthage will become wealthy again, because we will not have to pay for an army—Rome won't allow us to have one! What else could you want?"

I would want conquest, Salicar thinks. *Rome will not rest until we are gone.*

*   *   *   *   *

CIRTA, NUMIDIA 203 BCE. The golden eagle glides into its nest at the top of the towering mountain pine, its viselike beak carrying a fresh rabbit for her downy white hatchlings. Latching her powerful talons onto the branch, the mother tears off rabbit flesh and carefully feeds it to her cheeping charges.

Every time she drops a scrap of meat into an eaglet's gaping maw, the eagle darts her head about for danger. She scrutinizes the arid plains and turquoise coast below, her yellow-green eyes seeing everything.

There is no danger to her family. She has wisely chosen a tree near the thirty-foot walls of Cirta, atop a rugged granite pinnacle two thousand feet above the Mediterranean. The locale is so busy with human traffic that even the cheetahs and wild dogs avoid it. For centuries, Cirta has had few predators challenge it, be they man or beast.

Two wall sentries lean over the ramparts and watch the regal bird, enraptured. "She's as big as a dog," comments the first guard, an older man with a beard as large as his head. "Even bigger," the other replies, a boy barely into his teens. "She could carry off a dog, maybe even one of those kids down there."

The older sentry watches a dozen small children playing in front of the open gates. The tots roll a camel's-hair ball about with their forked sticks, chirping with laughter. "Nah, they're too big. Not the right size."

"You mean they are lion size rather than eagle size," the other quips, and they laugh.

"Here now, look over there!" the first sentry says, staring over the wall. "See those little bumps out there on the plain? Looks like old Syphax is coming back from the war."

The younger one peers out, straining his ice-blue eyes. "Those aren't just Numidians, old man. Those are Roman standards behind them, from what my father told me."

The veteran laughs. "Now what would Romans be doing up here? We haven't seen any since that Scipio fellow came to dine with Syphax. And they're our enemies now."

"I see what I see, and what you can't see. I'm calling the captain of the guard."

The young man clambers down the oak staircase and runs over to a limestone blockhouse that squats in the town square. Minutes later the muscular old captain hurries out from headquarters and up the staircase, peering over the edge of the wall.

"Looks like Romans, all right," the captain says. "Look at the bronze breastplate armor, and those helmet plumes. But those are Numidians with them."

The older sentry gapes. "Masinissa! It must be the rebel prince, come to conquer us!"

"We don't have enough men here," the young sentry whines. "They all went with Syphax." He brightens. "Perhaps our king made another truce with the Romans?"

The captain laughs. "After backing out of the last one? And all for the sake of some Carthaginian pussy? I think the only conciliation he'd get from Scipio is to choose the kind of wood he wants on his cross!"

The older sentry continues to watch the oncoming forces. "They don't act like they're coming to fight," he says. "They're riding in as a loose group, even those tight-assed Romans."

"Whatever their purpose, it's time to notify the town council." The captain clatters down the stairway. Soon the city horns are blowing the alarm. The children rush inside and the thick oak gates boom shut behind them.

Masinissa approaches the front entry with a squadron of his Numidians. The rest of the cavalry wait behind, barely a spear's throw from the prince.

The town council members pop their heads up above the gates. They are a quartet of portly older men with green linen robes, their gray beards laced with golden threads. They stare down at the immobile prince, waiting for him to say something. Soon, the walls are ringed with the people of Cirta, who watch apprehensively as Masinissa slowly draws nearer to the gates.

The Numidian prince raises empty hands above his head, showing he comes in peace. "I am Masinissa, Prince of the Massylii!" he shouts up to the leaders. "Surrender Cirta and none will be hurt."

The stoutest councilman hoots at him. "You think your puny band can breach our mighty walls? Out of respect for your father, I tell you to depart now, before Syphax returns and cuts off your head!" The other council members nod in agreement.

"His wrath will be fearsome," adds another, "and those ox-footed Romans will not save you. Go back to your caves and mate with your goats!" The council members laugh heartily, gathering courage from each other's' bravado.

Masinissa crooks an eyebrow at the portly politicians. He waves back at the rear lines.

"Bring him forward!" Masinissa orders. He turns back to the council members, a roguish smile upon his face. "I fear I have waited too long to retreat. Syphax is here!"

While the Cirta rulers watch, two Numidians lead a swaybacked old horse forward, bearing a slumped figure atop it. A disheveled Syphax stares up at the Cirta leaders. His hands are bound in chains, his bruised face discolored and puffy.

"Is this who you were waiting for?" Masinissa asks.

The townsmen's mouths drop open. They stare at each other. "Give us a bit of time to converse, Prince," the portliest man manages to say.

Masinissa bows deeply. "Why, of course! But do not tarry in your response." He points behind him. "My Roman friends are eager to destroy this town so they can return to their camp. They will do what I say, but I fear I cannot detain them much longer!"

The rulers disappear from the walls. Many of the townspeople hustle down the steps to their families, thinking how they can hide them from the cannibalistic Romans.

Syphax looks sideways at Masinissa. "You know this is my capitol. You're a fool if you think they will surrender to you. Or that you can take these walls."

There is a furious clattering and shouting behind the town gates, followed by the thumps of bodies being rammed against it. "Get them out of the way!" someone yells. Masinissa grins at Syphax.

There is the loud scraping of wooden bars being slid from their braces. The city gates are flung open. Masinissa and his men calmly trot inside. [lxxxvii] The Roman cavalry soon follow.

Masinissa's men lock Syphax into a blockhouse and surround it. Masinissa and his guards enter Syphax' grand palace.

Sophonisba peers out from her chamber above the palace entry, curious about the clamor. She sees Masinissa riding into the town square, with her husband in tow. Her heart leaps to her throat. *Oh my gods, he is here! He has come back to me, just as he promised!*

Sophonisba grows dizzy. She grasps the thick oak sill with her long fingers. *Steady. Do not fall to your death when you are so near your heart's desire.*

A Masaesyli guard appears, his hand on the pommel of his long curved sword. "My queen, it sorrows my heart to tell you: your husband has been captured by Masinissa. The city has surrendered to him."

Sophonisba's heart leaps with joy, but she knows she must play her role as Syphax' dutiful wife. Were Carthage to find out that she had betrayed them to the hated Romans, the Gisgon name would be forever disgraced, and her entire family put to the cross. She especially fears the wrath of the Romans, who have been known to humiliate captured enemy royalty before submitting them to an ignominious death or enslavement.

She knows that General Scipio appeared to be a man of kindness and respect when he visited her husband. But Scipio is still a Roman, and Syphax has told her of his brutality at Carthago Nova, Astapa, and

Locri. *I will not be humiliated by the men who destroyed my father*, she resolves.

"Yes, I saw that rebel, dragging in my king like a common beggar." She tosses her hair back and raises her chin high, the picture of anguished determination. "My heart breaks at the sight of him in chains. But I am Queen of Numidia, and I must do what is best for our people. Come with me."

Sophonisba motions for an attending slave to lace up her sandals. She hurries out the door, her six guards following her down the wide marble steps of the palace.

Masinissa enters the palace vestibule. Sophonisba rushes out to meet him. [lxxxviii] The Prince is flanked by his men and the town rulers, and he knows he must act like his beloved is an enemy, though his arms ache to enfold her.

Sophonisba flings herself at his knees and clutches them to her cheek. "The gods, and your own valor and good fortune, have seen that you have absolute power over us. I beg you, by the gods who preside over this palace, that you grant me a favor."

Masinissa takes her hand, willing himself to appear unconcerned, and raises her from the ground. "If it be in my power, my queen, I would grant it to you," he says, his voice quivering with repressed emotion.

"Had I been no more than Syphax' wife I would still prefer to rely on the honor of a Numidian, a fellow African, rather than that of a man born overseas. But you can understand what a daughter of General Gisgo has to fear from a Roman." She clutches his forearm. "I earnestly entreat you to save me from falling under the control of the Romans by letting me die now!" [lxxxix]

Masinissa's heart flutters with anxiety at these words. *Be calm. She is playing the role.* "You say you will rely on my judgment as a fellow African? Will you accept my decree, whatever it be?"

She bows her head. "I am under your power, Prince Masinissa."

Masinissa swallows. *There is only one way you can protect her from being dragged to Rome.* He faces the gathering. "It is time to unite our tribes. I would bind our two countries together in marriage, and bring peace to Numidia."

He points down at Sophonisba, his face stern. "I decree that you marry me." He gestures imperiously the steps she descended. "Return to your chambers, Queen Sophonisba. We shall be married tonight." [xc]

In later years, those watching Sophonisba tell of how she cried heavy tears when she heard the Prince's commands, anguished that she would be separated from her husband Syphax and wed to his enemy. They had no inkling that they were tears of joy, as the two lovers finally achieved their dream of being together, after years of being so hopelessly apart.

Sophonisba plods up the stairs to her chambers, dismissing her staff and leaving her guards outside the door. Once inside, she dances about the chamber. She flings open her trunks and pulls out her finest raiment, anxious to select her best gown as her wedding dress.

Sophonisba grabs her vial of poison and rushes to one of her chamber windows. She cocks her arm and flings it out to the towers below, where it shatters upon a roof.

"I will not be needing you now, my little friend," she declaims to the splotch below her.

Several days later, Laelius and his army arrive at Cirta, ready to celebrate his friend's bloodless triumph. Masinissa rises from his marriage bed and repairs to the throne room. He finds an angry Laelius waiting for him.

"Is it true?" Laelius shouts, the spit flying from his mouth. "Did you have the temerity to wed our enemy's wife? The woman who is a captive of Rome? Are you mad?"

Masinissa glowers at him. "You know my feelings for her. I was seeking to protect her from Roman enslavement. It is the one wish she asked of me, in return for all her services to us."

Laelius draws his sword. "Protect her? By all rights she should be taken back to Rome with her husband! Scipio's enemies will feast on this!" He starts for the stairs to her chambers. "I am tempted to drag her off that marriage couch myself and send her to Scipio." [xci]

Rage and fear fill Masinissa's heart. He whips out his sword and bares it at his friend, his hand quavering so hard the blade dances before him. "I cannot permit you to do that. Do not force my blade, I beg you!"

Laelius draws his gladius. His four guards step toward Masinissa, but he waves them off. He stares at Masinissa, thinking of his friend Sextus lying immobile, begging for death at his own' hand. He remembers how his trembling fists clenched the sword hilt, plunging it down, trying with all his might to pierce deep into Sextus' heart. *I cannot kill another friend. I cannot.*

Laelius sheaths his sword. "Two days hence," he says, looking away from Masinissa. "In two days we take Syphax back toward Castra Cornelia. We will exhibit him at the towns along the way to buy their capitulation." He looks sadly at his comrade. "I will grant you what pleasures you may find with her until then, Prince. Happiness is all too fleeting." *I curse you for making me do this to you.*

Masinissa sheaths his sword. "I accept. When we depart, please let me leave her here. She will not flee to Carthage."

Laelius nods. "She will be safe here—from your Numidians and my Romans." He raises his head and stares frankly into Masinissa's eyes. "I cannot promise what Scipio will do, once he discovers this betrayal."

* * * * *

CASTRA CORNELIA Marcus Silenus pushes himself upright from his sweaty sleeping mat in Scipio's command tent. *If I have to lay around anymore I will kill someone—or myself.*

Cursing his creaking knees, he pulls on his old military tunic, still dappled with bloodstains. He cinches his wide leather belt about his middle. *Where in Pluto are my sandals?* He scrabbles about until he finds them sticking out from under a pile of Scipio's scrolls.

Marcus laces his caligae about his feet and unrolls one of the papyrus rolls. He stares at a map of Macedonia from Alexander the Great's time, and sees Scipio's notes scrawled all over it. *Gods above, the man still acts like a schoolboy. Were he not a genius, I'd think him a fool.*

Marcus searches inside his goatskin pack bag hanging from the main tent pole. He grimaces with disappointment. *They took my sword, didn't even leave me a dagger. Did they think there would only be one assassin in camp?* With a grunt of disgust, the old warrior totters toward the tent's exit flaps.

A decanus steps in and blocks the exit. "You are not well enough to leave," the corporal says bluntly, his thick forearms crossed over his barreled chest.

Marcus fixes him with his baleful eyes. "Then I must prove to you that I am. Go ahead, try and stop me."

Marcus steps forward, his eyes fixed on the soldier's. His hands rest lightly at his sides but his fingers are splayed open, ready to grab. The decanus looks away. Marcus steps into him, his right hand effortlessly pushing him aside. *Well, that woke me up*, he thinks, as he steps out into the dawnlit camp.

The legate limps along a path that cuts through the endless rows of ten-foot long tents. He walks past the armorer's open air stalls, pausing to watch them hammering away at the orange-red gladius blades they drag out from their forges.

"Give them a good oil bath, they deserve it," Marcus says. "This new sword of Scipio's is a head-splitter."

Bored with watching their labors, he walks toward the open side gate. His walk changes to a march when he approaches the two guards standing by the gates. They quickly salute him, their eyes wide with surprise.

"Anything eventful last night?" Marcus inquires, as if he had never relinquished command.

One of the guards shrugs. "Only a drunken brawl between two centurions. Some teeth lost, that is all." The sentry sweeps his arm across the empty plain. "The scouts have not seen an enemy in days. There's no one left to fight!"

Marcus smiles thinly. "Soon, you will not be able to say that. Very soon."

He walks across the cleared plain outside of camp, heading toward a verdant stream that he noticed when he and Scipio first scouted this spot.

Minutes later, he hears the sound of babbling water. Marcus quickens his pace and pushes through the outlying plain grasses until he comes upon the rippling silver ribbon of a stream. For the first time in an eternity, Marcus smiles. He kneels into the rushes that line the frenetic little creek and cups his hand into the clear water, quaffing it as if it were nectar.

His thirst quenched, Marcus lowers himself onto a rounded boulder that is half immersed in the water, grunting with the effort. He fingers the green-throated stalks that undulate slowly in the morning breeze, enjoying the feel of their supple resistance. *I wonder how my crops are doing back home on the farm? I bet Prisca is watching the spring wheat come up.*

There is a tiny tapping sound behind him. With some effort he turns sideways and sees a tiny brown finch clattering on top of a creek boulder. The black-capped little bird totters on its feet. Its eyes are half closed, its feathers are rumpled and its huddled body shivers—clearly it is sick. Marcus watches the bird for a moment. He rises to a crouch and leans over, gently scooping up the bird with his man-killing hands.

Marcus eases back onto his seat, cupping the bird in his lap. The finch seems unalarmed with its change of location. Its tiny talons click faintly upon Marcus' hoary hands as it shifts about, pecking into his palm lines. Then it settles down, ruffling its feathers against a nonexistent cold, and closes its eyes. Marcus sits, immobile and expressionless, watching the shivering little bird. Morning creeps toward noon, and he

14427
27

74

continues his watch.

A young tribune stalks by, enjoying the glorious day. He stops near Marcus. An eager grin splits his face when he sees his commander holding the small bird. "What's that you have, sir? Have you caught yourself some breakfast?"

"Get the fuck out of here!" Marcus says, in a tone so menacing it sends the officer scurrying from the scene. The bird shivers, then squints its eyes. A tiny doot of shit appears on Marcus' calloused palm. He grins.

Soon Marcus again hears the crunching of caligaed feet. He turns with a glare that quickly vanishes when he sees it is Scipio himself, attired in cape and armor.

"What are you doing out here, Marcus?" Scipio asks softly, his voice full of concern. "The men say you have been out here for hours. They are afraid to come near you."

Marcus nods down at the bird, now lying on its side, its eyes mere slits.

"He shouldn't have to die alone," he says, his voice quavering. He looks back at the bird as if Scipio has vanished.

Scipio kneels next to his friend. He watches the two of them, saying nothing. Long minutes pass, as two of history's greatest warriors stand vigil. The sparrow shivers again. Its beak gapes and its tiny wings fall open.

The general sighs heavily. He looks into Marcus' face. "Come when you are ready," he replies.

Scipio walks away without looking back, hurrying to leave before Marcus betrays himself.

The old warrior sits a minute longer, breathing heavily, looking up at the sky. He rises and shovels out a tiny grave with his iron hands, and lays the finch inside. He pats the dirt mound until is it firm, carefully rounding its edges. He stands back and views it. *I hope it was a good life for you, little bird.*

Marcus turns and stalks purposefully back to camp, his shoulders straightening as he nears it.

There is tumult inside Castra Cornelia, with unarmed soldiers rushing toward the main gate. A Roman scout is there, pushing his horse through the crowd that has materialized to hear his news. Word has already spread that he has just returned from Laelius and Masinissa's army.

"What news, curse you, what news of the army?" barks an impatient centurion.

The scout raises his right fist skyward. "Victory, glorious victory! Now let me get to the General!" The scout does not have to wait long, for Scipio emerges from his command tent and trots toward the scout, eager for news of Laelius and Masinissa.

"What say you?" Scipio demands.

"Syphax' army is destroyed," the scout announces proudly. "He has been taken prisoner. The tribunes are bringing him to camp within the hour!"

"Where are Laelius and Masinissa?" Scipio demands. "What has happened to them?"

"Ap-apologies, General," the scout replies. Masinissa and Laelius were occupied with taking the garrison cities surrounding Cirta.[xcii] They will be here by dusk!"

Scipio's shoulders slump with relief. "I should be the one to apologize, I did not give you a chance to explain."

The scout nods self-consciously and pulls his horse toward the stables. Scipio turns to two of his tribunes. "Muster the men for a reception," he says eagerly. "Prepare our best wine and food. Tonight we celebrate!"

An hour later the tribunes arrive with their cohort of legionnaires. Syphax rides in the middle of them, his arms chained in front of him, a crown planted on his head to show onlookers that the Romans have caught a king. The camp soldiers cheer heartily when Syphax is dragged through the gates, as much for the upcoming feast as for his capture.

Scipio is there on his black stallion, clad in spotless formal armor, his blood-red cape flowing in the autumn wind. He sees Syphax covered with dirt and grimaces. *How far you have fallen. All you had to do was stay faithful to us.*

Scipio raises his right hand, speaking loudly enough that his men may hear him. "Greetings, King Syphax. Know that you will be safe from harm or insult here, on my honor."

Syphax raises his bedraggled head and manages a sarcastic smile. "You were ever a generous host to the defeated, General Scipio. I only wish I could have reciprocated your kindness, with you as my captive!"

Scipio chuckles, and shakes his head. *The old lion still roars, though he be in my cage.* "Get those chains off of him," Scipio orders. "Give him a bathing tub and proper clothing." Scipio returns to his tent, ashamed to see his former ally in such disgrace.

Later that afternoon, Syphax enters Scipio's tent. He wears an unadorned white tunic and Roman sandals, but he carries himself as though he is wearing robes of gold. Scipio wears a simple gray tunic bordered in purple. He motions Syphax to a reclining couch next to his.

"You are my guest here," Scipio says. "Albeit a guest with 'limited privileges,' shall we say."

He motions to a skinny local boy who is acting as his attendant. The youth brings a plate of olives, dates, olive oil and bread. The attendant pours wine into their cups and adds water to them. The two men recline on their couches and regard one another.

"I have only one question, King," Scipio says. "Why? After we signed a treaty to fight together, and Carthage lay before us. Why?"

Syphax waves his hands at Scipio. "I know, I know. You want to know why I did it." He shakes his cup for more wine. "Well, I can answer with one word: Sophonisba. Gisgo promised she would share my marriage bed if I joined forces with him. I could not refuse such beauty."

He drinks deeply of his refilled cup and glances defiantly at Scipio. "And I would do it again, though I know my kingdom would fall by doing it."

As Scipio ruminates over Syphax' words, the hawk-faced king reaches for a large dried fig and pops it all into his mouth. "You must excuse my greed. I have not had much in the way of good food for awhile, just dried cheese and grain." Syphax grabs for a flat speckled biscuit and bites into it.

Scipio watches him, a slight smile on his face.

Syphax chews the bread slowly, with loud crunches. He suddenly starts choking, and grabs for his wine goblet. Syphax quaffs deeply and drops the biscuit on the floor. "What in Ammon's name is that thing? It tastes like dust!"

"That was one of our famous buccelatum, my king," Scipio says, his eyes twinkling. "It's the army biscuit that all our men have, every day."

Scipio bites into one of the rock-hard salt biscuits, smiling with feigned pleasure. "All of us eat them. My men proudly call themselves the bucellarii, the 'biscuit soldiers.' "

"No wonder you Romans are so tough," Syphax exclaims, gesturing for more wine. "Your food accustoms you to serious deprivation!"

"At least we do not eat our horses," replies Scipio.

"Then you are missing a great delicacy," sniffs Syphax. "Roasted horse with pancakes is beyond compare. It was Sophonisba's favorite."

At mention of his wife's name, Syphax' eyes glow with anger. "I see it all now. Sophonisba, she is a seductive fiend. She resorted to all sorts of wheedling to turn my head and make me crazy, and to push me into battle and defeat." [xciii]

Syphax drinks deeply of his wine. He stares at Scipio. "Still, I have one consolation. I hear that she has passed into the arms of my greatest enemy—Masinissa. I could not wish for a better revenge."

He sees Scipio's look of dismay. "The gods be cursed, you are right to look concerned. Do you think she will not turn his head, as she did mine? You were a friend of mine, Scipio. I give you that warning as a final gift."

Scipio frowns. *If he speaks the truth, she endangers all our efforts. She could sway him back to Carthage's side.*

The two men are silent, each pondering the words left hanging in the air.

"What is to become of me?" Syphax finally says.

Scipio shrugs. "You know our traditions as well as I. You are part of my plunder. You will be led back to Rome with Sophonisba, because she is the queen."

Syphax laughs. "Ah, but she is not my wife now, is she? Masinissa married her! Laelius himself told me."

Scipio's mouth drops open. "He did truly take her to wife? And Laelius permitted it? What folly is this?"

"It is serious folly," replies Syphax. "I would say she somehow persuaded him to do it, to save her from being dragged to Rome." He cocks an eyebrow at Scipio. "And to keep her influence upon your precious little prince."

He laughs at Scipio, shaking his head. "My poor brilliant General Scipio, you have not had good luck with your Numidian allies, have you?"

Scipio feels a flush of embarrassment creeping up his neck. "Perhaps it is time for you to take your rest, King. You must be fresh for our victory celebration tonight." He smiles as he raises his cup. "You are, after all, the guest of honor."

Hours later Laelius and Masinissa breach a low rise by Castra Cornelia, leading in their cavalry and infantry. They find thousands of unarmored legionnaires arrayed below them on each side of the camp road. [xciv] The men cheer loudly as Laelius and his vanguard enter the space between their welcoming fellows. The two commanders wave and smile at the crowd, exulting as if Rome herself was giving them a triumph.

Scipio stands at the camp gates, looking like a father welcoming back two errant children. Laelius slides off his horse and hugs his childhood friend, who stiffly returns his embrace.

Laelius nods back toward Masinissa. "There he is, the future king of all Numidia! We have taken the surrender of a dozen towns and cities. They opened their gates once they learned that Syphax is ours. And now, Masinissa says he will..."

Scipio grabs Laelius' forearm, interrupting him. "Did he truly marry Syphax' wife?" he hisses. "What insanity is this? She is to be taken back to Rome with Syphax. They are both royal plunder!"

Laelius nods, shamefaced. "I know, I should have stopped him. But I was too late. And she is the love of his life."

Scipio snorts. "A war is no place to pursue infatuations. He has blundered seriously." He waves at the Numidian prince, beckoning him to descend from his horse.

"We will have a private discussion later, about this Sophonisba. But for now, you have to celebrate your victory." Scipio grimaces. "Quaestor Cato is already preparing a letter of complaint to Rome about the celebration's cost, so you know it will be lavish!"

Laelius shakes his head. "Good old Cato! It could be biscuits and vinegar, and he would still complain because we didn't serve sticks and water!" He claps Scipio on the shoulder and stalks off to bathe and dress.

That evening the camp is raucous with celebration. Food and wine are passed about liberally, with Masinissa's Numidians providing music from their bagpipes, oboes, and horns.

Scipio leads Masinissa and Laelius onto an improvised platform. He lauds the young commanders for their bravery and achievements, [xcv] paying particular attention to Masinissa. The Numidian prince is aglow with pride and happiness, and he embraces Scipio in a deep hug.

"Talk to me later in my tent," Scipio mutters into his ear.

Later that night, as music and laughter wafts through the air, Masinissa joins Scipio in his praetorium. Scipio dismisses his guards from the front of the tent, so he will not be overheard. When he is alone with Masinissa, he whirls to face him, his face flush with anger.

"Masinissa, I think it was because you saw some merit in me that you came to me initially, in Spain, to establish ties of friendship. But of those virtues for which you thought me worth seeking out, I would pride myself on none as much as my self-control and restraint. I wish, Masinissa, that you too could have added this quality to your other exceptional virtues." [xcvi]

Scipio walks over and picks up his black-plumed general's helmet, and holds it in front of Masinissa's face. "See this? I am a general, responsible for upholding Roman law! Syphax was defeated and taken prisoner under the auspices of the Roman people. By law, Syphax and his queen would have to be sent to Rome, even if the queen were not a Carthaginian citizen, and even if we did not discern in her father an enemy commander!" [xcvii]

Scipio places the helmet on the map table, his face softening, and puts his hand on Masinissa's shoulder. "I must follow our laws. To do otherwise would endanger our support from Rome. I am sworn to send Gisgo's daughter to Rome with her husband."

Masinissa bows his head, embarrassed. Tears well in his eyes. "I must abide by your decision, General. But I ask you to consider, I married her because I love her, I promised I would not let her fall into anyone else's hands." [xcviii]

Scipio steps back from his friend. He raises his chin, his face set. "You are to stay in camp with me. I will send some of our men to bring her here." He sighs. "I can at least give you a chance to see her before I send her away."

The words have barely left Scipio's mouth before Masinissa stalks from the tent. Scipio watches him go, then plunks down on a stool at his map table. He listlessly moves the cavalry and infantry figurines about, mixing Roman and enemy pieces together as a child might. Then he buries his face in his hands, trying to ignore to the revelry outside.

A half hour later, Marcus and Laelius enter the tent. Clad only in a cheetah loincloth and bone necklace, tipsy Laelius has a laurel victory wreath on his head. He nips from a bunch of maroon grapes, looking like a Numidian version of Bacchus, god of wine.

"You are not out celebrating," chides Laelius. "The men need to see you drinking with them, to bond them to you." He burps appreciatively. "Besides, that local wine is quite good. It was worth whatever you paid for it, though Cato looks as if he is shitting peach pits!"

Laelius clumsily sweeps his hand toward Marcus, who ducks his head and glares at him. "Why even this wounded old man was seen to down a cup or two of drink, though he be waiting for Pluto to lead him to Hades!"

Scipio shakes his head. "I am not of a mood for celebrating, though I am happy for you." He furrows his brows as Marcus. "Why are you on your feet? You are not well."

"I am well enough," Marcus states. "When you send Syphax and the rest to Rome, you can tell the Senate that I have resumed my duties as legate."

"They will be surprised," Scipio says. "As far as Rome knows, you are dead. I have kept your recovery a secret, so we can track down whoever hired Praxis to kill you. We have several of our best speculatores back there to spy on the Senate." He grins wryly. "Just in case one of our revered senators is prone to such mischief."

Laelius chuckles. "Ha! It would be more difficult to find one that is not!"

Marcus looks at Scipio, his eyes wide. "That means the person who hired this assassin may think I am dead." He looks away. "He may think he's free from those under my protection."

Scipio blinks at him. "So? You are worried about protecting someone back there?"

He has enough on his mind, Marcus thinks. "No, do not concern yourself. Just let them know that I am better. That I can still fight."

Scipio smiles at his friend. "That is good news, though I fear you overestimate your recovery. You will be needed, though. My informers say that Carthage has sent envoys to northern and southern Italia. Mago and Hannibal may soon be upon us."

Laelius walks over to a stool next to Scipio and drops onto it. He gazes blearily at the pieces. "You have the Roman and Carthaginian pieces mixed up together. Is this another of your revolutionary strategies?"

Scipio laughs, feeling the weight of his episode with Masinissa lift from his shoulders. "No, it was more of a revolutionary dream, that we would all be working in concert someday, toward a greater good."

Laelius nods appreciatively. "That is well. I worry about those fateful dreams you have at night. But I was worry more that you will lose your own dreams, the ones you have for your waking hours."

"Perhaps I do have time for a cup or two before I rest," says Scipio. "How about you, Marcus?"

Marcus nods "I can tolerate one more." The three step out into the feast, a cacophony of music, shouts, curses, and brags from warriors embracing their rare opportunity for silliness and excess.

Masinissa lies alone in his tent. He is face down on his sleeping mat, weeping convulsively into a straw-stuffed pillow. His spirit is torn with rage and sorrow. *Let the Romans rot*, his heart tells him. *You are the king now. Ride to Cirta and mass your tribesmen against them. Don't let them take her.*

He hears two centurions guffawing outside his tent, making rude jokes about what sexual punishments they would inflict upon Syphax if given the chance. *Syphax is gone,* He reminds himself. *You have all Numidia within your grasp; you can unite all the tribes. But you cannot do it without Rome. Even if you could, they would take the throne from you for your betrayal.*

Hours after midnight, Masinissa lets loose a groan so loud and painful that the men outside his tent can hear it.[xcix] He rolls off his pallet and wipes the sweat from his body, then steps out into the night.

"Fetch Hempol," he orders one of his men. Soon a middle-aged Numidian walks into the tent, a family slave who first served Masinissa's father. He is also the man who keeps Masinissa's poison, in the event the prince is taken captive by his enemies.[c]

"Hempol, I need you to leave camp immediately. Go now, under cover of night, while the Romans are lax with drink." He holds out a papyrus scroll. "Take this to Sophonisba."

The slave nods and heads for the door.

"Hempol," Masinissa says, his voice quavering. "Bring her a double draft of sleep poison. Place it in her hands."

The slave stares wonderingly at Masinissa. The prince turns away from him and faces the tent wall.

"As you wish," Hempol replies. He starts to leave, and stops again. "You will make a mighty king."

Masinissa stares at the camelskin wall, his face a stone. "King of what?" he says bitterly, as his vision blurs with tears.

*   *   *   *   *

CURIA HOSTILIA, ROME, 203 BCE. "I wish they'd hurry. My ass is getting cold!"

Pomponia is perched on a marble column pedestal near the bottom the Senate steps, waiting for the Senate to finish their session. She shivers as a late fall breeze wafts over her.

Jupiter is bringing winter early this year, she thinks as she pats back a loose strand of red hair. She motions for her attendants to bring her shawl. *I should visit my sons in Africa—it would be warmer there! But who would help Amelia take care of Cornelia?*

Finally, the senators pour out from their chambers, having concluded their brief session. Pomponia peers into the faces of the Latin and Hellenic party members, trying to read the results of their special vote, but she can detect no satisfaction on the faces of those she knows to be avowed Latins or Hellenics. She sees two red-faced senators gesturing angrily at one another. Their voices are rife with annoyance. *That's Crispus and Pompus, the two shipping magnates. They are displeased. That is good news!*

Lucius Metelius is one of the first senators to pick his way down the wide marble steps. Pomponia quickly strides up the steps to see the young man, the son of her closest friend.

"What news, Lucius? Did it pass?" she eagerly asks.

Lucius' handsome face splits into a broad grin. "Your campaign was a success! The Law of 218 has been stiffened.[ci] If any senators own ships that can carry more than 300 amphorae of goods, they can be imprisoned for indulging in overseas commerce. The law should open more trade to our common people!"

"And it will keep them from fomenting overseas wars for their own profit," adds Pomponia. She kisses him on the cheek. "Gratitude, Lucius. I appreciate your efforts to stiffen the penalty. Tell your mother I will see her soon, to celebrate."

The regal woman motions for her attendants and heads into the bustling Forum square, hurrying back to see Amelia and her new granddaughter Cornelia. Pomponia pushes her way through the crowds, aglow with pride in her achievement. Impulsively, she stops at a merchant stall several blocks from the square and buys a roast canary on a stick. *I deserve a reward!*

She skips along the street, biting into the sesame-covered treat while she ponders on the young haruspex' recent visit to see Amelia and Cornelia. *He said baby Cornelia was fated to be his bride, that their children would be legends of Rome. All that from a fresh augury!* She shakes her head. *Perhaps my son was right, the boy is not the most rational person on earth.*

"Ow!" Pomponia exclaims, feeling a sharp pinprick on her right arm. She looks at her bare shoulder and sees a tiny dot of blood there, which she quickly wipes away. She glares about to find the perpetrator, one hand inside her robe, fingering her throwing knife. But she only sees the wall-to-wall press of humanity that fills Merchant Street every business day, people of all classes flowing past each other like schools of fish: soldiers, slaves, patricians, farmers, priests, and prostitutes.

One figure catches her eye, a cloaked man hurriedly barging through the press of humanity, eliciting curses from those he jostles. The man disappears behind a baker's stall, but not before he glances back at Pomponia, his cold gray eyes staring at her as if she were his enemy—or prey. Pomponia pauses, taken aback by the cold hatred on the man's face.

Pomponia shrugs him off, motioning for her male attendants to stay closer to her. *That bastard Flaccus better not be stalking me again. I'll ram a pole up his ass this time!*

As Pomponia turns onto a side street she begins to stagger. She shakes her head to clear it, her vision blurring, and presses on towards her domus, the front doors beckoning her a mere block away.

Her legs grow heavy. *I must get the medicus at once. Cornelia must not catch this* is all she can think, her thoughts blurring.

Pomponia falls. Dimly, she hears the screaming of her attendants. Her cheek tingles against the cobbled street, feeling the vibration of scores of sandaled feet running in to stand about her. She tries to push herself up, but finds her arms are no longer hers—they are numb. Her heart pounds as she feels her breath slowing.

A strange peace comes to Pomponia. She feels as if her body no longer exists, she cannot sense it any more. Images flow dreamily through her mind: Scipio and Laelius as boys, playfully wrestling while Amelia giggles at them. Her husband Publius, arrayed in his purple-caped armor, kissing her deeply before he leaves for Iberia. Cornelia turning in her crib, waving her chubby arms at her wet nurse.

She sees two handsome young men standing at improvised rostrum in the Forum Square, speaking out for citizens' rights and benefits. Somehow, she knows they are her grandchildren, the democratic legends the haruspex predicted they would become.[cii]

Hope. There is hope she thinks, as the blackness softly descends.

*   *   *   *   *

BONONIA, NORTH ITALIA, 203 BCE. "Hiram! Get those elephants over here!" Mago barks, pointing to an open space in front of the Gauls. "Put them behind the Ligurians. And keep them ready!"

The young Carthaginian mahout bobs his turbaned head and rushes to herd in the two dozen war elephants, holding his twelve-foot elephant prod upright so he does not spear anyone.

Mago stomps about in his bearskin boots, surveying the wide river valley that sprawls to the foot of the rugged gray Apennines. He can see the Roman legions arrayed before him, strategically placed to block his army from passing between the mountains and down the coast. *I will have to go through them to get to my brother*, Mago decides.

"How many of those bastards are out there?" he asks Zinnridi, his lead commander.

"They have about forty thousand men, same as us," he replies, frowning at the well-organized rectangles of men below them. "There's four legions of Romans and twice that many allies, at least. And look over there! There must be three or four thousand cavalry when you count both flanks." He looks at Mago, concerned. "That's a lot of corpses to step over on our way to the Mediterranean."

Mago sniffs. "It's not as bad as it seems. That thirteenth legion is mostly slaves, whip-ass dogs that were given swords and sent up from their camp at Arminium. The fourteenth's got a lot of them, too."

He points to the thousands of legionnaires filling the Po River plain. "See there, all those men behind the legionary standards back by the river? They keep the thirteenth and fourteenth in the rear lines, behind the eleventh and twelfth—because they don't trust them." Mago rubs his hands in anticipation. "If we crush the front legions, the rear ones will follow."

Zinnridi grins, and leaps onto his roan stallion. "I hear you. We will press their center and break them!" He whirls off to check the front infantry lines.

I'm coming, brother, Mago says to himself. He chops his hand down to signal a call from the battle trumpets. The army's horns echo across the mile wide line, relayed from the brass Carthaginian trumpets to the ram's horns of the Gauls and Ligurians. The Iberians and Ligurians in the middle tramp forward, marching down a gradual incline towards the Romans.

The eleventh and twelfth legions stolidly await their adversaries, but the rear legions are not so placid. They are filled with men who want to fight for their freedom. They stomp about, at once nervous and eager.

"This is a fine state of affairs," grouses Thrax the Thracian, slapping his gladius blade onto his leathered palm. "They tell us we can go home if we fight well against Mago and his savages, but they stick us in the back lines where we can only watch!" He jabs his sword in and out with lightning speed, feinting an attack. "As if we Thracians weren't better fighters than those squatty little Romans."

"They don't trust us," says Rhesus, his rotund countryman. "They think their front legions are better than us because they fought in a few skirmishes with some drunken Gauls." He laughs. "We grew up fighting fiercer opponents—ourselves!"

Rhesus wrinkles his nose at his Roman sword. "Look at this little pigsticker, how's a man supposed to fight with this? It's a dagger!"

Thrax grins. "Well, I won't have to use it. See that velite up there, the one with the odd-looking javelin on his back? He is holding a special weapon for me. When the time comes I'll go get it, and show these Romans how a true Thracian fights!"

"You think you Thracians are the only ones that grew up fighting?" interjects lanky Kiro, a captive Macedonian. "We are given swords as soon as we can stand. And we know how to fight in formation, not like you wild-ass Thracians. We would not fear to take on the Libyans up there, much less a pack of bare-ass Gauls."

"Fah!" exclaims Thrax, "If you're so tough, what are you doing here?"

Kiro fingers his sword, and his mouth tightens. "Same as you. We were outnumbered, else I would not be here today."

The Thracians hoot at the young Macedonian's bravado. "We will get our chance," says Old Tose, another Macedonian. "Our commander, that proconsul Marcus Cornelius, [ciii] he is very ambitious. He will not be content to sit out the fight."

"Good," Thrax says. "I need my chance for glory, so I can free myself from cursed Italia!"

The Roman battle trumpets interrupt the slave soldiers' conversation, replying to the Carthaginians' horns. The thirteenth legion moves into cohort formation. The centurions check that each line is even, and that the men have maintained their three-foot gap between their linemates.

The legions' horns sound again, and the thirteenth marches forward to close the distance between themselves and the twelfth. To their right the fourteenth legion of slave soldiers marches alongside them, closing the gap on the advancing lines of the eleventh legion.

The veteran twelfth legion is on the left center of the mile and a half line of soldiers, heading toward the oncoming Ligurians and Balearics. The eleventh is at the Roman right center, preparing to confront Mago's staunch Libyan heavy infantry and the untested Carthaginian conscripts behind them. Each Roman legion is flanked with two legions of Italia allies. The allies to the left of the twelfth face the fierce Inguani Gauls. The allies on the right of the eleventh must contend with Mago's veteran Iberians.

The far flanks of both armies have thousands of cavalry riding about, with Mago's Gallic and Inguani riders on both sides. Mago holds his elephants, Gauls, and Numidians in the rear, waiting to deploy them when a weakness presents itself. Eighty thousand men are on the move. They tramp towards each other's destruction, stomping across the grassy fields of the fertile plains.

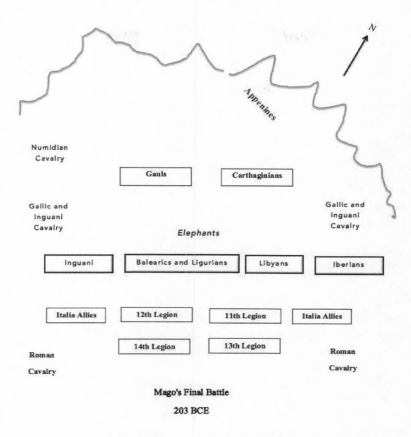

Mago's Final Battle

203 BCE

As the two armies approach one another, hundreds of unarmored velites trot out from the eleventh and twelfth legions. As ordered, they hurl all their javelins at the Ligurians and Libyans, Mago's most critical forces. The javelins arc down into the unwary back lines. Scattered screams erupt as the Roman's pila strike home.

On command, the young men hurl their second round directly at the front line of Libyans and Ligurians. Most bounce harmlessly off the enemy's sturdy shields.

The velites are readying their third throws when a horde of Balearic slingers breaks out from Mago's front line. The deadly warriors hurl round after round of river stones directly into the lightly armored velites, shattering the skulls and limbs of those too slow to raise their shields.

The velites do not break, however, they stand steadfast and hurl the last of their spears into the slingers. They dash back into the spaces between the oncoming legionnaires, leaving dozens of dying Balearic islanders scattered about the field. The Libyans and Ligurians march past their crying and moaning compatriots, their eyes fixed the front line Romans closing in on them.

The eleventh and twelfth's horns sound the charge. The twelfth legion sprints the last hundred yards to the Ligurians, pounding their shields and screaming defiance.

King Baelon rides out in front of his Ligurians, waving his thick-headed spear at the Romans. "At them!" he bellows.

With a mighty shout, the Ligurians rush forward with long swords upraised, heedless of order or restraint. They crash into the shield wall of the twelfth's front cohorts, swinging their heavy long swords at any Roman helmet or shield within arm's reach.

The Romans plant their sandaled feet and refuse to be knocked backwards by their heavier opponents, turning their bodies to leverage their attackers to the side. The dauntless centurions scream for their men to hold the line, even as they battle with the Gauls who are attacking them.

The twelfth's men carefully stab into openings between the Ligurians' body-length shields, aiming at their unarmored torsos. Their blades jab into ribs, stomachs, and shoulders, inflicting wounds that drain the strength from their foes. The Romans kill scores of the barbarians this way, but dozens of Romans fall with bashed-in skulls. The dead legionnaires are quickly dragged away and replaced with men from the second line, and the front rows hold.

Man-killing Korbis marches in, leading his army of Balearic islanders. His crazed eyes reveal that the battle lust is upon him. He is eager to take heads for his macabre collection.

"Come fight me, cowards!" Korbis bellows, pounding his oversized falcata against his oval shield. "I spit on your gods!" His silver scale armor gleams like the sun. His blue plume waves from high atop his domed helmet, daring any to attack him.

Korbis looks back at his men and beckons them with his sword. "Kill all now!" he shouts. "Into them!" The Balearics stalk forward, grimly determined to beat their way through the legionnaires in front of them.

"Legion, forward!" orders First Tribune, and the horns blare out his marching orders.

The Romans tramp straight into the Balearics. With a mighty shout, the two sides shove out their left arms and clang their shields into each other, their legs digging into the earth as they try to drive back their opponents.

"Push!" shouts the twelfth's First Tribune, as the legionnaires lean into their shields. One step at a time, the Romans force back the islanders. Then Korbis steps out in front of his men.

Korbis swings his cleaver-like falcata into the scutum of the centurion facing him. His blade cleaves halfway through the Roman's shield. "Hah!" he exults, and arcs his sword over his head. Another blow and the shield splits apart, falling in chunks at the centurion's feet. Undaunted, the centurion jumps forward and lances his gladius across Korbis' thick right forearm, gashing a deep cut into it.

Korbis roars with pain. "You pay for that, dog!" With a mighty sweep, Korbis chops his falcata into the base of the centurion's neck, cleaving him to his breastbone.

Even before the spurting corpse hits the ground, Korbis has yanked out his blade and attacked the next Roman in line. Korbis pushes the Roman's scutum aside with his own shield and rams his sword's pommel into the Roman's face, crushing his jaw.

"To me!" Korbis bellows as he steps farther into the Roman line. The chieftain's men hurry to his side. The lightly armored Balearics dart sideways to evade Roman thrusts, striking at the legionnaires' exposed sword arms. Their frenzied attack halts the Roman advance.

The eleventh legion joins battle with Mago's Libyans, a clash of two armies of battle-hardened veterans. The two front lines repeatedly batter their shields at each other, trying to knock their opponents to the ground. The din grows so loud that the Roman officers resort to hand signals, frantically gesturing their orders while their men continue to assault the front line Africans.

After the several bouts of shield clashes, the Libyans step back to reorganize their lines and catch their breath. They attack again, but this time the battle-wise Africans spring forward to jab their long spears through openings in the Roman shield wall. Cries of pain erupt from the Romans. Dozens of men fall wounded or dying. Gaps appear in the front line.

"Close on them! Block their spears!" the eleventh's legate commands. The tribunes lead their men forward. Many a Libyan spear thrust slides off an angled Roman shield, enabling the legionnaire to step inside his foe and stab into him. Soon, scores of Libyans retreat from the front line, gripping a bloody wrist or forearm. The Libyans behind them step into their place, spears at the ready.

The Roman cornu blare a new command. The front line hastati step to the rear and the veteran principes angle between them to the front. The fresh veterans batter the Libyans backwards, and the Africans' lines begin to break.

Mago rides in to exhort the Libyans. "Hold men, hold!" he screams. "Stay next to your brother, don't leave him alone!" Mago weaves among the men, shouting encouragement and flinging spears at the principes. The Libyans stand fast, refusing to yield any more space.

The Iberians fight to the left of the Libyans, at the edge of Mago's infantry line. The Iberians only number in the thousands but they are veterans of the Three Generals' wars against Scipio. They fight without hesitation or mercy, bunching their oblong shields close together while protecting their flanks with their heavy cavalry.

Ten thousand Italia allies fight against the Iberians. They hurtle into them with a concerted rush, but the tactic proves to be a costly mistake. The Iberians beat the allies back with slashes and stabs from their deadly falcatas, whooping with delight each time their blades strike home. They step over the corpses of the socii and slowly advance. Hundreds of allies fall, and the right flank of the Romans bends inward.

On the other flank, Asrix leads his Inguani into the teeth of sixteen thousand socii. The giant barbarians cut through the allied cohorts with their tree-felling battle axes. Asrix has tied his round iron shield to his arm stump, allowing him to wield his hand axe with deadly efficiency. He batters down every legionnaire that dares face him, his double-edged cleaver hewing through armor and bone.

The allied front loses scores of men to the relentless Inguani before fresh troops manage to replace them. The Roman allies constantly rotate men into the front lines, wearing down the outnumbered opponents. After a series of line changes, they finally halt the Inguani. The left flank of the Roman army has bent inward, but it has not broken.

Fighting fiercely in the center of the battle, the Balearics and Ligurians cave in the lines of the vaunted twelfth legion, and the Roman army center bends inward. Mighty Korbis fights like a man possessed, mad with battle lust. He hacks down one soldier after another, leading a wedge of Balearics through the front line hastati and into the principes backing them up.

Watching the Balearics advance ahead of them, the abashed Ligurians redouble their efforts. The chieftains mass their men together and launch forth with a swarming assault that breaks through the legion's front lines, enabling the mountain men to surround individual Romans and cut them down.

The Inguani deepen their own assault, heedless of the socii's stab wounds to their exposed backs and necks. Scores of allies fall, as the Italia fighters are pressed close together, too near one another to fight.

Praetor Publius Varus watches his lines cave in, and his heart leaps to his throat. *I'm going to lose the entire legion!*

"Retreat! Sound the retreat!" he shouts desperately. The cornu sounds the withdrawal.

"Maintain your lines or we'll all die," the centurions bellow to their centuries. "Face forward and stay next to your partners. Back up one step at a time, men. One step at a time."

The hastati and principes retreat, keeping their faces toward the enemy. The legionnaires pass through the waiting triarii. The middle-aged veterans bend down on one knee and plant their seven-foot spears firmly into the earth, creating a wall of death for any who would charge at them. A dozen impetuous Ligurians and Balearics impale themselves before the rest halt the attack, content to hurl spears and stones at the unwavering triarii.

Publius Varus waves over Proconsul Marcus Cornelius, who has left his thirteenth and fourteenth legions to spur on the front line hastati. "As you see, the battle is losing its momentum," says Publius. "The enemy's fear is being hardened into stubbornness—and there is a risk of it developing into boldness. We should get a brisk cavalry charge going." [civ]

Marcus Cornelius points to the left flank. "We should send all four turmae of our equites into the Ligurians. If we don't, our triarii will soon be overwhelmed!"

Publius nods his assent, and Cornelius dashes back toward his thirteenth legion, intent on leading an infantry advance to complement the cavalry charge.

Within minutes, twelve hundred Roman equites plunge into the Ligurian infantry, led by Publius' valiant young son, Tribune Marcus Varus.[cv] The patrician riders trample through the Ligurian front, leaning to the right and left of their mounts to spear down any foot soldiers who are near them.

The Ligurians fight back fiercely, pulling the riders down even as the Roman spears pierce their bodies. Scores of riderless horses stampede through the swirling melee' of man and animal, adding to the confusion.

"Follow me!" screams Marcus Varus, pushing his horse into the Ligurian force. The Roman riders plunge in after him. Their onslaught dissipates the loosely organized Ligurians, and chaos creeps into the barbarians' ranks.

When the Ligurians retreat from the triarii's spear wall, the twelfth legionnaires take heart and march back into the fray, the battle-tested principes now leading the advance. Attacked from two sides, hundreds more Ligurians fall. The barbarians begin a hasty retreat, even as Korbis and his Balearics continue to hew their way through the right side of the dwindling twelfth.

Marcus Varus ignores the Balearics' advance. He presses his cavalry charge deeper into the Ligurian ranks, seeking to chase them from the field so he can turn his riders upon the outnumbered Balearics. He can see victory unfolding before him, and he waves his sword back at his father, smiling triumphantly.

But Mago Barca is brother to Hannibal, and is an able tactician in his own right. Riding along behind the lines, Mago sees the tide of battle turn with the Roman cavalry charge. He summons commander Zinnridi and points to the dozen elephants waiting between the back line of the Ligurians and the front line of the unused Gauls.

"Bring them in, Zinnridi. Straight at the horses. Aim for that young bastard leading the charge over there." Zinnridi is galloping off even before Mago has finished his sentence.

Marcus Varus is fending off a Ligurian sword blow when he hears a mighty bellowing and screaming in front of him. He slices open the Ligurian's bicep and wheels his horse toward the tumult. As the Ligurian stumbles away, Varus looks up to find a herd of trumpeting elephants trampling toward him and his equites.

The monstrous beasts charge forward, heedless of the spears clacking off their chain-mailed bodies. The mahouts ride atop the elephants in their wicker battle towers, skillfully flicking their twelve-foot spears into the necks and arms of the fleeing Roman infantry. Many legionnaires are trampled beneath the onrushing beasts, their mortal screams cutting through the metallic din of battle.

The Roman horses rear back from the elephants' unfamiliar sound and smell, whinnying with terror. In the blink of an eye the tide of battle turns to Mago's advantage, as the equites' horses bolt from the field, pulling their cursing, yelling, riders far away from the conflict.[cvi]

Mago looks over at his Numidian commander. The African is carefully watching him, his eyes agleam with anticipation. Mago smiles and waggles his index finger toward the equites careening away onto the empty plain. *Go get them.*

In a flash, hundreds of Numidians hurtle after the escaping Romans. The African horsemen close easily on their slower-moving prey as the equites' horses dash erratically about the plain. Riding at full gallop, the Numidians expertly hurl their javelins into helpless young patricians, skewering them like fleeing antelope. When one Roman falls in front of them they dash past in pursuit another, glorying in their deadly hunt.

Three Numidians close in on Marcus Varus. The tribune decides he cannot outdistance the Numidians, so he spins his mount about and faces them. Laughing and shouting, the Africans take turns running at the young commander. Sword in hand, Marcus charges at whichever Numidian comes at him, only to see them dash from reach before his gladius can touch them.

The Numidians tire of their game. Circling around Marcus' horse, they nod at each other. With whoop of excitement the three attack at once, from different angles.

Marcus spurs his horse at the Numidian in front of him. He ducks under the African's spear and slashes him across the chest, drawing a thick ribbon of streaming blood. The slumping Numidian careens away from the fight. Marcus wheels his horse about for the next attacker, but he is already too late.

The second Numidian drives his iron spear through Marcus' thigh. The tribune screams out in agony, just as the third Numidian's spear buries itself in the side of his chest. Marcus Varus falls to the earth, struggling to push himself upright. A Numidian jumps from his horse and draws out his skinning knife.

With a practiced twist of the wrist, the African pushes his knife under the bottom of the young tribune's cuirass and disembowels him, reaching in with his hand to string Marcus Varus' intestines out onto the ground. Barking a disdainful laugh, the Numidian vaults back on his horse and gallops away, leaving Marcus to die groveling among his bowels.

The Ligurians regroup and press back into the remaining half of the twelfth legion, but they cannot break the ranks or the will of the principes and hastati. The legionnaires have massed together in a final stand and are held there by their fear of being dishonored by retreating again.[cvii]

The Romans relentlessly fight off the swarms of Ligurians, refusing to take a single step backwards. The surviving centurions and tribunes roam through the front, screaming for their men to hold their place.

The older triarii drop their spears and take sword in hand. They step forward and fill the ranks where their younger mates have fallen, knowing there are no other replacements—and no other choice. Dozens, then scores, of the dwindling twelfth fall, as the eleventh legion watches helplessly, occupied with their own enemies.

The battle trumpets sound behind the twelfth legion. Marcus Cornelius rides in front of the desperate legionnaires, striking down a Ligurian attacker. "Retreat, men, retreat in order," he screams, grinning at them as if they had won a victory. "My thirteenth is here to fight!"

The officers of the twelfth look behind their exhausted cohorts and see the advance of four thousand fresh legionnaires, Rome's infamous slave legion. The tribunes' blood-grimed faces flash with grins of relief. "To the rear," they shout, and the Roman survivors step to the rear, while Rome's captive Thracians, Macedonians, Moors, and

Iberians step forward to replace them.

The thirteenth legion marches directly into the tiring Ligurians and cuts through the first line as if they are not there, plunging their swords into them with all their strength. The slave infantry fights for their freedom, for the chance to return to their native lands, and they will not be denied. The officers of the thirteenth work desperately to keep their men from charging ahead recklessly and breaking ranks, so determined are they to wipe out their opponents.

Zinnridi sends a half dozen elephants rampaging into the slave legion. The African and Indian legionnaires are wise in the ways of elephants. They quickly spear down their mahouts and calmly herd the pachyderms away with spear jabs, driving them back into the Ligurians.

The eleventh legion sees the elephants being driven away and they charge into the remaining elephants that are near them,[cviii] hurling their spears from every direction. They drive the beasts back into Mago's own men, adding to his army's confusion.

Mago's army lines bend, but the Libyans refuse to break. They keep the eleventh legion at bay, along with the Balearics who fight next to them. The nearby Ligurians are overwhelmed and begin another retreat, with many running from the relentless thirteenth. As the Ligurians flee the front lines, the thirteenth legionnaires wheel in formation to surround the Balearics.

Korbis sees the envelopment and shouts for his back row fighters to follow him in. As they get through the front line, the giant Balearic sees the tall red crest of a tribune and heads directly for him.

The tribune notices Korbis' advance and strides out to confront him, wiping the blood off his blade as he stalks toward his towering foe. "Come on, fat boy," the stocky man shouts. "I'll have your balls for dinner!"

The tribune stabs for Korbis' exposed throat. The giant swipes the blade away with his shield and swings it back into the tribune's body, knocking him off his feet. Korbis straddles the tribune and arcs his falcata at the Roman's head. The legionnaire deftly blocks the killing stroke with his shield. Unfazed, Korbis batters upon the prostrate tribune, splintering his shield and denting his helmet.

The dazed Roman forces himself up to one knee, drunkenly stabbing at the Balearic. Korbis drops his shield, and grins. His hand snakes out and catches the Roman's sword arm in mid-thrust. "Now what you do?" he says to the tribune, grinning at him.

Korbis yanks the man's arm over his head and spins him backwards. His heavy sword flashes down and chops off the Roman's head with a single blow, cutting through the tribune's protective neck plate as if it were papyrus. Korbis bellows his triumph and flings the head into the front of the dismayed slave soldiers, halting their advance.

On the other side of the battle, Mago sees the elephants being driven into his men. He watches the dissolution of the Ligurians and the envelopment of the Balearics by the fresh Roman troops. Mago realizes his center is in danger of collapsing. It is time to deploy his last weapon.

Mago trots over to Morcant, the Gallic chief, and points his sword at the thirteenth legion massing in front of them. "Destroy those bastards and half the field plunder will be yours."

"We kill all!" Morcant bellows in his pidgin Carthaginian. Morcant swings his battle ax above his head three times. The Gallic horns sound the charge.

Thousands of Gauls rush forward from the rear. They knock the retreating Ligurians aside, lusting to take heads and plunder.

Mago waves over Zinnridi. "This is the moment, we rise or fall with our center. Bring all our Carthaginians to the fore, we'll follow in behind the Gauls!" He snaps the bridle onto his horse. "I'm going in with my elite guard, and you'd better have your men right behind me!"

Mago leads out his Sacred Band warriors, followed by thousands of Carthaginian citizen soldiers. The two waves march straight for the unbending lines of the thirteenth.

As Mago's Carthaginians charge forward, the Gauls crash into the slave legion, hammering at their shield wall with their heavy swords. Most of the thirteenth's slaves are former warriors and they are not easily cowed, even by the iron-thewed Gauls. The slaves ward off the down stroke of the Gallic swords with their spears, [cix] deflecting them from making a telling stroke on their shields or helmets, leaving the Gauls open to their counter thrusts.

The Gallic attack is fierce but brief. Morcant manages to break the front line of the thirteenth's hastati. Bellowing his battle fury, he hews down several Macedonians that dared to face him, pausing only long enough to chop off their heads. Morcant pulls off the helmet of a decapitated centurion and waves it about, its blood flowing down his sword arm.

"I fight any of you!" he bellows out across the field of battle. He throws down his shield and sword. "Here, I no use weapons! Come on!"

The Romans hold their formation, glowering at the blustering Gaul. "Pussies! We come get you!" Morcant shouts. He throws the head at the legionnaires and stomps forward. His Gallic tribesmen follow him into the havoc.

Back in the second line, Rhesus turns to his friend Thrax. "He's treating us like we are a bunch of cowardly slaves! I will show him what a Thracian can do."

"Stay in line, Rhesus," Thrax replies. "You'll get your chance."

"To Hades with waiting," Rhesus snaps, "I'm going to kill someone!"

Ignoring his centurion's cries to return, Rhesus pushes out to confront the oncoming Morcant. The Gaul waves his axe at Rhesus. "Come skinny man. Time to go to paradise!"

The Thracian abruptly charges forward. He ducks under Morcant's whistling ax blow and spears him in the side. Morcant roars in pain, and the Roman lines cheer. But the javelin sticks in Morcant's armor. The chieftain grabs the spear before Rhesus can pull it out, and yanks the Thracian off his feet.

Rhesus lands on his stomach and quickly covers his torso with his shield, trying to scramble to his feet. Morcant ignores the shield and chops off Rhesus' exposed leg below the knee, kicking the severed limb away as if it were a serpent. The Thracian screams in anguish and convulses on the ground, pouring out his life.

Morcant steps past his bleeding foe, looking for another victim. He does not have long to wait.

Thrax stands before him, naked blade in hand, furious at the sight of his friend dying on the ground.

"He was a good man," Thrax growls at the enormous Gaul. "Better man than you, who are now dead."

The chieftain sniffs disdainfully at the rangy warrior. He does not understand the Thracian's words, but he grasps their gist. "Come make it happen, if you can," he sneers, baring his broken yellow teeth. He bends over and rests his ax against one of his deerskin boots, daring the Thracian to attack him.

Thrax begins to shed his armor, keeping his eye on the Gaul. Soon he stands in tunic and helmet, bereft of shield, greaves, and chestplate.

"I fight as a Thracian now, with Thracian weapons," he brags, knowing the chieftain cannot understand him. "We know how to kill in an alley fight. Now I show you why the Romans fear us."

Thrax reaches behind his back and pulls out his sica, a curved dagger with an eighteen inch blade, elaborately scribed with figures of the Greek war god Ares, the Thracians' favorite god. He waves the sica in front of Morcant's disdaining face.

"You try to kill me with little sword?" Morcant laughs. "You stupid."

"That's not all, pig." Thrax replies. Reaching behind his back, the

255

Thracian slides out a Thracian rhomphaia,[cx] a five foot polearm with half its length a daggered blade created for arm's-reach slashing and cutting. He grabs the long wooden handle in his left hand, dangling his dagger in his right. Thrax walks straight at the ax-wielding behemoth waiting for him.

Morcant still stands without his weapon. "Come on, slave," he sneers, impatiently waving his shield. Thrax stomps forward. When Thrax is within arm's reach, Morcant moves with stunning speed. He grasps his ax and swings it at Thrax' unprotected throat.

Thrax had served years in the gladiatorial pens, fighting as a thraex with the same weapons he now holds. He is not easily fooled. He snaps his torso backwards and the blade whistles by him, etching a thin cut along his chest.

As Morcant's ax passes by, Thrax jabs out with his rhomphaia, puncturing the Gaul's pectoral muscle. Morcant seems to hardly notice as he rushes at the Thracian, shoving out his shield to block Thrax' dagger thrust.

Morcant blocks the dagger's thrust with the edge of his shield, colliding with its hilt and almost knocking Thrax off his feet. The Thracian' levers his curved blade over the shield's edge, slashing a deep furrow along Morcant's lower forearm.

The Gaul roars with pain. He swings wildly at Thrax with his head splitting ax, apoplectic with frustration. The rangy Thracian darts about with the elusive grace of a gladiator, dodging Morcant's whistling ax.

Soon, time and temperature join Thrax in his duel against Morcant. The Gaul's swings begin to lose their momentum, and he holds his ax lower to his knees. Thrax continues to dodge Morcant, watching him carefully. He sees several Gauls heading across the field to aid their leader, and he knows he must act quickly.

When the Gaul aims a killing side cut at the Thracian's stomach, Thrax leaps forward. He shoves his polearm into the Gaul's blade, deflecting it off course. The force of the blow knocks the rhomphaia from his hand.

In one desperate move, Thrax scrambles in and collides chest to chest with his foe. Morcant wraps his thickly muscled arm stub around Thrax' back, pinning him close for a killing axe chop.

Thrax jabs upward with his sica. The curved blade delves into the underside of the Gaul's chin, burrowing deep into his skull. Morcant arcs back his head and screams to the heavens. He scrabbles at his face, trying to pry out the agony within it, his nose and mouth gushing blood beneath his bulging eyes. As Thrax yanks out the blade, Morcant's arms fall limp to his sides. The chieftain crashes to the ground like a fresh-hewn oak.

The legionnaire leaps back and grabs his fallen polearm. He dashes from the approaching Gauls, and merges with the rest of his cohort to resume battle formation. Looking in front of him, he sees Morcant's inert body being dragged off by his tribesmen.

Like wildfire, word spreads among the Gauls that their leader has died. Morcant's chieftains call for a retreat, and the disheartened barbarians trudge back from the battle, ignoring the Carthaginian officers' calls to attack.

Thrax watches them depart with great satisfaction. He turns to his centurion. "You see me kill that bastard? You see them go away? I win this battle for us! I get freedom!"

The centurion nods. "You will be a hero in Rome, but best you try to stay alive first. Here come the Carthaginians!"

Mago charges forward with his Carthaginians and Sacred Band warriors, delving through the retreating Gauls. He sees Morcant being dragged from the field, and he knows the tide of battle is turning against him.

"At them!" Mago screams to his elite guards. "Hit the center!" Mago spurs his horse into the front of the infantry battle, churning about like a madman, his curved sword flashing down like lightning bolts upon the doughty slave soldiers. Hundreds of the deadly Sacred Band warriors attack en masse to join Mago, with the Carthaginian citizen soldiers following them.

Fighting with cool efficiency, the well trained Sacred Band warriors fell scores of the thirteenth's hastati and principes, halting the Roman advance. Mago continues to lead the attack, screaming encouragement, promising lands and gold to those felling the Roman officers.

To his left he sees that the methodical Libyans have finally pushed back the eleventh legion, even as Marcus Livius leads the slave legion of the fourteenth to relieve them. To his right he sees that the battle-loving Inguani are repulsing the resolute Italia allies, though the northerners stand in mounds of their own dead.

The cavalry battles are swirling stalemates of Gallic, Inguani, and Iberian cavalry against the Roman allied riders, with most of the Roman equites driven off by the Numidians. Mago's eyes light with excitement. He knows he has but to hold the center and victory will be his. Exultant, he plunges his mount deeper into the Romans, and his Band follows.

A small, slender Moor slips through the melee' in front of him, his eyes fixed on his chance for glory. The dark little legionnaire hides behind a knot of his battling linemates until Mago draws near him. When Mago rides past his front line, the Moor dashes out toward the general, his sword held high.

The Moor stabs his gladius into Mago's leg, slashing his thigh to the bone. Mago screams and clutches his gouting wound, shouting for help. The frightened soldier runs back into the lines of his fellows without delivering the telling blow, seeking safety over glory.

Mago screams with frustration and dismay as his officers dash toward him, ripping strips off their linen tunics to form bandages. *I'll die if I stay to fight, but these barbarians will be torn apart if I'm not here to control them.* He clenches his teeth as another wave of pain convulses him, and turns to Zinnridi.

"Sound the retreat," he mutters through clenched teeth. "Gods damn me, sound the retreat!" As the Carthaginian horns sound, Mago's Sacred Band warriors surround him. Mago is carried from the field, with his main army following. [cxi]

Zinnridi gallops furiously across the entire line of battle, screaming orders to Asrix and the other chieftains. Zinnridi urges them to withdraw in order, facing the enemy. The Inguani, Iberians, and Libyans gradually withdraw from the field, their flanks dashing out to skirmish with any who pursue them.

As he rides over to the left flank, Zinnridi and his guard are surrounded by a squadron of allied cavalry. The Italia fighters swarm over his guards and kill every one of them until Zinnridi is alone.

The Carthaginian nobleman takes one look at the scores of warriors around him and drops his sword, knowing he will be taken prisoner and ransomed at a later date. As the socii rope his hands together in front of him, Zinnridi glances back to the center lines. *May Baal save you, General. I will be back to join you before the year is out.*

Korbis and his men are battling through the first lines of the fourteenth legion replacements when he hears Zinnridi's order to retreat. With a cry of anguished disappointment, Korbis redoubles his attack on the Romans, hurling himself any Roman he can find, even as he eases back to rejoin the main army.

"I come back and kill you pigs!" he shouts, his eyes tearing with frustration. As he walks up the rise, Korbis looks back over the field of battle. He sees hundreds of his men strewn across it, taken down by the thirteenth legion's flank attack. *Too many of them for us to win today. I will kill them later.*

Dusk drifts across the battlefield. Publius Varus sees the futility of trying to destroy Mago's army before night falls. He calls over Marcus Cornelius and the two order the men to return to camp.

Thousands of Romans are counted dead, most of them from the unfortunate twelfth legion. Marcus Cornelius and Publius Varus are thankful, however. They estimate that twice as many of Mago's men have perished. [cxii]

Mago's march to Hannibal has been halted and a great victory has been won, but there also is much grieving in the two Roman camps. Many officers and centurions were lost, including those trampled to death by Mago's dreadnaught elephants.[cxiii]

Publius Varus is inconsolable for the loss of his son Marcus. He spends the night prostrate in front of the camp altar while his men celebrate throughout the camp. At dawn Varus rises from the ground and vows vengeance upon Mago and his Numidians. He cajoles Marcus Cornelius into preparing an attack on Mago's camp, so that Varus can meet the Carthaginian in single combat.

Two days later the Roman armies march upon Mago's emplacement. They arrive in front of empty walls—Mago's army abandoned the camp the night of the battle. Only a few luckless Carthaginians are in the camp, volunteers who patrolled the walls to foster the appearance of an army.

By steps and stages, the grievously wounded Mago leads his men back toward Genova, intending to regroup and recruit. *I will not desert you, brother*, he swears as he bounces along. Every bump makes him to wince with pain—and steels his resolve.

*　　*　　*　　*　　*

CIRTA, NUMIDIA. "This looks queenly, don't you think, Jezebel?"

Sophonisba's fifty-year old slave looks at the drape of the gown held against her young mistress' nude body. "It needs a pinch in the waist," the rotund attendant replies, impatiently tapping the floor with her wooden leg. "It bags too much because you have no belly!"

Jezebel spreads out the waist material as far as it will go, pulling it from Sophonisba's hips. She grins at her mistress, her white teeth shining in her nut-brown face. "After you have babies you will get fat like me. Then you can let out the dress!"

Sophonisba smiles. "That will never happen. My king loves my slim body, he has caressed every inch of it with his hands!" Jezebel whoops with delight and the two break into laughter.

Sophonisba's chamber door booms with the pounding of a heavy fist.

"Quiet! We are busy in here!" Jezebel snaps.

"Go see who it is, Jezebel. It might be important."

The Numidian Queen carefully lays her gown next to the others on her bed. She slips into her long linen shift and smoothes down the stray strands of her flowing raven hair.

Jezebel clops to the door and pulls it open. She glares at the tall, rangy messenger standing in front of her, his body speckled with trail dust. The man looks about uncertainly, his eyes weary and bloodshot.

"What you want?" she spits. "Look at you! You come to your queen looking like a dusty cur!"

The messenger shifts. He swallows hard and sets his jaw. "I have a message from King Masinissa." He extends the scroll to Sophonisba, the message shaking in his hand. "It is for you, my queen."

Sophonisba's eyes light up. "Oh, good! I have been waiting to hear from him! She hurries over to the messenger and snatches away the papyrus roll. Sophonisba breaks the seal and reads the message, her lips moving silently. She slaps the back of her hand to her mouth, not believing what she reads. She teeters on her feet, her eyes glazed with horror.

The messenger reaches into his pouch. "Please excuse me, my queen. I also have this." He holds out a small sealed urn.

Sophonisba pulls out the cork from the top of the urn and sniffs it. *It is wine, oddly scented wine.* Her mouth tightens. *You know what that scent is.* She delicately closes the urn and nods, her eyes shiny with tears.

The messenger looks at her, then averts his eyes. "I must tell you. The

Romans are not far behind me. They are coming for you."

The scroll falls to her feet, and Jezebel rushes to pick it up. She glances at it and gasps, shaking her head at what she reads.

My Beloved Wife and Queen:

I promised I would not let you fall into Roman hands, to be humiliated at Rome. I truly thought our marriage would protect you, but Scipio will not rest until you are returned to Rome as a captive, conjoined with your former husband.

I have failed to protect you through marriage, but I offer you the other path. Drink this and find blessed surcease from this world of endless disappointment. Wait for me in the land of Melqart, I shall soon come to you.

I love you forever,

Masinissa

Sophonisba beckons for the scroll to be returned to her, willing her heart to cease its hammering. She reads it one more time to confirm its words, then crumples it up and gives it to her attendant. "Burn this. The Romans must not see it." The slave scurries out the door to the main hall, looking for a wall torch.

Sophonisba stares at the walls for several long moments. *The Romans are coming take you back to Rome, the men who helped kill your father. What would he think of you being paraded about in chains? What will your ex-husband do to you, if you are kept together?*

A cough startles her reverie, and she looks over to see Masinissa's messenger still waiting for her.

She takes a deep breath and straightens her shoulders, "You have done well, brave one, although your news is most, uh, most unexpected. Your king will want a reply."

Sophonisba steps over to a flat table filled with writing supplies, and pulls out a papyrus scroll and stylus. She dips the stylus into a pottery jar of octopus ink and hastily completes a letter in her flowing hand, her breath catching in her throat as she writes.

My Love:

As the daughter of a Carthaginian general, I know the ways of the world. I venture that you were offered a choice between your kingdom and my life, nothing else could stay you from standing here by my side to protect me from such a loathsome fate.

Your choice between power and love is not the one I would have made, were it mine to make. I know you are forsworn to reclaim your father's kingdom. I hope, somehow, it justifies your decision in your mind.

Sophonisba starts to roll up the message. She pauses, unrolls, it and adds a final line, biting her lower lip as she writes it.

I must say, my death would be more acceptable to me, had my marriage not coincided with my funeral. [cxiv]

Sophonisba shakily rolls up the scroll and stamps it with the phoenix seal of the Gisgon family. She waves the messenger over to her and presses it into his hands.

"Go now, before the Romans come, and worry about me no more."

The messenger nods and rushes to the chamber doors. He starts to close them when Jezebel barges in, weeping loudly. Sophonisba's attendant throws herself into her mistress' arms, desperately clutching her.

"We can escape, mistress! I have family in the far west, you will be safe with my tribe. Send the guards away, we can take horses and go." She peers into Sophonisba's face, looking for an answer, and is horrified at what she sees. "No! Do not do this!" she begs.

Sophonisba disengages from her treasured servant, kissing her gently on the lips. "You are right about escaping, but it will be you who leaves. I flee no Roman." Wiping her eyes, she composes herself and steps to the door, beckoning in her two senior guards. She points to Jezebel. "Get this woman an escort back to the land of the Moors."

Sophonisba turns to her slave and presses a purse of gold coins into her hands. "Take this, and go. Do not look back!"

The slave starts to reply when she sees the beseeching look on her mistress' face, and knows her mistress can barely hold on to the stern look she has mustered to control the guards. Jezebel bows deeply, her lips trembling, and hurries out the door.

As the guards start to close the door Jezebel glances back at Sophonisba, who stands alone in the room, her hands balled into fists. Sophonisba crosses her hands over her heart, and mouths a kiss to her. Jezebel's head droops, and she closes the door.

Heaving a deep sigh, Sophonisba walks to her marble refreshment table and fills a cup of dark red wine. She puts the cup back on the table and goes to her large wicker basket of ceremonial clothes, rummaging deep into them, her fingers probing. "Ah! There you are!" she exclaims.

Sophonisba extracts a small bottle and uncorks it. She sniffs it to affirm its potency. *Thank the gods I got some more after Masinissa left. I knew something like this would happen when he joined the Romans.*

She smirks. *At least I will have the final mockery.*

The queen picks up Masinissa's urn and throws it out the window, enjoying the sound of its crash. *If the cursed Romans want to drag me back to Rome they will find me appropriately prepared to receive them,* she muses, enjoying the ghastly image that comes her mind.

Sophonisba walks back to her bed and holds up the gown she had worn a few minutes—an eternity—ago. She slips out of her shift and stands nude before her beaten-metal mirror. She runs her hands down her peerless body, recalling the pleasures she has given and received.

Sophonisba slides the gown over her head, and slips on her silver-inlaid sandals, running her fingers across the silver phoenix birds that top each one of them. *Oh, if only I could be reborn from my ashes like you. That would make things so much easier.*

Sophonisba dons the gold diadem that Masinissa gave her, pinning it tightly into her hair. *Wouldn't want it to fall off, that would not befit a queen.*

She picks up the small glass bottle and empties its contents into her wine, stirring it slowly with her finger, her eyes distant.

Carrying the wine carefully, she walks out from her chamber, smiling at her two remaining guards, and steps down the wide stone steps that lead from the upper chambers to the throne room. The Numidian queen clacks across the polished marble floor and seats herself on the throne Masinissa had installed next to his just before he left—when he swore to protect her from the humiliating clutches of the Romans.

Sophonisba eases into her chair. She grabs her sacred yew wood scepter and cradles it in her lap. She spies a passing house slave and has a flash of inspiration. She snaps her fingers, summoning him over. "Riad! Get me a long string of rope. Now!"

The slave dashes off and soon sidles back, clutching a skein of rope. "Bind me to my throne. Go behind it and wrap the rope around me." He stares confusedly at her. "Do not fear, Riad. All is as it should be. As it was fated."

The slave steps behind her and loops the soft rope over her head. She pulls it around her waist. He pulls a second loop between her breasts. Bemused, she smiles faintly at how they jut from her tightly bound gown. *That will titillate those pigs.* "Tie it tight," she commands, and the slave tugs in the knots.

"Go now, and tell no one what you did!" The slave dashes from the room. Sophonisba looks about the throne room, at the draped finery and gilded columns. She shakes her head. *So close, my prince. We were so close to having it all.*

Sophonisba grabs the cup and downs its contents in one long gulp.

Coughing, she flings the cup off to the side, where it clangs across the gleaming marble floor. *No sense waiting. Hasten its arrival.* She takes a dozen deep breaths and blows them out, staring at the door.

Soon, very soon, the tremors come...

Three hours later, twelve of Scipio's guards ride into Cirta, towing a litter for Sophonisba's transport. The men pull up in front of the palace and quickly trudge up its steps. They halt in front of the Numidian sentries standing on each side of the entry.

"Where is Sophonisba?" the centurion commands.

One guard looks at the other, a cryptic smile on his face. "In the throne room," he says flatly. "She is waiting for you."

The Romans march across the wide entryway, their hobnailed caligae clacking on the wide stone tiles. They stride into the throne room, pushing past the strangely passive guards stationed by its doors. Inside they find Sophonisba.

Sophonisba sits grinning on her throne. Her teeth are bared in a rictus of mocking death.

The *Sardonicus* plant has long been the favored suicide poison of the Celtiberian tribes. When hopelessly surrounded, the fierce warriors take it as a final jape upon their conquering opponents. Their dead faces would contort into a skeletal smile so frightening that even the bravest enemies would not come near a warrior who died from it, fearing that demonic spirits inhabited their grinning faces.

Years ago, when her father Gisgo told Sophonisba about the poison, she knew it would be her preferred method of suicide, should the Romans ever overwhelm Carthage and come after her. Little did she dream she would use it as a Numidian queen.

Now the mover of nations sits bound to her throne, her scepter resting askance her cold bosom. Now the Roman's intended captor sits bolt upright, staring into infinity, mocking their intents with her frozen smile.

The centurion finally finds his voice. "Cut her down, we will take her corpse with us. They can parade it across the Forum." The Romans step up to the throne with drawn daggers. They hear a loud shuffling behind them.

The hall fills with scores of armed Numidians, silently staring at the Romans. The tall, lean warriors step in farther and fill the throne room, stopping a mere sword's thrust from the centurion who stands beneath Sophonisba.

An old Numidian steps in front of the grim warriors, wearing armor two sizes too large for his withered frame. He pushes his helmet back from his face and points at Sophonisba. "She stay here, Roman," he says in broken Latin. He bares his toothless gums. "You do us that favor, eh?"

The centurion gauges the number of the Numidians blocking his progress. fists clenched about their swords, belying the calm of their faces. He notices they stand on the balls of their feet, ready to spring into action.

"Come on, men. We don't need to drag a stinking corpse all the way back to camp. Leave it here with the savages."

The old man spits a few words to his fellows. The Numidians part in the middle, leaving a wide passage to the door. The legionnaires slowly walk through the massed warriors, glancing nervously at the bright curved swords in their ready hands.

Once the Romans exit the gauntlet, their pace quickens to a run. They leap onto their horses and hurtle out the gates of Cirta, racing to give their dire news to Scipio.

And to Masinissa.

VIII. TRUCE AND TREACHERY

ROME, 203 BCE. Laelius stumbles away from the Scipio family tomb, his eyes filled with tears. He is overcome by his visit to see Pomponia's urn, a simple black enameled repository resting in its niche inside a wall frescoed with a woodland scene. The taste of the ceramic urn is still on his lips; his final kiss to the only mother he ever knew. He places his hand on his breast. *Oh Charon, give her blessed passage across the Styx to Hades, that she may achieve her rest!*

The news of Pomponia's death struck Laelius like a thunderclap, the ill-fated message arriving just as he boarded his quinquereme to take Syphax to Rome. There was only time to halt the trip for a night and repair to Scipio's tent. He spent the night in his beloved friend's arms as Scipio cried out his grief. Marcus Silenus sat stolidly in the rear of Scipio's praetorium, awkwardly watching the two men cry.

"She is gone because I was here playing soldier," Scipio curses, throwing his maps and scrolls about the room. "The haruspex was right, People die because of me."

Marcus Silenus rises and places his hand on Scipio's shoulder. "It was not you. She died because of me. I swore to protect her and failed." The two gape at him.

Scipio wipes the tears from his eyes and stares at him. "What do you mean?"

Fool! Marcus tells himself. *He has enough on his mind. Take care of it yourself.*

Marcus shrugs noncommittally. "It was just a thought. Who knows who did it, and why?" He glares sternly at Scipio. "You are vain to think you are the cause of all her troubles. She was a very powerful woman. She begat her own enemies."

Scipio blinks at him, uncomprehending. He throws himself on his sleeping pallet. Soon, after several cups of unwatered wine, Somnus comes to Scipio, and the God of Sleep blesses him with temporary forgetfulness.

At dawn Laelius helps Scipio stumble to the latrines. After taking Scipio to the improvised camp baths he forces him to eat breakfast, insisting he will not depart for Rome until Scipio has taken nourishment. With a final kiss and embrace, Laelius rides away from Scipio's tent, leaving him in the company of a heavily bandaged Marcus Silenus. *They are both so wounded,* Laelius thinks as gallops off. *Will either be himself again?*

Now Laelius is in Rome, back at the center of his world. The ragged orphan is now cloaked with honor, his captive the king of a vast empire.

A week ago Laelius had thought this trip would be filled with triumph and laughter. Now the brokenhearted hero receives the Senate's accolades and awards with dulled gratitude. Even as he describes Scipio's victories to the citizen's Popular Assembly, where his words are almost drowned by the people's ecstatic cheers,[cxv] his mind is elsewhere.

His mission is accomplished, but he cannot leave. The Senate has received a message that a Carthaginian peace delegation will come to Rome after they meet with Scipio in Castra Cornelia. They enjoin Laelius to wait until the envoys arrive in Rome and meet with the Senate,[cxvi] that he may offer his counsel about the terms.

And so Laelius spends his waiting days with Amelia, helping her to care for baby Cornelia, who has already become the love of his life. Today, having paid his final respects to Pomponia, he returns to Amelia with a heavy heart.

Laelius enters the Scipio domus and walks to the sunny central atrium, looking for Amelia. Seeing no one there he heads for her favorite room in the house, the garden. She is there by the rear wall, carefully watering the carnation that Scipio brought from the Iberia battlefield

269

three years ago, a living token of his love. The slender plant has grown into a fully flowering bush. This greatly pleases Amelia, who takes it as a sign that their romance has blossomed, however distant he is from her.

"Amelia," Laelius says softly, "The libitinarius gave this to me at the tomb." He unwraps the indigo cotton square and takes out the undertaker's work: a wax death mask of Pomponia, every face detail evident. Amelia looks at it and nods her satisfaction.

"That is her: noble, strong, and beautiful. She was a great defender of the people, the equal of any in Rome," Amelia looks at the Scipio masks that line the atrium. "Certainly she deserves her place among the Scipio generals. Put her next to her husband Publius. She would like that."

Laelius walks into the adjoining atrium, stepping over to the wall lined with masks of generations of Scipio generals and senators. He sees the empty hook next to Publius solemn mask, and carefully slides Pomponia's image onto it, lightly caressing it before he steps back.

"The first woman on the wall, eh? Well, progress is slow."

"How is he?" he hears Amelia say as he steps away from the mask. "Has he changed?"

Laelius takes a deep breath and continues to stare at the wall. "He is the same, but he is different, I don't know. He wants peace, but he is determined to make war until he gets terms that will protect Rome forever." He looks at Publius' mask. "Terms that will fulfill his promise to his father." Laelius walks to a low couch next to the fish pond, and beckons in Amelia. She pads over and sits next to him, taking his hand in hers.

"He has won so many battles, against incalculable odds," Laelius continues, "But the victories have changed him. There is a hardness to him now, a cocksure confidence that he can defeat anyone. He is very suspicious of achieving peace by negotiation or diplomacy, when he would have avidly sought that before. Now he trusts to his military might to get what he wants."

He edges near to Amelia, and puts his hand on her arm. "I fear I am a danger to him, because of my ... lifestyle. Cato and the Latins, they spread rumors that he is my consort. They use my sexual preferences as a weapon against him."

Laelius looks pleadingly at Amelia. "Hannibal is coming back to Africa, I am sure of it. A great battle looms, and I fear I will not survive it. If I do not, please tell him I always knew of his sacrifices for me, though he never spoke of them. And I love him above all others. Above my own life."

Amelia leans over and softly presses her lips to his hand. "I have lost my commander, too. With Pomponia gone, I must redouble my efforts for the plebs and slaves." She smiles. "Both of us will be very busy, eh? We have a war to win and a child to raise!"

Laelius kisses her on the cheek and they sit silently for a while. Then he rises, a jaunty smile on his face. "Apologies, I have been somber too long. If the Senate will make me a prisoner in my own city, I might as well savor its bounty!" He grins as he strides out of the room. "I shall be late, carissime. Do not wait up!"

Laelius repairs to his room and changes into a battered gray tunic and worn sandals, looking every bit like a common citizen. He hurries out into the street and walks the half mile over to Rome's largest public bath. He undresses inside the entrance and gives his tunic and sandals to a slave.

Wearing only a scant subligalculum, he pads over to the large adjoining gymnasium, eyes alight with eagerness. There Laelius finds what he seeks; dozens of young men engaged in a series of free form wrestling matches. The men grapple until one throws or pins the other, only to part and dash over to another opponent, locking arms about each other's torsos.

Laelius jumps into the fray, wrestling with a wiry youth who is easily thrown. He follows with a match against a broad-beamed man that barely budges when Laelius shoves against him, so unmovable that Laelius can only laugh at his futile efforts to throw him. The yard echoes with the athletes' laughter and curses, with Laelius contributing more than his share.

For a while, for a brief respite, Laelius is no longer an admiral or legate, no longer a man-killing warrior. He is the orphan boy from the Ostia docks, enjoying the combative community of men stripped of rank or privilege, measuring each other by only by their strength and skill.

Laelius spends several gloriously exhausting hours in the gymnasium. He finishes with a steaming hot bath followed by his favorite luxury, an olive oil cleansing. A muscular Nubian slave expertly massages olive oil into Laelius' nude body, and scrapes the oil off with his bull's horn knife.

Relaxed and exhilarated, Laelius strolls through the cobbled streets off the Forum, heading for his favorite wine bar. *Might as well treat myself to a goblet of good Falernian, it will help me sleep. I have to be ready to defend Scipio tomorrow. That Senate meeting will be a cockfight.*

Laelius hears a stick tapping against a wall. He looks down the darkened side street from whence the sound came, but he sees no one. The tapping comes again, louder and more insistent, down by his feet.

Laelius looks down and sees a black-cloaked older woman sitting on the street among the garbage and offal, her lank gray hair shrouding her lined and angular face.

She again taps her tree branch walking stick. Her watery blue eyes stare up at him, pleading. She points a veined finger at the tufa stone tablet next to her. Laelius bends over and squints at the chiseled tablet.

The sickness took my hearing. My husband died at Cannae. A coin please.

Laelius grabs into his belt pouch with both hands, his hands trembling with urgency. He bends over and cascades a double handful of silver and gold coins into her lap.

His breath quickens and shakes. His left hand scrabbles desperately inside his battle-worn pouch, looking for more. He drops another denarii into her lap.

The woman's eyes bulge with amazed pleasure. She presses two grimy fingers to her lips and holds them toward Laelius, smiling. He reaches down and gently squeezes them. He bows his perfectly groomed head at her and walks away.

Something calls within him to pause. He turns back and sees the woman beaming at him. *I love you*, she mouths.

Laelius walks quickly to the next corner and pivots around it. Then the feeling rushes onto him, an overwhelming mix of gratitude and sorrow. He leans his hand against the mud wall of a rickety insulae, steadying himself as the deep sobs wrack his body.

His shaking hand wipes the tears from his face. He clenches it into a fist. *What the fuck is wrong with you? Summon yourself.*

Laelius pulls out a linen scrap, wipes his face, and blows his nose. Straightening his shoulders, he marches firmly down the street.

Gratitude, Beautiful. Now I am ready for anything the Senate may do.

He manages a small grin. *Thank the gods Marcus didn't see me. He'd think me a sentimental weakling.*

*   *   *   *   *

CASTRA CORNELIA, NORTH AFRICA. Masinissa sits upon his U-shaped seat in Scipio's enormous new praetorium, looking every bit a king in his robes and posture. But his eyes stare into nothingness and his face is empty of emotion.

Scipio sits next to the prince in an identical chair. He turns to tell Masinissa a joke, but his smile vanishes when he sees Masinissa's withdrawn expression. *He acts as if I were not here.* Scipio turns back to the tent entrance and waits for the next petitioner.

Scipio has tried everything to win back his friend's regard after Sophonisba's suicide. He called a celebratory assembly of the entire camp, at which he placed a golden crown upon the prince's head and gave him an ivory scepter, referring to him King Masinissa.[cxvii] Scipio then gave him an ivory curule chair, shaped like a curved X, the same magisterial chair that Scipio himself now uses to rule over camp affairs. Masinissa received the gifts and accolades with courteous gratitude, but his voice and actions were those of a man whose soul has left his body.

He has lost his spirit and I have lost him, Scipio thinks.

The next petitioner is a centurion who has been jailed for stealing money from his subordinates. As a crime of theft, he is due to be tied into a sack of snakes and thrown into the river, in accordance with Roman camp law. The terrified centurion pleads that two legionnaires under him bore false witness, that he won this money by gambling. Several legionnaires from the adjoining century testify that they lost money in dice games with the centurion, as did the two accusers.

Scipio declares the centurion in innocent. He decrees that the two liars be flogged in public on the morrow, be given barley instead of wheat in their rations, and have their year's pay given to the centurion. When the centurion leaves the tent, Scipio turns to Masinissa. "I cannot take your silence any more. What is wrong, friend?"

"You are my commander," Masinissa says, his voice cold and distant as he stares straight ahead. "And we are allies." He turns blank eyes on Scipio. "But I no longer call you friend, General. My heart is empty of you."

Scipio stares at him, searching for words. "I regret the loss of our bond, but I do not regret what I did. I had to honor the law and send her back to Rome. I also did it to protect you, whether you believe me or not. I want nothing more than to see you King of all Numidia."

Masinissa crosses his arms over his chest and stares away from Scipio, saying nothing. Scipio purses his lips. "Well, then. I will honor my promise to support your kingship. Ten cohorts will join you when you leave for Numidia." [cxviii]

Masinissa's head turns slightly toward Scipio. "Can they be ready in two days?" he asks flatly.

Scipio blinks at him. "You want to leave in two days? Don't you want to stay for the peace talks with Carthage's envoys? They will be here the same day you would leave."

"My business here is done. I would depart." He looks blankly at Scipio. "That is, with your approval, Imperator," he says, his voice tinged with sarcasm.

I have lost him, Scipio thinks. *I have saved him but I have lost him.* Scipio starts to reach for Masinissa's shoulder, then lets his hand drop to his side. "Ten cohorts, two days. As you wish."

Masinissa nods, and rises from his seat. "Gratitude. I am off to prepare my men." He walks toward the exit, his shoulders stiff as a stone.

"We are not yet done," Scipio blurts. "I will need your assistance when Hannibal comes."

Masinissa pauses and looks over his shoulder. "Of course," he says, smiling sarcastically "I am, after all, a friend ... to Rome." Masinissa steps out of the tent, leaving Scipio alone in the large room.

Two days later Carthage's fifty envoys debark from a trireme in Utica's harbor. The purple-robed men trot down the wide dirt road to Scipio's camp, flanked by retinue of armed slaves and guards. Scipio greets them a mile from his gates, poised atop a coal black stallion with a blood red saddle blanket. His senior tribunes and Honor Guard form a semicircle about him, each carrying a silver headed ceremonial javelin.

"Welcome, Carthaginians. I am honored with your presence," Scipio says. "I hope our talks will be most productive."

"The honor is hours," says Durro, the senior representative. "We have brought you this token of our respect." Durro gestures to a man behind him. A stout young African trundles out a small wagon, with a linen covered shape lying prone inside it. He halts in front of Scipio and whisks off the cover. A four-foot statue of Mars, Rome's god of war, reclines on purple linen. Durro bows.

"Hasdrubal the Fair captured this in the last war between our nations," Durro says. "I thought we should return it to you, as a gesture of conciliation." He chuckles. "Anath, our goddess of war, was becoming very jealous of him!"

Scipio grins. "Take it to my tent. The god can preside over our talks tomorrow, although I would prefer we had one of Pax, our goddess of peace!"

Scipio turns his stallion to camp. "Please come to my camp. I have provided food and sleeping quarters. We can meet on the morrow."

"We Elders would appreciate that," Durro replies, rubbing his bony neck. "The trip was short, but the seas were most unkind." He snaps the reins on his horse and leads in his entourage.

Leaving the Carthaginians with his tribunes, Scipio repairs to his tent to ponder the envoys' words. *They call themselves "Elders?" Many are not even thirty! Still, if they are willing to accept my proposals, I might craft a peace that the Rome will approve—without destroying Carthage.*

Scipio summons Lucius and Marcus Silenus. Their meeting lasts long into the night. They argue over the peace terms they will present, ones that will end Carthage's military threat to Rome but have enough trade concessions for them to maintain their commerce and culture.

The next morning a drowsy Scipio presents the peace terms that he feels will protect Rome from Carthaginian dominance. Carthage must hand over all prisoners of war and renounce all claims to Iberia and the Mediterranean islands. Rome will be paid five thousand talents of silver for its financial losses, and Carthage must surrender all but twenty of its warships, which they may retain for their own protection. [cxix]

In exchange, Carthage is allowed to resume its normal business and military operations, unless they conflict with Rome's own interests.

"Outlandish!" blurts one of the younger men, a Barca senator. "You would turn Carthage into a fishing village!" The council leader steps in front of the young man, and shoves him back into the rest of the delegation.

Scipio looks at Lucius. "Perhaps we should not consider peace at all."

Lucius nods. "We can march back out on a day's notice," he says, playing his part.

The envoys stare at one another. "Apologies, mighty Scipio," interjects Durro. "This fool of a Barca does not see what you could have demanded." He looks at his fellow delegates, his question unspoken. Each nods their agreement or shakes their head in denial, as the Durro takes a voiceless vote of them. He turns back to Scipio.

"We agree to those terms, General. But we should discuss some additional details about our army, and the shipping lanes. Details covered in the first treaty with Rome."

By the gods, there is a chance for peace, after all. "It will be done, I am sure the Senate will favor most of that treaty's agreements. I suggest some of you stay with me to finalize those details, while others go to Rome with a signed version of our treaty, that the people may approve it."[cxx]

"I think we should take the matter up with our Senate before we do," Durro replies. "That may take another month."

"Or longer!" Scipio replies angrily. He stares imperiously at them. "If it be peace, I will have it as soon as possible, or I will resume this war."

Durro is silent for a moment. Scipio and his officers watch him silently, their faces expressionless. "We will return to Utica tomorrow," Durro answers, his voice tinged with anger, "and depart for Rome the day after that."

"It is well that you do," Scipio says. He raises his right arm. "We are done here." The envoys file from the room. Scipio waves his arm toward the tent exit, and his own men leave.

Scipio sits in his empty praetorium, looking at the legionary pennants and weapons that decorate the walls. His gaze lingers on the marble statue of Mars. *Peace. After sixteen years we have made a peace with Carthage. I should celebrate, but Laelius is gone, Masinissa has left me, and Marcus is half dead. Not much to celebrate.*

He rubs the back of his neck, trying to ease its tension. "Guard! Bring me my cup-bearer," he calls to the front of the tent. "And get my brother Lucius!"

The sentry returns with Lucius and one of Scipio's trusted tribunes, the man who ensures Scipio's wine is free of poison. Praxis' attempt on Marcus life has made Scipio more cautious of his own.

The tribune pours a large cup of wine for Scipio and Lucius. He samples both and then gives them out. The two brothers raise a cup to each other and drink.

Lucius drains his cup. "Apologies, brother. But it is time for me to check on our fleet and get some sleep."

Scipio slumps in his command chair, moodily sipping his wine. *At least Laelius is having fun.*

*   *   *   *   *

TEMPLE OF BELLONA, OUTSKIRTS OF ROME. *Ah gods, they kept me here for this circus? Kill me now, and save Hannibal the trouble!* Laelius is sprawled out in the front row of the temple steps, defiantly clad in a Greek style black and gold toga. He wears the laurel wreath of victory that was conferred upon him, hoping it will give him more credence with the senators.

Laelius is listening to the thirty Carthaginian envoys who have arrived from their meeting with Scipio. By law, enemies are not allowed within the city limits, and so the Senate has ventured out to meet with them on the steps of this beautiful little temple.

Laelius' face is pinched with disgust at what he hears. *Lies*, he thinks. *Lies and betrayal. Their Senate is no better than ours.*

"Let me reiterate what my older fellows said a little while ago," says a curly-haired young Carthaginian senator. "Carthage wants peace. Our citizens want peace, we have always wanted peace. Now, this Hannibal Barca, he attacked your allies at Saguntum without the Senate knowing about it.[cxxi] He crossed the Alps without our permission. Carthage itself has faithfully held to the peace terms of our first war. But Hannibal, he has his own mind in the matter."

The pudgy Carthaginian Senator takes a deep breath and draws himself up to his full five feet and two inches. "We have recalled Hannibal from your homeland, and we are here to sue for peace, the peace that Scipio has approved. We ask only for the same terms as contained in the treaty of our first war—and that you cease all hostilities immediately."

One of the eldest Roman senators rises, a thirty-year veteran whose back is still ramrod straight. He fixes his keen gray eyes on the speaker. "You say you want the same terms as the original treaty. Does that include our control of the shipping lanes?"

The young Carthaginian Senator looks beseechingly at his fellows. They nod their agreement. "Uh, yes. Whatever those conditions were," mumbles the envoy. "As I said, we agree to whatever the treaty specified."

"But what about Sardinia and Sicily?" queries another elder. "I was here when the treaty was signed. Land ownership of those lands has changed in the forty years since that treaty!" His response provokes a round of angry muttering among the Senate.

Several Romans spring to their feet. "These men seek make peace with a treaty they know nothing about!" blurts one.

"They think their lies will do what their sword cannot—stop Scipio's advance!" declares another.

"Carthaginian duplicity," yells a third.[cxxii]

"Apologies," says the praetor in charge of the meeting. "We must discuss your proposal in private," He summons a guard to usher the envoys to a nearby temple while the Senate confers.

When the envoys have left the chamber, the elegant Quintus Metelius rises to speak. "I do not think we should be the ones to make peace with the Carthaginians," the former consul says. "No one can more accurately appraise their intentions than the man who is at their gates, Publius Cornelius Scipio himself!" [cxxiii]

Another former consul, the estimable Marcus Valerius Laevinus, jumps up from his seat. "You know how tricky the Carthaginians can be. I do not think these men are envoys, I think they are spies! We should order them to leave. Tell Scipio to continue his fight against Carthage." [cxxiv]

Listening to the two senators, Flaccus' face flushes with alarm. *They are going to turn the entire war over to Scipio! If he wins, the Hellenics will have all the glory and power!* Flaccus rises from his seat and stands next to Metelius, who yields the floor to the senior senator.

"Do you hear yourselves, giving all our power to a soldier?" Flaccus chides. "Would you abrogate our duty to a fledgling general far away from our control? We should be the ones to make the decision, and insist Scipio abide by it!" The Senate is quiet as they mull Flaccus' words.

Laelius senses the Senate is on the cusp of backing away from the treaty. *Oh, no! They're going to waste months chewing on this, and then give Carthage some kind of intolerable proposal.* He sees that many of the senators look confused. *Play to their fears, boy, that always works.*

"Do I have leave to address the Senate?" Laelius asks of the Senate Leader. The seventy-year old Senator merely nods. Laelius stands up and strolls out from the temple steps, smoothing down his lavish tunic.

"General Scipio made his peace agreement when Hannibal and Mago were still in Italia, and Carthage was at its most vulnerable," Laelius says. "Now, we hear that Hannibal and Mago are being recalled to Carthage. It is well they are gone from Italia, but their presence in

Africa means another outbreak of war. And who knows what Fortuna will bring to us if we wait, inactive, suspended between peace and war? We had best make a decision, here and now."

"What is to stop them from breaking the treaty?" asks a senior senator. "They are Carthaginians, after all."

Laelius nods. "Nothing. As with all treaties, we must trust them." His face darkens. "But I swear this to you, if Scipio finds they have violated any of the terms, his vengeance will be swift and terrible. You have all heard about what he did at Astapa. And Sucro. And Carthago Nova!

"You heard consul Quintus Metelius, who is a most honorable and sagacious man. He said no one is more qualified to make a treaty with Carthage than Scipio. And Scipio has made that treaty. We deny it at our peril." With a theatric swirl of his glittering toga, Laelius marches back to his place on the steps.

The Senate Leader rises. "Thank you, Admiral Laelius. I think we have all heard enough. I call a vote on ratification of the treaty. Those in favor of approving the treaty, walk to the left and stand next to the statue of Bellona. Those against will walk to the right."

Within a few minutes, the goddess statue is thronged with treaty supporters, the decision evident before the senators in the rear can descend the steps. Flaccus and a group of Latins stand to the right, fuming at their overwhelming loss.

Watching the vote unfold, Laelius smiles with satisfaction. *I hope this peace is what you wanted, my friend. Hannibal will return and Mago will join him, and the treaty may be broken. Can you overcome the both of them?*

*　　*　　*　　*　　*

CROTON, SOUTH ITALIA, 203 BCE. "Are the transports finished?" queries Hannibal as he stares out into the Mediterranean, watching two of his quinqeremes patrolling past the docks.

"We have four more to finish, but we are weeks late," replies the

Carthaginian shipwright, wiping his gnarled hands on a rag. "We lost over forty Bruttian workers in the last two weeks. I think the bastards deserted to the enemy."

"Bruttians!" spits Hannibal. "Some leave every day!" He shakes his fist at Maharbal, his second in command. "I tell you this, I'm only bringing the best of them back to Africa. The rest can go sit on a spear, for all I care!"

"You are sure we are going back home?" asks the shipwright, unable to keep the eagerness from his voice.

Hannibal glares at the man. "I was told a delegation from Carthage was coming here," he says coldly. "The message said nothing of troops or supplies. I fear the worst." He shakes his head forlornly. "They would be playing right in to that Scipio's hands, pulling me out from Italia."

"They'll take Mago, too," adds Maharbal. "At least you can join armies against him."

Hannibal shrugs. "Perhaps, if they can find him. I have not heard from him for a while. He should have passed through Bononia by now."

Maharbal idly picks at a string dangling from his sword belt. "We might as well go home. Lately we haven't done anything here but raise taxes and bully people into paying them. I would relish a good fight, wherever it is!"

Hannibal laughs, and smiles at Maharbal. "You have always been so impetuous! We were ordered to stay here until the delegation came, and that is what we will do. In the meantime, we collect money to pay the mercenaries, so we do not lose any more of them. More of those damned Gauls deserted last week. Thank Baal the Iberians have nowhere to go, or they'd be gone, too!"

Maharbal snorts. "You think I am impetuous? If you had listened to me after Cannae, we would have stormed Rome's gates while they were most vulnerable! We were right there, amidst forty thousand of their dead, a day's ride from conquest!"

"You will not forget that, will you?" Hannibal retorts. "We were exhausted and Rome was days away, with four Roman legions between us and the city. I will hear no more of it. If you want action, take the Numidians and Bruttians north to Paterunum. Engage that consul Gnaeus Servilius. He has been seducing our allied towns to the Roman cause.[cxxv] We can show the Bruttians that we are the stronger power."

"That I will gladly do," Maharbal responds. He hurries back to camp.

Hannibal turns to the master shipwright. "You must finish all the ships within the month. We may have to leave in short notice, and whatever cannot be taken—whoever cannot be taken --- must be disposed of." He looks intently at the builder. "And you will be responsible."

The shipwright's eyes widen. "I will finish them, I promise!"

Hannibal gives him a grim smile. "Yes, you will. Or you will be one of the disposed."

Six days later Maharbal returns to Croton at sunset, riding to Hannibal's command tent outside of the city. He finds Hannibal outside, preparing to sleep on the ground near his men, as is his custom. Hannibal rises from his small cooking fire and watches Maharbal expectantly. He notices Maharbal's white linen cuirass is spotless, and grimaces. "You missed them?" he asks Maharbal.

The cavalry commander slides from his saddle and tromps over to the fire, rubbing his hands in front of it to warm himself. "The consul wouldn't fight, and we couldn't trap him," he growls. "As soon as his scouts sent word we were coming, he garrisoned his legion inside the nearest town, and he wouldn't come out."

Maharbal looks at Hannibal. "I think the Romans are content to contain you here in Bruttium, like a lion in a pen," he says. "They wait for Scipio to win the war for them."

"Hmph! This old lion still has some teeth!" Hannibal stalks into his tent and Maharbal follows him. Hannibal stoops over his map table, staring at the map of the Bruttium region, scrutinizing its features as if it holds some secret to victory.

Maharbal walks to the back of the tent and pours himself a glass of wine. He knows Hannibal is strategizing his next move, and may not speak for hours.

As night settles over the camp Hannibal pours over the map, refusing both food and wine. He runs his finger along the Neto River that separates Croton from Servilius' legions in the north, then over the Sila Mountains to the west of his camp.

Finally he stands up, his eye agleam with excitement. He gestures Maharbal to his side. "We are going to break out of here and join Mago, before we lose any more Bruttians. We march north to Sybaris, to head along the coast and then along the Via Appia toward Rome."

He runs his finger along the Neto River. "This will be low country beneath the Sila Mountains. Send our cavalry into the Sila Plateau the night before, up in that thick forest at the top, where they cannot be discovered. They can follow us along the plateau as we march in the lowlands to Sybaris. If Servilius' legions try to stop us, our riders will descend on him and cut into his flank."

Maharbal drains his wine cup. "Excellent! If Servilius won't fight, we head north and rejoin our allies in Lucania and Apulia." he smirks. "We have enough Roman-haters there to build another army!"

Hannibal nods. "We muster out in three days." Satisfied, the two old comrades in arms sit over the map table late into the night, plotting their campaign and drinking wine.

The next day Hannibal is shaken awake by one of his Sacred Band officers. He rises groggily from the ground near his cooking fire. "What is it, Akbul?"

"General, the scout ship has just docked. They say there is a Carthaginian ship coming in to port."

Hannibal grits his teeth. "One? Only one ship? Is it a transport?"

The shipwright shakes his head. "No, just a trireme."

Hannibal sighs with disappointment. "Not even a quadrireme? Well, that is our answer about Carthage's plans. Fetch me the master shipwright!"

The officer trots off and Hannibal walks into his tent, preparing himself to receive the trireme's occupants. The shipwright enters Hannibal's tent as a slave is scraping the olive oil from Hannibal's naked body, a cleansing habit he adopted from the Italians.

"I want those ships finished within two weeks," he orders, not bothering to rise. "I don't care if you have to chain those Italians to the docks and work them night and day!"

The old man stares at Hannibal, incredulous. "You said a month just a few days ago, General."

"I am aware of my own words, builder." Hannibal barks. "Gods help me, we may need to load the ships very soon, or leave much of our army behind. Including you!" The shipwright scurries from the tent.

By early afternoon the Carthaginian trireme is stroking into the docks of Croton, furling up its proud purple sail. Arrayed in his best ceremonial armor, Hannibal marches along the wide dockway, just in time to meet the six old men who are stepping down off the gangplank.

A heavy, loose-limbed older man stumps out from the gathering on his one good leg. Hannibal knows him to be General Yutpan Magon, a veteran of the first war against Rome.

Hannibal frowns when he sees Yutpan. *They would not send a general unless it is news I don't want to hear.*

Never a man for words, the decorated old officer knocks across the wood planks and places his hand on Hannibal's shoulder.

"My son, I am sorry. You are recalled to...." Yutpan begins.

"No!" Hannibal blurts. "Another year! I just need another year! I am leaving to join Mago and march on Rome!"

Yutpan purses his lips and shakes his head. "It is not possible. Mago is returning, too. We have sent delegates to get him. The Senate wants you two back. You have to destroy Scipio before he takes Carthage."

Hannibal throws back his head and erupts into loud, bitter laughter, startling all around him.

He has gone mad, Yutpan thinks. *We'll have to chain him inside the hold.*

Hannibal continues laughing, wiping a tear from the corner of his eye, and looks at the old general.

"Do you not see? We are playing into that boy's hands. He does not have the army to overthrow Carthage,[cxxvi] were he to lay siege to it for a thousand years! No, he went there to draw us from here, to draw me from the shores of Italia."

"The Elders Council has signed the decree I bear you," Yutpan continues doggedly. "We need you back to protect Carthage."

"You mean to protect the merchants' interests, don't you?" growls Hannibal, looking at the noblemen behind him. "They are all begging for peace, aren't they? They want to get back to getting rich."

"You are under orders to leave as soon as possible," squawks a wizened delegate, his gold chains heavy about his neck. "We will wait here until you go."

Another soft-assed businessman. Hannibal glowers at the banty-sized nobleman. "I have some transports that will be finished in two weeks. I need them to take our best men with me. The rest I will send to our garrisons.[cxxvii] Perhaps we can still hold on to Bruttium, in spite of your best efforts to the contrary."

Yutpan sees the futility of further discussion. "It has been a long journey, General. Perhaps you will favor us with some rest and refreshment?"

Hannibal bows his head, embarrassed at his breach of manners.

"Forgive my incivility. My heart breaks with your news, though it was not totally unexpected."

Hannibal spins on his heel and stalks from the docks, his guards trailing behind him to escort the Elders. Yutpan hobbles up to join Hannibal. "Think of it this way. Scipio awaits you. You have a chance to conquer the unconquered, and become an immortal hero."

Hannibal merely sniffs. "For years past they have been trying to force me back by refusing me reinforcements and money. Now they recall me no longer by indirect means, but in plain words. Hannibal has been conquered not by the Roman people whom he defeated in battle so many times and put to flight, but by the envy and disparagement of the Carthaginians." [cxxviii]

With those words the two generals trudge back up the docks, each wrapped in his own thoughts.

*   *   *   *   *

GENOVA, NORTH ITALIA. Durro sits patiently at the meeting table in Mago's headquarters, waiting for the general to come in. The Elders' senior envoy sips the date wine he has brought with him from Carthage, savoring its sweet taste and fragrance. *As you get older you learn to appreciate the things you oft overlook when young*, he muses ruefully. *Such as being alive.* He looks idly about the room's tall timbered walls and taps his foot impatiently, growing irritated that Mago has not yet arrived.

The Elder has been at Mago's headquarters for five days now, waiting for him to return from his sally against the Roman legions. Mago's army returned yesterday, but Durro has not seen any trace of the doughty Carthaginian commander. After being turned away from Mago's private quarters, Durro was forced to summon an audience with him by Senate decree. *He delays because he suspects what I will tell him*, Durro thinks. *As if one more day would change the Senate's mind. Or mine.*

Durro is finishing his wine when the chamber doors boom open. A quartet of Mago's elite guard marches into the room, carrying Mago on a litter bed suspended between two stout poles. Mago lies atop the litter, plush pillows pushing his head upright, his face drawn and pale. With every bump and jostle he grits his teeth, yet no cry issues from his mouth. His men ease him from the litter and place him in a pillow-lined chaise prepared for him. Mago nods weakly at Durro.

"I see you have met some misfortune on your venture against the twelfth and thirteenth," Durro notes dryly.

"There were four legions," Mago says dourly. "And there are three more in the region. Their numbers surprised us. Next time we'll break through."

Hannibal's army had defeated twice that many up here, Durro thinks, but he only nods sympathetically. He brandishes a camelskin scroll sealed in purple wax, bearing the merchant-ship seal of the Senate Council. "You have new orders, General. You are to return to Africa, there to join Hannibal in his war against Scipio."

Anger, resentment, and hope rage inside Mago. He is furious to be recalled from his mission when victory is so close, resenting the cowardice of the Senate at recalling both him and his brother to fight Scipio's small army. But he is delighted to join his brother. For the first time, they can fight together.

"I only need the rest of the winter to recruit more men," Mago growls, in between gasps of pain. "There are thousands more Gauls and Ligurians up in the northern mountains. Hardy warriors who live to fight Romans!"

Durro shakes his head. "Carthage's safety comes first. You are to leave at once."

The businessmen's money comes first, Mago thinks. "I need to take all my Balearics, and the Libyans too, of course. And more money to pay the Gauls and Ligurians to come with me."

Durro waves his hand dismissively, as if Mago asked for a new sword. "It will be done. But three days hence we depart."

"Then it will be as you decree. I will call the chieftains tomorrow. Now let me go, I must rest."

Durro rises from the table. "I will be at my ship on the third morn. I will wait there until you join me."

Mago grimaces at Durro's words. *I need a month to recover. But Hannibal needs me. Perhaps the sea voyage will heal me.* [cxxix]

Three days later the Genova docks are filled with thousands of soldiers marching onto Mago's flotilla of troop transports and warships. Korbis stalks onto the gangway of a mossy old ship, leading his Balearic warriors into the hold.

The Libyans file into their transports. They are grateful to be heading home from the chill climate, but they regret losing the chance to loot more Italia towns.

Mago's mahouts direct the loading of his six surviving elephants. The beasts draw up next to a transport specially prepared to carry them, the deck mounted with a large platform to tie them down. Trumpeting their protests, the elephants are wrapped in enormous bolts of sailcloth and hauled up by pulleys onto the deck.[cxxx]

Once aboard, they are chained onto the platform, with each of their mahouts taking a pallet next to the elephants under his care. The mahouts will stay close to their charges for the three-day voyage, knowing that a frightened elephant can quickly destroy a ship.

Finally, all the ships are loaded and scores of transports and warships sail out into the late afternoon sun, heading south for the Carthaginian coast.

Inside his flagship, Mago tosses and turns on his sweaty pallet. He can smell the pustulent stench from his wounded leg. Worse, he can no longer feel its stabs of pain because the leg is numb. Mago ignores his fear by planning how he and Hannibal will attack Scipio. *We'll send the elephants first, to wreak havoc on the front lines. Then the Gauls and Ligurians as shock troops. When the Romans tire, the Libyans will cut through them.*

His trembling lips tighten into the rictus of a smile, as his mind drifts from plans to dreams. *We'll ride in the center, him and me. I'll fight Scipio myself, disembowel that patrician bastard. Hannibal, he'll be proud of me.*

Hours later, grim reality comes to Mago. He can feel his strength fading, his body shaking with chills. *Baal help me*, he prays. *I know it is my time. Just keep me here until dawn. At least give me that much.*

Mago attendants stand in somber vigil over the frail shell of their once-mighty commander. No words are spoken.

Dawn peeps through the cracks in the deck timbers over Mago's chamber. His pale eyelids flutter open, and he looks about the lightening room, staring at his officer's faces as if they were strangers. He weakly raises his hand and looks upward.

"Not here," he rasps. "Take me to the decks."

The Sacred Band guards gently lift their commander and carry him up to the deck. Mago gestures toward the ship's prow, and the men take him there. With the last of his strength, Mago lifts his head to face an unseen Carthage.

I am sorry brother is his final, fading, thought.

The last of the Three Generals perishes as his fleet sails past the tip of Sardinia.[cxxxi] Mago dies without knowing that the mere presence of his fleet here will do more to change the course of the war than any of his efforts while alive.

*　　*　　*　　*　　*

ISLAND OF SARDINIA, 203 BCE. The scout ship captain shifts about in front of the praetor, nervously twisting his hands. "There may have been a hundred of them, Praetor. All heading south toward the African coast." He wipes the spittle from his mouth. "Apologies for my excitement, but I think it is Mago Barca's fleet, going out to attack Scipio's army."

Publius Lentulus scrunches up his golliwog face, irritated that this news is disturbing a day that promised to be very uneventful. He knows that a Carthaginian fleet's presence in his sphere of influence means he must take action to prevent it from damaging Scipio's campaign. If he does not, he risks dishonor back at Rome. But what to do? His loose lips flap as he mutters to himself.

Lentulus' officers watch patiently. They are accustomed to their praetor's anxious and indecisive ways, and are careful to hide their disdain. Neither soldier nor seaman, this son of a wealthy slave trader has many influential friends in Rome. His battle-tested subordinates respect Lentulus' position more than the man. They duly follow his commands, albeit with liberal interpretations of what he orders.

The rotund patrician suddenly jumps up from his seat at the meeting table and stares excitedly at his men. "We have to send our fleet to help Scipio!" He turns to his navy commander. "We'll send him a hundred stocked ships!" he says proudly.

The admiral forces himself to remain calm, though his voice edges with irritation. "And exactly what will be stocking on these ships, Praetor? Men, food, money—women?" Several tribunes snicker. Publius silences them with a cock-eyed glare they have learned to obey, on pain of being assigned to the other end of the island.

"The winter winds are upon us, Commander," says the admiral. "It would be a dangerous journey."

The praetor waves his words away. "Psh! It is early winter, and is but a journey of one day from here to Africa, as you are well aware." He makes a disapproving face at the rest of his officers. "As to your sarcastic question, we will send him food, horses, and money. Just what you would expect, were you not so intent upon making a joke of it!"

Lentulus dismisses his men. He is watching them file out when he has a burst of inspiration. "Send for my scribe!" he yells to the backs of the departing officers. The praetor tramps outside into the morning sun, energized with determination to help the war effort—and secure accolades from the Senate.

A young Roman trots up to Publius, lugging a straw basket of writing tools. "You sent for me?" the boy asks anxiously.

"Write a message to Praetor Gnaeus Octavius in Sicily. Inform him that Mago's army is sailing back to Africa to attack Scipio. Tell him I am sending a hundred freighters of supplies to Scipio's landing at Cape Farina, and I urge him to do the same."

Lentulus points toward his headquarters. "Go in there and write it now, and bring it for my signature. I want it out on a bireme to Sicily within the hour!" The scribe rushes inside to write the orders, while Publius repairs toward a nearby thermopolium, deciding to reward his efforts with a second breakfast of boiled eggs and ham.

A week later, Publius' hundred freighters sail out from Sardinia, to be followed by two hundred from Gnaeus Octavius in Sicily.[cxxxii] Lentulus' supply ships arrive uneventfully in Africa, and Scipio gratefully receives the ships' stores. He writes a commendatory letter to Rome, as Publius had hoped he would.

Gnaeus' fleet does not fare well. His ships fall victim to the capricious winter winds, and his transports are swept off course. Many are blown to the southwest, where they strand themselves on an island near the Bay of Carthage. Others are forced into the bay itself. [cxxxiii]

The stranded Romans hastily abandon their ships and repair toward Scipio's camp near Utica, leaving a trove of supplies within eyesight of Carthage's walls.

The local fishermen soon inform the citizens of Carthage that a Roman bounty awaits any willing to sail out for it. Heady with their navy's previous victory at Utica, the citizens angrily storm the Senate steps, demanding that they send troops to plunder the Roman ships.

The Senate bows to popular demand, even though they know that plundering Roman ships would violate the truce Scipio has approved with them. Days later, the Carthaginian warships return to the Port of Carthage, towing strings of captured Roman supply ships.

The citizens of Carthage wildly celebrate their fancied triumph, their victorious mood fomented by the militaristic Barcas. Meanwhile, other Carthaginian Senators visit the temples and offer sacrifices to peace, praying their plundering will not anger Scipio. They do not have to wait long to find out.

*   *   *   *   *

CASTRA CORNELIA. "They did what?" Scipio blurts angrily at his brother Lucius, his face reddening.

Lucius, the acting fleet admiral, throws open his arms to emphasize his own disbelief. "You heard me. The Carthaginians took at least fifty Roman transports back to Carthage. A group of supply ships blown off course from Sicily." He stares at his brother. "Ships intended for us."

Scipio pounds his fist on his throne-like chair. "So we lose tons of food and weapons and Carthage takes them? What happened to our truce, to our agreement?"

"This is theft, pure and simple," says Lucius.

Scipio rubs his forehead. "Fortuna be cursed! Our messengers just told us that Rome approved the peace proposal we made with them. The Carthaginian Senate must have known that! What would prompt such treachery?" He snorts. "We were so close to peace."

Lucius looks at the floor and nervously fingers his tunic. He glances uncertainly at his brother. "Perhaps we should send someone to talk to them before we resort to war." His eyes grow clouded with memories. "Before more women and children die."

Scipio sits silently, his face cradled in his hands. "This truce is our chance for a lasting peace without war. But I cannot sit idly while Carthage ransacks our ships. It will only embolden them when Hannibal comes."

"There are so many lives at stake, brother," Lucius says, his voice breaking. "Can you try once more?"

Silence hangs between them.

"Very well. We'll send a delegation," Scipio replies. "Perhaps there is an explanation for this that escapes me, though I cannot fathom what it would be."

Relief washes across Lucius' face. "That is wise, brother. Maybe they will make reparations. Or crucify the perpetrators."

Scipio summons three of his most trusted lieutenants and sends them on a quinquereme to Carthage. He commissions the three as legates and authorizes them to act as his peace envoys. By making them delegates for peace, Scipio indicates that he knows the peace treaty was ratified by Rome and that he is ready to hold to it.[cxxxiv]

Two days later, the Roman ship pulls in to the Carthaginian docks, escorted in by two Carthaginian triremes. The envoys and their guards march from their ship under the protection of Carthage's Sacred Band.

Once they enter the city, they walk into bedlam. The townspeople are emboldened by their plundering of the Roman ships. They hurl rocks and imprecations at the Romans, who huddle in the midst of the stoic Sacred Band warriors. The Romans are led towards the Carthaginian Senate chambers. The envoys goggle at the soaring marble buildings that encircle the enormous city square.

"This makes our Forum look like a stable," quips Lucius Sergius, dodging a rotted fig.

"It won't look so beautiful when we level this viper's den," mutters Lucius Baebius. "Look at all this shit flying at is! Cato was right, Carthage must be destroyed!"

The envoys clamber up the hundred steps to the chamber entrance. They stride through its massive open doors and find the Carthaginian Senate waiting for them, attired in their finest purple robes. After the customary sacrifices and prayers to open the meeting, two Elders lead the envoys to an adjoining amphitheater where the People's Assembly awaits them; a hundred elected delegates of the Carthaginian people.

"Our Senate cannot ratify any treaty unless the Assembly approves it," says one of the Elders. "You must speak to them first."

Ever the boldest in battle, Lucius Baebius steps in front of his fellows. "I'll be glad to talk to them," he says. He walks up the steps to the prow-shaped speaker's rostrum.

"Based on your actions, Carthaginians, we are justified to inflict any punishment we desire, but we Romans are a generous people." His words prompt a scattering of hoots and derisive laughs, but Baebius remains unruffled.

"General Scipio thinks you may be relying on Hannibal's arrival to change the course of this war. But that would be ill-advised. Remember, we drove Hannibal's army to an inconsequential promontory in South Italia, and he just succeeded in saving himself by leaving for Africa." [cxxxv] Baebius grins. "Elsewise, there would no Hannibal at all!"

The legate's words evoke a chorus of angry denials from the Assembly. "Roman pig!" blurts a portly, red-faced wine merchant.

"Remember Cannae!" shouts one of the Barcas planted in the crowd, and others echo his call.

"Baebius!" Lucius Sergius hisses, "Think of what you say! You are insulting them."

The brash young warrior only winks at his older compatriot, and spreads his hands in fake bewilderment. "Do you people disagree with my viewpoint? Do you deny its plausibility?" He grins at the senators standing to his right. They glare back at him.

Baebius smiles beatifically at the citizens, thoroughly enjoying his baiting of them. "Even if Hannibal's army were about to give battle to us, who have beaten you in two successive battles, your expectation of success should be quite uncertain and you should not only contemplate the prospect of victory but that of a further defeat!" [cxxxvi]

"Lies!" a delegate shouts. "Kill the pigs!" shouts another.

A handful of angry citizens surge toward Baebius. The Carthaginian guards rush out in front of the rostra and use their hand-sized cudgels to beat back the attackers.

A rail-thin Elder bangs his walking stick upon the floor. "No more violence," he shouts in his shrill voice. "Our laws say they may speak their minds!"

Sergius steps to the fore, and shoulders Baebius aside. He nods respectfully at the delegates, and then towards the senators. He stands calmly with his hands at his sides, his stance communicating calm and respect.

"Forgive my brash young colleague," he says, as soon as the din has subsided. "He is proud of Rome and its military history. Surely you can understand such vulnerabilities in a warrior, those of you who have fought for mighty Carthage."

He shakes his head and grins, bemused. "Rome and Carthage, Carthage and Rome. With Greece fading, we are the two most powerful empires in the world. Yet we would risk it all over some minor territorial issues."

Sergius waves his arm about the amphitheater, taking in its many ornate columns and walls. "When I walked through Carthage today I was amazed at the beauty of your temples and homes—at the presence of so many statues and frescoes! Your city is truly a paradise on earth."

As Sergius speaks the Assembly delegates sit down, save for a group of that stands with arms crossed, signifying their rejection of Sergius' words. The Barca senators smile at the group, satisfied with the demonstration they have paid for.

Baebius looks at Sergius. *You are a pussy*, he mouths silently, as he steps forward to speak.

"General Scipio also admires the art and education of your people. He strives to develop such culture within Rome. Certainly, he would not want to destroy your city, Even though he will do it if provoked!"

"You dare threaten us?" shouts a Barca senator. "We will send back your head!"

"Throw him into chains!" shouts another.

Baebius waves his hands. "I did not mean to say that Scipio desires your destruction. My Imperator only asks this of you: that you restore our ships and supplies you have brought to your port. If you do that, it will be the end of the matter." [cxxxvii]

Amid catcalls and insults, Baebius steps back. "We anxiously await your decision," he concludes.

The amphitheater is filled with a susurrus of voices, as the representatives argue about the two legates' words. The Senate Elder stands up, tall and muscular despite his sixty years, holding his staff of command bolt upright. He faces the three envoys.

"Thank you for addressing us," he says tonelessly. "Permit us to discuss this among ourselves. We will give you our answer tomorrow, after we conclude our morning session."

The legates glance at each other and nod their heads. "That is acceptable," replies Baebius. "But do not tarry beyond that. Dread Scipio grows restless."

The elegant Lucius Fabius steps to the fore for the first time, his gold neck chains flashing as he inclines his head. "Honored Assemblymen and Senators, I have a request," he croons in his deep baritone. "May we have an escort when we depart your fair city?" He rubs a stone bruise on his arm. "We were received somewhat rudely on our arrival."

The Senate Elder rises from his seat and pounds his staff. "Forgive our people's manners, Rome has inflicted much deprivation and grief. Your request is granted. Our ships will escort you as far as Utica. Now take your rest until tomorrow."

A knot of Sacred Band guards appears and leads the three legates toward a cavernous adjoining room. As they exit, Baebius looks back over his shoulder, smirking at Carthage's august body.

That night, the Barcas call a covert meeting of Senate militants. [cxxxviii] They meet at the city manse of Kanmi Barca, a retired general of the first war. The decorated veteran is furious at Baebius' public disparagement of Hannibal, his favorite nephew. With a coastal map before him, Kanmi outlines his plan to destroy the truce.

"We cannot settle for peace now, not after our naval victory at Utica and our capture of their ships. Scipio's army is weaker than it's ever been, and our soldiers' confidence has never been higher! Hannibal and Mago will soon arrive with twice his number. When they do, they'll wipe him from the face of the earth!"

"So we will vote to deny Scipio's proposal?" asks one of Hasdrubal Gisgo's uncles. Since Gisgo's suicide, many of his relatives have longed for revenge. The Gisgons and Barcids are united in their desire to defeat Scipio.

Kanmi shakes his head. "No, there is no chance of winning a vote— those gutless merchants hold the voting majority, and now they have been told that Rome has ratified their peace treaty. We have to act before our envoys return from Rome and finalize the treaty with in our Senate. If we can get Scipio to break the truce, we break the peace."

"He is not an impetuous man," notes an elder Gisgon. "He would likely seek negotiation before action. The Senate won't just declare war."

Kanmi grins wolfishly. "With my plan, it will be Scipio who will declare war on us! Our Senate will vote for a resumption of hostilities."

"How can we get him to declare war?" asks one of the Gisgons. "Do we burn his captured ships?"

"Scipio will not declare war over a few ships," says Kanmi. "But he would if we capture his envoys!" He waves his hands about, excited. "Then we will get the Senate to dither about their release until Hannibal has organized his army over here!"

"Brother, the envoys will be under Carthaginian protection when they leave," says another of the Barcas. "We would have to kill our own men to get them."

"Our men will only go as far as Utica.," says Kanmi. "I'll send a message to the fleet admiral, his ships are near there." Kanmi grins. "The admiral is sympathetic to our cause, and anxious to take a victory before peace breaks out. He will intercept the Romans when the escort departs from them."

The old Barca stares at his compatriots, seeing their reluctance. "We do that, or watch our empire destroyed by peace. Who approves?"

The militants raise their hands in silent votes of agreement.

One of the Hannonid family shakes his head. "Be not so sure of this. What if our Assembly delegates agree to finalize the peace treaty coming to us from Rome? The Senate would notify the admiral to halt all aggression."

"We have to stall for time," replies Kanmi. "Tomorrow morning the Senate will confer with the People's Assembly. Our propagandists will be scattered throughout the crowd. They will demand that there be no agreement until they can see the full terms of the treaty signed by Rome." He smirks. "With enough of an outcry, our spineless senators will not approve anything until the official treaty arrives here."

Kanmi stands up. "Enough talk, we have only a few hours for action. If you have some citizens in your purse, or some who owe you a favor, go to them now. Shake them from their beds and demand they protest tomorrow. Go, before Rome wins the peace!"

Late the next afternoon the Roman envoys are called into the Carthaginian Senate. The Senate leader faces the three legates as they stand before him, his face stern. "We have consulted with the popular assembly of our citizens. Many demanded that we see the signed treaty before we take action. So we have decided not to decide. In the interests of all concerned, we must send you back to your commander without a reply." [cxxxix]

Lucius Baebius is flabbergasted. "You cannot decide? Did you hear nothing of what I said yesterday? Your decision is whether or not you want to be destroyed! Is that so difficult to make?"

Lucius Sergius tugs at Baebius' elbow. "You gain nothing with your threats. We have to get back and tell Scipio."

"We have two triremes waiting to escort your ship," the Senate leader says evenly. "We trust you will have a safe journey."

The leader motions to his left and a knot of Sacred Band guards surrounds the Romans, leaving an open path to the Senate chamber doors. The Romans march out the door, their shoulders slumped.

Kanmi Barca watches from the back row of the Senate seats, his eyes shining with delight.

Hours later the Roman quinquereme sails past the Bay of Carthage and rounds a rocky promontory where the Bagradas River empties into the sea, approaching Utica. The two triremes veer off into open waters, circling back to Carthage. The envoys watch them from the deck.

"They seem to be leaving early," Lucius Fabius says. Baebius snorts. "Hmph! Afraid to get too close to our fleet, I'd wager. They'd probably run if a little fishing boat came out from there."

Sergius shakes his head. "You underestimate our enemy, the very thing our commander Scipio has warned us about. Their ships are faster than ours, they have no reason to fear." He frowns at Baebius. "Perhaps they are tired of protecting the very people who insulted them at the Senate meeting yesterday."

Baebius peers out into the empty sea. "Nevertheless, we should be watchful. There are Carthaginian ships out there, somewhere."

The quinquereme coasts along the open seas. The bored legates lean over the deck rail and study the faint outline of the coast. They chat and argue as they watch the distant shore, trying to spot signs of enemy activity.

Their shore watch is interrupted by the sound of marines hustling about the fifteen-foot wide deck. The ship's captain comes striding toward them, his face grave.

"There are ships approaching," he reports, pointing out to the open seas.

Baebius faces the captain, still grinning from a joke about Libyans' sexual proclivities. "Is it a Roman welcoming party, Mamercus?" The thick bodied older man shakes his head. "Three quadriremes are coming at us. Their sails are purple."

The legates look at one another, anger washing across their faces. "That's why those triremes sneaked off so early," sneers Baebius. "They wanted to say they honored their 'promise' while someone else springs the trap!" He waggles his finger at Fabius. "See what I mean about Carthaginians? Not to be trusted!"

"Right now we have more immediate concerns, such as our survival," replies Sergius. He faces the captain. "What can we do about this?"

Mamercus looks anxiously over his shoulder. "There are too many of them, and more may be coming in behind them. We have to make a run for our camp by Utica." He grimaces. "We are closer to it than they are, but they are faster."

Baebius frowns. "Then make haste for camp. But we are not surrendering if those cowardly pigs catch us, you hear? We have a century of marines, get them ready to fight." He smirks at his two fellows. "We'll see if they are as good as Laelius claims they are!"

"They are already piling up missiles on the deck," replies Mamercus dryly, offended that an infantryman would presume to tell him naval tactics.

The captain hurries off, shouting orders to hoist both sails and to increase the oarsmen's' pace. The three legates silently don their battle armor. They watch the Carthaginian quadriremes angling toward their heavy ship as it surges toward the distant outline of Utica's walls.

"There's going to be a fight," Sergius says. "And war is going to follow."

The quinquereme's three banks of oars slash into the water, and the ship gains speed. The Carthaginians' narrower and lighter quadriremes stroke even faster. They soon close on the Romans. When the three Carthaginian warships draw closer, they aim their bows at the quinquereme's side. The thick, curved rams on their prows explode through the blue waves in front of them, washing seawater across decks that are a scant six feet above the waterline.

The Roman oarsmen stroke on below decks, their sweat-streamed arms yanking furiously on the oars. The armored marines dash back and forth from the storage chambers below deck, piling up javelins and stones.

A squad of marines carefully maneuvers the ship's three small catapults onto the deck, ones that remained from the ship's siege of Utica. They face the ballistae at the decks of the Carthaginian ships, two hundred yards away and closing. The Romans can see the decks bristling with Carthaginians, shields and javelins held at the ready, preparing to release their deadly showers upon the quinquereme.

Baebius' face flushes with anticipation. He draws his sword and waves it over his head. "Get all the soldiers on the decks!" he shouts at the ballistarii. "Aim your javelins at the men on the deck!"

"I'm the commander of this ship, Legate. Get out of the way!" Mamercus shoves Baebius back from his men, glowering at him.

"Aim for the rowers," Mamercus orders. "Ignore the men on the top deck."

He whirls upon Baebius, his fists clenched. "Your order was stupid. We must wound the wings of the beast, not the claws!"

Sergius and Fabius pull Baebius back from the captain. "Just shut up for once and let him do his job," snarls the mild-mannered Fabius.

"Fine," Baebius barks, "But get them to do something!" He straightens his shoulders and strides over to the pile of javelins near the prow. Baebius hefts one in his hand and draws it back, ready to fling it at his despised enemy. Sergius and Fabius look at each other, shrug, and follow Baebius to the javelins. The three legates stand with the marines and sailors, ready to fight as common soldiers.

The Carthaginian ships speed up their oarstrokes, building to ram speed. Mamercus watches the ships close on him. *We will have to get them at the first blow, or they'll sink us.* He raises his hand, looking back at his officers to ensure they are attending to him. When the Carthaginian ships close within a spear's throw of the ship, Mamercus shoves down his hand.

"Now!"

The ships' sails are immediately angled sharply to one side. The banks of oars facing the Carthaginians stop rowing while the rowers on the opposite side speed up, delving their oars deep into the waters.

The ship pivots away from the quadriremes' rams. The enemy ships arrow past them, veering off to come about and attack again. Two ships draw close to the starboard side of the quinquereme, and pass by the port railing.

As the Carthaginian ships slide past the quinquereme, scores of marines hurl javelins at the open side railings where the oarsmen row. The spears rain down from each side of the taller vessel.

Scores of Carthaginian rowers fall screaming upon the exposed lower decks, their limbs and torsos pierced by the pitiless bronze. The Carthaginians return fire with their own spears and slings, but they must throw theirs upward and their volleys are less effective. Even so, several Romans fall with crushed skulls and lanced bodies.

"Take heart men," Mamercus shouts. "They can't reach us!"

The words have no sooner left Mamercus' mouth than clusters of clay pots shatter onto the quinquereme's deck, hurled by the Carthaginians' slingshot catapults. Knots of poisonous snakes slither out from the shards, crawling about the deck.[cxl]

"Cobras!" shrieks a marine. Another flight of pots crashes onto the deck. "Adders!" cries another. Battle-hardened Romans dash frantically about the confines of the deck, begging their fellows to remove them.

Some collide with colleagues who are holding their shields above their heads, leaving them prey to the cascading spears of the Carthaginians. Several terrified men dive into the sea, shedding their armor before they fling themselves overboard.

"Get rid of them!" screams the captain. Six rural-born Romans wrap their arms and hands with leather strips. They scramble furiously about the deck, plucking up snakes and pitching them over the side rail.

Screams erupt from the Roman oarsmen; the snakes have found their way below. The Roman ship slows and veers off course. The Punic warships head back toward the foundering quinquereme. One ship draws along the port side and hurls hooked ropes onto the Roman deck railings, preparing to pull themselves closer and board.

Mamercus rages about the ship, working frantically to restore order. "Cut those ropes!" He screams, using his gladius to lean out and chop through one that has hooked into the railing. He shoves his men into rows along each side of the deck. "Keep your shields up!" he bellows. "Throw all your pila at them! Throw anything!"

The captain runs over to his three catapult crews and points toward the port side quadrireme. "Into the oarsmen!" he shouts. The crews crank back the thick sinews of the bow-like catapults and drop an arm-thick iron arrow into their hurling slots. The bowstrings twang, and three bolts fly into the unfortunate oarsmen lined along the exposed sides of the quadrireme.

The missiles explode through timbers and bodies. Four volleys follow the first. The Carthaginian quadrireme becomes a floating abattoir of corpses and screaming wounded. The ship founders, circling crookedly like a bird with a wounded wing.

The Roman captain has no time to savor the victory. He rushes to help turn the catapults toward the other side of their craft, targeting a warship that is closing on them. The ballistarii repeat their deadly launches but with less effect, as the alert Carthaginian captain turns his ship so the prow absorbs the brunt of the onslaught. Even so, several rounds of the dreadnought missiles hurtle lengthwise into the rowers, cutting a bloody swath through the front rowers.

The port side quadrireme limps off course while its officers shuttle oarsmen to the damaged side, rolling bodies over the lower railing and into the sea. Soon the Punic ship resumes its coordinated pace, and circles back toward the quinquereme.

The third quadrireme loops out of catapult range, giving Mamercus the opportunity to break out from the encircling trio. "Half pace on the left oars, double on the right!" he orders. He whirls to the deck officer. "Haul the sails to landward!" The Roman ship slides out from its pursuers, its nose angled toward the distant shore.

Mamercus starts to rush to the fore of the ship when he feels his chest explode. He looks down to see a javelin's barbed point jutting from his breast. Coughing blood, Mamercus falls to one knee, eyes wide with shock. He tries to push the point back out of his chest but it sends a white bolt of agony through him, and he drops his hands away from it.

The captain struggles upright, swaying on his feet, staring bewilderedly at the men rushing to help him. "Get to your posts!" he mutters dazedly, even as his legs fold beneath him. Captain Mamercus crumples to the deck and lies still, as his stunned officers stare down at him.

Baebius sees the ship's officers standing around their fallen leader. *By Jupiter's cock, they're standing about like cows! The fools will kill us all!*

He rushes over to them. "As legate of Rome and the right hand of Imperator Scipio," he blusters, "I take command of this ship!"

Mamercus' second-in-command looks at the deckside chaos, his eyes glazed. "What can we do?"

Baebius scans the deck, his mind racing. He sees half of the crew lying dead or wounded, with a scant pile of javelins and rocks as their only ammunition. He looks aft to see the three quadriremes closing in on their ship. *So what will you do, fool?*

Looking to shore, Baebius spies a thick line of ant-like shapes moving along the shore, with mules and carts in tow. *That might be a Roman foraging party. Or not. What else is there to do, swim? Fuck it, just do it!*

"Head for shore! Full speed toward the beach!"[cxli] he thunders. The officers look at one another. One junior officer finally points toward the beach, his face incredulous. "Legate Baebius, where are we to go? There are rocks sticking out everywhere!"

Baebius steps into the principale and slaps him. "You can die while floating out here or live by crashing in there! Get to it! Run this ship to the beach, like you were running for your lives! Go!"

The officers rush away to give orders. The oarsmen row for all they are worth, and the sailors work the sails to catch every bit of wind. The quinquereme lunges toward the rocky shore, splashing heavily into the outgoing waves. The quadriremes bear down on the Roman's stern. The Carthaginians catapult fist sized stones onto the deck, clouting down the marines who are flinging their remaining missiles at them.

Sergius steps near Baebius. "You are going to run us aground? Are you insane?" Baebius rolls his eyes and shrugs. "Perhaps insane, but not uncertain, which is a lot fucking worse! They all were standing around with their fingers in their asses!"

In the fields above the beach, a sharp-eyed centurion notes the faint outline of a ship heading toward them. He leaves his foraging party and heads across the rocky beach toward the sea. The centurion wades into the water, squinting at the hazy outline of masts and sails coming into view.

Then he sees a blurry double-eagle shape on the lead ship's sail, with three purple blotches behind it. "Roman ship!" he shouts to his fellows, running back to shore. "One of our ships is coming in! It's being chased by Carthaginians!"

A hundred tunic-clad legionnaires race for the few weapons they've brought along, grabbing every spear and stone they can carry. They rush into the shallow water at shore's edge and string themselves out along the shoreline, tracking the oncoming quinquereme.

"Come on, you bastards, get in here!" yells a grizzled legionnaire.

"I bet ten denarii they will make it!" his young companion shouts.

The lead tribune turns to one of his centurions. "Get the men back, Cassius, they're going to run that thing right into us!"

On board the quinquereme, the crew prepares to hit the shoals. The young principale regains his aplomb and marches along the deck. "Take off all your armor and leave your weapons," he orders. "Prepare to swim for shore." He rushes to the front of the prow and stares at the jagged rocks which jut from the waves like claws. His eyes grow large. "Grab the rails!" he screams.

With a resounding, splintering, crash, the speeding quinquereme rams into the rock shelves lining the shore. The prow shatters, and the ship lurches sideways into the lapping blue-green waves. Its oars and side rails crack apart as it settles into the sandy bottom.

The marines tumble from the deck into the shallow seas, followed by the oarsmen. The water fills with Romans thrashing toward the beach.

Up to his neck in water, Baebius shouts orders until he realizes no one is paying attention to him. "Fine! To Hades with all of you!" he yells, as he swims toward the shore.

Like sharks toward a kill, the three quadriremes circle the wounded quinquereme, counting on their shallower draft to bring them near. The Carthaginians close in on the fleeing Romans and lean over the deck railings with spears in hand, prepared to throw them into the foundering seamen. But they have not counted upon the legionnaires on the beach.

The camp soldiers rush into the water, hurling pila and rocks at the approaching Carthaginians, raining volley after volley upon the surprised sailors. Dozens of dead and wounded Africans tumble over the ship railings.

"Get them!" cries the centurion. The ablest Roman swimmers paddle towards their foundering enemies, their swords clenched in their teeth. They plunge their blades into the wounded Carthaginians, ignoring their pleas for mercy.

The quinquereme's survivors crawl in to shore, dodging the few enemy spears that fly by them.

"We can't get them now," growls the Carthaginian captain. "Return to port." The three ships angle back toward Utica.

The beachside legionnaires prance and cheer, dancing along the gravelly sand while they pull the last of the crewmen from the water.

By dusk Scipio is meeting with the three legates in his camp tent. Marcus Silenus attends and Laelius is there, having just returned from Rome with the signed peace agreement.

Baebius, Sergius, and Fabius take turns explaining the Carthaginians' treachery to their commander. Scipio listens to their reports with his fist under his chin, scowling with every word. He says nothing as they speak, but his eyes glitter with repressed anger. Baebius finishes by awkwardly attempting to explain his orders to beach the ship. Before he concludes, Scipio jerks up his hand. Baebius falls silent.

"Enough, I have heard enough!" Scipio says. "They have not only broken their truce with me, they violated the peace agreement so recently made with Rome. Treachery twice made!" He rises from his curule chair and paces the room, stalking about like a caged lion.

"I thought we had a chance to build a lasting peace with our victories here, a peace that would protect Rome forever." He rubs his eyes. "Ah, gods, I was a fool. We have accomplished our objective, to draw Hannibal from our homeland. But now the Carthaginians have gained false hope with his arrival, and have renewed hostilities."

"You are saying that further peace talks are out of the question?" Laelius asks. "I was held in Rome for nothing?"

Scipio laughs derisively. "Peace talks are out of the question while

Hannibal remains in the field. That is very clear to me now. Words were always a waste, while he was there to give them false hope. As the ancient saying goes, 'deeds, not words.' We have to act."

Marcus totters to his feet, still favoring his wound. He walks over to face Scipio. "My men are ready to fight. They need to fight. This truce is dulling their fighting edge. They are bored, and mutiny springs from inaction." He smiles grimly. "Which do we take next, Utica or Tunis?"

Scipio reflexively reaches inside his belt pouch. His fingers brush the figurine of the Nike, goddess of victory, the inspiration that Amelia gave to him years ago. *Deeds, not words. Final deeds.*

He looks at Marcus and slowly shakes his head, as if ridding himself of niggling thoughts.

"No more cities, no more sieges, no more towns. We march out to crush Hannibal, wherever he lands. We are going to end this folly, once and for all."

IX. ZAMA

LEPTIS MINOR, SOUTHEAST TUNISIA, 203 BCE. "Careful with him," Hannibal growls, "I didn't bring him all the way from Italia just for you to knock him into the sea."

Hannibal glowers at the mahout guiding Surus down the dock walkway toward land, tapping the sides of the seven-ton beast with his long spear. Hannibal watches the guide carefully, ignoring the hundreds of transports that are bobbing about in the harbor behind him, filled with the fifteen thousand men he has brought with him from Italia. There are Gauls, Numidians, Iberians, and Bruttians, all hand-picked to join him for what he knows will be his final, decisive battle.

Hannibal follows Surus, making sure his pet is safe. He has a special plan for his favorite juggernaut. Hannibal is going to build an army of war elephants to destroy Scipio's army, and Surus will show them how to fight.

Hannibal follows his elephant along the docks, stroking his trunk and cooing reassurances. Maharbal joins him, running down the gangplank of his quinquereme.

"We are finally back home," Maharbal exclaims, trying to catch his breath.

Hannibal looks at the low shelves of hills about the port city. "Well, we are a hundred miles southeast of Carthage, but we are close enough to call it such."

"We could have landed closer, I tell you," Maharbal grumps. "Then we could have camped by Carthage, and I could have seen my family. It has been sixteen years since I have seen them!"

He shakes his head in wonderment. "A third of my life spent in war and we are back where we started!"

"You know we could not go there," Hannibal retorts. "The fields near Carthage area have been ravaged by Carthage, to sustain itself for a siege. This is the only area that has enough food and forage to sustain our army."

Hannibal chuckles ruefully. "You think *you* have spent a lot of years at battle? I joined my father in Iberia when I was only nine years old. My entire life has been war without end." He sighs. "But all that will be ending soon, now that I am here. It will be good to see Mago again."

The two brothers-in-arms walk toward the city's wide harbor street, the dock timbers groaning with Surus' every step. They see a tall, gaunt figure waiting for them, his hands tucked inside his robe. In a few more steps Hannibal recognizes Durro, the chief emissary for Carthage's Council of Elders. As always, the old man has a dour expression on his creased brown face, as if waiting to predict impending doom. *I should have Surus grab him with his trunk, just to crack the expression on that stone face.*

"Hail, Durro," Hannibal shouts good-naturedly, raising his right hand. "What news bring you today?"

Durro blinks several times and avoids Hannibal's stare. For the first time in his life, Hannibal sees doubt on the man's face, as if he does not know what to say.

"Hail, mighty Hannibal. Carthage exults that you have returned." Durro looks behind him, fidgeting. "There is good news. Mago's army is coming to join you. There are fifteen thousand Ligurians, Gauls, Balearics, and Iberians. And the Numidian cavalry."

"That is good to hear," Hannibal responds. "Especially about the Numidians. I have so few cavalry. I had to slaughter four thousand of my horses so the Romans would not get them. They would not fit onto our transports. Most of my horsemen are hiding in garrisons at Bruttium."

He frowns at Durro. "Had I another month before I was called back here, those riders could be here with me." He shrugs. "But my time for regret is past, I have an army to build."

Hannibal looks over Durro's shoulder. "Where is Mago? Is he still with his army?"

Durro bows his head so low Hannibal can only see the top of his head. When he raises it his face is a mask of sadness. "I do not know how to tell you this, General."

Oh gods no! Hannibal feels tears welling into his remaining eye. "I think you already have," he mumbles, struggling to contain himself. "How?" he manages to say.

"On the passage here from North Italia, near Sardinia." Durro smiles faintly. "He was grievously wounded in a battle, but he was determined to come see you as soon as possible." His mouth tightens. "He should have waited. We could have given him more time."

Maharbal steps to Hannibal's side. "I will see to the ship's unloading," he says softly. "Take your time here." Maharbal clasps Hannibal's shoulder and nods for Durro to follow him. The two head for the adjoining dock, where the Lucanians and Bruttians are marching down from the gangplanks of the troop transports.

Hannibal stands alone. He remembers the times that he, Mago and Hasdrubal played soldier together, tutored under the stern eye of their father Hamilcar. *All dead*, he thinks. *All dead from war with Romans*.

A great weariness settles upon Hannibal, the weight of sixteen years of constant strife. *Now I am home, but what do I have to come home to?*

Hannibal walks over to Surus and strokes his trunk, lost in bewildered sorrow. Surus senses his master's mood. He inclines his head and gently wraps his trunk around Hannibal's chest, softly rumbling his sympathies.

Hannibal stares into space, absently stroking Surus hide, looking around but seeing nothing. He squeezes Surus' man-killing trunk. *You*

*are the last of my family, old friend. I pray you are with me until the
end.*

*   *   *   *   *

SIGA, FAR WEST NUMIDIA. "It is true, then? Hannibal has
returned to Carthage?" Vermina stares at the Numidian messenger
standing below his throne, nervously twisting his head scarf in his
leathery hands.

"Yes, Prince Vermina. That is why they sent me, to inform you of
Hannibal's arrival. And to request your assistance." The lanky young
African holds out a goatskin scroll stamped in the purple wax seal of
the Carthaginian Senate.

"I am to help them? Like they helped my father Syphax?" Vermina
sneers. "All they did was help him onto a prison ship to Rome! I will
have to spend a fortune to ransom him back."

The Numidian messenger shrugs, not knowing what to say. Vermina
breaks the seal and hastily scans the message. He shows it to Galus, a
loose-limbed man with a wide body and short arms, a soldier whose
clownish looks belie his deadly skills as a horse warrior. "You should
know about this, Galus. As the captain of my cavalry, you would be
responsible for the lead."

The Numidian nobleman scans the scroll and nods enthusiastically.
"So, if we fight for Hannibal, Carthage gives us a thousand talents of
silver and their entire army in support your attack upon Masinissa. Not
such a repulsive arrangement."

"I am not enthused about fighting Scipio," Vermina says. "My father
thought he was the reincarnated spirit of Alexander the Great."

"Masinissa has Rome on his side," Galus counters. "We have to fight
them both sooner or later."

Vermina flips the scroll to the side of his chair. "But Scipio and
Masinissa destroyed my father's army. Our Masaesyli are scattered to
the four winds! We need time to rebuild."

"Just tell him we will come as soon as we are ready. Hannibal has already asked your cousin Tychaeus to join him, and he has several thousand of the best horsemen in the country.[cxlii] We have several months to recruit and train a larger force."

"It will not just be a larger army," Vermina replies, "It will be monumental! I'll send our officers to every tribe. Any Masaesyli that they see upon a horse, they are to bring them to me regardless of age or station. We will amass more cavalry than the world has ever seen. Ten thousand, maybe twenty thousand! An army of nothing but cavalry!"

Vermina vaults from his chair and paces about. "We'll get enough men to destroy all the sluggish Roman cavalry in one battle. Then we can move on to Masinissa, with Hannibal's army behind us!"

Galus eyes him skeptically. "That many men will take longer. Maybe a year to get them here and prepare them."

"I don't care," retorts Vermina. "My father's defeat has shown me the folly of using green troops. We will not fight until they are ready."

"We can teach them the way of sword and spear, Prince, but how can we make them seasoned warriors, when they have not yet fought?" asks Galus.

Vermina picks up the cast off scroll, rolls it up, and pantomimes using it as a sword. "Why, in the best way you could imagine," Vermina says thrusting his scroll at Galus' face. "Fighting Masinissa's men!"

*   *   *   *   *

PELLA, MACEDONIA. King Philip lowers his golden goblet onto the marble tabletop, his manicured hands caressing its inlaid scenes of frolicking centaurs and satyrs. The dashing, dark-haired man chuckles.

"So Hannibal has been recalled from Italy? Poor bastard! I bet it was by a bunch of merchants who want him to run off big bad Scipio so they can get back to making money.

He sighs heavily. "Ah, it seems like yesterday when he and I met in

Italia. He was rampaging across the country, destroying Roman armies as he went." Philip runs his long delicate fingers through his thick locks, clearly distressed. "We have to help him, Josif. The last time I sent him troops, I gave him my word I would provide more. He has been a good friend to Macedonia."

Philip's chief aide furrows his brow, worried. "Is that a wise move, my king? Our treaty with Rome is barely two years old; they still watch our every move. You send him an army, they could regard it as an act of war."

Philip frowns petulantly. "Oh, and I would half welcome the opportunity to fight those upstarts again. They think they can supplant Macedonia as a world power. We will show those overweening farmers what the descendants of Alexander the Great can do!"

Josif waits for his king to finish, being used to his tirades against Rome. "You repudiated Carthage as part of the treaty agreement.[cxliii]If you join them now you will have their allies fighting against us!"

He looks pleadingly at Philip. "It would be suicidal, don't you see?"

"Well gods curse it, I am going to do something!" Philip declares. "I cannot watch him fight the Romans without my help!"

Josif knows that look, Philip's mind is made up—all Josif can do is control any potential damage. His mind races for a compromise solution.

"Perhaps you could send Hannibal a small but potent force of warriors. Just enough to fit onto one or two ships that escape into the night, undetected."

Philip purses his lips. "Yes, that may work. It would be a good gesture. But who could I give him? Cavalry take too much space. He has plenty of mercenary infantry already."

Josif smiles. "Send him the type of soldier he doesn't have, the ones that have caused problems with the Romans before." The aide holds four fingers in the air. "Maybe, oh, four thousand of them."

"Four or five thousand of who?" Philip demands. "Quit playing games."

Josif looks at him, disappointed. "You know who. Your favorite warriors." Josif mimics a forceful upward spear thrust.

"You mean the phalangites?" Philip asks. "You want me to give him four thousand of my best spearmen?" [cxliv]

"Yes, that is exactly who I mean. Scipio has not fought their like, they would give him some problems. Remember what our phalangites did to the Aetolians? They used those eighteen-foot pikes to stick them like pigs on a skewer!"

Philip grins, feeling himself relax. "Ah, Josif, I knew there was a reason I have kept you alive! That is an excellent idea. They do me no good in this horrid peace we are under. Perhaps they will do us some good fighting for an enemy of Rome."

"See to it," Philip orders. "Send them out on the first moonless night. Sopater will lead them."

As Josif shuffles off to attend to the matter, Philip stretches out in his silver and gold throne, desultorily quaffing from his goblet. *The Romans think their triarii are so fierce with their little spears. Wait until they meet my phalangites. Pigs on a skewer, hah!*

*　　*　　*　　*　　*

CURIA HOSTILIA, ROME 202 BCE. *He's still alive!* Flaccus stumbles his way out of the Senate meeting chambers, his eyes glassy with fear. The Senate has met to formally retract the Carthaginian peace agreement they had signed weeks ago, and one of the attending praetors casually mentioned that Marcus Silenus had recovered from a grievous wound and was again the commander of Scipio's infantry.

Flaccus froze with terror when he heard these words. His expression so alarmed that the senators next to him inquired about his health. *He'll come to revenge her!* is all he can think, recalling Marcus Silenus' threat if anything tragic befell the Scipio household.

Zama

"Where is Scipio's army at?" Flaccus had asked the praetor.

"He has collected his forces at Castra Cornelia, in preparation for an encounter with Hannibal," said the old commander.

"Will Scipio or any of his officers be coming back to Rome soon?" Flaccus persisted, prompting a puzzled look from the officer.

"No, I would not think that a good idea," the praetor replied slowly. "They will have to move against Hannibal as soon as possible."

Flaccus bobbed his head. "Yes, I can see that. Thank you." He had settled heavily into his seat, repressing the waves of nausea from his knotted stomach. It was all he could do to stay long enough to cast his vote to revoke the peace treaty.

Now Flaccus hurries down the Senate steps and heads for the Aventine Hill, a rough section of Rome populated with immigrants, laborers—and gangs. Though he is a wealthy patrician, Flaccus is not a stranger to the area. On more than one occasion he has visited to hire one of the local collegios of thugs for some special work. Now, Flaccus is looking for one man in particular, and he is not hard to find.

Decimus Cherlius is holding court at his space among the Aventine merchant stalls, sprawled on a throne of piled grain sacks. He is a thick and pale man, wearing a dirty brown tunic that is incongruously belted with a silver chain. His calloused and dirty fingers gleam with gold and silver rings. Jeweled necklaces dangle beneath his two grimy chins.

Seeing Flaccus approaching him, Cherlius raises a meaty arm and beckons the Senator forward. His broad face splits into with a yellowed grin.

"Ah, revered Senator Flaccus!" he bellows. "What a welcome surprise to see you here—in the daylight!"

Cherlius shoves his fist at one of his burly underlings, a man dirtier than he, if such is possible. "You! Get our senator some sacks to sit on! Where are your courtesies?"

317

Flaccus rolls his eyes. *Patience. He has been very serviceable.*

"Gratitude, but I have been sitting all day," says the Senator, eyeing the stain-mottled bags. "I have just stopped by to request some security assistance."

Decimus crosses his legs and studies his hoary toenails, waggling his feet back and forth. "A disposal job, yes? Who is he? Or is it a she again?"

Flaccus' eyes dart about the milling commoners, frantic someone has overheard. "No! Nothing like that! Do not speak of that again!"

The gang leader waves his hand dismissively. "Phah! What you fear? You know me. No tales, even if tortured. Same for my men. What you need?"

"I need some protection, just protection," Flaccus replies. "Someone may be after me." He shudders. "Someone very fearful. I need three strong warriors to follow me around." He eyes Cherlius. "Men who would not be afraid to kill a Roman soldier."

Cherlius laughs heartily. "Not afraid? I have men who would pay *you* to do it! Yes, I have men you seek. All good with dagger or sword. One in particular, he fight for Romans but he hate them. He get wounded so he come back here. The man walk funny, but he fight like lion."

"That sounds excellent," Flaccus says eagerly. He gives Decimus Cherlius a small purse bulging with coins. Decimus peers into it and nods. "Good. You have them for month. One die on you, you get two months for the rest."

"Can they start now?" asks Flaccus, looking over his shoulder. Decimus shrugs. "Yes, sure." He turns to his attendant. "Go get Septimus and Crispus. Tell them bring things to stay for a month." The attendant disappears. Decimus shakes the purse, listening to its silver jingle.

"I thought you said there were three?" Flaccus says. "I paid for three."

Cherlius grins. "No worry. I keep the best one near me, he great killer." The man pushes himself up and looks back into the empty merchant stall behind him. He waves his hand peremptorily. "Come out here."

A lean, muscular man limps out of the shadows, wearing an immaculate gray army tunic with the Roman double-eagle stamped on it.

Decimus chuckles. "Don't let eagle fool you, he not Roman, he Thracian, was slave to Romans. He kill anyone who come for you."

The dignified man steps forward and faces Flaccus. He looks him straight in the eye, unfazed by Flaccus' dress and rank.

A bit dismayed, Flaccus nods at the man. "I am Senator Marcus Fulvius Flaccus," he says.

The warrior gives the barest of nods in return. "I am Thrax, the Thracian. Late of the Thirteenth Legion." He fingers the pommel of his sica. "It will be my pleasure to serve you."

As Flaccus completes his transaction on the Aventine Hill, Amelia's housemaster Cassius is busily hobbling about the Scipio domus on his tree-branch crutch, overseeing the slaves who are cleaning it from top to bottom. *You'd think a horde of wild boars came through here* he grouses, surveying the aftermath of Amelia's feast.

Amelia had just hosted a large memorial feast for Pomponia. All the Hellenic Party members attended, staying long into the night. Now the house is covered with wine and oil stains, broken pottery shards, mussel shells and chicken bones.

I hope they didn't eat one of Gracchus' sacred chickens, the old centurion thinks, recalling that the young haruspex brought several of them for divinations. *Ah well, a good time was had by all, although the mimes were a bit tedious.*

"You there!" Cassius barks at a boy slave. "Take those wine amphorae to the kitchen and have them washed out, especially that one with vomit on it! And I will check on you!"

These Illyrians, you have to keep an eye on them every minute! Cassius walks into the atrium and nods his head approvingly at its immaculate floor.

Senator Aurelius had splashed water all over the carved marble tiles when he fell into the pool. *At least Amelia got the drunken bastard to donate more money to Italica,*[cxlv] *so more of her husband's veterans can retire there.* He grins. *Might move to Iberia myself. Heard those women love us Roman liberators!*

Cassius' reverie is interrupted by the sight of a one-armed army messenger standing in the vestibule, holding a goatskin pouch in his hand.

"The mistress is out at market," Cassius says.

"I am looking for Centurion Cassius Paullus," the messenger replies.

Cassius blinks in surprise. "Me? You have a message for me?"

The man smiles dryly. "Only if you are he." He eyes Cassius' crutch. "But I suppose you are. How many one-legged war veterans could be in this house?"

"Give it to me," Cassius growls, in his best centurion's voice.

The messenger stuffs the pouch into his wooden hand and extends it to Cassius. As soon as Cassius pulls it from the messenger's prosthesis, he marches back toward the door.

"Where did it happen?" Cassius asks. The messenger looks over his shoulder. "Iberia. Battle of Ilipa. A Celtiberian chopped it off at the elbow." He grins. "I put a sword through the bastard's mouth. You?"

"Cannae." Cassius replies.

The messenger blows out his cheeks. "Whew. That was a horror, wasn't it?" Without waiting for a reply, he walks toward his waiting horse.

As the horse's hoofs fade into the distance, Cassius opens the pouch and breaks the seal on the papyrus scroll inside it, noting it bears the owl's head seal of the Scipio clan. When he unrolls the scroll a smaller one falls to the floor. Cassius props himself on one arm and bends to retrieve the small note, holding it in his hand as he reads the three scrawled lines in the larger one:

My brother-in-arms:

There is a matter I have left unsettled in Rome, a debt of honor that I must resolve.

In the event I do not return, and only if I do not return, open the enclosed scroll and follow its instructions. You will find money to do what needs to be done.

My gratitude is with you,

Marcus Silenus

Cassius smiles at the sight of Marcus' blocky signature. *Anything for you, old friend. You gave me back my life. But I pray to Jupiter I will not need to do this, for all concerned.*

*   *   *   *   *

CARTHAGE, 202 BCE. "Join Hannibal's army today! Drive out the vile Roman invaders!"

The Carthaginian officer shouts out his recruiting slogans, standing in the back of a mule drawn wagon that rumbles towards the temple zone.

"Follow us to get your arms and armor!" shouts a Sacred Band soldier next to him, resplendent in gold-rimmed white linen armor. "Defend your family against the child-raping Romans! Put Scipio's head on a spear!"

Ignoring the winter drizzle, hundreds of Carthaginian men follow the recruitment wagons. They come from every part of the vast city, heading for the central temple of Anath, goddess of love and war.

The volunteers are fishermen, stable hands, slave merchants and noblemen, all eager to join the army and fight in the Final Battle, as it has come to be called. They want to pit themselves against the Roman general who has brought their mighty empire to its knees.

Carthage has turned to actively recruiting its own citizens instead of hiring mercenaries. The Assembly and Senate unanimously agreed to follow Hannibal's request to muster every available man and send them to his camp.

Hordes of Carthaginian men swarm into the gigantic city square. They gather beneath a sixty-foot statue of a woman in an ankle length tunic, a feather crown on her head and a war club held high in her right hand. A dozen wood tables encircle the foot of Anath. The tables are staffed by priests. Only holy men can be the recruiters, because the Senate has declared this a sacred war.

The priests take each man's name and place of origin, asking them about their skills with horse and sword. Their few questions answered, the priests give each man a white or purple scrap of linen and direct them to show up three days later.

When the recruits return, they find the square filled with scores of Carthaginian soldiers, massed under a white or purple banner at opposite ends of the square. The recruit shows his scrap to the waiting soldiers.

The ones with the white scrap are infantry. They are given a spear, short sword, white linen cuirass, round shield, and domed helmet. The new infantrymen jump onto the back of a thirty-foot troop wagon and trundle off to Hannibal's winter camp at Hadrumentum.

The men with a purple scrap are given a horse, small shield, spear, and short sword. After demonstrating that they can properly guide the horse, they are led outside the city gates. After hundreds of riders have gathered, a Carthaginian cavalryman leads them out toward Hannibal's camp. For weeks the recruitment continues, and Hannibal acquires four thousand more Carthaginians for his battle.

While the Carthaginians are filling the ranks of Hannibal's growing army, Senator Salicar and General Kanmi Barca are three days' march southeast of Carthage, meeting with the chief of Libya's largest coastal tribe. Following an exchange of gifts and the downing of several flagons of wine, an agreement is quickly struck: the chief will be given a measure of silver for every warrior he sends to Hannibal.

Four days later, Kanmi Barca leads out a contingent of four thousand Libyan warriors, heading to Hannibal's camp to be equipped for battle.

The old officer smiles as he leads the battle-tested tribesmen toward his Barca kinsman, savoring his contribution to the war. *Hannibal will destroy Scipio. Then we'll see who begs for peace. To think, those soft-assed senators almost finalized that peace treaty!*

He looks back at the stern and muscular tribesmen marching behind him. *I may get in this fight myself. Who better than a Barca to lead these barbarians?*

*   *   *   *   *

ATLAS MOUNTAINS, NORTHWEST AFRICA. "I've got another one here!" exclaims the dark and wiry little man, looking over at the monstrous beast he has just lassoed from the top of his elephant. [cxlvi]

"Come on, men, get the ropes," the mahout yells. "Get them on his front feet before he bolts!" When the wild elephant's feet are contained, the mahout tows the beast into the timbered pen constructed at the base of the peaks.

"That's sixty three so far," says the leader. "We need seventeen more for Carthage." He turns his specially trained elephant away from the pen, heading to the south foot of the heavily forested mountains, where an elephant herd was recently sighted. The other mahouts ride their horses alongside him, carrying their ropes and herding poles.

"What are they going to do with all these elephants?" shouts up one of them.

"They are going to give them to Hannibal. We are to get them to his camp before the spring rains start. He'll have the greatest elephant army ever!" He grins a gap-toothed yellow smile. "Those Romans will shit themselves when they see a wall of these beasts coming at 'em!"

"But they are all wild," declares the mahout. "We need time to train them! And train some riders!"

The leader spits over the side of his elephant. "Well, that's why we're going with them. We'll have to get these pretties in battle shape, get them used to noises and spear pricks. And used to those smelly Romans! Come on, let's get the rest of them before Scipio's pissing on the walls of Carthage!"

The old mahout snaps the reins on his horse and gallops ahead, out to find the southern elephant herd. He laughs. *Eighty elephants! They are going to make one fucking mess of that battle, one way or another...*

*   *   *   *   *

TESTOUR, TUNISIA. Hassan peers out from the side of his litter, searching for the rear lines of Scipio's army. "How far away are they?"

"An hour or two away from us," the Moroccan replies. "The Romans have surrounded Testour. It will only be a matter of time."

Hassan smiles broadly at the scout's report, the gold wire flashing in his ivory dentures. *When Testour falls, I will have hundreds more slaves to buy.* The portly Moroccan slave trader has followed Scipio's army since it left Castra Cornelia, tracing the legions' path of destruction south.

Hassan is delighted at the Roman general's change of heart. Scipio was known to release a captured town to its inhabitants, and Hassan could only buy the odd lots of soldiers that the Romans had not killed or maimed. Now, this oddly moral general has turned into a vengeful engine of destruction, pillaging one town after another and selling its inhabitants into slavery[cxlvii] as he marches towards Hannibal's camp seventy miles southwest.

"March on," Hassan orders his litter-bearers. "I must be there for the

Testour's fall, before those cursed Nubians show up to outbid me!" The eight slaves shoulder his litter and pick up their pace. Hassan's camel caravan moves across the edge of the Great Plains, heading up into the hills of the Medjerda Valley.

Two hours later the leader halts caravan at the top of a small rise. "We are here," he shouts.

Hassan parts the white linen curtains and lumbers out of his cab, eyes alight with greed. He pulls his silver embroidered indigo robes above his thick ankles and shuffles across the packed sand to the top of the rise.

Below him sprawls Scipio's army, battering at the timbered gates of the town's main entrance, the rammers shielded by a shell of Roman shields. Hassan watches scores of escaladers pitch their ladders upon the twenty foot walls and scramble up toward the top. They hold their small round shields over their heads to deflect the townsmen's desperate stones and spears. The escaladers are eager to win the gold corona muralis for being the first to scale the walls, and they will not be detained by the townsmen's futile efforts to defend themselves.

Testour is the fifth conquest of Scipio's new campaign. By now the legionnaires are very practiced in their assaults. Less than two hours later, the gates buckle beneath the iron ram's head and the escaladers fill the ramparts.

The Cannenses from Sicily are the first maniples to march through the splintered gates. The old veterans cut through the terrified militia that has massed to stop them. After the first two lines of defenders lay writhing on the ground, the rest of the Africans throw down their swords and shields, begging for mercy.

The legionnaires rope the men together about their ankles and middles. Two centuries lead the captives out of town while the rest of the Cannenses move through the city, rounding up the inhabitants. By late afternoon the screams of terror and death have subsided. The last of its populace is herded out onto the plains, waiting to be sold like cattle.

Scipio stands at the top of a low hill in front of Testour, surveying its capture. Marcus Silenus and Laelius trudge up the hill to join him, Laelius wiping flecks of blood from his mirror-bright breastplate.

"It is done," Marcus says. "The town is ours. Less than a dozen of ours are dead, mostly the escaladers."

"How many did we capture?" Scipio asks dully, watching the last of the captives being herded over to Hassan's waiting caravan. "Over two thousand," replies Laelius. "I hear that Cato fetched a good price for them. At least the pesky little bastard is good for something."

"Send the money to Rome as soon as possible, just like before," Scipio says wearily. "We have to give them evidence we are winning this war, lest their support diminish."

Laelius laughs. "Are you mad? The plebs voted you Imperator, to stay in Africa until the war is won."

Scipio purses his lips in disgust. "You underestimate the machinations of Flaccus and his Latins. The Senate has acceded to one of the new consul's demands to be part of the war. That Latin Party dog, Tiberius Claudius, he will be coming here with a fleet of fifty quinqueremes full of soldiers.[cxlviii] He wants the glory of ending the war before I do, and I fear he would levy brutal demands upon Carthage. We must not give him that opportunity."

"Then why don't we use the money to get some horses and train more cavalry?" Laelius presses. "We don't have nearly enough to fight Hannibal, especially if our spies are correct, and Syphax' son is coming with thousands more!"

"We cannot," Scipio says. "We have neither the time nor the resources."

"So we will go fight the Carthaginians when their riders may outnumber ours ten to one?" asks Marcus flatly. "You have ever preached that cavalry is the arm of decision in battle, yet you would fight the Carthaginians with a weak arm."

"Masinissa," Scipio replies patiently. "Masinissa has to bring men to join us, as he promised." He shrugs at his two commanders. "If not, we do not have much chance, no matter where we are."

Laelius shakes his head. "I don't like it. We have our entire army out here with us, save for the cohorts you left with that lunatic Baebius back at camp. We have overextended our lines of supply. Don't you think it's time to return to Castra Cornelia?"

"You have not heard me!" Scipio bellows, taking them aback. "We have to get to Hannibal before the winter comes. He would use it to recruit more men, and to train those he has just acquired. Our men are veterans. We need to catch him while we still have the edge in experience."

"As you command," Laelius replies testily. "But what about Testour town?" We can use it as a garrison, to store supplies for our army. We are fifty miles from Castra Cornelia, so we need something closer."

Scipio shakes his head. "We do not need garrisons to win this war, we need fear. I will convince Carthage that I am out to devastate their homeland, leaving nothing for them to rule. They will demand that Hannibal attack us. He will have to fight before winter sets in."

Scipio takes a final look at the immaculate little city. *These people had a quiet life. Until you came.* Scipio recalls his vow to his father, and his mouth tightens with resolve.

"There is no one left to live here. Burn it and level it, same as the others. We march for Teboursouk, on the Plains." His eyes grow distant, and a grim smile comes to his face. "I hear it is a rich and beautiful little city. Its destruction will be especially irksome to the Carthaginians."

Scipio turns and trudges back toward his tent as Laelius and Marcus watch him disappear.

"I love him, but he's turning into monster," Laelius says to Marcus, his voice distressed.

Marcus' mouth tightens. "He's turning in to a conqueror," he says with a trace of pride. "He learned a lesson when he took Carthago Nova. Some must die so that others will live."

Laelius sniffs. "A lesson in murder."

Marcus glares at Laelius. "And part of him is dying with the doing of it. Be not so harsh on your friend, I wager he is harsher on himself."

Marcus strides off, following Scipio's path. He limps slightly with his wounds, but his gait is strong.

*   *   *   *   *

HADRUMENTUM. NORTHWESTERN COAST OF AFRICA, 202 BCE. As the wild elephants watch, Surus kneels down so the mahout can clamber onto his back. The monstrous elephant rises and stalks into the herd. The intelligent beasts observe Surus' docile behavior. Their massive heads follow his every move.

Hannibal watches from outside the tree-trunk pen that contains the pachyderms, with Maharbal by his side.

"They are progressing," comments Maharbal. "Some of them will take a man on their backs now."

Hannibal nods. "Next we put a mahout upon them when they go to forage in the fields. If they allow that, they will be ready for battle training."

Maharbal snorts. "Would our Carthaginians learned as fast as the elephants! I swear, those civilians use a spear as if it was a camel prod, jabbing without artifice or artistry!"

Hannibal grins. "Well, that shows Carthage's wisdom in hiring mercenaries to fight our wars. Perhaps we'll hire some of Scipio's Romans for the next one—if there are any left!"

He shoves himself away from the thick pen rails, reluctant to leave his beloved elephants. "Come on, Maharbal. The Elders waiting for us. I cannot stall them any longer."

"What do they want this time?" asks Maharbal.

Hannibal shrugs. "Baal may know, but I do not. Perhaps they have bribed Philip to send us more of his Macedonians. Now those men know how to use a spear!"

The two old war mates stalk back inside the camp gates. They watch the recruits being trained out in front, laughing at their awkward sword movements. The two head for Hannibal's camp tent. The six purple-togaed Elders are sitting inside on cushions, sweating in the late spring heat. Durro stands in front of them. His face is free of perspiration, though he wears a thick white robe.

The man must be a spirit, muses Hannibal, wiping his own brow. Or *maybe he's just a skeleton under there.*

"Hail, Durro. What brings this august body to my humble camp?"

Durro spreads his bony hands. "Scipio has razed Teboursouk, one of the gems of our empire, and sold them all into slavery. Then he leveled several towns to the southwest of it. The country is in a panic. You have to stop him!"

Hannibal nods. "It is my intention to end him and his army, Durro. As soon as the winter rains subside early next year, we will march on him."

"Gods, no. Not that long," replies a portly young merchant. "You must fight him soon, within the next two moons!"

"That is not possible," Hannibal says.

The Elders retreat several paces and huddle together. They mutter among themselves. Durro steps out from the group and faces Hannibal.

"You promised your father you would protect Carthage, and forever be an enemy to Rome," says Durro. "Do you think you are fulfilling your promise if Scipio is laying waste to our empire, selling our people into slavery?"

Hannibal flushes with anger. He stands up and glares at the thin old man. "For sixteen years I have labored to fulfill my promise, and now you seek to rush me into battle because of your womanish fears? Is that what you did to Mago?"

He grasps the pommel of his sword. "Your proposal is treachery. I should kill you where you stand!"

Durro merely blinks at Hannibal, though the Elders cower behind him. "The Hundred and Four will judge you derelict in your duty if you do not attack," says Durro, wiping Hannibal's spit from his face. "The cross could await you. You would become am eternal disgrace to the Barcid clan."

Hannibal stares at Durro, his breath slowing. He swallows. "I will march out after the next two full moons, and set a new camp near Scipio. But not before. I need time to prepare my army. Winter or not, I will destroy the Romans."

Durro looks back at the Elders. They give the barest of nods, and Durro turns back to Hannibal. "Gratitude for the accommodation, General. We will relay the news to Carthage."

"Get out," Hannibal says, his body rigid with anger.

Durro and the Elders file out. Hannibal spits in their direction and turns to Maharbal.

"Get me the Numidian scribe. I must send a message to Vermina. We need all his Numidians, in case Masinissa rejoins Scipio."

*   *   *   *   *

CIRTA, NUMIDIA. Masinissa pitches the scroll to the floor. "He wants me to come to his aid? The man who was going to send my beloved to Rome in chains? I have no answer for him, get out!"

The Roman messenger nods. He marches out the open palace doors as the Numidian guards glare at him, their hands fingering their swords.

Masinissa turns to Afra, the old Cirtan magistrate who has become his advisor. "I sent his damned cohorts back to him," Masinissa remarks petulantly. "Doesn't he understand what that means?"

"He fulfilled his commitment to help you regain your throne," the old man says. "Have you fulfilled yours to him?"

"Commitments, pah! If he had not insisted on following his precious 'military law' and dragging Sophonisba back to Rome, she would be sitting by my side now, on her throne."

"If Scipio had not sent Laelius and his soldiers to help you, there would be no throne to sit on," Afra replies. He waits a second then adds, "You may have need of Scipio's help again, my king. Vermina controls much of his father's western tribes."

Masinissa glowers at him. "Sometimes your vaunted honesty is more a hindrance than a help. Leave me. I must think about this."

The mentor bows and shuffles out the palace door. Masinissa sprawls on his gold-gilt throne, brooding.

Late that night, Masinissa rides out alone through the city gates, trotting his horse down the citadel's winding road to the plains below it. There, at the base of a tree-covered hill, he dismounts in front of a twenty-foot high stone pyramid.

He makes his way over to a large block in the center of the pyramid; a massive stone with a dancing elephant carved into it. Four words are chiseled into the top of the block: *Sophonisba, Queen of Numidia.*

Masinissa lays a thick sheave of orange-red hibiscus flowers at the foot of the stone. He kneels before it, his tears glistening in the full moonlight.

"There is not a day passes I do not grieve for you. All my wealth and power are nothing when I see the throne where last you sat, mocking the Romans who came to capture you." He sighs. "You were a queen to the end."

He presses his long fingers to his face, wiping the tears away. "I am distressed, my love. Do you remember Vermina? The one you said looked like a jackal, and acted worse? He is making an army to join Hannibal. If they defeat the Romans they will come after me next, I am sure of it. The only way I can stop them is if I return to help Scipio. Do you see my dilemma?"

The prince looks at the dancing elephant figure and nods his head. "I remember what you told me. Our lives are but a brief dance, we cannot let fear spoil the music. I do not fear to lose my new kingdom, or my life. But I cannot bear losing what you sacrificed your life to give me."

Masinissa stands up, staring intently at the tomb, as if listening. He nods morosely, as if being chided. "Yes, the Roman holds our dreams in his hands. A united Numidia, with peace upon the land." He returns to his horse and vaults effortlessly upon it, staring at the moonlit sky. He looks back at the tomb.

"You were ever the wisest of us," he says. "I shall work for our dream. That much I can give you."

With a snap of his reins Masinissa dissolves into the night. The moon plays it rays upon the tomb, where the elephant dances for all eternity.

*   *   *   *   *

HANNIBAL'S CAMP, ZAMA, NORTHERN TUNISIA, 202 BCE.
The old leopard lies still, very still. He crouches down in the esparto grasslands, knowing its prey will soon come to it—knowing its prey must come if it is to live.

For three days the beast has stalked the gazelle herd across the grasslands by the river, staying downwind as it creeped toward the fleet young beasts. The ancient hunter is still wily and strong, but not as quick as once he was—and oh, he was so quick!

The predator knows he must bide his time before he strikes, though he is starved. Winter is coming, and game will be scarce. He must gorge on his kill, and hide the rest for harsher times. The wind blows past his feral yellow-green eyes, wafting his scent away from the gazelles. The grazing herd moves closer to him, and he tenses for the final plunge.

The earth trembles faintly beneath the mighty beast. A rumbling gathers in the distance, echoing in from the dawnlit west. The gazelles raise their heads and stare about. The leopard sees them tensing to run. He knows this is his final chance.

The predator summons his remaining strength and leaps forward, just as the herd bolts from the rising thunder of hooves in the distance.

There is a desperate dash through the three-foot grass, and a swipe of a fatal paw. The leopard has its prey; he will live to hunt another day. Grasping the hundred pound gazelle in its mighty jaws, the leopard bolts toward the hillside, fleeing from the oncoming rumbles.

Riding in the forefront of his two thousand Numidians, Prince Tychaeus spies the leopard dashing off to his right. The rangy young man grins at the sight of the sleek beast gracefully carrying along its prey. *We will be the leopards in this battle*, he thinks. *We will chase the Romans down and clamp our jaws upon them. They have not seen the likes of my men!* His grin broadens as a new thought occurs to him. *If I can help Hannibal defeat the Romans without Vermina being here, Hannibal will be obligated to help me. I could kill Vermina and Masinissa, and be king of all Numidia.*

"Tubbal!" he shouts over his shoulder, "Bring me my leopard skin!" The attendant gallops up to Tychaeus and gives him a flowing leopard skin cape with the head fashioned into a loose cap. Tychaeus pulls the head over his short domed helmet and rides on, the skin rippling down to the back of his Numidian pony.

Within the hour Tychaeus draws near to Hannibal's vast, sprawling camp. The elephants are the first thing he sees. Eighty beasts are ranged across the plains foraging for their tons of daily food, their mahouts walking alongside them. Tychaeus trots through the fields of tents and huts that sprawl for miles across the plain. Thin plumes of countless cooking fires curl up into the sky.

A lone tent stands in the center of camp, with a thirty-foot open space around every side. *That can't be his, it's too small.* Maharbal stalks out from the tent, followed by Korbis the Balearic and several Macedonian, Gallic, Ligurian, and Numidian officers. The last person to emerge is a statuesque older man with a worn black eye patch, a short linen tunic covering his scarred and muscular frame. The man fixes the Numidian commander with his penetrating gaze. He nods once, and strides forward.

It's him! Tychaeus gasps. *Look at the way he carries himself. He is a god on earth!* Tychaeus bites his lower lip. *I must turn him from Vermina and bring him to my side.*

"Hail, General Hannibal," Tychaeus shouts over the ring of Sacred Band guards that has suddenly materialized to block his approach. "I am Tychaeus, cousin to Vermina, son of Syphax." He sweeps his arm behind him. "I bring warriors. Two thousand of my finest horsemen!"

Hannibal says nothing, but he waves over a Numidian captain who is standing by his tent. Hannibal points to Tychaeus and looks inquiringly at his officer.

"He is truly Tychaeus," the captain replies.

Hannibal nods, satisfied. "Welcome, Prince. Your cavalry are sorely needed. Come join me in my tent."

Tychaeus enters the tent and looks about, surprised at its austerity— there is nothing in it save for a map table and a stand with a water flagon. Hannibal waves him over to the table. He puts his finger on a point northwest of his camp.

"Scipio's army is somewhere near here. They are moving toward us. We will have to fight him." Hannibal taps his finger on the map, impatient. "Where is Vermina? He said he would be here by end of autumn."

Tychaeus shrugs. "I cannot say. I wager he is gathering a larger army—he is very cautious about getting into a fight." He bows deeply to the commander. "I heard of your plight, and came at once with all my men."

Hannibal frowns. "That is most unfortunate about Vermina. I was counting on his help."

"I will send my fastest messengers to him, and urge him to join me as soon as he can," Tychaeus replies. He grins at Hannibal. "Fear not. My men are the best riders in Africa."

Hannibal grins. "That is good. I have need of experienced fighters. With your cavalry I have about four thousand horsemen. That will suffice—unless Masinissa joins Scipio."

Tychaeus waves his hand dismissively. "Masinissa? He might have taken much of Numidia right now, but his men are untrained peasants from the mountains, I can overcome whatever forces he has."

Hannibal nods. "Do that, and you will find me very grateful."

"I only desire to rid ourselves of the Roman menace," Tychaeus says. He glances to the tent exit. "I saw all sorts of officers just leaving. How many men do you have?"

"Forty-two thousand," Hannibal answers. "Thousands more than the Romans, I would guess. I sent three scouts to spy on Scipio's camp.[cxlix] We will soon know exactly how many he has."

"Very good, General. We will be ready to fight at your command."

"It is not a command I relish to give," Hannibal replies morosely. "The slaughter could be tremendous on both sides. Peace would best suit us both."

Tychaeus laughs derisively. "From what I heard, Romans use peace to prepare for war. They cannot be trusted."

"Perhaps, perhaps," Hannibal says, scratching his graying hair. "This Scipio is a strange one. He does not act like a typical Roman, he seems more ... thoughtful."

He smirks. "Who knows? He might be that rarest of humans, a Roman who will listen to reason!"

*   *   *   *   *

NARAGARA, NORTHERN TUNISIA. "Look what I found!"
exclaims Laelius. He drags in three woebegone Carthaginian scouts,
small, thin, men wearing hooded cloaks of darkest gray, their hands
roped in front of them.

Scipio rises from his breakfast table and looks quizzically at Laelius.
"You found them here? How?"

Laelius laughs sheepishly. "Well, actually, our sentries caught them.
They were trying to sneak over the brush walls by the stables." He
glares at Scipio in mock anger. "I told you we should have put up
palisades and a trench!"

Scipio chuckles dryly. "You were ever a genius where hindsight is
concerned. We are moving to a spot by the river tomorrow, we will
build a more fortified camp over there."

"What are we to do with these three mule-heads?" Laelius asks,
glancing at the fearful scouts. Ransom or crucifixion?"

"Neither," replies Scipio. "I will give them something that Hannibal
will remember for the rest of his days."

Scipio draws his dagger and stalks toward the terrified scouts. "This
won't take long," he says to Laelius.

Scipio grabs the front of the spy's ragged cloak and bends over. With
a quick slash of his razored blade, he severs the ropes that binds the
first man, setting his hands free. He strides over to the next man and
cuts him free, and then the third. Laelius gapes at him, too stunned for
words.

"You want to learn about my camp, Carthaginians? I would be happy
to show you, I am quite proud of my army!"

Scipio turns to one of his officers. "Tribune, give these men a camp tour, take them wherever they want to go. When they have seen all they want, give them as escort back to their camp."[cl] The puzzled tribune can only nod mutely. He motions for the spies to follow him from the tent.

When they are gone, Laelius whirls upon Scipio. "Are you are as crazy as Cato says? You would give Hannibal our emplacements and numbers? What are you up to this time?"

Scipio smiles. "All Roman camps have the same layout, and Hannibal knows what it is. They will overhear no secrets, now that we know they are here. Let Hannibal wonder why we did this. It may distract him from more important things. And there is something even more important for us."

Scipio gives Laelius an open message. "This arrived late last night. Masinissa is coming with his men. He's not here yet, and I want these spies to report his absence to Hannibal. It will give us another element of surprise."

"I see your logic, but his other scouts will see the Numidians arriving," Laelius says.

Scipio shakes his head. "I have sent Masinissa a return message. His men are to enter our new camp under cover of darkness, in small units. When daybreak comes they will all be inside."

Late that night Hannibal's three scouts report back to him. He listens raptly to their tale.

"What hubris this man has! I have never seen his like."

"The man is a brazen fool," Maharbal grunts. "Now we know we have at least five thousand more infantry than he does, and twice as many cavalry. We should attack before that new consul Tiberius Claudius brings his legions to join him."

Hannibal is quiet for several long moments. "I want to meet Scipio," he blurts. "Get my messenger."

Maharbal shakes his head. "Why lay with a snake, when you know he will bite? Strike now, while we have the advantage."

Hannibal crosses his brawny arms and stares at Maharbal, his mind made up. "We can wait a couple of days. Vermina may come by then. Besides, Scipio may be amenable to a negotiated peace."

"You would surrender to the Romans?" Maharbal exclaims.

"I would preserve Carthage, as I vowed to my father." replies Hannibal testily. "Rome will never surrender, no matter how many men we kill. They will just keep sending their legions at us. I should have realized that after Cannae."

"So you want to make another treaty with them?" Maharbal snipes. "Scipio broke the last one, when those idiots came after his three delegates. It is futile."

"It's only futile if I don't try. If I have to destroy him to get Rome out of Carthage, I will do it. But the fighting would not end there, Rome would come again. This way, there's a chance both our empires can survive."

He shrugs. "Besides, it's raining. The Zama Plains are too muddy for a battle."

"You go have your talk with the Romans," Maharbal snipes, stomping from the tent. "I'm going to stay here and train our men to kill them. I wager my right arm they will need to do so very soon."

*   *   *   *   *

OUTSKIRTS OF ZAMA. Lucius pulls his cloak over his head as he strides out from the camp kitchen, shielding his head from the morning rain. He picks his teeth with a split twig. *That antelope tastes pretty good when you get used to it, but there's nothing like a good roasted boar.* He begins to shiver, and pulls his cloak closer about him.

What a way to celebrate the new year, freezing my ass off in this dismal land. Back home they are feasting and drinking for the

Saturnalia, and the consul candidates are giving their windy speeches before the elections start. Mother would have prepared a lavish feast, to woo the candidates to her side. Gods, I miss her!

He stomps about, trying to warm his feet. *Who would think a desert could be so cold? If I ever get back there I'm never leaving. My brother can be the big hero in the family. Father always treated him like one, anyway.*

One of Scipio's Honor Guard marches up to Lucius, and salutes. "General Scipio requests your presence immediately," he says, then marches away without waiting for a response.

"Curse the gods, another meeting!" Lucius mutters. He pitches away his twig. *I wonder what my crazy brother wants now.* He slaps through the muddy main street of camp, hunched against the rain.

Lucius sees Marcus Silenus striding toward Scipio's tent, and he veers over to join him. "What is this about, Marcus?" Lucius asks.

"Battle preparations, I would hope," Marcus states. "It is time to end Hannibal and end this war."

"I agree," Lucius whines. "I want to go home!"

Marcus gives Lucius a sideways glance. "I long for Rome, too," he finally says, his voice a feral growl. "I left a matter unsettled there, with another foe."

Lucius looks curiously at his stern friend, but says nothing. He steps ahead of Marcus and pushes past the soggy guards at the tent's entrance.

Scipio is seated on a stool at a long low table. Laelius sits on a bench to his right, desultorily chewing on a fig, his eyes puffy from lack of sleep. To Lucius' surprise Masinissa is there, sitting next to Laelius. He nods at Lucius and Marcus as they enter, his face cold and austere.

"King Masinissa arrived last night," comments Scipio, answering their unasked question. "He has brought six thousand infantry and four thousand cavalry with him.[cli] Our forces are not so overmatched now."

Lucius smiles shyly at the regal Numidian. "I am blessed to see you, Masinissa."

The Numidian gives the briefest of nods. "I am here to fulfill a promise, so that Rome will fulfill its promise to me," he says coldly, looking at Scipio. "Romans are, after all, so very concerned with holding to their laws."

Scipio's mouth draws into a tight line, but he does not reply. He waves a goatskin scroll in front of Lucius and Marcus. "This is from Hannibal. He has asked me to meet with him."

Lucius and Marcus look at each other, dumbfounded.

"Why?" stammers Lucius. "Does he want to make peace?" he adds hopefully.

"It could be treachery," growls Marcus Silenus. "They just broke our truce with them, they could be out to put a dagger in your back."

"Carthage broke the truce and the treaty," Scipio says. "It was not Hannibal, whom I believe to be an honorable man."

"He may be," Laelius says, "but he cannot guarantee the honor of his Senate, or the citizenry. They are the ones who stole our ships and attacked our envoys."

Scipio rubs his chin, and looks at his trustworthy officers. "He is the greatest general in the world," he says,. "I would regret it forever if I did not take this chance to meet him without a sword in my hand. I will go."

The general rises from the table. "Leave me. I must think about this."

Masinissa is the first to leave, walking past Scipio as if he is not there. Lucius lags behind, waiting for the others to depart. He walks over to Scipio, his face somber.

"Just remember, brother," says Lucius. "Your dream was to forge a lasting peace, one that would preserve Rome and Carthage for years. Do you think you can get that while mighty Hannibal remains as a beacon of hope to them?"

"I know, brother." says Scipio. "That thought has long occupied my head."

Lucius beats his arms about his shoulders, shivering. "It's cold. I want to go home and I want to see Mother's tomb, but I would take the time to see this through properly, for your sake."

"This was never a fight you wanted," says Scipio. "Father pushed you into this, though Mother tried to push you out." He kisses Lucius on the cheek and eases him toward the door. "I need to think on this."

When all have gone, Scipio picks a fig off Laelius' plate and chews moodily upon it. He reaches into his belt pouch and pulls out Amelia's figurine of Nike, goddess of victory, its facial features worn smooth by his constant rubbing. *You promised to defend Rome. You have come so far, and are so close. What is the best path toward your end?*

He swooshes the winged figurine through the air as a boy might, his features softening. With a final whirl, he clacks it upon the table.

"Gods be cursed!" he says resignedly to himself. "I know what I have to tell that old bastard."

*　*　*　*　*

ZAMA, 202 BCE. "Stop here and wait," Scipio says to his anxious guards. "You will be but a spear's cast away, in case I need you."

Laelius frowns with disappointment. He insisted on coming with Scipio, but now he is to be left behind, in accordance with Hannibal and Scipio's agreement—their conversation will only be between the two of them.

"Look, double-chin, you don't have to do what old Hannibal says," Laelius grouses. "I won't say anything. I'll just stand right behind you."

Scipio looks up at the mist-shrouded morning sky. "It looks like another day of rain, doesn't it?" he says, ignoring his friend's request.

Laelius smirks. "Very well. Go on, then, but don't blame me when you are writing to Amelia from a Carthaginian prison."

"As opposed to having to talk to you if we are both in one of them?" he says with a grin.

Scipio is nervous but in a good humor—he is going to see the military genius he has studied for years. *This is more a meeting between colleagues than enemies*, he tells himself. Then he grins. *A colleague who would destroy my army.*

Scipio motions for his interpreter to follow him. The two slowly trot forward to the solitary duo waiting for them on the gray-brown sandy plains, shadowed silhouettes of a man with a plumed helmet on a tall gray stallion and a thin cloaked figure huddled on a dappled pony.

Scipio stares anxiously at the upright figure before him, feeling his heart thump in his chest. His mind races. *If we agreed to peace, would Rome even consider it? Or would they replace me with that dull-witted Tiberius Claudius—he would undo all I have achieved! But if I go to battle, the haruspex' prediction might come true, and another loved one would die for my cause. Or more.*

Scipio wills his breath to slow. *Easy. You are the conqueror here. You have never lost a battle.*

As Scipio approaches, the mounted figure raises his hand in greeting, and his face comes clear from out of the mist.

Scipio gasps. *It's Hannibal!*

Scipio sees a strikingly handsome man with a penetrating green eye flashing from a bearded face of graying curly black hair, a bronze eye cap over his empty socket. His countenance is seamed with the scars and cares of seventeen years of war, but his back is unbowed and his chin held high. Though he is alone with his interpreter, Hannibal conveys an aura of absolute command. And absolute confidence. *He is like a god come to earth,* Scipio thinks. *No wonder all those barbarians and mercenaries follow him so willingly.*

"Salus, Publius Cornelius Scipio," says Hannibal in his deep baritone, using the Roman greeting. "I am Hannibal Barca." Scipio rides next to him and firmly clasps his forearm.

"Salve, General. It is a true honor to meet you." Scipio nods toward the ground. "Shall we discuss this on foot?"

Hannibal slides from his saddle blanket and thumps onto the ground, and Scipio follows suit.

"Regrets about your mother's death," Hannibal says. "I have heard she was an admirable woman."

Scipio nods his acknowledgement. "I am sorry you lost your brother Mago." Scipio smiles slightly. "He was a brave and relentless leader, as well I should know."

"This war has cost us both loved ones, and I would not see more depart," says Hannibal. "That is why I wanted to meet you." He grins. "And to see about this man they call the Scourge of Africa."

"I have learned much from you," Scipio replies, to which Hannibal arches an eyebrow.

"Not too much, I trust. I would like to think I have some surprises left, in case I need them!" Both chuckle, and there is an awkward silence. Then Hannibal raises his head.

"But perhaps there is no need for further battle," Hannibal continues. "We have went to war for the possession of Sicily and Iberia. Refusing to listen to the admonitions of Fortuna, we have gone so far that your land was once in imminent danger, and now mine is. What remains, but for us to consider how we can avert the anger of the gods and resolve our present contention? I myself am ready to do so, as I learnt by actual experience how fickle Fortuna can be."[clii]

"You think we could consider peace," bristles Scipio, "after your countrymen's treachery to our envoys? After I now control the countryside?"

Hannibal sighs wearily. "You are very young and success has constantly followed you—so far. Fortuna has not yet turned her head from you. But just consider this: after Cannae I was the master of Italia and ready to throw down Rome's walls. And now here I am back in Africa, negotiating with you, a Roman, for the safety of my country."

"That is just it," replies Scipio. "I am here, and Italia is safe from your depredations. What have I to lose?"

"If you conquer you will add but little to the fame of your country and your own, but if you suffer defeat you will utterly efface the memory of all that was grand and glorious of your past.[cliii] Is it worth the risk?"

Scipio looks into the distance, his jaw set. "I made a promise to my father, and I will not disrespect it."

At those words Hannibal is silent for a moment, taken aback. "Your goddess Fortuna indeed has a sense of humor," Hannibal says softly, as if his mind is elsewhere. "I made a promise to my father, too, and I would not disrespect it. But I have changed my mind about how to fulfill it. Now I know I can do it by peace, not conquest."

"Knowing you are a Barca, that is very surprising to hear, though I doubt not your honesty. I, too, have changed my mind. Most recently, in fact. I realize that peace can only be attained by subduing Carthage. And that means defeating you. Until your army is subdued, Carthage cannot be trusted to keep the peace."

Hannibal is silent, thinking of what he can offer Scipio to change his mind. Unconsciously, Scipio reaches to his belt and feels the outline of his Nike figurine. *You need victory, do not settle for less.*

"Perhaps not," Hannibal finally replies. "But hear me out. I propose that all the countries that were formerly a subject of dispute between us—Sicily, Sardinia, and Iberia—and all the islands between Italia and Africa, they shall all belong to Rome."[cliv]

He's offering less than the treaty terms they broke, Scipio thinks. *The Latins would throw it in my face.*

"Put yourself in my place and tell me, shall we withdraw the most onerous of the conditions we originally proposed. That would reward your countrymen for their treachery, and teach them to continue to betray their benefactors. Consider this: the moment Carthage conceived the slightest hope of victory by your return, they again treated us as enemies and foes." [clv]

Scipio looks steadily into Hannibal's face, his expression that of a proud conqueror. "Either put yourselves and your country at our mercy or fight and conquer us." [clvi]

Hannibal rubs the back of his neck and looks at Scipio. "The idea that I would put myself at your mercy is repugnant to me, and a dishonor to my empire." He smiles grimly. "You have chosen to let Fortuna decide our fate instead of rational negotiation, Roman. I will see you on the battlefield."

Without another word, the two sides turn and trot back to their waiting retinues. Scipio's head is held high, but he trembles from released tension—and mounting anxiety. *Mother of Jupiter, what have I done?*

* * * * *

BATNA, ALGERIA, 202 BCE. Vermina's army wends its way down the winding saddle that divides the Atlas Mountains. His scouts roam up and down the flanking mountainsides, searching every hiding place that might hold Masinissa's men.

Vermina is not overly concerned, however. He has twenty thousand cavalry with him, and his spies have told him that the Numidian prince has ventured out to join the Romans. *What a sweet victory it will be*, thinks Vermina. *I can ally myself with Hannibal, wipe out Masinissa, and drive the Romans from Africa!* He reminds himself to sacrifice a young camel to Ammon after the victory.

A lone rider gallops across the fertile valley below them, heading straight for Vermina. The man is riding a Numidian pony, and bears the cheetah skin banner of Tychaeus' tribe. Vermina waves the man in, and the Numidian leader's vanguard parts to allow him to ride up to their leader.

"I bear urgent news from your cousin Tychaeus," announces the messenger. He hands Vermina a crudely drawn papyrus map, bearing Tychaeus' mark and leopard symbol. "The Romans have moved their camp, and Hannibal has followed suit. Tychaeus requests that you go to this river plain near Tebessa, where Hannibal and he will join you." [clvii]

Vermina stares at the map. "This is almost three days' march from Zama. Why are they moving down there?"

The messenger shrugs. "I do not know, but Tychaeus said it was urgent that you go south to meet him there."

Vermina sucks on his lower lip, staring at the map. He brusquely folds it and hands it to one of his guards. "Tell Tychaeus we will join him there." He looks suspiciously at the messenger. "But I am sending my own scout to follow you back, that he may report to me on Hannibal's progress."

The messenger nods at Vermina, a slight smile on his face. "An excellent idea, Commander. Rest assured, I will take care of him."

*　　*　　*　　*　　*

HANNIBAL'S CAMP. Hannibal's officers circle around him in his barren tent, eager to receive their final instructions. There are commanders of the Balearics, Iberians, Ligurians, Numidians, Libyans, Macedonians, Bruttians, and Carthaginian citizens—all the parts of Hannibal's diverse army. Tomorrow Hannibal will march out to battle Scipio, knowing he has to defeat him or lose the war.

There are so many officers in his tent that Hannibal has had to suspend his large battle map from two poles held by his guards, so that all can see it. The chart is a jumble of small squares and circles that designates the placement of all the Roman infantry and cavalry, with only three wide rectangles for the Carthaginian side, each stacked behind the other. It is a puzzling arrangement.

"Three armies," Hannibal explains. "We will defeat Scipio by throwing three armies against him." [clviii] The officers converse intently with their interpreters and look back at Hannibal, puzzled. Maharbal perceives their confusion.

"Do not you see?" the crusty commander says, staring at them as if they were dull children. "We come at them in waves. Mago's front army will tire them out. The second army of Macedonians and recruits will inflict more damage, if any Romans are left by then. Then Hannibal and me, we come in finish them off!" *Or we can retreat to camp if you are all destroyed.*

Hannibal steps in front of his commanders. "It is more than that. We have to lure his riders away from the fight. My spies found out that Masinissa has joined him. Scipio has at least a thousand more cavalry than we do. But we have at least six thousand more infantry. For once, our infantry will decide the battle."

Tychaeus bristles at these words. "What is our role, then? Are we to stand by and watch the foot soldiers fight?" Hannibal shakes his head. "You have the most valuable role of all."

He takes his burnt-wood drawing tool and etches out a circle next to the flank of the first rectangle. "You are bait. You will draw his cavalry away from the battle."

"What! Bait?" splutters the young commander, "I have the finest horsemen in the world! We can run all over those stodgy Romans, no matter how many horsemen they have!" Hannibal walks over and gently but firmly places his hand behind Tychaeus' shoulder guiding him to the front of the map. He points to the nest of circles with the label "Masinissa" on them.

"The Numidians are our worry, not the Romans. Your men will be set opposite his. You are his tribal enemies, he will be eager to kill you. You engage him and flee, drawing his men from the battle as he chases you across the plains. With the Numidians out of the battle, we can exercise our infantry advantage."

He squeezes Tychaeus' shoulder. "You are not the only one. Our Carthaginian riders will do the same to the Romans."

Gigantic Korbis barges forward.. "We be in the front line?" he asks. "We fight Roman army first?" He looks back at the Carthaginian, Bruttian, and Libyan officers, and points a thick finger at them. "Why they hide in back like women, not join us to fight?"

"Those men will defend your flanks. If Scipio is as clever as they say he is—or he thinks he is—I expect he will try to 'surprise' me by rushing his principes and triarii to attack our flanks. That is what he has done in his conquests of Syphax and Gisgo."

Korbis looks at the Iberian, Ligurian, and Gallic commanders from Mago's old army. "We all fight Romans while Carthaginians hide," he growls. Hannibal sees them step forward to join Korbis and he becomes worried. *How can I tell them my new Carthaginians are too weak to fight in the front? Their commanders are standing right in front of me!*

Hannibal makes a line of dots in front of the first rectangle. "Look here, Korbis. We will run the elephants out ahead of you, to sow disorder in their front lines before you attack. That should make it easier for you to penetrate their lines."

He arches an eye brow at the giant Balearic. "Remember, the first to attack gets first pick of the plunder."

Korbis bites on his thick lower lip for a minute, then grimly nods. "I kill many Romans, you give me plenty gold?" He leers a grin. "And women?"

It is all Hannibal can do to keep from rolling his eyes. *Balearics and their women!* "Yes, yes, women, too."

Korbis' broad face lights up. "Good! We do it."

"So, we are to break their front lines so the rear line Romans cannot outflank us?" asks the Ligurian captain, chewing on the end of his pigtail.

"Oh no," remarks Hannibal with a grim smile. "We will let him accomplish exactly what he wants. And we will be waiting for him when he does..."

While Hannibal meets with his squadron of officers, Scipio has ridden out onto the wide flat plains, joined by Laelius, Lucius, Masinissa and Marcus Silenus. They sit quietly for a moment, surveying tomorrow's battle site.

"He has eighty elephants, you know," Marcus says.

"Of course I know," Scipio snaps. "That's why we changed our legion formation. We'll make space for them to run." He points out toward the low-slung hills toward the north. "We'll have the maniples of the principes standing a hundred feet behind the hastatis, with the triarii maniples another hundred behind them.[clix] That will give them room to run away from us, front to back and side to side."

"Hannibal will notice that the principes and triarii are arranged differently. He will execute a countermove," says Laelius.

"No, he won't," says Marcus. "I'm going to have my velites filling the gaps between the front line maniples, it will look like a solid line at the start of the battle. He won't see past them."

Scipio nods. "When the velites rush out and start the battle, it will be too late for Hannibal to change his formation. Then we can use the principes and triarii to rush to the sides and outflank his men, as we did to Gisgo and Syphax." He looks hopefully at his captains. "With Fortuna's blessing, he will not be expecting that."

"He may not," replies Decimus Agrippa, senior tribune of the Cannenses. "But he will adjust to it with his own tricks." He looks down at his feet. "I know, I watched him do it at Cannae." The room is quiet, the officers embarrassed at Decimus' mention of his legion's defeat.

"If he does, we will adjust to his adjustments!" Scipio quips. "More than ever, we must be ready to adapt our formations to the tide of battle." After reviewing the placement of the principes and triarii, the

Roman and allied officers leave to meet with their centurions.

Scipio pours over his Zama map for hours, nervously drawing out infantry flanking tactics, absently chewing on some bread dipped in olive oil. He studies the horse figurines placed on the wings of his infantry pieces. *For once we have the numerical superiority of cavalry. But Hannibal knows that. What will he do about it?* He looks over at his wicker scroll basket, and grimaces. *They won't do me any good. He will invent and adapt. I have to do the same.*

Scipio rubs his weary eyes and leans his head into his hands. He feels his brow warming. *Oh gods no, not the fever. Not now.*

Scipio pushes himself away from the map table. He pours a half cup of wine and adds some water to it. Sipping his evening drink, Scipio settles near a small table that holds the latrunculi game board. Its black and white stones are scattered across the board grid, left in position when Scipio and Laelius abandoned their game to meet with the officers.

Scipio desultorily moves his white pebbles to the sides of the board, trying to counteract Laelius' moves to corner two of his pieces. He moves Laelius' black pebbles to counteract his spread. He swipes them away and stands up, too tired and feverish to concentrate. *Leave it, you need strength more than strategy.* Scipio drains his cup and falls onto his sleeping mat, plunging into a feverish sleep.

Late that night the fever dreams come to Scipio while he tosses and turns on his sweat-stained mat. He sees himself in front of a field-sized latrunculi board with hundreds of squares, its grid populated with scores of life sized white figurines— his infantrymen. His pieces are arranged in a rectangle four rows deep, with spaces between each row of eight figures.

Hannibal stands on the far side of the enormous board. His side has black figurines for his Carthaginian warriors, similarly arranged.

Scipio waves his arm and watches his back pieces move to the side squares where they filling the squares on the front sides. Hannibal waves his hand to the right and left, and his pieces move farther out to the sides of Scipio's.

Scipio sees Hannibal is about to corner his rows of pieces. He waves his hand to the right and left, not knowing what to expect. His pieces in the back move out to the edge of the board in a solid single line, filling in the spaces on each side of his front line figures, stretching out of sight.

This is silly, Scipio chides himself. *You can't play like this, you're breaking the rules.*

Hannibal rages at Scipio, calling him a cheat and a coward. Scipio watches in horror as his pieces move of their own volition, the entire front row moving forward. Hannibal screams at Scipio and waves his hands madly about, and his pieces swarm all over the board, creating a jumble of figures banging into one another.

I have upset him. No one plays like this.

The morning horns wake him from his nightmare. Scipio props himself up on his elbows, groggy but strangely relaxed. *He knows the way we play the game*, Scipio reflects. *I will have to break our rules to surprise him.*

Scipio rolls out from his bed and stands over the latrunculi board, arranging its few pieces into a semblance of his nightmare game. He moves his pieces into a rectangle and then into a single line. *One thin line? It would be foolish to do it. But he wouldn't expect foolish from me, would he?*

X. THE BATTLE OF THE FOUR ARMIES

SCIPIO'S CAMP, ZAMA, 202 BCE. For the third consecutive morning, the day dawns bright and clear. The flat scrabbly ground has dried from the December drizzles of the previous days, and the plains are a flat firm table that ranges to the surrounding hills. The birds chirp merrily in the scrub trees scattered throughout Scipio's camp, blessedly unaware of what the day portends.

Tullius crawls out from his heavily patched eight-man tent, bending his legs to loosen up his creaky knees. He draws in the crisp morning air and contemplates the sunrise horizon. *What a glorious day—too glorious to be killing people! But one more battle and we can go home. At least that's what those plumed helmets keep telling us.*

The sturdy little legionnaire walks to the stables and gathers some twigs from the camp woodpile. He returns to his tent and kneels near the back of it. Shivering, he piles his sticks into a rude pyramid. *Minerva's cunt, it's still cold out here!*

Tullius builds a small cooking fire and boils a large portion of barley porridge, sprinkling in some extra dried cheese. *Going to need all my strength today. But maybe I'll be in the back lines, and I won't have to fight. As if that bitch Fortuna has ever favored me!*

While Tullius chews on a dried date, he massages the last of his pack urn's olive oil into his sturdily muscled body, proofing himself against the morning chill.

His toilet complete, Tullius draws his sword and runs his thumb over the steely blade, ascertaining that its point and edge are razor sharp. *This will be it boy,* he tells his wasp-waisted gladius hispaniesis. *One more fight, win or lose.*

Nervous with anticipation, Tullius takes out his sharpening stone and runs it across his weapon. It is an unnecessary act but it makes him feel better prepared to fight—and to win back his integrity. Tullius is a member of the disgraced Cannenses legion. A victory today will restore his legion's tarnished honor. *Scipio has put us in the center, the place of honor. Best we die there than retreat—again.*

Tullius has been in a dozen combats, but he is most fearful of this one's outcome—and consequences. If they defeat Hannibal today, Carthage will be broken and he will go home. If not, Hannibal will slaughter them as he did at Cannae, which Tullius remembers all too well. Most of all, he fears dying while so close to living a life of honor with his family. *Just one more battle.*

The porridge burbles and thickens. He sprinkles in some cinnamon he bought from one of the ubiquitous merchants that follow the army, inhaling its spicy fragrance. While he waits for his food to finish, Tullius scrabbles into his leather pack and takes out the clay figurines of his wife and two boys. He arrays them near the fire, as if to warm them from the chill.

I shall not die today, he swears to the figures. *I will return to Sicily and join you.* He slowly stirs his breakfast with a stick, stifling the sob that rises in his throat. *I will.*

Tullius pours the porridge into his mess tin and shovels it into his mouth with his wooden spoon. He washes down the last of his porridge with his daily red wine allotment, and hurries off to get in line for the latrines. The latter is an important visit, for voiding oneself in the lines is a sign of fear and a serious loss of dignity.

Tullius walks over to the small stone altar in the center of camp, joining the hundreds of men who watch while the camp priest sacrifices a white ox to Victoria, goddess of victory. *Goddess, let me make it through this day,* Tullius prays.

He returns to his tent and grabs his sword and shield. Knowing that they will be mustered soon for battle, he and the rest of his century hurry over to the armorers' stalls to get their special weapons.

The camp armorer gives each of them a shiny new tuba, a four-foot long trumpet designed to blare a loud brassy sound. General Scipio himself selected Tullius' century to use this strange instrument, telling them it may hold the key to victory.

Tullius is worried because they have not practiced on these instruments, but he remembers that they are not required to make music, only to blow as hard as they can, when the order is given. He sees other veterans grabbing the horns, and he is comforted. *At least I won't be the only one looking silly.* Tullius rushes back to his tent with his tuba.

While his army arranges itself for battle, Scipio marches out from his praetorium, followed by Laelius and Marcus Silenus. All are arrayed in their choice battle armor. Scipio has a gleaming new helmet with a dark purple plume, his cheekpieces shining like the sun. Laelius wears a silver-plated breastplate and helmet, his sword belt studded with captured gold coins. Marcus Silenus' plain bronze armor is dented and beaten from a half hundred battles, but it is immaculate.

Scipio faces his two friends. "Fortuna be with you," he says. He grasps Marcus' forearm in a tight grip and receives a grip that makes him gasp.

"Victoria will be with you, General," says Marcus. He trudges off toward the front line of battle.

Scipio smirks. *Actually, I prefer Nike as my goddess of victory,* he thinks, fingering his Greek figurine.

Scipio turns to Laelius to find that his friend's eyes are moist, though he smiles jauntily at him.

Laelius sweeps his hand across the mile-wide lines of infantry stretching into the distance on either side, with the cavalry barely visible on the distant flanks. "There they are, my friend. All of them waiting to finish this battle, so they can go home and bugger someone other than each other!"

Scipio surveys the vast field in front of him. *Hannibal is out there, waiting for me.* He bolts back to his tent and he vomits into one of the wine flagons by his map table.

Laelius sticks his head into the tent. "Let's not drink from that one during our victory celebration," he remarks. Scipio wipes his mouth and washes it out with vinegar.

He holds his hand up in front of Laelius. "Look, my hand is shaking like a leaf. I feel like a student going against the master."

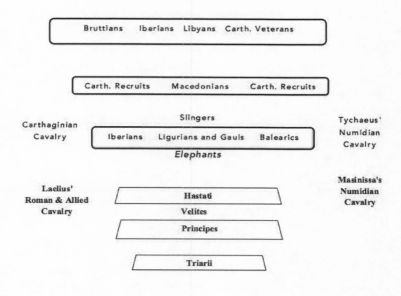

**Battle of Zama
202 BCE**

Laelius laughs. "Ah, boy, years from now, men will be studying how you kicked old one-eye's ass!"

Scipio laughs nervously. "As long as they aren't talking about my glorious death in battle!"

Laelius walks over and faces Scipio. He squeezes his wrist. "You know I love you, brother. Though I have never said it enough."

Scipio clasps Laelius' hand, and their grip lingers. "Whatever befalls me today, it cannot alter that you are the gift of my life."

He quickly kisses Laelius, and pulls on his helmet. Laelius wipes the corners of his eyes and smiles. "Well, then. It's time to end this stinking war. Let us get to it!"

The two friends walk out of the tent and jump onto their horses. Laelius rides over to Scipio's left flank, where he will lead the Roman and Italia cavalry. Scipio trots through the center of his army, riding across the hundred yard gap that separates the maniples of the triarii and principes, then through the one that separates the principes and hastati.[clx] He joins Marcus Silenus in the front and center of his army, next to the double-eagle standard of the Cannenses legion.

"Is all in order?" Scipio asks his legate.

Marcus' smile is grim. "We but await your order to wreak their destruction."

Scipio withdraws his gleaming gladius and waves it thrice over his head. The cornicen sound the call to march. With a deafening shout, the front-line hastati lead the march across the tan African plains toward Hannibal's waiting army.

The legions close within a quarter-mile of Hannibal's minions. Scipio calls a halt, and trots past his lines to assess Hannibal's formations. As he had expected, Hannibal has arranged his eighty elephants across the front of the Carthaginian army, prepared to use them as shock troops. *They'll be like a living wall coming at us. Our tuba players had best be up to their task.*

Scipio scrutinizes the front line for any sign of mass movement, waiting for his scouts to arrive before he executes his opening assault. Soon a bedraggled young rider races through the gap in the Roman front. He pulls up next to Scipio and describes the arrangement and composition of Hannibal's three armies, the last two arrayed hundreds of yards behind the one in front of it. Scipio's eyes widen with surprise. *He is going to fight a war of attrition. He's prepared to fight three battles just so he can win the last one!*

Scipio waves over Marcus Silenus and describes Hannibal's strategy. "We may not be able to outflank him at the outset," he says to Marcus. "Our infantry will have to fight our way through front army until the cavalry can get to their sides." He looks over at the Carthaginians. "His second army has a lot of raw recruits. If we can get past the elephants and deal with Mago's old army on the front lines, we have a chance to win this."

"I will keep my men moving forward through them, or I'll be dead myself," Marcus replies. "Just get rid of those cursed beasts for me."

"I think our trick will work," Scipio replies. He glances at the towering wall of elephants. "Gods help us if it does not!"

Scipio takes a deep breath, and waves his hand. "Commence!" he shouts to his tribunes. The battle horns sound. Thousands of Scipio's velites dash toward Hannibal's waiting force.

The Carthaginian horns blare out from behind the elephants, and the massive beasts begin to stir about, restless for action. Surus trumpets his defiance, and the others repeat his challenge. The battlefield echoes with their roars.

Hannibal's Balearic slingers run out between the elephants, whirling their weapons over their heads. The islanders dash within a hundred yards of the Romans. They halt, plant their feet, hurl their rounded stones, and dash forward again. Hordes of the deadly missiles rocket toward the light infantry.

The velites crouch down and raise their shields for protection, but not before hundreds of the stone missiles find their way into Roman chests and stomachs. Scores of the lightly armored young fighters fall dead from crushed skulls and caved chests, while others writhe on the ground from broken bones and limbs.

"After them!" shouts Marcus Silenus. He waves the velites forward as he stalks in behind them.

The light infantry closes in on the Balearics and flings a thick volley of javelins into the unarmored slingers, their spearheads piercing many of them.

"Again!" bellows Marcus. The velites fling another volley, draw their swords and trot toward the islanders.

The Balearics wheel about and dash for the safety of the elephants. Aroused with battle lust, the vengeful velites chop into the wounded Balearics lying about them. Many a prostate Balearic raises an arm in supplication, only to be kicked flat and transfixed by the remorseless steel of a Roman sword.

The slingers reform behind the elephants and reload their slings. Hannibal's Numidian and Carthaginian light infantry trot out toward the Romans. As soon as they pass the elephants they fling their spears at the oncoming velites, who are roaming about to kill the last of the Balearics.

As dozens of their brothers fall about them, the Romans respond with their own javelin volleys. The sky becomes clouded with spears, and the plains are filled with screams.

The Roman battle horns sound the charge and the Carthaginian bugles reply. The two light infantries dash into each other. The battle field is speckled with hundreds of individual combats. The battle-hardened velites take a heavy toll on their newly trained adversaries. They patiently fend off the enemy sword blows until they find an opening for a quick stab or slash, bleeding out their opponents.

Hannibal watches the opening of the battle from the vantage point of a slight rise in the plain. He is stationed in front of his third army, surrounded by his veterans from the Italia wars. When the Roman velites dash out from between the maniples, Hannibal gasps with surprise at what he sees.

The Roman legions are not typically arranged with the rear maniples staggered to fill the maniple gaps in front of them. Instead, the groups are directly behind one another, with wide open lanes between them.

What is he up to? Hannibal wonders. *Is he going to run his principes out through the lanes? Or the triarii?*

The Carthaginian general notices that his light infantry recruits are getting the worst of the opening skirmish. He recalls them. *Time for the real battle to start, may Baal protect us.*

He turns to Maharbal. "Bring on the elephants, and get the second army ready."

Maharbal grins. "I will enjoy watching this little show."

The Carthaginian trumpets blare three long blasts. The elephant drivers pick up their ten-foot guide spears and prod their elephants forward.

Clad in blood red mail, Surus appears like a malevolent beast from the underworld. More than one velite quails at the sight of the enormous elephant bearing down on him, the monster's body shining like fresh-shed blood. Several legionnaires involuntarily step back from the onrushing horde, only to be shoved into place by their ever-watchful centurions.

Scipio sees that the elephants are rampaging toward his unprotected velites, closing on them with remarkable speed. "Retreat, tell them to retreat!" he yells, knowing it is already too late.

The elephants stampede through the fleeing light infantry. The heavy feet of the rampaging beasts pulverize scores of young warriors before they can scatter from their path. [clxi] Seeing the elephants rumble toward them, the hastati clench their javelins in white-knuckled fists, waiting for the order to defend themselves.

The African mahouts prod the beasts straight toward the Roman heavy infantry, eager to destroy the front ranks of the hastati. Hannibal's horns sound again. His Ligurians, Gauls, and Balearics tramp forward, ready to penetrate the impending breaks in the Roman front.

If we can break their front and get into the back lines, we have them, Hannibal thinks, craning his head forward in anticipation.

Tullius dashes out into the space between the maniples. He is followed by centuries of the other veterans who were handpicked for their swiftness, and were held in reserve for just this moment. Carrying only a tuba, javelin, and shield, the soldiers dash straight at the elephants stampeding across the space between the two armies.

The runners swarm around the sides of the beasts, blaring a cacophony of notes into the elephants' sensitive ears. Those without instruments draw out their swords and stab down the mahouts who are guiding the pachyderms. Tullius blows his tuba until his ears pop, dodging about through the startled beasts.

With their mahouts gone, the elephants panic. Dozens whirl about and trample back the way they came, flattening scores of Hannibal's warriors. Others rumble sideways across the space between the two armies, scattering skirmishers from both sides. Trumpeting with fear, the elephants thunder past the cavalry on the flanks and flee out into the vast empty plains.

Back in the center of battle, young Tullius runs alongside the head of the fearful Surus, blowing so hard his cheeks are crimson with effort. The giant beast heads toward the wide lane between the center maniples, lumbering along to escape the noise. *It works, I'm herding this monster*, Tullius exults.

Tullius blows harder, his eyes bulging with the effort. He is so intent he does not see a velite's decapitated head lying at his feet. He steps upon the head and his foot rolls out from under him, pitching him sideways into the path of the terrified animal.

The elephant's table-sized rear foot crushes into Tullius' spine. The legionnaire screams in agony and rolls onto his stomach. He lies there, broken and dying.

Coughing blood, Tullius props himself up on an elbow. He scrabbles for his belt pouch and fumbles out the three figurines of his family, staring at them as his eyes cloud over. *I am so sorry,* he thinks. His nightfall descends.

With blares and prods the tuba-carrying soldiers herd Surus and the rest of the elephants through the open columns and into the wide open rows separating the hastati and principes. Once between the two rows of maniples, the elephants seek the path of least resistance and dash toward the flanks where Scipio's cavalry await their turn to battle.

Laelius sees dozens of elephants stampeding toward his cavalry, led by the frightening vision of Surus. *Now we'll see if this crazy plan works*.

"Get your javelins out," he orders. "Line up along their left side and do what I told you."

The elephants close in, and the Roman riders back up a short distance from them. When the elephants' left sides are opposite the riders, they hurl their javelins into them.[clxii] The animals bellow in pain and stampede to the right, directly into the outlying Carthaginian cavalry, scattering them like sheep.

Bleeding from a half dozen wounds, mighty Surus tramples down two Carthaginian riders and rumbles out toward the distant hills, never to be seen again.

Laelius and his men plunge in after the elephants, cutting into the dispersed Carthaginian riders. On the other flank, Masinissa follows behind the other elephants, and charges into Tychaeus' Numidians.

Now the battle has shifted from the center to the flanks, as Scipio's cavalry fight swirling battles on both sides. Tychaeus and his men bravely ride into Masinissa's larger force, hurling their spears into them before they close with their swords. The expert horsemen circle one another in a swirling dance of death, jabbing their short swords at any perceived opening.

Masinissa fights in the center of the maelstrom. He is a whirlwind of destruction, stabbing men to the right and left. As Masinissa yanks his sword from the thigh of a passing rider, he spies the leopard-skin cap that covers Tychaeus' helmet.

"After me!" Masinissa shouts to his nearby riders. He weaves his mount through the knots of horse battles about him, his eyes fixed on the leopard's head.

Tychaeus sees the grim prince fighting his way toward him, slashing down any who dare oppose him. *This is a good time to follow Hannibal's directive,* he decides.

"Fight and retreat!" Tychaeus screams, "Fight and retreat!" His cavalry disengage from their foes and race toward the open plains. Masinissa regroups his men and leads them out in pursuit of Tychaeus, drawing his four thousand fighters away from the heart of the conflict.

On the other flank Laelius and his heavily armored cavalry fight a more deliberate battle, trotting forward in line formation. The equites crash into the Carthaginian fighters. Dozens of Hannibal's inexperienced cavalry fall beneath the equites' practiced blades, as the Romans easily fend off their awkward thrusts.

But many of the Carthaginian noblemen are expert riders and are more maneuverable than their civilian counterparts. Their spears find their way into Roman throats and torsos. Six, then eight, then twelve of Laelius' men fall from their mounts.

The outnumbered Carthaginians abruptly turn and flee. Laelius leads his men on a chase after them. The two cavalries shoot past the rear echelons of Hannibal's army, out into the wide open plains.

Hannibal watches Scipio's Romans and Numidians dashing away from the center of battle. He nods with satisfaction. *Now, while their cavalry are gone.* He sends one of his messengers to the front line army commanders. The battle horns sound a long and a short blast.

Hordes of Balearics, Ligurians, and Gauls stride across the gap between their men and the Romans, led by the bearlike Korbis. The barbarians chant and shout in their various tongues, clashing their weapons against their shields.

The Romans march silently forward, led by Marcus Silenus. He stalks along with drawn sword, his eyes flashing with determination to cut through the enemy ranks in front of him.

First Tribune Decimus Agrippa marches next to Marcus. "Time for honor! Time for glory!" he shouts back to the disgraced exiles of the Cannae and Herdonia battles. The legionnaires pick up the pace, eager to vanquish the general who destroyed them.

When the Romans close within a spear's cast of their enemy, Marcus shoves his sword upright into the air. "Attack them, men!"

As one, the Romans scream out a war cry and bash their spears upon their shields, raising a tumult that drowns all other noises in the battlefield. The barbarians halt, momentarily taken aback. Seeing their hesitation, Marcus sprints at the Ligurians in front of him and the rest of the hastatis follow, acting more like Gauls than Romans. With a fearsome crash the main battle starts, as the Romans bash into Hannibal's first army.

In the army center, the Cannenses fight with a deadly controlled fury, determined to regain their honor. Using the falcata-like gladii fashioned by Scipio, their steel blades shatter the long iron swords wielded by the Gauls and Ligurians. Hundreds of the northern barbarians are cut apart by the fearsome cleavers. The legionnaires step over their dismembered bodies, pausing only to kill any who writhe near their feet.

Marcus calls Decimus to his side. "We are becoming too disorganized. Men are scattered all over the place!" Decimus nods. "You take the tribunes, I will find the centurions."

Marcus and Decimus range across the front. "Keep your lines together!" Marcus says to every tribune he finds.

"Maintain formation, don't overpursue," Decimus shouts to the centurions. "I don't care if they drop their weapons and run, we have to keep together!" The Romans return to a more methodical assault, and the Cannenses gradually beat back the fierce Northerners.

While the center legions advance, the right side of the Roman army is deadlocked with the Balearic infantry. Korbis rages across the front lines, hewing through shield and helmet with his oversized falcata. He leads his elite Balearics wherever the front lines start yielding to the

Cannenses' advance, charging recklessly into their hastati and principes. After an hour of furious fighting, the islanders push back the Romans.

"No quit now!" bellows Korbis. "You follow me!" He pushes his way through the conjoined shields of two hastati, battering them sideways with blows from his heavy sword.

"Mercy! I beg you!" screams a voice to the right of Korbis. Korbis looks over to see one of his Balearics lying on the ground, begging for mercy from a centurion who stands over him.

"Coward!" spits the centurion, savoring his victim's plight.

With a roar of anger, the chieftain crashes his way toward the centurion. He hews his falcata into back of the unwary Romans's neck, splitting him from shoulder to stomach. As the legionnaire falls at his feet Korbis swoops down his falcata and beheads the Balearic who was begging for mercy, sending his head spinning across the battlefield. The soldier's blood gouts over Korbis' legs as he stares balefully at his men. His message is clear: there will be no surrender. The islanders redouble their attack.

On the Roman left wing, the veteran Iberians hold their tall oblong shields out in front of them, using their long spears to fend off the Romans' sword thrusts. Try as they might, the staunch legionnaires cannot penetrate their enemy's unwavering shield wall, and the Romans' left wing advance grinds to a halt.

Directing the center attack, Marcus Silenus receives a messenger's reports that both infantry wings are stalemated. *Gods curse those sag-butts, we've got to go help them!* Marcus fumes. *Where's that damn Decimus?* He sees Decimus fighting a Gallic chieftain off to his right and strides over to him.

The Gaul slashes his long sword at Decimus' head but the tribune ably ducks underneath it. Marcus darts in and sticks his shield between the Gaul and Decimus, deflecting Gaul's next sword swipe. As the blade screeches off his shield, Marcus' snakes his sword point under the

Gaul's guard and carves open the underside of the barbarian's sword arm. The Gaul's forearm floods with blood. He drops his shield and runs behind his lines, howling with rage and pain. Marcus grabs Decimus' breastplate and pulls him near his face.

"We must not advance any farther into the center because our flanks cannot move forward," he shouts over the din. "We are in danger being enveloped." He points to his left. "You hold the center. I'm going to the left wing and break those Iberians."

Marcus waves behind him, and a velite brings him his horse. He gallops behind the hastati lines until he arrives opposite the Iberian phalanxes. He sees what he has been hoping for—a kill that will help him turn the tide of battle.

Commander Zinnridi is there, riding atop his snow white stallion, coolly directing the Iberian defense. After being captured at Mago's defeat in North Italia, Mago's former commander was ransomed by Carthage. Now he has returned to battle the Romans, as he swore he would do. Zinnridi rides behind the front line Iberians, calling for fresh troops wherever the Iberians fall.

That bushy bastard's what's holding that shield wall together, Marcus concludes. *He needs to die.*

Marcus sees a velite who is gripping his half-severed right hand, staring at it in shock. "Soldier!" Marcus barks, "Give me those weapons and get back to camp!" He takes the dazed youth's two javelins and pushes him toward the back lines. "See to your wound!"

The legate surges his sturdy little Numidian horse through a narrow space between two front maniples, heading straight for Zinnridi. Marcus spies a tribune in the second line of the hastati, and wheels his mount toward him.

"Get two centuries of your men and follow me!" he shouts to the tribune, and plunges his horse toward the Iberians. Marcus hears the battle whistles blowing behind him. He glances back to see scores of infantry following him. Satisfied, he pushes on.

Marcus Silenus crashes his sturdy little horse into the narrow space between two Iberian infantry stationed in front of Zinnridi, splitting open their shield wall. The Iberians are knocked aside but they quickly recover, hurling their spears into the neck of Marcus' escaping mount.

The stricken horse rears onto its hind legs and falls backwards, whinnying out its life. Marcus leaps sideways from his horse as it falls, sprawling onto the ground. His brittle knee joints scream with pain at the impact. *Curse the gods for making us old!*

Marcus plants an iron hand in the ground and shoves himself upright, spears and shield clenched safely in his other hand. The two Iberians grab their second spears and run at him.

Marcus drops one of his javelins and stands still, anticipating the Iberians' direction of attack, watching their spear arms. The nearest Iberian jumps forward and thrusts his spear at Marcus' unmoving head.

Marcus darts inside the thrust. He stabs his javelin deep into the Iberian's ribs, bringing the man to his knees. In one swift motion, Marcus genuflects, hauls his right arm back, and delves his spear through the fallen Iberian's neck, splitting open his throat. The Iberian clasps his neck with both hands and curls into a ball, gurgling out his final minutes on earth.

Roaring in anger, the second Iberian leaps at Marcus and jabs his spear at Marcus' unprotected back. Still on his knees, the old warrior whirls about and clangs the iron sleeve of his spearhead against the descending blade, deflecting it past him. He jumps up and faces the stout young Iberian.

"Come on, boy. Come try to kill me." The two circle one other like two gladiators, spears at the ready for a killing stroke.

Marcus looks behind the barbarian and sees Zinnridi leading his men out towards the left wing. *That hairy bastard's going to get away!*

Marcus charges the Iberian. The barbarian leaps at him and shoves out his spear. Marcus turns sideways and the spear flashes past his chest. He rams his shield into the Iberian's, leaving him open for the javelin thrust that stabs through his bowels. The barbarian screams in agony and crumples to his knees, clutching at his stomach.

Without a backward look, Marcus runs toward Zinnridi. He halts in front of the Iberians fighting in front of their commander.

Marcus digs in his feet, hauls back his right arm, and hurls his javelin at Zinnridi's head. The spear burrows into the shoulder of Zinnridi's horse. The veteran animal bellows in pain but does not buck. Glowering at Marcus, Zinnridi leans over and yanks out the spear.

What a horse! Marcus marvels. He draws his gladius and dashes forward, dodging past several Iberians. Hemmed in by thick circle of fighting infantry, Zinnridi can only turn his horse about to face his oncoming nemesis.

"Come on, Roman filth," he sneers, drawing out his shining blade.

Marcus nods. "It will be my pleasure." He strides forward, his eyes fixed on the expanse of bare neck between Zinnridi's cuirass and helmet.

A bearish Iberian infantryman charges out from the fight and rams into Marcus' side. Marcus stumbles to the ground, cursing as his sword flies away from him. He rolls sideways, narrowly avoiding the falcata blow that would have split his neck.

The Iberian rushes at Marcus, who grabs his shield and pushes himself to one knee. *Where in Hades is my sword? Gods curse me, I've lost it!*

He sees the Iberian coming at him and grabs his shield with both hands.

The barbarian stabs his falcata at Marcus' heart. The legate batters the heavy blade aside with his scutum and rams its bottom into the Iberian's chest, knocking him off his feet.

Marcus leans over and rams his stony fist into the Iberian's chin. The stunned Iberian claws at Marcus face. Turning his head back and forth to avoid the scratches, Marcus yanks out one of his throwing knives and plunges it into the Iberian's eyes, stabbing him until the hands drop from his face.

Marcus shoves himself upright and pushes the bloody knife back into its belt slot. He runs after Zinnridi, who is plowing his way through the infantry fight, heading for the left flank.

"Commander!" shouts an Iberian. "There's a man behind you!"

Zinnridi looks over his shoulder and sees Marcus charging at him, carrying only his shield. "You going to try to slap me to death?" Zinnridi chortles. He spurs at his horse at Marcus, grinning with anticipation.

Marcus's hand darts to his belt. His throwing knife flashes at Zinnridi's head. Quick as a cat, Zinnridi ducks down his head. The knife clangs off the top of his helmet. Zinnridi plunges toward him..

The legate searches the ground for a sword or spear, but there is none to be found. The Carthaginian closes on Marcus, leaning sideways to stab him down with his six-foot spear. Marcus grabs his shield with both hands.

As the Carthaginian rears back his arm for the fatal spear thrust, Marcus leaps forward and rams the top of his shield into Zinnridi's breastplate. The enemy commander tumbles backwards from his horse.

As Zinnridi rises from the ground, Marcus steps in and kicks him in the head with his hob-nailed sandals, stunning him. Marcus grips his shield on the bottom and side. With all the force of his iron-thewed arms, Rome's greatest warrior arcs his scutum down into Zinnridi's unprotected neck, delving through flesh and bone and into the ground.

Zinnridi's head rolls to Marcus' feet. He watches its eyes blink at him, uncomprehending, and turn glassy. Marcus stares at the gory bottom of his shield. *Maybe I should sharpen the edges and forget about using a sword.*

Marcus grabs the commander's head and runs back to the front lines of his men. He brandishes Zinnridi's bloody head at the Iberians, and then at his hastati.

"Zinnridi is dead," he yells in Iberian, facing the commander's infantry.

He turns to face his legions. "Their leader has fallen!" he shouts. "Press your advantage!"

The Romans cheer Zinnridi's fall, even as the Iberians cry out in dismay. The energized maniples finally break through the Iberian lines and drive them back. The Iberians slowly retreat, but as more fall of them to the Romans they run—and the rout begins. The barbarians dash toward Hannibal's second army, with most heading toward the thousands of Carthaginian recruits on the wing opposite them.

Marcus runs back toward the Roman lines, passing the advancing infantry, and commandeers a wounded equite's stallion. He gallops over to join Decimus Agrippa in the Roman center.

"The Iberians are broken. Take over the center, and attack the Balearics on the right!"

The Cannenses see that their compatriots are chasing the Iberians from the field. The weary veterans attack the Ligurians and Gauls with renewed vigor. They smash into their enemies with their shoulders and shields, moving them ever backward. The principes and triarii follow the battling hastati, waiting for their chance to move into the fray.[clxiii]

Scipio leads the principes forward, carefully attending to the progress of the infantry wings and center. He watches the Iberians break apart on his left, followed by dissolution of the center lines of Gauls and Ligurians. Looking to the right flank, he sees that the Balearics still stand firm, beating back the legionnaires that assault them.

Scipio pulls his horse to a halt and takes off his helmet. He wipes the sweat from his brow and rubs the back of his neck. *Their first army is broken, but two still wait to fight us. Better hold back on the flanking maneuver until I reach Hannibal, we may need fresh veterans. But first I've got to break those cursed Balearics.*

Scipio dons his helmet. He gallops across the back of his battle lines until he reaches the far right flank. Six thousand Numidian infantry are arrayed there, waiting for their chance to be called to battle.

The general rides up to the stout little Numidian captain and points toward the Balearic infantry. "Break that line, that is all I ask of you. Break that front line!" He mimes the attacking action, unsure how much Latin the African understands.

He understands enough. The Numidian captain grins, his broad teeth glowing in his sun darkened face. He trots his horse out in front of his men and begins barking orders, gesticulating wildly and pointing at the Balearics in front of them. The lightly armored Numidians trot across the plain. The riders chant their traditional war song about the glory of death in battle, heading for the fight raging between the Balearics and the legionnaires.

Scipio trots back towards the center lines. He waves at Marcus Silenus until he catches his eye, and points to the right.

The legate sees the Numidians drawing near the Romans on the right flank, and nods at Scipio. *Now is the time to break those island bastards.*

Marcus rides over to the right flank. He sees the massive Korbis standing in front of his men, challenging the Romans to come out and fight him. *There he is again.* Marcus thinks, recalling their last fight.

Marcus eases down from his borrowed horse and strides toward the giant Balearic, assessing the man's stance, build, and moves. *He is likely a berserker. He depends on brute strength to batter down his opponents.*

The Balearic sees the legate approaching him and disdainfully hammers back the centurion he was fighting. "Kill him!" he shouts back to his Balearics, pointing his falcata at the centurion. The islanders swarm over the young soldier and stab him down.

Korbis stalks toward Marcus Silenus. His feral grin shines through his black bushy beard, his blue plume nods from the top of his domed silver helmet.

"Your head will be a great prize," Korbis shouts. "I will stick it outside my tent and watch the flies eat it!"

Marcus pitches a javelin at Korbis, studying the islander's reaction. Without breaking stride, the Balearic commander deftly catches the throw on his shield. He yanks it out and flings it back. The battered spearhead thunks off Marcus' shield.

He's fast, Marcus notes, *but he favors his right.*

Then the two warriors are upon each other. Marcus darts his gladius at Korbis' wide middle, but the Balearic blocks the thrust with his round shield. With a roar of effort, Korbis delivers a ringing blow to Marcus' scutum, knocking him to his knees and splitting his shield.

Marcus blinks in surprise at the sheer force of the blow. He vaults to his feet and jumps inside the Balearic's guard, arcing back his gladius. He stabs his blade at a finger-wide gap in the Balearics' silver scaled chest armor. The point cuts deep into Korbis' pectoral.

With a bellow that is more rage than pain, Korbis backhands his shield into Marcus Silenus. The Roman catches the blow on his damaged shield but is again knocked sprawling. Korbis wipes his hand across his chest and stares at the blood. He smiles, his eyes alight with eagerness. "I going to piss on your head every day 'til it rot!"

Marcus shoves his chest armor into place and stalks toward the waiting islander, planning his death strike.

While the two heroes battle, the Numidian infantry arrives and swarms into the Balearics' flanks, hurling clouds of spears upon them. Hundreds fall beneath the pitiless iron of the Numidians, and the front line hastati press their advantage, marching forward to cut their way into the disrupted islanders.

Korbis hears his men shouting and screaming. He sees his troops being enveloped from the front and rear, as the battle turns into a riotous conflict of attackers swarming over the Balearics from three sides.

"I kill you later, little man," he shouts at Marcus, and lumbers off to join his men.

Marcus stands in the opening between the front lines, catching his breath and willing his heart to slow. He watches Korbis lead his men on a retreat around the flank toward the second army. He sheathes his sword and grins. *Next time I'll be more prepared for you.*

The legate casts off his shattered scutum and bends to take a shield from a dead hastati. He places a denarius deep inside the dead man's throat so it will not fall out. *Gratitude, soldier. Here is a coin for Charon, that he may guide you safely to the underworld.*

Marcus hefts up his new shield and marches back to the center of the pursuing hastati, ready to lead the rout.

*   *   *   *   *

Hannibal's first army is now in full retreat, scattered across the two-hundred yard gap between the remains of their troops and the second army. Mago's veterans cast off their weapons and armor as they flee the pursuing hastati, desperate to get out of spear range.

Maharbal is atop his horse in the center of the second army, his Carthaginians, Macedonians and Libyans fresh and organized. He dourly observes the defeat of Hannibal's first force, waiting impatiently for his chance to attack the Romans and score the victory. He does not have long to wait.

Hannibal's messenger delivers a hastily written papyrus scroll with two terse orders. *Attack at will. No retreat.*

Maharbal grins. *Finally, we can get at those bastards!* He trots over to the Macedonian general, who is standing in front of his four rectangular phalanxes of a thousand spearmen each.

"You must preserve the center," Maharbal says, waving the papyrus under the general's nose. "There is nowhere for you to retreat, and

372

Hannibal will kill you if you try. You win or die."

The thin-faced young noble raises the face piece of his helmet and stares disdainfully at the wiry old commander.

"We will not die today, and woe to those who try to kill us."

Maharbal signals his trumpeters and they sound the call to attack. Twelve thousand men march down the plain's gentle incline, a mile-wide forest of Carthaginian and Macedonian spears, their bronze heads glinting in the afternoon sun.

The survivors of Hannibal's first army run toward Maharbal's approaching forces. Many of them loop around the flanks of the second army, seeking safety with the third force or hoping to escape to the hills. Others rush into the second army itself, trying to hide behind the front lines.

Fearing these demoralized men will disrupt their staid ranks, the second army commanders order their men to drive them away. Hundreds of desperate Gauls, Ligurians, Balearics and Iberians battle with the second army forces. Chaos reigns along the second army's front lines, except for the Macedonian center.

The imperturbable Macedonians stab out with their eighteen-foot pikes, cutting down any refugees who flee toward them. The first army remnants abandon their attempts to penetrate the Macedonian formations. They flee through the open spaces between the four phalanxes.

The second army's Carthaginian and Libyan recruits on the flanks do not fare as well against the first army invaders. Scores of them fall as the internecine battle continues along the second army's front lines.[clxiv]

Marcus and his tribunes lead Scipio's legions into the enemy's distracted front lines, eager to strike at a weakened foe. Once again, the aging Cannenses are at the center of the battle, their maniples vainly trying to break through the thick Macedonian spear walls.

With the infantry center deadlocked with the staunch Macedonians,

Scipio's left and right flanks march in toward the second army's Carthaginian and Libyan recruits. The Roman veterans slash into their legs and arms, disabling their untrained foes before they administer fatal thrusts to their bodies.

Within an hour, Scipio's men have cut down thousands of the young Africans on the second army flanks. The terrified recruits ignore their captains' commands and flee the Roman's relentless attack, following the first army's retreat to the rear of Hannibal's third army.

Maharbal gallops about the retreating Carthaginians, furious at their cowardice. "Turn around and fight," he screams, striking his men with his spear. "I'll have you all crucified!" It is all to no avail. The recruits pitch away their weapons and run to the rear.

In his embarrassed rage Maharbal fails to notice the maniples edging in around him, until he is confined within a circle of Roman troops.

"Get off your horse and throw down your weapons," a centurion commands, gesturing the meaning of his words. The centurion has no desire to kill Maharbal, knowing he is a prize that will bring Rome much ransom—and bring him much honor.

Maharbal wheels his horse about, looking for an opening. All he sees is a circle of arms and armor that is three men deep. He spits at the centurion and grins.

"I have slain your men, fucked your women and eaten your babies," he shouts in a mocking tone. "Life has been good!"

Hannibal's commander draws his sword. "For Ammon and Carthage!" he screams, and plunges his horse at the centurion.

A dozen legionnaires leap forward. They jab their sharp spears into Maharbal's legs and stomach, levering their spearheads to slash across his bowels. Maharbal bellows in pain. "Pig fuckers!" he manages to shout, as the reins fall from his grasp.

Maharbal topples sideways from his horse, clutching at his protruding intestines. The Romans plunge their pila into him again and again, until the dread Maharbal becomes just another unrecognizable corpse.

With the second army flanks destroyed, the tribunes direct their men toward the staunch Macedonians in the center. The maniples encircle the four phalanxes, staying carefully out of reach of their fearsome thicket of spears. Several sorties at the Macedonians leave scores of wounded and dead Romans about their perimeter. The frustrated tribunes confer and agree upon a new tactic—they will retreat to conquer.

The Romans rush the Macedonian front again, only to encounter the same staunch resistance. After a half hour of futile assaults and spear throws, the tribunes call for their front lines to retreat. The exultant Macedonians press their advantage. Their phalanxes move forward, pushing the Romans farther back.

The Romans retreat passes through the location of the first army battle, where the ground is mounded with corpses and weaponry. The Macedonian phalangites crawl, push, and step around the layers of the dead, lowering their spears to maintain their balance. The phalanxes' organized lines and spacing breaks up. The spear walls lose formation, leaving the Macedonians vulnerable.

Seizing their advantage, the tribunes direct their men to charge into the Macedonians' ragged perimeter. The Romans delve into the Macedonians' inner lines, where the phalangites' unwieldy spears are more liability than threat. The legionnaires dart under the spears and stab down hundreds of the proud warriors.

The Macedonians pitch down their spears and draw their swords, but the spearmen are no match for the gladii of Scipio's battle-tested veterans, men practiced in close combat kills. Philip's men die where they stand, far from home, contained by walls of vengeful legionnaires.

Decimus Agrippa leads his men into the remains of the Macedonian front, stepping over the furrows of densely packed corpses. He pulls off the black-plumed helmet of the dead Macedonian general and brandishes it for all the Cannenses to see, exulting in his disgraced legion's symbol of victory. "Victory! Honor! Glory to Rome!" he shouts triumphantly.

A dying Macedonian sees Decimus standing near him, brandishing his beloved general's helmet. The phalangite summons the last of his fading strength and pushes up from the pile of corpses he has laid upon, propping himself up with one hand. Wiping the blood from his other hand, he grabs a dead companion's spear.

The Macedonian lunges forward and shoves his eighteen foot lance deep into the side of Decimus' stomach, wedging it between the two halves of the tribune's cuirass.

Decimus gasps and bends over. He falls to one knee. Two of his fellow tribunes rush to surround him while another one splits the skull of the dying phalangite. Decimus is carefully bandaged, eased onto a litter, and given the Macedonian general's helmet.

As he jounces toward the rear ranks Decimus turns on his side to look back at the battlefield, clutching his victory symbol. *Thanks be to Mars, our honor is restored.* He lies back on the litter, listening to the clashes and screams.

*　　*　　*　　*　　*

Hannibal watches the destruction of the second army unfold, the men rushing across the plain toward his reserve force. He gnashes his teeth. *Those soft-handed recruits weren't ready for this. The elephants weren't ready. I should have told those Elders to go fuck themselves and taken another month.*

He waves over three of his infantry commanders. "Strato, order our officers to drive off any of those cowards who try to get into our front lines. Haggith, get over to the right flank and muster the survivors into some semblance of order. They are to block any flank attacks. You, Baalhan, you do the same for the left. Kill any who resist. Do you hear me?" The captains nod and ride off to their tasks.

Hannibal smirks. *Scipio will think twice about sending those back lines on a flanking maneuver. He will have to fight my best after exhausting himself on the recruits.* He kicks his heels into his horse and gallops to the right flank, eager to ascertain that his men are placed correctly.

Marcus Silenus has left his horse and marches on foot, leading the weary hastati toward Hannibal's staunch army of veterans. The legionnaires stumble over the weapons and bodies of the sixteen thousand dead strewn about them, slipping on the blood and gore that lies beneath their every step. The hastati lose their organized ranks as they scramble over the mounds of dead and dying, some stopping to plunder a choice item from the enemy dead. The principes who follow fall into disarray as they scramble to get closer to the advancing hastati.clxv

From atop his horse behind the principes, Scipio can see his army losing its formation and discipline. He shakes his head, darkly amused at the turn of events. *Hannibal's dead are doing what his living could not, they are breaking our ranks.* He sighs. *We're not organized enough to fight his fifteen thousand veterans.*

Scipio sees Hannibal's first and third army survivors massing along the sides of Hannibal's army, led by a phalanx of Balearics on his right. *The old fox anticipated my flanking tactics. By the time the principes and triarii cut their way through those herds of survivors, his real army would be ready for us. And our hastati will be exhausted. Shit!*

Scipio waves over a messenger rider. "Tell Marcus Silenus to halt the advance. Our legions are turning into a mob." The messenger dashes to the front, and Scipio follows him with his retinue of guards, his right hand twitching with anxiety. *His line is widening past our wings—he is going to outflank me!*

Then Scipio remembers his dream, about his playing pieces spread out in a long single line. *I've got to spread my men across the front and stop him from outflanking me. The Cannenses will have to hold until our cavalry comes. If he breaks them, we are lost.*

Scipio stares anxiously into the plains beyond Hannibal's waiting army. *And where in Hades are my cavalry? Has the earth swallowed Laelius and Masinissa?*

Far out to Scipio's left, far behind Hannibal's army, Laelius and his men are swarming about the hundreds of Carthaginian cavalry who have halted their flight to turn about and fight. The equites and socii cut down a dozen of the enemy riders before the Carthaginians abruptly gallop away again, fading into the distance.

Laelius calls in his men to regroup before they resume their chase. *Why in Jupiter's cock are they running away? They act like Numidians, they run and fight then fight and run.*

Laelius looks back at the distant dust clouds of the infantry battle, and it finally dawns on him. *Idiot! They are luring you away from the battle!*

Laelius whirls in his saddle, searching for his second in command. "Cassius! Forget chasing them, we have to find Masinissa. Get our men together and follow me!"

Laelius races away from his men, galloping east across the plains, desperate to reach Masinissa in time.

Scipio has little time to reflect on the loss of Laelius and Masinissa. He rides out to join Marcus Silenus in the quarter-mile gap that separates his men from Hannibal's third army.

"We will reorganize here, where the ground is level and free of the dead," he tells Marcus. "Bring up our fresh principes and triarii. Line the principes on the wings, that they may support our hastati.[clxvi] Put the triarii on the very edges, to prevent a flank attack.[clxvii] When we have them aligned, we attack."

Marcus stares at Scipio. "You will have no reserves behind our front lines? If the Hannibal's men break through, they can attack from the front and rear."

"I know that, but it is our only chance," Scipio replies. "I have faith our men will not break. And our cavalry will return."

"Gods help us all, General," says Marcus, as he turns to go.

While the principes and triarii line up on each side of the hastati, Laelius closes in on Masinissa's men. The prince's men are engaged in a swirling battle with their tribal enemies. Masinissa is in the center, hacking his short sword to the right and left, fighting his way towards a man with a leopard skin cap on his helmet.

Laelius dodges through the battling Numidians, his silver-bossed shield deflecting the spear jabs of several charging enemies. He draws up behind his friend.

"Masinissa, Masinissa! We have to get back to the army, Hannibal's going to trap them!" he yells.

Masinissa shakes his head. He points his sword at Tychaeus. "That one needs killing. I go nowhere."

Laelius grimaces. *Stubborn bastard.* "Very well," he says. "Let us be quick about it!"

Laelius puts heels to his horse and surges ahead of Masinissa, hurtling towards Tychaeus.

"Wait, you fool!" Masinissa curses, fearing he will lose the honor of killing the Numidian general. He puts heels to his horse and careens through the cavalry duels about him, closing in on Laelius.

"Get away! He is mine!" he bawls.

Laelius ignores Masinissa. He levels his javelin and charges, desperate to kill Tychaeus and return to Scipio. "You there, with the smelly helmet!" Laelius shouts. "Time to meet your gods!"

Tychaeus sneers at Laelius. He gallops towards the heavily armored Roman. As they close on each other, the nimble Numidian ducks under Laelius' sword swing, and bashes him sideways with his small round shield. Laelius is thrown off balance. He fumbles for his horse's reins and finally pulls his mount to a stop, but Tychaeus has already wheeled about and is charging back into Laelius.

Laelius yanks on his horse's rope to turn him about, but the swift

Numidian is already upon him. Tychaeus shoves his spear into Laelius' back until the point juts out below his ribs.

Laelius twists around in agony. His sword and shield drop from his hands. A grinning Tychaeus yanks at his spear to retrieve it for a final blow, but the point catches momentarily in Laelius' silver scaled armor.

A moment is all Masinissa needs. As Tychaeus yanks at his spear, Masinissa charges in and jumps onto Tychaeus' back, riding him off his mount and onto the ground. Leaping up from his stunned foe, Masinissa pulls out his long dagger and kneels onto Tychaeus' arms, pinning him to the earth.

"Would you were your uncle Syphax," Masinissa says to the struggling Masaesyli, "but you will just have to do."

The Numidian plunges his dagger into the left side of Tychaeus' throat and pulls its razored blade across his squirming neck, watching Tychaeus' eyes start from his head. Blood gushes over Masinissa's hands as he finishes his grisly task, sawing open his entire throat.

Masinissa pulls off Tychaeus' leopard skin cap and wipes his arms on it. "No more hunting for you," he mutters, flinging the bloody skin onto Tychaeus' lifeless face.

Masinissa rises up from the corpse of his tribal enemy, giving it a final kick to the head. He rushes over to Laelius, who clings to the neck of his mount, his blood streaming down the horse's neck.

"We have to get back to the infantry," Laelius mutters. "Hannibal wanted to lure us away from them."

"In a minute," Masinissa replies. He carefully extracts Tychaeus' spear and unstraps Laelius' cuirass. The prince saws off strips of his tunic and wraps Laelius' bleeding middle, tying a firm knot to seal it.

"Enough, Mother," Laelius says, pushing Masinissa away. "If I die, I die—but we have to get back!"

Laelius puts heels to his mount and dashes back toward the battle.

Masinissa yells orders for his captains to follow him. He surges after Laelius. The arriving Roman cavalry merge with the returning Nubians. Five thousand riders pour across the plains, hurtling toward Hannibal's rear echelon.

Scipio's realigned army is now a mile and a half line of seasoned veterans, with none held in reserve. The legions tramp in unison toward Hannibal's war-tested Carthaginians, Gauls, Libyans, Iberians, and Bruttians. The Romans do not shout or chant as they close with the third army; their time for bravado is past. They are quietly determined to end these men and end their time in accursed Africa.

When Scipio's army is within a spear's cast of the Carthaginian front, Hannibal's battle horns trumpet the attack signal. The Carthaginian mercenaries march forward, ready to wipe out the Romans. The two armies meet with a crash of shield and sword.

The Cannenses in the center clash with Hannibal's relentless Iberians and Libyans, men who fight fearlessly and deliberately, waiting for a fatal opening. The mercenaries' judicious spear thrusts strike home, and dozens of tired Cannenses fall during the first minutes of battle, dragged from the front as others step in to relieve them.

Hannibal's Bruttians are on the Romans' left wing, dueling with their Italia countrymen. The right wing is a melee' of Romans against Carthaginians and Gauls, with Korbis' Balearics rushing late into the fray.

Hannibal gallops behind his front line fighters, yelling orders and encouragement, wading in to the fight wherever the lines seem to be bending.

The left wing of the Romans is the first to gain advantage. The fresh legionnaires use their shoulders and shields to press their Bruttian opponents backwards and shove them into each other.[clxviii] Their battering tactics limit their opponents' space and mobility, allowing the Romans to stab down most of the front-line defenders. Desperate, the Carthaginian captains push the refugees of the first and second army into the left wing conflict. The Roman advance slows, if only because there are more men for them to kill and more bodies to negotiate.

The right wing is at standstill. The principes cut through the initial onslaught of the rampaging Gauls, littering the battle space with their large bodies, and drive the Northerners into retreat. But Hannibal's veteran Carthaginians maintain their ranks, skillfully stabbing their spears into the advancing principes. The Roman advance halts. The triarii on the far right flank fends off Korbis and his attacking Balearics, using their long spears to form spear walls when the islanders quickly counterattack.

Bleeding from a half-dozen spear pricks, Korbis leads his men on four charges against Scipio's elder soldiers, but he and his men are repelled by the spear walls of the senior legionnaires.

The Cannenses in the middle are fighting their third battle of the day. Most are older men from the Cannae and Herdonia defeats of years ago. They fight without fear, taking a heavy toll on the staunch Iberians and Libyans, but they become very weary. Their ranks slowly thin from casualties inflicted by the fierce tribesmen, and there are few men left to replace them.

Hannibal sees that the Roman center is beginning to bow inward. He rides to the rear and summons the remains of the second army's Ligurians and Gauls to come to the front, hoping to break the Roman middle before his Bruttians collapse and the Romans outflank him. The Libyans and Iberians in the center step back to rest as Hannibal's reserves march in to engage the hastati, giving them no respite.

The legionnaires of the beleaguered center are now worn to exhaustion. Their arms and legs grow heavy, and they hold their swords and shields ever lower. Many valiant front liners fall to the Ligurians' and Gauls' beserking attacks.

Noticing their weariness, Hannibal calls for another charge by the refreshed Libyans and Iberians. The Roman center bows farther inward.

Another strike should do it, he thinks. He raises his arm to summon a concerted charge by the all his troops in the center, determined to break through Scipio's thinning center and attack his wings from behind.

Hannibal feels the cavalry attack before he sees it. The ground tremors reverberate through his mount and into his feet.

Hannibal looks over his shoulder and beholds his defeat.

Five thousand Roman and Numidian cavalry are rolling in upon his rear lines, with the pursuing Carthaginians faint dots in the distance.

Hannibal frantically waves over his officers. "Quick, quick! Turn the rear lines around! The cavalry are coming!"

Led by Laelius and Masinissa, the Numidian and Roman riders flood into the unsuspecting rear infantry like a tidal wave of death.[clxix]

Masinissa's Numidians are everywhere, swarming through the rear of Hannibal's third army. Their deadly spear thrusts fell men right and left as they dash from one victim to another.

The armored Roman cavalry are more deliberate but no less effective. Each squadron of thirty attacks as a group. They hew holes through the Hannibal's back lines, jamming the survivors into his front line defenders. Hannibal's men begin to mill about, trying to protect themselves from simultaneous front and rear attacks. Confusion and disorder become Scipio's allies.

A deathly pale Laelius leads several squadrons on an attack into the Libyan phalanxes on the flanks, breaking into their stolid ranks.

"Come on, boys. One more charge and we have them!" he shouts. He blinks his eyes, suddenly dizzy.

Laelius starts to slide off his horse. He grabs the mane of his steed and kicks it forward, leading his men into the confused Africans. With a grunt of effort, he wobbles a javelin into the enemy riders.

A rangy young squadron leader grasps Laelius' horse by its neck rope. "We have the battle, Commander. Please come with me." The equite pulls Laelius' horse into an open space behind Hannibal's dissolving rear lines, just as Laelius starts to topple from his horse.

The squadron leader eases Laelius off his mount and onto the ground. His men stand guard over their fallen leader, watching the carnage of defeat unfold before of them.

The Bruttians are the first to break. They dash from the battlefield, throwing down their weapons in order to run faster across the plains. The first and second army survivors follow them.

Hannibal's entire right wing is soon in flight, leaving the principes and triarii free to outflank the Iberians and Libyans in the center. In a matter of minutes, Hannibal's center lines are encircled. The mercenaries fall by the hundreds, fighting with the doomed desperation of men with no escape.

Scipio sees the Carthaginian center caving in, and his heart thuds with excitement. *We have them, if we but press our advantage.* Scipio charges recklessly out from the rear and across the front lines, his gladius in his hand. He stabs down a Carthaginians who rushes up to block his way, even as his Honor Guard hurries to catch up with him.

Approaching the center, Scipio can see the fatal encirclement of Hannibal's best fighters. He knows the battle is won. Scipio rides to the tribune leading the Cannenses.

"Tell our men to withdraw. Offer the Libyans and Iberians the chance to surrender. Kill those who do not throw down their arms." The tribune departs to notify his fellows. Scipio rides toward his right flank, hoping to end the last pocket of resistance.

Masinissa and three thousand of his Numidians encircle Hannibal's wing of Carthaginians, Gauls, and Balearics. The rest of his riders sweep across the plains to hunt down the thousands who are fleeing across it. The left wing of Hannibal's army is pressed ever closer together, and the men begin to throw down their arms.

Scipio rides to the front line of advancing principes and triarii, prepared to halt the slaughter and offer surrender terms. He dismounts and walks over to the tribune directing the principes' onslaught.

"Septimus, take the men back ten paces. We can make the rest our captives."

Septimus' reply is interrupted by a loud roar of voices in front of him, shouts of battle and cries of pain. He and Scipio gape at a wedge of Balearics rampaging through the Roman lines in front of them.

Korbis stalks out from the front line of his men. He heads straight for Scipio, with murder in his eye...

Korbis realizes the battle is lost. His Balearics have nowhere to escape in this strange land, and the slave markets await if they are captured. When he sees Scipio himself riding up near the front lines he lifts his eyes skyward. *Gratitude for the opportunity of a glorious death*, he prays. *Grant me time to take my prize.*

Korbis waves over his surrounding elite Balearics. "Follow me to death, glorious death. We go take Scipio's head!"

The chieftain lumbers forward, his falcata raised high, beckoning his men to their fate. The Balearics charge headlong into the principes in front of Scipio. They slash and stab at any who oppose them, heedless of the Roman blades that take their lives.

Korbis hews his way through two soldiers blocking his way, leaving them writhing on the ground. His eyes fix on Scipio while his remaining men swarm at the Romans around him.

My gods, that monster is coming after me! Scipio thinks. He withdraws his sword and stands waiting. His shield hand clenches his Nike figurine.

Korbis closes on Scipio, ready to batter him to the earth. Septimus steps in front of Scipio.

"Get away from him, Septimus!" Scipio orders. "This is my fight!"

"I cannot do that, General," Septimus replies. The burly tribune marches forward and rams his scutum into the Balearic's bossed shield with all his might. Korbis does not break stride as he plows the tribune to the earth, shoving his falcata through Septimus' breastplate armor and into his heart. He plants his foot on the dead man's chest and yanks out his thick sword, savoring the blood dripping from it.

Korbis grins at Scipio. "You see what I have for you?"

Scipio's right hand trembles but he extends his sword and beckons Korbis forward. "Come on, fat man."

"You beat Hannibal, but you not beat me," Korbis blurts in crude Latin. The Balearic charges, his helmet-splitting falcata raised high over his head.

Korbis skids to a stop, yelling with pain. He grabs at the base of his neck and pulls out a small throwing knife, his plate-sized hand covered with blood. Enraged, he glares about for the thrower.

"You!" he snarls. "This time I kill you sure!"

Marcus Silenus marches forward, his predator eyes fixed on Korbis. "Get back, General," Marcus says as he closes on Korbis. "This man is mine."

Quick as a cat, Marcus jumps in and chops his gladius at Korbis' head. The Balearic deftly blocks it with his shield, but the force of Marcus' blade knocks him back a step. The chief's eyes widen. Then he grins.

"You are strong little man, eh?"

The Balearic springs forward and whooshes his heavy sword at Marcus' neck. Marcus angles his shield sideways and deflects Korbis' fatal blow, but the falcata hews away a quarter of his shield, knocking him backwards. Korbis follows his advantage and swings his sword at the gap in Marcus' shield, caving in the shield's boss and splitting it into two useless chunks.

Marcus scrambles away and flings off the remains of his shield, shaking off the numbness in his shield arm. He stands with feet apart and arms spread wide, watching Korbis' eyes to see which way he will move.

The grinning Balearic throws away his shield. "You try stop this, little man," he snarls in Latin. He grasps his mighty sword in both hands, and rushes forward, raising it over his head.

Surprise is the only way, Marcus decides. He darts forward, straight at the onrushing giant. The heavy sword slices down towards Marcus' head, but the old warrior has already dropped to the ground and is rolling beneath Korbis feet. Marcus stabs his razored gladius upward, cutting open Korbis' thigh artery.

The barbarian bellows with pain. "You little dog!" he yells, and kicks Marcus sprawling. As he falls to his back, Marcus grabs Korbis thick leg with one arm and jams his gladius up into Korbis' rectum and bowels. He buries his blade to the hilt and twists it back and forth.

Korbis roars with anguish. He kicks Marcus and staggers backwards. Korbis yanks out the gladius and flings it away. Groaning, Korbis glares at Marcus. He takes a step toward him, then another.

"I kill you!" Korbis splutters. Then he falls.

Korbis writhes on the ground, swinging his falcata about until Marcus walks over pries it from his hamlike fist.

"You deserve a better death," he says, looking into Korbis' reddened eyes.

"Fuck you," Korbis replies, spitting blood onto Marcus shins. "Do it."

Marcus grabs the falcata with both hands and crunches it through Korbis' forehead, splitting open his skull. The Balearic's eyes bulge from his head. He convulses for a minute, then his massive body lies still.

Shaking and dazed, the legate steps back and puts his hands on his knees. "Little man, eh?" he gasps, and spits on the corpse.

Preoccupied with killing the man who would kill his friend and general, Marcus does not see the Balearic who has crept in behind him. He only feels his deadly spear.

Marcus convulses backward, yelling in pain. A leaf-shaped spearpoint explodes from his chest, punching through his battle-weathered breastplate. Marcus whirls about, the spear sticking from his back like a giant quill, looking for his assailant. But the principes have already gotten to him, and all Marcus sees are three Romans jamming their swords into a twitching body.

Rome's greatest warrior falls to his knees. His men ease out the spear and lay him on the ground. They hurriedly rip up the ends of their tunics to make bandages, sobbing unabashedly.

Scipio pushes through the men and falls to his knees next to Marcus, tears streaming down his blood-grimed face. He touches Marcus' brow.

"You were always the best of us," Scipio says, watching in horror as Marcus yellow-green eyes begin to dim.

Marcus raises his hand. Scipio grasps it, feeling the tremors that rush through his body. The legate looks deeply into Scipio's eyes. His mouth twists into a tight smile.

"...my honor to serve you," Marcus mumbles. "I am glad you were here with me. I did not die alone." Then he stares to Olympus.

Scipio rises, oblivious to the battle around him, wiping the tears from his face. "Take him to the rear," he orders. "Protect his body with your life."

Scipio stumbles over to the front lines. The principes and triarii have rallied and are battering down the last of the Balearics. The remainders the Carthaginians are running from the field. Scattered cheers erupt from the exhausted legionnaires.

Scipio glances dully at the carnage, watching Korbis' men being cut down all about him. *Good. Destroy all of them. Kill every fucking one of them.* Then he thinks of the men he would lose in such unnecessary slaughter, their lives given for Scipio's revenge. *Marcus would be ashamed of you.*

Scipio raises his arm and waves it in front of his face, as if shooing away a bothersome insect. "Take the rest prisoner," he tells his senior tribune. "No one else has to die today."

Behind his center lines, Hannibal watches the seventeen-year war die with the death of his army. He sees the Romans surrounding his troops, his men throwing down their arms, his proud veterans running away in every direction. He sees the Roman cavalry trotting up the plain towards him. *Carthage will need you. There is much work yet to do.*

Hannibal swallows a sob and turns to his Sacred Band captain. "Back to Hadrumentum." [clxx] Hannibal spins his horse around and gallops for the low hills behind him. A hundred of his men follow, their hearts mixed with sorrow and relief.

Dusk light washes over the battlefield. Its gray light mercifully shrouds the fields of carnage. Scipio weaves his horse through the serried rows of the dead, looking for Laelius.

After a dozen anxious queries, one of the cavalrymen points Scipio toward the back of Hannibal's erstwhile third army, which has become a half-mile line of roped captives. Scipio sees a squadron of cavalry standing about a prone figure in shining armor.

Oh my gods, no!

Scipio gallops madly to the gathered equites and leaps from his slowing horse. The somber Romans step aside. Laelius is lying on the ground, his waist bandage splotted with blood. Scipio falls to his knees and gently grasps Laelius' shoulders, tears starting from his eyes.

"Oh, please, not you too," he sobs. "All this is nothing without you."

Laelius' lidded eyes flicker. His hand rises, and he feebly shoves Scipio in the shoulder. "Gods no, boy." Laelius mumbles. "The medicus says the spear did not strike home." His mouth wrinkles into a grin. "But I could use a day or two from my duties, if it is not too much trouble."

Scipio looks about him and up into the sky, looking for someone to thank. He buries his face into Laelius' chest and cries.

Laelius' fingers stroke Scipio's hair. "Jupiter's cock, you act like we lost!" he murmurs. Minutes later, his hand falls as he drifts off to sleep. Scipio's Greek army doctor gently pulls him from the sleeping warrior.

"He needs to rest," the old medicus says. "But he will recover in time."

Scipio impulsively kisses the wizened old man and walks back to his horse, shaking with relief. He looks at his attending guards. "I want to know of his welfare, every hour," he says sternly. "Whether I be asleep or awake." His eyes sadden. "Do not tell him of Marcus yet."

Two tribunes walk up to Scipio, wearing weary smiles on their dust grimed faces. "Congratulations, General." We estimate over twenty thousand of theirs are dead, and less than two thousand of ours.[clxxi] It is a great victory. You will be forever known as the man who defeated Hannibal."

Scipio manages a tight smile. "Yes, quite an honor. I defeated a weary old man armed with untrained troops and elephants. Thank the gods he was not the Hannibal of ten years ago."

Scipio rides away from the two bewildered officers, trotting up onto a rise above the battlefield. He looks across the dusky acres of bodies strewn across the plains of Zama, the grim harvest of his victory. He watches the hundreds of ravens that speckle the killing fields, their feasting caws punctuated with the despairing shrieks of wounded enemies being dispatched by the plundering Romans.

He offered me peace, an honorable peace. All of them would be alive if I just said "Yes."

Scipio recalls Marcus' words at Carthago Nova, when a young Scipio massacred innocent citizens to save his own soldiers. *Someone has to die, that others may live.*

He sighs. *I fear you were right. Oh gods, I will miss you.*

Scipio begins to tremble with relief as the day's tensions leave him. His eyelids begin to droop. *One more hour. You've still got work to do.*

Scipio waves over one of the passing cavalry officers. "Get our cavalry over here, and the Numidians, too. We have not finished this battle."

Within the hour, the Roman and Numidian riders are storming through Hannibal's camp. They drive the hundreds of remaining Carthaginians and mercenaries out into the plains. The survivors are still dazed with their defeat and humiliation.

The once-proud warriors are bound and held next to the captured horses and elephants—beasts destined for a life of slavery.

After piling up hills of weapons and valuables in front of the camp, Masinissa's men ride back in with torches. They set fire to every corner and space, as per Scipio's orders.

The flames tower into the moonless sky, a beacon of triumph and tragedy that broadcasts its three dire messages throughout the indigo African night.

Hannibal has lost.

Carthage has been defeated.

The war is over.

XI. SCIPIO RISEN

ROME, 201 BCE. "You are but a man," the slave whispers in Scipio's ear. "Nothing but a man."

The wiry little Egyptian straightens Scipio's purple toga, and evens up the laurel wreath about his head. Satisfied with the Imperator's appearance, the slave resumes his role of holding the bejeweled golden crown of triumph over Scipio's manicured curls.

Scipio does not notice the slave's ministrations, nor does he hear the young man's ritual chant of humility. He is too engaged with waving at the thousands of plebians that throng about his four-horse chariot, screaming their love for the man who has finally brought peace to Rome. *By Minerva's shield, just look at them. They are happier than I am!*

Scipio beams at them. He is pleased by their adulation but he is more delighted at the sight of Laelius riding behind him, resplendent in the new silver armor that hides his heavily bandaged stomach. Most of all Scipio savors the sight of Amelia and Cornelia riding in a small gold-trimmed chariot behind Laelius, his wife holding their child at arm's length to view the spectacle.

For the hundredth time since he landed in Sicily last month, Scipio grips his Nike figurine, now worn to an indistinct lump. He turns and smiles at his white gowned wife and shows it to her. *Victory is ours. I fulfilled my promise to Father.*

Amelia smiles at Scipio. She nods. *I know.*

King Syphax marches far in front of Scipio's laurel-festooned white chariot.[clxxii] The chained king holds his head high, ignoring the captive Carthaginian officers around him and the garbage that flies past his head.

Syphax is rudely nudged along by two oxen pulling the lead wagon of the fifty that follow, each one filled with Scipio's plunder of captured Carthaginian artwork, jewels, and gold—a smidgeon of the spoils destined for the Senate's vaults.

Scipio frowns at the sight of his erstwhile friend in chains, and for a moment his triumphal joy is clouded with regret. *He was a loyal ally until he became enraptured with Sophonisba.* He sighs. *I will soon have to tell him we caught his son Vermina's army and destroyed it.*[clxxiii]

He waves at the boys hanging from the statues at the Temple of Victoria. *At least Vermina escaped alive. Thank the gods he was late in arriving at Zama, though I cannot guess why did not get there on time.* He smiles to himself as raises both hands high. *Hannibal was right. Who knows what Fortuna will bring?*

The Roman Senate marches in front of Syphax, garbed in snow white tunics with broad purple borders. Flaccus marches next to Cato, both looking as if they are captives themselves.

"Do you know what his victory will do for the Hellenic Party?" Flaccus grouses. "They'll use Scipio to raise taxes and lower wheat prices, I am sure of it." He looks over his shoulder at the trumpeters blaring behind him. "For Jupiter's sake, shut that noise up for a while!"

"Scipio has not won yet," Cato replies. "He has stolen money from this war plunder. And spent more on lavish feasts for his men. As his former quaestor, I will take him to trial for it." [clxxiv]

Flaccus nods, mollified. "We do not have to win the case. As long as he is being tried for it, the accusations will be all the propaganda we need."

"I care not for fostering propaganda," Cato snorts. "I want him for corrupting Roman soldiers with his wastefulness and luxury."

Flaccus rolls his eyes heavenward, but he nods. "Yes, there is certainly that corrupting influence issue, Cato." *The man would have us all living in huts and eating turnips. But he is useful—for now.*

393

Scipio's army marches at the rear of the parade, filling the Via Sacra's main street all the way back to the Gate of Triumph, from which the procession started. Released from their years-long fear of death and capture, the war veterans are gloriously, deliriously, drunk. They march along in loose ranks, laurel wreaths dangling from their tousled heads, singing obscene songs about Scipio's sexual endowments and proclivities. The Cannenses lead the march, their standard bearers stretching their arms heavenward to extend their banners as high as they will go, proud men at last.

The triumph wends its way past the thronged temples and government buildings, and finally terminates at the Forum steps. Rome's two new consuls are waiting for Scipio, grinning from ear to ear.

"Lo, triumphe, Scipio!" shouts Cornelius Lentulus. "As consul of Rome, I am delighted to see you have returned safely."

Scipio smiles at Lentulus' words, knowing that the newly-elected consul had lobbied mightily to be given Africa as his province, that he might depart for Carthage and secure the peace treaty himself, thereby gaining the honor of ending the war.[clxxv]

Well, the people told him what they thought of his little gambit, Scipio muses, recalling that all thirty five plebian tribes voted for Scipio to be retained until he secured the peace.[clxxvi]

A young woman rushes to the side of Scipio's chariot, shouldering her way through his veterans as if she were Marcus Silenus reincarnate. She carries a sallow-faced infant in her arms. Her pleading expression tells Scipio of her desperate purpose—she wants him to cure her child with his godlike powers.

Scipio orders his men aside. He bends over the side of the chariot and raises the swaddled infant into his arms, kissing it softly on each sickly cheek. He gently returns it to the mother, who tearfully kisses his scarred, man-killing hands.

"Gratitude, Imperator," she mumbles tearfully. "May your ancestors smile upon you and your family!"

He strokes her veiled head. "It was nothing. I but repay my debt of gratitude to another," Scipio replies, recalling Hannibal's dramatic intervention during Scipio's peace negotiations with Carthage.

Three months ago, Scipio stood at the floor of the Carthaginian Senate, repeating the peace terms he had given to the Elders that came to his camp shortly after Zama. The terms embodied Scipio's dream of protecting Rome from future assaults while preserving beautiful Carthage from utter destruction. Carthage would keep its African lands and a small fleet of ten triremes. They would pay their vast war indemnities over the next fifty years, softening the immediate blow to their economy.[clxxvii]

At that meeting, a haughty senator from the Gisgon faction stood up and walked to the speaking dais in front of the Senate. There, the former general bellowed his protests at Scipio's terms, inciting many senators to voice their agreement with him, jeopardizing the peace settlement. [clxxviii]

Hannibal himself rose from his Senate seat and stalked up to the dais, where he promptly threw the astonished Gisgon from it.[clxxix]

"It seems to me," Hannibal said, looking at Scipio and then at the Senate, "astounding and quite incomprehensible that any man who is a citizen of Carthage and is conscious of the designs that we all individually and as a body have entertained against Rome, does not bless his stars that now that he is at the mercy of the Roman he has obtained such lenient terms!" [clxxx]

Hannibal's words were the end of the dispute and, much to Scipio's relief, the treaty was signed. *He always had Carthage's welfare first in his mind*, Scipio recalls. He playfully waves his ivory scepter at the Roman citizens. *Would he were one of our consuls.*

The procession resumes from the Forum and finally stops at Jupiter's temple on the Capitoline hill. Scipio steps down from his chariot and walks up the temple steps to the waiting priests, there to deliver his oration about the valiance of his troops.

The priests sacrifice two white oxen to the gods. The second new consul, the famous war veteran Lucius Manlius, steps to the prow-shaped speaker's rostra.

"As you know, General Publius Cornelius Scipio, your victory has earned you the title of Man of Triumph, and you join the illustrious Romans who have earned that honorific." He smiles. "But for the first time in history, we have a new title for you. A title given to you by our people."

The people roar their approval of Manlius' words, knowing what he will say next. And he does not disappoint. The stocky older man spreads his hands and looks up to the sky.

"The Senate has voted to give you an honorific named after the country you have conquered, that history may remember your achievement. From this day forward you will be known as Scipio Africanus, the man who conquered Africa!"

Amid the people's delirious shouts, Scipio steps up to embrace Manlius, and kisses him on each cheek. Scipio Africanus turns to face the citizens of Rome, tears streaking the triumphal red paint that covers his face.

"I accept this honor as recognition for my men's victory in Africa, for the restored honor of the valiant Cannenses and the falsely disgraced legionnaires of Herdonia." He pauses in front of the silent throngs, choking back his tears. "And in honor of the greatest Roman of them all, Marcus Silenus!" Scipio stands with bowed head, allowing the crowd to thunder out their joy. A few minutes later, he raises his hands to speak.

"Now that I am a Man of Triumph, my first act is to reward those who truly earned our peace, our valiant legionnaires and allies. I am giving 400 asses of silver to each of our men in Africa." [clxxxi]

He grins at the crowd. "I have also brought 123,000 pounds of silver for the Senate coffers, so there is still plenty of money for them to waste!"

Amid the laughter, Cato turns his angry face to Flaccus. "You see? He wastes more money on his men!"

Flaccus shakes his head. "I am more worried that he curries favor with the plebians—we must soon rid ourselves of him."

Cato glares at Flaccus, reading his mind. "Yes, we will. But it will be by legal means, Senator."

The ceremony finally ends with a feast for the magistrates and senators, with Scipio presiding as the guest of honor. The hours wind long and the wine flows freely. Finally, the patrician celebrants wobble their way to their city manses or ride out to their country estates.

Flaccus takes a small carriage back to his city domus, drunkenly cursing the rattling wheels and bouncing ride. Thrax rides behind him, accompanied by Flaccus' other two guards.

"This concrete stuff they are using among the cobblestones, it is worse than riding on dirt!" Flaccus grouses.

"We will go ahead of you, Master," says Thrax. "To make sure no one is lurking about." The three guards disappear into the night.

"Faster, Otho!" Flaccus spits at his driver. "I have to take a piss!" The slave snaps the reins and the carriage speeds up, adding more distress to Flaccus' bouncing bladder. He does not notice the two hooded figures riding on horseback a block back from his carriage.

"Oh, fuck it, just pull over here!" he says, spying a dim alleyway between two insulae. Flaccus jumps from the carriage and pads over to the alley entrance. He raises his robes and pisses on the wall of an apartment building, looking about to make sure he is not seen.

Flaccus hears a thump and a scraping behind him, and immediately drops down his toga. "Otho? Is someone coming?" He hears no reply.

The senator hurries back to his carriage, only to find it empty. "You can piss at home," he yells out into the empty street, "let's get going."

Flaccus steps up into the back of the covered carriage. He pauses and peeks inside but it is empty. Nervous, he scans the empty street. The senator sees a stray sandal lying on the street on the other side of the carriage. A man's sandal.

"Thrax! Guards! Get back here!" Flaccus cries. Silence is his only answer.

An iron forearm clamps across Flaccus' neck. A thick sack falls over his head and is roped tight, muffling his outcry. Flaccus twists against the four hands holding him, until a club ends his struggles.

When Flaccus awakes he finds himself lying on the floor of the Scipio tomb, his hands bound behind him. A lone torch burns in the corner, its flames casting flickering shadows across the urns of the Scipio ancestors. He sees the dim outline two figures standing in the darkness by the tomb door, watching him.

"Yes, you are in the Scipio tomb," says a deep voice from the shadows. "It is only fair that Pomponia observes what will happen to you."

"Take me back now, and I will spare your lives. You have my promise," says Flaccus.

The voice laughs. "A promise from noble Senator Flaccus! How much is that worth? Too bad General Fabius is not here to witness this, I wonder how he would value your word?"

The voice tinges with anger. "We are not sure if you were responsible for Pomponia's death, or for the attempt on Marcus Silenus," says the voice. "But one thing we are most assured of—your kind should not be allowed to reproduce. And we will accomplish what Pomponia Scipio had oft wished for you..."

A large, fleshy, hooded man steps out from the dark, his hairy stomach pouring down over his filthy loincloth. The thick-armed man carries a curved dagger in one melon-sized fist and a thin cord in the other. "Tie them up and cut them off," orders the voice in the shadows.

Flaccus' eyes widen with dawning realization. He licks his lips. "A thousand denarii to each of you. Just let me go."

The voice barks a laugh. "Ah, but that would be a breach of my promise," it replies. "It would be difficult for you to understand, but that makes it impossible."

The burly man yanks up Flaccus' purple bordered toga and rips off his snow white subligalculum, exposing Flaccus' thin white legs and flaccid genitals.

"Five thousand denarii!" Flaccus wails. The man cinches a thin cord around his testicles. The man tugs the loop tight, and Flaccus howls in pain. Minutes later, his pleads turn to screams, then keening wails. A soft plop echoes on the tomb floor. Then another.

"Stuff a rag in his mouth and cover his eyes," says the voice from the shadows, and it is done.

When the strip is tied over the Senator's eyes, Cassius Paullus limps out from the shadows, his crutch bound on the bottom to conceal its thump. He leans over the sobbing patrician.

"No one will know you are a eunuch, Senator, if you but behave yourself," Cassius says in an affected voice. "Should any mischief befall the Scipios, your secret will become known, and your career will be ended."

Cassius starts to walk away, and then turns his head back to Flaccus. "And I will tell Scipio Africanus of my suspicions."

The one-legged old tribune drops a heavy purse into the burly man's waiting hand. "Stitch him up, put him to sleep, and dump him at the front of his estate." He waggles his finger at the hooded castrator. "Be careful, we don't want him dying. That would be too merciful."

Cassius limps up the steps and out into the cool predawn air. He takes a deep breath and then another, as if ridding himself of evil humors. He looks down at the ground, as though staring into Hades. *Your wishes are fulfilled, Marcus. He will live out his days in pain and shame.*

Cassius carefully sheathes his crutch in a saddle sleeve and clambers awkwardly on top of his mare. He snaps the reins and leisurely clops out from the cemetery, heading toward the city entrance. He watches the twinkles of the merchants' torches as they bustle about their stalls inside the gates, preparing for a new day.

*   *   *   *   *

BRUNDISIUM, SOUTHEAST ITALIA, 201 BCE. *Where is that cursed ship? That old bastard better not have lied to me, I'll go back and flay him alive. I had to kill those two guards for this.*

Thrax stomps along the small oak-plank pier at the terminus of the Appian Way. The Thracian stares into the Adriatic's fog-shrouded waters, searching for the outline of a ship's sail, or sound of oars sloshing into the waters.

He looks back toward the roadway, listening for the sound of marching feet. Looking for the silhouettes of Roman soldiers. *What if Flaccus is dead, and they figure out I killed his guards? I'll be on a cross the day they catch me. Ah, it was worth the risk. I'm going home.*

Thrax walks over the edge of the pier, dragging his careworn sack of belongings. He pulls up his gray tunic and pisses into the murky waters, listening to its faint splashing. *Maybe I should steal a boat and take my chances. Yes, that's a great idea! Drown like an idiot after surviving the ring and the battlefield.*

A small trade ship materializes in front of him, it's ghostly shape gliding toward the front of the pier. Thrax stares at the prow's insignia. *It's a Greek ship. He told me it would be Greek, but I thought it would be a warship!*

He can see two men furl up the sail and back paddle with the oars in the rear. A stout man stands in the prow, gold chains dangling from his shaggy black tunic.

Thrax shakes himself off and grabs his bag. He limps over to stand next to the head of the pier as the ship pulls alongside. Two deckhands pitch looped ropes over the timbers, and pull the boat next to the pier.

"Salve, stranger! Are you Cassius' friend?" shouts the captain in his pidgin Latin.

"Yes. I am Thrax."

"Good. I take you across the sea. Get other half of money from that crazy man Cassius. We go now."

"This will make it across the sea?" Thrax asks, eyeing the thirty-foot boat.

"I do it every day of the week, and twice on Dies Solis, just to celebrate the sun day!" brags the captain. "Besides, what choice do you have?"

What choice, indeed? says Thrax to himself, looking back at the empty Via Appia.

He leaps from the pier and lands with a thump onto the deck. The ship lurches sideways with the impact, spilling Thrax onto his back. He rolls across the deck until he collides with the olive oil amphorae that are roped into the railing. The captain laughs.

"Cassius say you were in military, but you were not in the navy, eh? You sure you ready to leave Rome and bounce across the sea?"

"I have been slave, gladiator, and soldier to Rome," retorts Thrax. "And my reward was a crippled leg and a handful of coins. I am ready to be gone, and I will not look back."

"Then we are off for Aulon, in Illyria. We will be there by nightfall!"

"Good. I can find my way to Thrace from there," says Thrax.

"Cast off," the captain orders. The two deckhands snap the ropes off the pier timbers and push away with their paddles, easing out into the open waters.

Once the prow is pointed east, the sailors unfurl the rectangular sail and watch it billow out with the morning wind, pushing the boat towards the rising sun.

*　　*　　*　　*　　*

CIRTA, NUMIDIA, 201 BCE. Masinissa stands at the tomb of Sophonisba, pressing the point of his double-edge sword into the pit of his stomach, angling it toward his heart. *Just lean forward, quickly, and then you will be with her.*

He looks at the dancing elephant carved over her tomb entrance. *You were ever a creature of joy, beloved. Until your father needed Syphax to be his ally.*

"I am coming to join you in paradise." He leans back, mustering himself to pitch forward.

No, comes a voice in his head. *Not now.*

Masinissa's eyes roam around the tomb, looking for someone. *It was in your head*, he concludes. His eyes widen. *She is in your head.*

"Why not go?" he says out loud. The answer murmurs inside him. *You will soon unite all of Numidia. It is your destiny.*

"There is no honor in doing it!" he shouts up to the starry skies, spreading his arms in supplication. "Cursed Scipio gave me Numidia as part of the peace treaty, I did not win it." [clxxxii] He knots his fists. "I should have killed him in his camp, while he lauded me with his false favors."

The Roman only gave you an opportunity. Vermina is alive, the tribes are rising in revolt. You are the only one who can stop them. I will be watching.

Masinissa listens for more, but hears nothing. "Sophonisba? Are you there? Don't go, Beloved!"

He hears nothing. Masinissa stares at the tomb, half expecting her to appear. His naked sword dangles from his hand. He turns it about, watching it gleam in the moonlight.

After several long minutes, Masinissa sheaths his blade and walks to the copse of trees where his horse is tied. He leaps onto the back of the Numidian pony. He stares at the tomb.

"I will not marry. You will be my only queen. Two years hence, I will bring you your crown—and you will rule a united nation."

Masinissa wheels his horse and trots up the winding road to his Cirta fortress, already planning his assault upon Vermina.

* * * * *

ROME. "Grrrrr, glabglabglab!" Lucius babbles, as he makes faces at his niece Cornelia. The child laughs and waggles her hands in the air. Lucius breaks into one of his rare smiles.

Scipio exchanges a grateful look with Amelia and reaches across the dining couch to squeeze her hand. *He is finally coming back to us,* he thinks, *the horror is fading from him.*

"Caring for children will be in my future," Lucius says, as Cornelia wraps her pudgy hand around his proffered finger. "Perhaps I can be a tutor like our Asclepius."

He smoothes Cornelia's curly hair and looks at his brother. The smile vanishes. "Teaching them would help compensate for that time in Iberia, when ... you know..."

Scipio grips Lucius' shoulder. "You could not have known there were children hiding under those shields. No one could have known." Lucius bows his head to hide his face. He hurries from the room.

"It will take him a while longer," Amelia says. "Perhaps years."

Scipio sighs. "I have to help him, somehow. I promised Mother. What can I do?"

"For now, just let him heal." Amelia runs her fingers over Scipio's face. "There are lines on your face and gray at your temples. You have already given so much of yourself, it is time for you to give something to yourself."

She gently pokes his cheek. "Lucius, the Hellenic Party, the Senate—they can all wait a while." She shakes his shoulder. "Go to the baths, get drunk, do something fun!"

Scipio laughs. "I hear and obey, Wife. But there is one more thing to do before I rest."

The next day Scipio drops on a worn gray tunic and summons a nondescript mare from the nearby stables. He rides out to the rolling Sabina Hills, watching the people working the olive groves and new growth wheat fields, reflexively searching for signs of a potential ambush.

Scipio meanders past the wheat fields where Dentatus' hut still stands, commemorating the humble origins of early Rome's savior. Taking a dirt road to the north, he trots past Cato's farm, where he sees his former quaestor working side by side with his field slaves, as squalidly dressed as they.

Cato pauses to drink some watered vinegar from the slaves' flagon. He notices Scipio and glares at him, his steely gray eyes following him down the road.

Scipio catches Cato's stare. He musters a fatuous grin and waves his hand at Cato. "Salve, old friend! I'm having a lavish feast tonight, paid for with all my stolen plunder! And a reading of fine Greek poetry! Want to come?"

With a final scowl Cato returns to his hoe, levering out rocks from the freshly furrowed field.

Laughing, Scipio kicks his horse forward. *The nettlesome little bastard is not a hypocrite, anyway. He lives the austerity he preaches.*

A half hour later, Scipio approaches an immaculate little villa on the side of a hill, its freedmen working its lush olive groves. A one-legged man busily hobbles about the rows. He barks instructions as if he were commanding troops, jabbing out with his crutch to emphasize his orders. Scipio grins at the sight and rides toward the old man, who eagerly stumps over to him.

Scipio juts out his right hand in a military salute. The old soldier gravely returns the gesture.

"What news Cassius? Is everything well here at Marcus' estate?"

The old man runs a hoary hand through his tousled gray hair. "Ah, these field hands are as lazy as my recruits used to be! Always looking for a shady rest."

"Perhaps I should lend you my old training cudgel," Scipio says. "It stood me in good stead in Iberia."

Cassius chuckles. "In truth, everything is fine. Mistress Prisca has the farm as efficient as one of your legions. Her son Florus has grown to be as a large as a Gaul, and twice as crazy!" His voice grows wistful. "Marcus would be very proud of them."

Scipio swallows the lump in his throat. "I am pleased to hear that. If anything is needed here, anything, come back to your other home and see us."

"As you command, General," Cassius says, snapping out another salute. "And what of you now, First Man of Rome?" [clxxxiii]

Scipio scratches the back of his neck and shrugs. "Well, my veterans have returned to find their work taken by slaves and foreigners. While my popularity is still high, I will persuade the Senate to allocate land to them. They can restore the farms ravaged by Hannibal." [clxxxiv]

"What, no more war campaigns for you?" blurts Cassius. "You are the greatest general in history, Rome needs you! That prissy Philip of Macedon has been stirring up trouble on the coast, and Antiochus of Syria is not far behind him."

"Ah yes, there is always another war, isn't there? But Flaminius and the other young generals can handle them. My wars are here in Rome, to promote the public good while my name still carries weight."

Scipio looks toward Africa. "A great man once told me that Fortuna is fleeting and fickle, and I have come to see the wisdom of his words."

Cassius wrinkles his nose. "With respect, I cannot believe you will not fight again. And when you go on your next campaign, don't forget to bring me along. You will need someone to replace Marcus, though I could not pretend to offer the protection he gave your family."

Scipio bores into Cassius' eyes. "I know someone was hired to kill my mother, Cassius." He gazes south across the fields, where Flaccus' estate is perched atop a hill. "I think I know who did it, although I cannot be certain."

Cassius vigorously rubs one of his front teeth with a calloused index finger and inspects its results, ignoring Scipio's stare. "And if you were certain who it was, what would you do?"

Scipio blinks at him. "I would be honor bound to kill him, of course."

Cassius nods, a slight scowl on his face. "And you would be tried for murder. And Rome would lose the one man who can guide it forward to the future."

"I hardly think I am indispensable."

The old man's bright blue eyes burn into Scipio's, his mouth a line of conviction. "I too, know something certain. Pomponia's killer is dying a hundred deaths. I am honor bound to say no more."

Scipio's face reddens. "Who is it, Tribune? I will not be denied my revenge!"

Cassius shakes his head forlornly. "I don't know," he lies. "Marcus arranged for Pomponia's revenge, should he not have lived to accomplish it himself." He shrugs. "Her killer has been brought to justice, that is all I know. I hope it eases your mind."

Scipio is quiet for a while, his anger fading. "That seems cruel to do that," he finally says. "Death would be more merciful."

Cassius shrugs. "Perhaps it was for other crimes unpunished. Who knows? Marcus knew what you would do if you knew who it was. He was the best killer I have ever seen, but he would not let you venture into that world."

Scipio's face softens. "Times are changing. We will never see his like again."

Scipio Africanus tugs his horse about, and slaps it on its haunch. "You want me to fight again, Cassius? I fear I will disappoint you. For now my contests will be with Laelius. He is waiting at a wine bar for a game of latrunculi. I dare not lose that battle, I would have to pay!"

About the Author

Martin Tessmer is a retired professor of instructional design and technology. He also worked as a training design consultant to the US Navy and Air Force.

The author of twelve nonfiction and fiction books, his most current endeavor is the Scipio Africanus Saga, which includes *Scipio Rising*, *The Three Generals*, and *Scipio's Dream*.

He lives in Denver, Colorado, with his two Australian Cattle Dogs, Hector and Rita.

[i] Bagnall, p. 275.

[iii] Marcus Porcius Cato, *De Agri Cultura*.

[iv] Ibid.

[v] Ibid.

[vi] Gabriel, 158.

[vii] Livy, 29, 29, p. 550.

[viii] http://askville.amazon.com/history-phrase-divide-conquer/AnswerViewer.do?requestId=29595554

[ix] Gabriel, 158.

[x] Several military historians, including Richard Gabriel, have questioned the wisdom of Scipio's siege of Africa, when Tunis was a more strategic and vulnerable target.

[xi] Ibid.

[xii] http://www.britannica.com/biography/Agathocles

[xiii] Livy, 29, 34, 556.

[xiv] Ibid.

[xv] Ibid.

[xvi] Livy, 29, 35, 557.

[xvii] Livy, 22, 51, p. 120.

[xviii] http://www.therthdimension.org/AncientRome/Roman_Army/On_the_March/on_the_march.htm

[xix] Livy, 29, 36, p. 559.

[xx] Livy, 29, 35, p. 559.

[xxi] See Waterfield's note in Livy, about Livy's exaggeration of the number and circumstance of Hannibal's losses. In Livy, page. 698.

[xxii] Gabriel, p. 157.

[xxiii] Livy, 29, 35, p. 558.

[xxiv] Livy, 29, 23 & 24, p. 544.

[xxv] Martin Tessmer. *Scipio's Dream*, Chapter IX.

[xxvi] Livy, 29, 35, p. 558.

[xxvii] Livy, 29, 35, 558.

[xxviii] Gabriel, p. 163.

[xxix] Livy, 29, 38, p. 562.

[xxx] Bagnall, p. 278.

[xxxi] Plutarch, p. 11.

[xxxii] On several occasions, Livy has remarked about Cato's criticisms of Scipio's easy treatment of his men.

[xxxiii] Gabriel, p. 163.

[xxxiv] http://www.quotationspage.com/quote/28737.html

[xxxv] Polybius. *The Complete Histories of Polybius*, trans. W.R. Paton. Book XIV, "Scipio in Africa." DigiReads.com, 2014.

[xxxvi] Gabriel, p. 164.

xxxvii Livy, 30, 4, p. 566.

xxxviii Gabriel, p. 163.

xxxix Ibid.

xl Livy, 30, 4, p. 567.

xli Livy, 30, 4, 567.

xlii Bagnall, p. 279.

xliii Ibid, 568.

xliv Waterfield, in Livy, p. 701.

xlv Gabriel, p. 165.

xlvi Livy, 30, 6, 569.

xlvii Gabriel, p. 170.

xlviii Livy, p. 569.

xlix http://penelope.uchicago.edu/Thayer/E/Gazetteer/Places/Africa/Liby a/_Texts/MATCIS/Sabratha*.html

l Livy, p. 569

li Gabriel, p. 160.

lii Ibid, 570.

liii Livy, p. 579.

liv Gabriel, p. 167.

lv http://dalby.pagespersoorange.fr/extra/SalammboFeast.html

[lvi] Polybius, XIV, 6, p. 378.

[lvii] Yardley, in Livy, p. 702.

[lviii] Livy, 570.

[lix] Gabriel, p. 169.

[lx] Gabriel, 238.

[lxi] Livy, p. 570.

[lxii] Gabriel, p. 169.

[lxiii] Livy, 30, 9, 571.

[lxiv] Ibid.

[lxv] Gabriel, p. 171.

[lxvi] Gabriel, p. 162.

[lxvii] Ibid.

[lxviii] Ibid, p. 162.

[lxix] Livy, 30, 10.

[lxx] Ibid.

[lxxi] Ibid.

[lxxii] https://en.wikipedia.org/wiki/Leon_of_Salamis

[lxxiii] Livy, 30, 10, 572.

[lxxiv] Ibid.

[lxxv] Ibid, 573.

[lxxvi] Ibid.

[lxxvii] Livy, 30, 11, 574.

[lxxviii] Ibid.

[lxxix] Italicus, in Gabriel, p. 173.

[lxxx] Ibid.

[lxxxi] Gabriel, p. 173.

[lxxxii] Livy, 30, 12, p. 575.

[lxxxiii] http://www.indiana.edu/~ancmed/midwife.HTM

[lxxxiv] According to Plutarch, among other sources, Cato distrusted doctors, especially Greek ones.

[lxxxv] Livy, 30, 16, p. 581.

[lxxxvi] Ibid.

[lxxxvii] Livy, 30, 12, p. 575.

[lxxxviii] Ibid, 576.

[lxxxix] Ibid.

[xc] Ibid, 577.

[xci] Ibid, 577.

[xcii] Yardley, in Livy, p. 703.

[xciii] Livy, 30, 13, 578.

[xciv] Ibid.

[xcv] Livy, 30, 14, 578.

[xcvi] Ibid

[xcvii] Ibid, 578-9.

[xcviii] Ibid, 579.

[xcix] Ibid.

[c] Ibid.

[ci] http://www.mariamilani.com/ancient_rome/ancient_roman_ships.htm

[cii] These are the legendary Gracchus brothers, Tiberius Gaius, champions of the common man.

[ciii] Livy, 30, 18, 583.

[civ] Ibid

[cv] Ibid, p. 574.

[cvi] Ibid.

[cvii] Ibid.

[cviii] Ibid.

[cix] Hall, William Henry. *The Romans on the Riviera and the Rhone: A Sketch of the Conquest of Liguria and the Roman Province.* 1974, Ares Publishers, Page 42.

[cx] https://en.wikipedia.org/wiki/Rhomphaia

[cxi] Livy, 30, 18, 584

[cxii] Ibid, 585.

[cxiv] Livy, 30, 15, 580.

[cxv] Livy, 30, 17, 582.

[cxvi] Ibid. 30, 21, 588.

[cxvii] Livy, 30, 15, 580.

[cxviii] Gabriel, p. 174.

[cxix] Bagnall, Nigel. *The Punic Wars Rome, Carthage, and the Struggle for the Mediterranean.* New York: Random House, 2008. p. 284.

[cxx] Livy, 30, 16, 582.

[cxxi] Ibid.

[cxxii] Ibid, 589.

[cxxiii] Livy, 30, 23,589.

[cxxiv] Ibid.

[cxxv] Livy, 30, 19, 586.

[cxxvi] Gabriel, p.

[cxxvii] Livy, 30, 20, 586.

[cxxviii] Peddle, p. 229.

[cxxix] Livy, 30, 19, 585.

[cxxx] See, for example, John Kistler's *War Elephants*. Lincoln, Nebraska: University of Nebraska Press, 2007, pp. 83-84.

[cxxxi] Livy, 30, 19, 585.

[cxxxii] Ibid, p. 590.

cxxxiii Peddle, p 246.

cxxxiv Polybius, Book 15, p. 380.

cxxxv Ibid.

cxxxvi Ibid

cxxxvii Gabriel, 177.

cxxxviii The proper term for the Barca family is "Barcid," but I use the former to avoid confusing our readers.

cxxxix Polybius, 15, p. 380.

cxl https://en.wikipedia.org/wiki/History_of_biological_warfare

cxli Livy, 30, 25, 591.

cxlii Polybius mentions that Tychaeus was a relative of Syphax, but the exact relationship is unknown.

cxliii https://en.wikipedia.org/wiki/Treaty_of_Phoenice .

cxliv Livy, 30, 26, 502. Historians disagree on whether Philip sent troops to Hannibal or not. Livy mentions them, Polybius does not. Yardley considers it a fiction, but Gabriel argues for its possibility.

cxlv https://en.wikipedia.org/wiki/Italica

cxlvi This is a traditional elephant capture method referred to as *mela shikar*. https://en.wikipedia.org/wiki/Mela_shikar

cxlvii Polybius, 15, 1, p. 381.

cxlviii Livy, 30, 27, 593.

cxlix Polybius, 15, 1, p. 382.

[cl] Livy, 30, 29, 596.

[cli] Ibid.

[clii] Polybius, 15, 1, p. 383

[cliii] Ibid.

[cliv] Ibid.

[clv] Ibid, p. 384.

[clvi] Ibid.

[clvii] No one knows the exact path of Vermina's army to Hannibal, but records indicate he showed up days late for the battle, indicating he may have gotten lost or been misdirected.

[clviii] I am indebted to Richard Gabriel for the three armies metaphor for Hannibal's line arrangements.

[clix] Gabriel, p. 186.

[clx] Gabriel, p. 186.

[clxi] Livy, 30, 33, 603.

[clxii] Polybius, 15, 1, p. 388.

[clxiii] Gabriel, p. 193.

[clxiv] Livy, 30, 35, 604.

[clxv] Ibid.

[clxvi] Polybius, 15, 1, 388.

[clxvii] http://www.roman-empire.net/army/zama.html

[clxviii] See Yardley's comment about this tactic in Livy, Note 34, p. 711.

[clxix] Livy, 30, 35, 605.

[clxx] Ibid.

[clxxi] Ibid.

[clxxii] Livy indicates that Syphax died before he could be marched in the triumph, but Polybius says he was in the procession. See Livy, 30, 45, 617.

[clxxiii] Livy, 30, 36, 606.

[clxxiv] Cato did instigate charges against Scipio for misappropriation of funds, among other charges. See Gabriel, p. 232.

[clxxv] Bagnall, p. 298.

[clxxvi] Ibid.

[clxxvii] For a more extensive list of peace terms see Livy, 30, books 37 and 38.

[clxxviii] Ibid.

[clxxix] Ibid.

[clxxx] Polybius, 15, 1, p. 388.

[clxxxi] Bagnall, p. 299.

[clxxxii] Livy, 30, 37, 607.

[clxxxiii] Gabriel, p. 203.

[clxxxiv] Gabriel, p. 205.

Manufactured by Amazon.ca
Bolton, ON